THE QUANTS

Scott Patterson worked for several years as a financial reporter at the *Wall Street Journal*. He lives in New York.

Praise for *T*

'Mr Patterson is onto a big story that already begs follow-up'
New York Times

'A riveting account' *Financial Times*

'The Quants . . . radiates with hubris, high stakes and pricey toys'
BusinessWeek

'Patterson paints a clear picture of the history and evolution of
quantitative trading on Wall Street, before shifting focus to the
"crisis before the crisis" in which a number of quant funds almost
collapsed in 2007 . . . definitely worth reading for an in depth
analysis of one of the points in recent financial history where
things may have started to go awry' *Insider*

'[An] intriguing history of the quants' Stephen Fay, *TLS*

'Scott Patterson has the ability to see things you and I don't notice.
In *The Quants* he does an admirable job of debunking the myths of
black box traders and provides a very entertaining narrative in the
process' Nassim Nicholas Taleb, author of *Fooled by Randomness*
and *The Black Swan*

THE

QUANTS

The maths geniuses who

brought down Wall Street

. . .

SCOTT

PATTERSON

rh

BUSINESS
BOOKS

Published by Random House Business Books 2011

6 8 10 9 7

First published in the United States in 2010 by Crown Business,
an imprint of the Crown Publishing Group,
a division of Random House, Inc., New York

First published in Great Britain, with the subtitle *How a small band of maths whizzes took over Wall Street and nearly destroyed it*, in 2010 by

Random House Business Books
Random House, 20 Vauxhall Bridge Road,
London SW1V 2SA

www.rbooks.co.uk

Addresses for companies within The Random House Group Limited can be found at: www.randomhouse.co.uk/offices.htm

The Random House Group Limited Reg. No. 954009

A CIP catalogue record for this book
is available from the British Library

ISBN 9781847940599

Penguin Random House is committed to a sustainable future for our business, our readers and our planet. This book is made from Forest Stewardship Council® certified paper.

Printed and bound in Great Britain by Clays Ltd, St Ives plc

For Mom and Pop

Contents

The Players ix

1 • ALL IN 1

2 • THE GODFATHER: ED THORP 13

3 • BEAT THE MARKET 27

4 • THE VOLATILITY SMILE 47

5 • FOUR OF A KIND 64

6 • THE WOLF 102

7 • THE MONEY GRID 118

8 • LIVING THE DREAM 151

9 • "I KEEP MY FINGERS CROSSED FOR THE FUTURE" 183

10 • THE AUGUST FACTOR 209

11 • THE DOOMSDAY CLOCK 242

12 • A FLAW 262

13 • THE DEVIL'S WORK 289

14 • DARK POOLS 301

Notes 313

Glossary 323

Acknowledgments 327

Index 329

The Players

Peter Muller, outspokenly eccentric manager of Morgan Stanley's secretive hedge fund PDT. A whip-smart mathematician who occasionally took to New York's subways to play his keyboard for commuters, in 2007 Muller had just returned to his hedge fund after a long sabbatical, with grand plans of expanding operations and juicing returns even further.

Ken Griffin, tough-as-nails manager of Chicago hedge fund Citadel Investment Group, one of the largest and most successful funds in the world. In the years before the crash, Griffin's indulgences included the purchase of an $80 million Jasper Johns painting and a Paris wedding at the Palace of Versailles.

Cliff Asness, sharp-tongued, hot-tempered founder of AQR Capital Management, a hedge fund with nearly $40 billion in assets under management at the time of the crash. Mere days before the crash, Asness's hedge fund was on the verge of filing the final papers for an initial public offering.

Boaz Weinstein, chess "life master," card counter, and powerful derivatives trader at Deutsche Bank, who built his internal hedge fund, Saba (Hebrew for "wise grandfather"), into one of the most powerful credit-trading funds on the planet, juggling $30 billion worth of positions.

Jim Simons, the reclusive, highly secretive billionaire manager of Renaissance Technologies, the most successful hedge fund in history, whose mysterious investment techniques are driven by scientists poached from the fields of cryptoanalysis and computerized speech recognition.

Ed Thorp, godfather of the quants. As a math professor in the 1950s, Thorp deployed his mathematical skills to crack blackjack, unifying the key themes of gambling and investing, and later became the first math genius to figure out how to use similar skills to make millions on Wall Street.

Aaron Brown, the quant who used his math smarts to thoroughly humiliate Wall Street's old guard at their trademark game of Liar's Poker, and whose career provided him with a front-row view of the explosion of the mortgage-backed securities industry.

Paul Wilmott, quant guru extraordinaire and founder of the mathematical finance program at Oxford University. In 2000, Wilmott began warning of a mathematician-led market meltdown.

Benoit Mandelbrot, mathematician who as early as the 1960s warned of the dangers wild market swings pose to quant models—but was soon forgotten in the world of quants as little more than a footnote in their long march to a seemingly inevitable victory.

"We have involved ourselves in a colossal muddle, having blundered in the control of a delicate machine, the working of which we do not understand. The result is that our possibilities of wealth may run to waste for a time—perhaps for a long time."

—JOHN MAYNARD KEYNES,
The Great Slump of 1930

THE
QUANTS

ALL IN

Peter Muller stepped into the posh Versailles Room of the century-old St. Regis Hotel in midtown Manhattan and took in the glittering scene in a glance.

It wasn't the trio of cut-glass chandeliers hung from a gilt-laden ceiling that caught his attention, nor the pair of antique floor-to-ceiling mirrors to his left, nor the guests' svelte Armani suits and gem-studded dresses. Something else in the air made him smile: the smell of money. And the sweet perfume of something he loved even more: pure, unbridled testosterone-fueled competition. It was intoxicating, and it was all around him, from the rich fizz of a fresh bottle of champagne popping open to the knowing nods and winks of his friends as he moved into a room that was an impressive lineup of topflight bankers and hedge fund managers, the richest in the world. His people.

It was March 8, 2006, and the Wall Street Poker Night Tournament was about to begin. More than a hundred well-heeled players milled about the room, elite traders and buttoned-down dealmakers by day, gambling enthusiasts by night. The small, private affair was a gathering of a select group of wealthy and brilliant individuals who had, through sheer brainpower and a healthy dose of daring, become the new tycoons of Wall Street. This high-finance haut monde—perhaps Muller most of all—was so secretive that few people outside the room had ever heard their names. And yet, behind the scenes, their decisions controlled the ebb and flow of billions of dollars coursing through the global financial system every day.

Mixed in with the crowd were professional poker players such as T. J. Cloutier, winner of sixty major tournaments, and Clonie Gowen, a blond Texan bombshell with the face of a fashion model and the body of a *Playboy* pinup. More important to the gathering crowd, Gowen was one of the most successful female poker players in the country.

Muller, tan, fit, and at forty-two looking a decade younger than his age, a wiry Pat Boone in his prime, radiated the relaxed cool of a man accustomed to victory. He waved across the room to Jim Simons, billionaire math genius and founder of the most successful hedge fund on the planet, Renaissance Technologies. Simons, a balding, white-bearded wizard of quantitative investing, winked back as he continued chatting with the circle of admirers hovering around him.

The previous year, Simons had pocketed $1.5 billion in hedge fund fees, at the time the biggest one-year paycheck ever earned by a hedge fund manager. His elite team of traders, hidden away in a small enclave on Long Island, marshaled the most mind-bending advances in science and mathematics, from quantum physics to artificial intelligence to voice recognition technology, to wring billions in profits from the market. Simons was the rare investor who could make Muller feel profound respect.

The two had known each other since the early 1990s, when Muller briefly considered joining Renaissance before starting his own quantitative hedge fund inside Morgan Stanley, the giant New York investment bank. Muller's elite trading group, which he called Process Driven Trading, was so secretive that even most employees at Morgan weren't aware of its existence. Yet over the previous decade the group, composed of only about fifty people, had racked up a track record that could go toe-to-toe with the best investment outfits on Wall Street, cranking out $6 billion in gains for Morgan.

Muller and Simons were giants among an unusual breed of investors known as "quants." They used brain-twisting math and superpowered computers to pluck billions in fleeting dollars out of the market. By the early 2000s, such tech-savvy investors had come to dominate Wall Street, helped by theoretical breakthroughs in the application of mathematics to financial markets, advances that had earned their discoverers several shelves of Nobel Prizes. The quants applied those same breakthroughs to the highly practical, massively profitable practice of calculating predictable patterns in how the market moved and worked.

These computer-driven investors couldn't care less about a company's "fundamentals," amorphous qualities such as the morale of its employees or the cut of its chief executive's jib. That was for the dinosaurs of Wall Street, the Warren Buffetts and Peter Lynches of the world, investors who focused on factors such as what a company actually made and whether it made it well. Quants were agnostic on such matters, devoting themselves instead to predicting whether a company's stock would move up or down based on a dizzying array of numerical variables such as how cheap it was relative to the rest of the market, how quickly the stock had risen or declined, or a combination of the two—and much more.

That night at the St. Regis was a golden hour for the quants, a predators' ball for the pocket-protector set. They were celebrating their dominance of Wall Street, just as junk bond kings such as Michael Milken had ruled the financial world in the 1980s or swashbuckling, trade-from-the-hip hedge fund managers such as George Soros had conquered the Street in the 1990s.

Muller flicked a lock of sandy brown hair from his eyes and snatched a glass of wine from a passing tray, looking for his friends. A few nonquants, fundamental investors of the old guard, rubbed elbows with the quant crowd that night. David Einhorn, the boy-faced manager of Greenlight Capital (so named when his wife gave him the green light to launch a fund in the 1990s), could be seen chatting on a cell phone by a tall, narrow window overlooking the corner of 55th Street and Fifth Avenue. Just thirty-seven years old, Einhorn was quickly gaining a reputation as one of the sharpest fundamental investors in the business, putting up returns of 20 percent or more year after year. Einhorn was also an ace poker player who would place eighteenth in the World Series of Poker in Las Vegas the following year, winning $659,730.

The next billionaire Muller spotted was Ken Griffin, the blue-eyed, notoriously aggressive manager of Chicago's Citadel Investment Group, one of the largest and most successful hedge funds in the business. Grave dancer of the hedge funds, Citadel was known for sweeping in on distressed companies and gobbling up the remains of the bloodied carcasses. But the core engines of his fund were computer-driven mathematical models that guided its every move. Griffin, who sported a no-nonsense buzz cut of jet-black hair, was the sort of man who could trigger a dark sense of foreboding even in close associates: *Wouldn't want to mess with Ken in a dark alley. Does he ever smile?*

"Petey boy."

Muller felt a jolt in his back. It was his old friend and poker pal Cliff Asness, manager of AQR Capital Management, among the first pure quant hedge funds. Asness, like Muller, Griffin, and Simons, was a pioneer among the quants, having started out at Goldman Sachs in the early 1990s.

"Decided to grace us tonight?" he said.

Asness knew Muller wouldn't miss this quant poker coronation for the world. Muller was obsessed with poker, had been for years. He'd recently roped Asness into a private high-stakes poker game played with several other traders and hedge fund hotshots in ritzy Manhattan hotel rooms. The game had a $10,000 buy-in, couch cushion change to topflight traders such as Asness and Muller.

The quants ran the private poker game, but more traditional investment titans joined in. Marc Lasry, manager of Avenue Capital Group, the $12 billion hedge fund that would hire former first daughter Chelsea Clinton later that year, was a regular. Lasry was known for being a cool investor whose icy demeanor belied his let-it-roll mentality. He was said to have once wagered $100,000 on a hand without even looking at his cards. And won.

The real point of Asness's needle was that he never knew when the globetrotting Muller would be in town. One week he'd be trekking in Bhutan or white-water rafting in Bolivia, the next heli-skiing in the Grand Tetons or singing folk songs in a funky cabaret in Greenwich Village. Muller had even been spotted belting out Bob Dylan tunes in New York's subway system, his keyboard case sprinkled with coins from charitable commuters with no idea the seemingly down-on-his-luck songster was worth hundreds of millions and flew around in a private jet.

Asness, a stocky, balding man with a meaty face and impish blue eyes, wore khaki pants and a white tee peeking out from his open collar. He winked, stroking the orange-gray stubble of his trimmed beard. Though he lacked Muller's savoir faire, Asness was far wealthier, manager of his own hedge fund, and a rising power in the investment world. His firm, AQR, short for Applied Quantitative Research, was managing $25 billion and growing fast.

The year before, Asness had been the subject of a lengthy and glowing profile in the *New York Times Magazine*. He was a scourge of bad practices in the money management industry, such as ridiculously high fees at mutual funds. And he had the intellectual chops to back up his attacks. Known as one of the smartest investors in the world, Asness had worked hard for his success. He'd been a standout student at the University of Chicago's prestigious economics department in the early 1990s, then a star at Goldman Sachs in the mid-1990s before branching out on his own in 1998 to launch AQR with $1 billion and change, a near record at the time. His ego had grown along with his wallet, and so, too, had his temper. While outsiders knew Asness for his razor-sharp mind tempered by a wry, self-effacing sense of humor, inside AQR he was also known for flying into computer-smashing rampages and shooting off ego-crushing emails to his cowed employees at all hours of the day or night. His poker buddies loved Asness's cutting wit and encyclopedic memory, but they'd also seen his darker side, his volatile temper and sudden rages at a losing hand.

"Here comes Neil," Asness said, nodding toward Neil Chriss. A quiet, cerebral mathematician with degrees from the University of Chicago and Harvard, Chriss had cut his teeth on Wall Street at Morgan Stanley, where he'd met Muller. In 1998, he took a job at Goldman Sachs Asset Management just after Asness had left. By 2004, Chriss was quietly building a cutting-edge quant machine at a giant hedge fund called SAC Capital Advisors, run by the eccentric and reclusive tycoon Steve A. Cohen. He was also a member of the quants' poker-playing inner circle.

"Seen Boaz?" Chriss asked, scanning the room.

They looked for the fourth member of their private poker game, Boaz Weinstein. Just thirty-three, Weinstein was head of all credit trading in the United States at Deutsche Bank, the German behemoth. A chess "life master," he'd made vice president at Deutsche in 1999 at the tender age of twenty-five. Two years later, he was named a managing director of the firm, one of the youngest in the bank's history. He ran a wildly successful internal hedge fund at Deutsche that he planned to name Saba, Hebrew for "wise grandfather" (in honor of his own saba). A few times a year, Weinstein jetted off to Las Vegas along with members of MIT's secretive blackjack team, several of whom had worked on Deutsche's trading floor. The team had already gained fame in the bestseller *Bringing Down the House* and was soon to get the Hollywood treatment in the movie *21*. People who knew him said Weinstein's name was on more than one Vegas casino's blacklist. He didn't care. There were plenty of casinos, none better than the one he played in every day from his third-floor office in downtown Manhattan. Wall Street.

"Over there," said Muller, pointing to Weinstein, dough-faced, brown-haired, typing rapidly on a BlackBerry while chatting up Gowen. Asness whistled and cleared his throat.

The players soon got down to business. A melodic chime summoned stragglers into the main room, where vested dealers waited behind scattered rows of card tables, fresh decks arrayed in wide rainbows before them. The game was Texas Hold'em. The action was cordial on the surface, cutthroat between the lines. It was a charity event, after all. Nearly $2 million in proceeds would go to support a math program for New York City's public schools—a fitting beneficiary, as the players were Wall Street's glorified mathletes. Muller, Asness, Griffin, and Weinstein were all quants. Math was the very air they breathed. Even the custom-made poker chips at the event were stamped with the names of mathematical river gods such as Isaac Newton.

The potent combination of their mathematical brilliance, feverishly competitive natures, and out-on-the-edge gambling instincts led to an almost fanatical obsession with poker—the odds, the looping mental games, the bluffing (*if I bet this much, he'll think that I think that he thinks* . . .). Asness didn't take the game as seriously as Muller, Weinstein, and Chris did. He'd picked it up in the past few years after an internal tournament at AQR (which he happened to win). But the guys he was playing against were *insane* about poker. Muller had been frequenting poker halls since the 1980s during his days as a young quant in Berkeley, California. In 2004, he'd become so serious about the game—and so good at it—that he joined the World Poker Tour, pocketing nearly $100,000 in winnings. He played online poker obsessively and even toyed with the bizarre notion of launching an online poker hedge fund. Weinstein, more of a blackjack man, was no slouch at the poker table, having won a Maserati in a 2005 NetJets poker tournament. Griffin simply hated to lose to anyone at anything and approached the poker table with the same brainiac killer instinct that infused his day-to-day trading prowess.

No matter how hard they might play elsewhere, no poker game mattered more than when the gamblers around the table were their fellow quants. It was more than a battle of wits over massive pots—it was a battle of enormous egos. Every day they went head-to-head on Wall Street, facing off in a computerized game of high-stakes poker in financial markets around the globe, measuring one another's wins and losses from afar, but here was a chance to measure their mettle face-to-face. Each had his own particular strategy for beating the market. Griffin specialized in finding cheap bonds through mathematical formulas, or, via the same logic, cheap, down-on-their-luck companies ripe for the picking. Muller liked to buy and sell stocks at a superfast pace using Morgan Stanley's high-powered computers. Asness used historical tests of market trends going back decades to detect hidden patterns no one else knew about. Weinstein was a wizard with credit derivatives—securities whose value derives from some underlying asset, such as a stock or a bond. Weinstein was especially adept with a newfangled derivative known as a credit default swap, which is essentially an insurance policy on a bond.

Regardless of which signature trade each man favored, they had something far more powerful in common: an epic quest for an elusive, ethereal quality the quants sometimes referred to in hushed, reverent tones as the Truth.

The Truth was a universal secret about the way the market worked that could only be discovered through mathematics. Revealed through the study of obscure patterns in the market, the Truth was the key to unlocking billions in profits. The quants built giant machines—turbocharged computers linked to financial markets around the globe—to search for the Truth, and to deploy it in their quest to make untold fortunes. The bigger the machine, the more Truth they knew, and the more Truth they knew, the more they could bet. And from that, they reasoned, the richer they'd be. Think of white-coated scientists building ever more powerful devices to replicate conditions at the moment of the Big Bang to understand the forces at the root of creation. It was about money, of course, but it was also about proof. Each added dollar was another tiny step toward proving they had fulfilled their academic promise and uncovered the Truth.

The quants created a name for the Truth, a name that smacked of cabalistic studies of magical formulas: alpha. *Alpha* is a code word for an elusive skill certain individuals are endowed with that gives them the ability to consistently beat the market. It is used in contrast with another Greek term, *beta*, which is shorthand for plain-vanilla market returns anyone with half a brain can achieve.

To the quants, beta is bad, alpha is good. Alpha is the Truth. If you have it, you can be rich beyond your wildest dreams.

The notion of alpha, and its ephemeral promise of vast riches, was everywhere in the hedge fund world. The trade magazine of choice for hedge funds was called *Alpha*. A popular website frequented by the hedge fund community was called Seeking Alpha. Several of the quants in the room had already laid claim, in some form or another, to the possession of alpha. Asness named his first hedge fund, hatched inside Goldman in the mid-1990s, Global Alpha. Before moving on to Morgan in 1992, Muller had helped construct a computerized investing system called Alphabuilder for a quant farm in Berkeley called BARRA. An old poster from a 1960s film noir by Jean-Luc Godard called *Alphaville* hung on the walls of PDT's office in Morgan's midtown Manhattan headquarters.

But there was always a worry haunting the beauty of the quants' algorithms. Perhaps their successes weren't due to skill at all. Perhaps it was all just dumb luck, fool's gold, a good run that could come to an end on any given day. What if the markets weren't predictable? What if their computer models didn't always work? What if the truth wasn't knowable? Worse, what if there wasn't any Truth?

In their day jobs, as they searched for the Truth, channeling their hidden alpha nerds, the quants were isolated in their trading rooms and hedge funds. At the poker table, they could look one another in the eye, smiling over their cards as they tossed another ten grand worth of chips on the table and called, looking for the telltale wince of the bluffer. Sure, it was a charity event. But it was also a test. Skill at poker meant skill at trading. And it potentially meant something even more: the magical presence of alpha.

As the night rolled on, the quants fared well. Muller chalked up victories against Gowen and Cloutier in the early rounds. Weinstein was knocked out early, but Muller and Asness kept dominating their opponents. Griffin made it into the final ten before running out of luck and chips, as did Einhorn. The action got more intense as the hour grew late. Around 1:30 A.M., only three players were left: Muller, Asness, and Andrei Paraschivescu, a portfolio manager who worked for Griffin at Citadel.

Asness didn't like his first two cards on the next deal and quickly folded, happy to wait for a better draw, leaving the pot to Muller and Paraschivescu. The crowd fell quiet. The incessant honking city whir of Fifth Avenue penetrated the suddenly hushed room.

Breaking the silence, Griffin shouted a warning to his underling:

"Andrei, don't bother coming into work next week if you don't knock Pete out." Some in the crowd wondered if he meant it. With Griffin, you never knew.

The room went quiet again. Paraschivescu lifted a corner of the two cards facedown on the table before him. Pair of fours. Not bad. Muller bent the corner of his two cards and eyed a pair of kings. He decided to go all in, sweeping his chips into the pot. Suspecting a bluff, Paraschivescu pushed his mound of chips forward and called, flipping over his pair of fours. Muller showed his kings, his only show of emotion a winsome glint in his blue eyes. A groan went up from the crowd, the loudest from Griffin. The other cards dealt in the hand couldn't help Paraschivescu, and he was out.

It was down to Muller and Asness, quant versus quant. Asness was at a huge disadvantage. Muller outchipped him eight to one after having taken Paraschivescu to the cleaners. Asness would have to win several hands in a row to even have a chance. He was at Muller's mercy.

Griffin, still smarting from his ace trader's loss, promised to donate $10,000 to Asness's favorite charity if he beat Muller. "Aren't you a billionaire?" Asness chortled. "That's a little chintzy, Ken."

After the deal, Muller had a king and a seven. Not bad, but not great. He decided to go all in anyway. He had plenty of chips. It looked like a bad move: Asness had a better hand, an ace and a ten. As each successive card was dealt, it looked as though Asness was sure to take the pot. But on the final card, Muller drew another king. Odds were against it, but he won anyway. The real world works like that sometimes.

The crowd applauded as Griffin rained catcalls on Muller. Afterward Muller and Asness posed for photos with their silver trophies and with Clonie Gowen flashing a million-dollar smile between them. The biggest grin belonged to Muller.

As the well-heeled crowd of millionaires and billionaires fanned into the streets of Manhattan that night, they were on top of the world. The stock market was in the midst of one of the longest bull runs in history. The housing market was booming. Economists were full of talk of a Goldilocks economy—not too hot, not too cold—in which steady growth would continue as far as the eye could see.

A brilliant Princeton economist, Ben Bernanke, had just taken over the helm of the Federal Reserve from Alan Greenspan. In February 2004, Bernanke had given a speech in Washington, D.C., that captured the buoyant mood of the times. Called "The Great Moderation," the speech told of a bold new economic era in which volatility—the jarring jolts and spasms that wreaked havoc on people's lives and their pocketbooks—was permanently eradicated. One of the primary forces behind this economic Shangri-la, he said, was an "increased depth and sophistication of financial markets."

In other words, quants, such as Griffin, Asness, Muller, Weinstein, Simons, and the rest of the math wizards who had taken over Wall Street, had helped tame the market's volatility. Out of chaos they had created order through their ever-increasing knowledge of the Truth. Every time the market lurched too far out of equilibrium, their supercomputers raced to the rescue, gobbling up the mispriced securities and restoring stability to the troubled kingdom. The financial system had become a finely tuned machine, humming blissfully along in the crystalline mathematical universe of the quants.

For providing this service to society, the quants were paid handsomely. But who could complain? Average workers were seeing their 401(k)s rise with the market, housing prices kept ticking ever upward, banks had plenty of money to lend, prognosticators imagined a Dow Jones Industrial Average that rose without fail, year after year. And much of the thanks went to the quants. It was a great time to be alive and rich and brilliant on Wall Street.

The money poured in, *crazy* money. Pension funds across America, burned by the dot-com collapse in 2000, rushed into hedge funds, the favored vehicle of the quants, entrusting their members' retirement savings to this group of secretive and opaque investors. Cliff Asness's hedge fund, AQR, had started with $1 billion in 1998. By mid-2007, its assets under management neared $40 billion. Citadel's kitty topped $20 billion. In 2005, Jim Simons announced that Renaissance would launch a fund that could juggle a record $100 billion in assets. Boaz Weinstein, just thirty-three, was wielding roughly $30 billion worth of positions for Deutsche Bank.

The growth had come rapid-fire. In 1990, hedge funds held $39 billion in assets. By 2000, the amount had leapt to $490 billion, and by 2007 it had exploded to $2 trillion. And those figures didn't capture the hundreds of billions of hedge fund dollars marshaled by banks such as Morgan Stanley, Goldman Sachs, Citigroup, Lehman Brothers, Bear Stearns, and Deutsche Bank, which were rapidly transforming from staid white-shoe bank companies into hot-rod hedge fund vehicles fixated on the fast buck—or the trillions more in leverage that juiced their returns like anabolic steroids.

The Great Hedge Fund Bubble—for it was a true bubble—was one of the most frenzied gold rushes of all time. Thousands of hedge fund jockeys became wealthy beyond their wildest dreams. One of the quickest tickets to the party was a background in math and computer science. On Wall Street Poker Night in 2006, Simons, Griffin, Asness, Muller, and Weinstein sat at the top of the heap, living outsized lives of private jets, luxury yachts, and sprawling mansions.

A year later, each of the players in the room that night would find himself in the crosshairs of one of the most brutal market meltdowns ever seen, one they had helped to create. Indeed, in their search for Truth, in their quest for alpha, the quants had unwittingly primed the bomb and lit the fuse for the financial catastrophe that began to explode in spectacular fashion in August 2007.

The result was possibly the biggest, fastest, and strangest financial collapse ever seen, and the starting point for the worst global economic crisis since the Great Depression.

Amazingly, not one of the quants, despite their chart-topping IQs, their walls of degrees, their impressive Ph.D.'s, their billions of wealth earned by anticipating every bob and weave the market threw their way, their decades studying every statistical quirk of the market under the sun, saw the train wreck coming.

How could they have missed it? What went wrong?

A hint to the answer was captured centuries ago by a man whose name emblazoned the poker chips the quants wagered with that night: Isaac Newton. After losing £20,000 on a vast Ponzi scheme known as the South Sea Bubble in 1720, Newton observed: "I can calculate the motion of heavenly bodies but not the madness of people."

THE GODFATHER: ED THORP

Just past 5:00 A.M. on a spring Saturday in 1961, the sun was about to dawn on a small, ratty casino in Reno, Nevada. But inside there was perpetual darkness punctuated by the glow of neon lights. A blackjack player sat at an otherwise empty table, down $100 and exhausted. Ed Thorp was running on fumes but unwilling to quit.

"Can you deal me two hands at once?" he asked the dealer, wanting to speed up play.

"No can do," she said. "House policy."

Thorp stiffened. "I've been playing two hands all night with other dealers," he shot back.

"Two hands would crowd out other players," she snapped, shuffling the deck.

Thorp looked around at the empty casino. *She'll do whatever it takes to keep me from winning.*

The dealer started rapidly shooting out cards, trying to rattle him. At last, Thorp spied the edge he'd been waiting for. Finally—*maybe*—he'd have a chance to prove the merits of his blackjack system in the real-world crucible of a casino. Twenty-eight, with dark hair and a tendency to talk out of the corner of his mouth, Thorp resembled hordes of young men who passed through Nevada's casinos hoping to line their pockets with stacks of chips. But Thorp was different. He was a full-blown genius, holder of a Ph.D. in physics from UCLA, a professor at the Massachusetts Institute of Technology, and an expert in devising strategies to beat all kinds of games, from baccarat to blackjack.

As night stretched into morning, Thorp had kept his bets small, wagering $1 or $2 at a time, as he fished for flaws in his system. None was apparent, yet his pile of chips kept shrinking. Lady Luck was running against him. But that was about to change. It had nothing to do with luck and everything to do with math.

Thorp's system, based on complex mathematics and hundreds of hours of computer time, relied primarily on counting the number of ten cards that had been dealt. In blackjack, all face cards—kings, queens, and jacks—count as tens along with the four natural tens in every deck of fifty-two cards. Thorp had calculated that when the ratio of tens left in the deck relative to other cards increased, the odds turned in his favor. For one thing, it increased the odds that the dealer would bust, since dealers always had to "hit," or take another card, when their hand totaled sixteen or less. In other words, the more heavily a deck was stacked with ten cards, the better Thorp's chances of beating the dealer's hand and winning his bet. Thorp's tens strategy, otherwise known as the hi-lo strategy, was a revolutionary breakthrough in card counting.

While he could never be certain about which card would come next, he did know that statistically he had an edge according to one of the most fundamental rules in probability theory: the law of large numbers. The rule states that as a sample of random events, such as coin flips—or hands in a game of blackjack—increases, the expected average also becomes more certain. Ten flips of a coin could produce seven heads and three tails, 70 percent heads, 30 percent tails. But ten thousand flips of a coin will *always* produce a ratio much closer to 50–50. For Thorp's strategy, it meant that because he had a statistical edge in blackjack, he might lose some hands, but if he played enough hands he would always come out on top—as long as he didn't lose all of his chips.

As the cards shot from the dealer's hands, Thorp saw through his exhaustion that the game was tipping his way. The deck was packed full of face cards. *Time to roll.* He upped his bet to $4 and won. He let the winnings ride and won again. His odds, he could tell, were improving. *Go for it.* He won again and had $16, which turned into $32 with the next hand. Thorp backed off, taking a $12 profit. He bet $20—and won. He kept betting $20, and kept winning. He quickly recovered his $100 in losses and then some. *Time to call it a night.*

Thorp snatched up his winnings and turned to go. As he glanced back at the dealer, he noticed an odd mixture of anger and awe on her face, as if she'd caught a glimpse of something strange and impossible that she could never explain.

Thorp, of course, was proving it wasn't impossible. It was all too real. The system worked. He grinned as he stepped out of the casino into a warm Nevada sunrise. He'd just beaten the dealer.

Thorp's victory that morning was just the beginning. Soon he would move on to much bigger game, taking on the fat cats on Wall Street, where he would deploy his formidable mathematical skills to earn hundreds of millions of dollars. Thorp was the original quant, the trailblazer who would pave the way for a new breed of mathematical traders who decades later would come to dominate Wall Street—and nearly destroy it.

Indeed, many of the most important breakthroughs in quant history derived from this puckish mathematician, one of the first to learn how to use pure math to make money—first at the blackjack tables of Las Vegas and then in the global casino known as Wall Street. Without Thorp's example, future financial titans such as Griffin, Muller, Asness, and Weinstein might never have converged on the St. Regis Hotel that night in March 2006.

■   ■   ■

Edward Oakley Thorp was always a bit of a troublemaker. The son of an army officer who'd fought on the Western Front in World War I, he was born in Chicago on August 14, 1932. He showed early signs of math prowess, such as mentally calculating the number of seconds in a year, by the time he was seven. His family eventually moved to Lomita, California, near Los Angeles, and Thorp turned to classic whiz kid mischief. Left alone much of the time—during World War II, his mother worked the swing shift at Douglas Aircraft and his father worked the graveyard shift at the San Pedro shipyard—he had the freedom to let his imagination roam wild. Blowing things up was one diversion. He tinkered with small homemade explosive devices in a laboratory in his garage. With nitroglycerine obtained from a friend's sister who worked at a chemical factory, he made pipe bombs to blow holes in the Palos Verdes wilderness. In his more sedate moments, he operated a ham radio and played chess with distant opponents over the airwaves.

He and a friend once dropped red dye into the Plunge at Long Beach, then California's largest indoor pool. Screaming swimmers fled the red blob, and the incident made the local paper. Another time, he attached an automobile headlight to a telescope and plugged it into a car battery. He hauled the contraption to a lovers' lane about a half mile from his home and waited for cars to line up. As car windows began to fog, he hit a button and lit up the parked assemblage like a cop with a spotlight, laughing as frantic teens panicked and sped away.

During high school, Thorp started thinking about gambling. One of his favorite teachers returned from a trip to Las Vegas full of cautionary tales about how one player after another got taken to the cleaners at the roulette table. "You just can't beat these guys," the teacher said. Thorp wasn't so sure. Around town, there were a number of illegal slot machines that would spit out a stream of coins if the handle was jiggled in just the right way. Roulette might have a similar hidden weakness, he thought, a *statistical* weakness.

Thorp was still thinking about roulette in his second year of graduate school physics at UCLA, in the spring of 1955. He wondered if he could discover a mathematical system to consistently win at roulette. Already he was thinking about how to use mathematics to describe the hidden architecture of seemingly random systems—an approach he one day would wield on the stock market and develop into a theory that lies at the heart of quant investing.

One possibility was to find a roulette wheel with some kind of defect. In 1949, two roommates at the University of Chicago, Albert Hibbs and Roy Walford, found defects in a number of roulette wheels in Las Vegas and Reno and made several thousand dollars. Their exploits had been written up in *Life* magazine. Hibbs and Walford had been undergraduate students at the California Institute of Technology in Pasadena, and their accomplishments were well known to astute denizens of Caltech's neighbor, UCLA.

Thorp believed it was possible to beat roulette even without help from flaws in the wheel. Indeed, the absence of defects made it easier, since the ball would be traveling along a predictable path, like a planet in orbit. The key: because croupiers take bets after the ball is set in motion, it is theoretically possible to determine the position and velocity of the ball and rotor, and to predict approximately which pocket the ball will fall into.

The human eye, of course, can't accomplish such a feat. Thorp dreamed of a wearable computer that could track the motion of ball and wheel and spit out a prediction of where it would land. He believed he could create a machine that would statistically forecast the seemingly random motion of a roulette wheel: an observer would don the computer and feed in information about the speed of the wheel; a bettor, some distance away, would receive information via a radio link.

Thorp purchased a cheap half-scale wheel and filmed it in action, timing the motion with a stopwatch that measured in splits of hundredths of a second. Thorp soon realized that his cheap wheel was too riddled with flaws to develop a predictive system. Disappointed, he tabled the idea as he worked to finish graduate school. But it gnawed at him, and he continued to fiddle with experiments.

One evening, his in-laws visited him and his wife, Vivian, for dinner. They were surprised when Thorp didn't greet them at the door and wondered what he was up to. They found him in the kitchen rolling marbles down a V-shaped trough and marking how far the marbles spun across the kitchen floor before stopping. Thorp explained that he was simulating the path of an orbiting roulette ball. Surprisingly, they didn't think their daughter had married a lunatic.

The Thorps made their first visit to Las Vegas in 1958, after Thorp had finished his degree and begun teaching. The frugal professor had heard that the rooms were cheap, and he was still toying with the idea of beating roulette. The smoothness of the wheels in Las Vegas convinced Thorp that he could predict the outcome. Now he just needed a solid, regulation-size wheel and suitable laboratory equipment.

Thorp had also decided to try out a blackjack strategy he'd recently come across. The strategy was from a ten-page article in the *Journal of the American Statistical Association* by U.S. Army mathematician Roger Baldwin and three of his colleagues—James McDermott, Herbert Maisel, and Wilbert Cantey—who'd been working at the Aberdeen Proving Ground, a military facility in Maryland. Among blackjack aficionados, Baldwin's group came to be known as the "Four Horsemen," although no one in the group actually tested the strategy in Las Vegas. Over the course of eighteen months, the Four Horsemen punched a massive amount of data into desktop calculators, plotting the probabilities involved in thousands of different hands of blackjack.

Ever the scientist, Thorp decided to give Baldwin's strategy a whirl in Las Vegas. While the test proved inconclusive (he lost a grand total of $8.50), he remained convinced the strategy could be improved. He contacted Baldwin and requested the data behind the strategy. It arrived in the spring of 1959, just before Thorp moved from UCLA to the Massachusetts Institute of Technology.

At MIT, Thorp found a hotbed of intellectual creativity that was quietly revolutionizing modern society. The job he stepped into, the coveted position of C. L. E. Moore Instructor, had previously been held by John Nash, the math prodigy who eventually won the Nobel Prize in economics in 1994 for his work on game theory, a mathematical approach to how people compete and cooperate. (Nash later became known as the subject of *A Beautiful Mind*, the book and movie about the competing forces of his genius and mental illness.)

That first summer in Cambridge, Thorp crunched the numbers on blackjack, slowly evolving what would become a historic breakthrough in the game. He fed reams of unwieldy data into a computer, seeking hidden patterns that he could exploit for a profit. By the fall, he'd discovered the rudimentary elements of a blackjack system that could beat the dealer.

Eager to publish his results, he decided on a prestigious industry journal, *The Proceedings of the National Academy of Sciences*. The trouble: the journal accepted papers only from members of the academy. So he sought out the only mathematics member of the academy at MIT, Dr. Claude Elwood Shannon, one of the most brilliant, and eccentric, minds on the planet.

On a November afternoon in 1960, Ed Thorp walked briskly across MIT's leaf-strewn campus. A cold wind whistled off the Charles River. The freshly minted mathematics professor shuddered, and his nerves jangled at the very thought of sitting down face-to-face with Claude Shannon.

Few figures at MIT were more intimidating. Shannon was the brains behind two of the twentieth century's greatest intellectual advances. The first was the application of the binary number system to electronic circuits, which laid the groundwork for the birth of the computer. Shannon's great breakthrough had been to take a two-symbol logic in which problems are resolved by the manipulation of two numbers, 1 and 0, and apply it to a circuit in which a 1 is represented by a switch that is turned on and a 0 by a switch that is turned off. Sequences of on and off switches—essentially strings of 1s and 0s—could represent nearly any kind of information.

Shannon was also a founding father of information theory: how to encode information and transmit it from point A to point B. Crucially, and controversially, Shannon asserted at the start that while messages "frequently have meaning ... [such] semantic aspects of communication are irrelevant to the engineering problem." In other words, information, as a technical matter, is completely devoid of meaning and context. Instead, it is purely statistical, and therefore encodable.

This was highly counterintuitive. Most scientists prior to Shannon had assumed that the fundamental element of communication was meaning, and nothing but meaning. Shannon changed all that.

Thorp didn't want to talk to Shannon about the binary code or information theory, however. He wanted to talk about blackjack. He was still on edge as he stepped into Shannon's office. Shannon's secretary had warned him that the busy professor had only a few minutes to spare.

Thorp spat out his blackjack results as quickly as he could and showed Shannon his paper. Shannon was impressed and said that Thorp had made a significant theoretical breakthrough. He agreed to submit the paper, which was called "A Winning Strategy for Blackjack." But he had one suggestion.

"I think you might want to change the title."

"Okay," Thorp said, confused. "Why?"

"The Academy can be a bit stodgy. And this title has a bit too much of a whiff of the casino. How about 'A Favorable Strategy for Twenty-One'? That should be boring enough to pass the smell test."

Thorp agreed, and his few minutes were up. As he stood, Shannon asked, "Are you working on anything else in the gambling area?"

Thorp paused. He'd kept his roulette research largely secret, and he hadn't worked on it for months. But maybe Shannon would find it interesting.

"I've been conducting some studies of the game of roulette," he said, "and have had some . . . interesting results."

"Really?" Shannon said, his eyes lighting up. He gestured for Thorp to sit down again. "Continue."

Several hours later, Thorp left Shannon's office into the darkening November night.

Thorp started paying regular visits to Shannon's home later that November as the two scientists set to work on the roulette problem. Shannon called his home "Entropy House," a nod to a core concept in information theory, borrowed from the second law of thermodynamics. The law of entropy essentially means everything in the universe will eventually turn into a homogenous, undifferentiated goop. In information theory, Shannon used entropy as a way to discover order within the apparent chaos of strings of seemingly random numbers.

Shannon's three-story wooden house overlooked the Mystic Lakes, several miles northwest of Cambridge. One look indoors told Thorp why Shannon likened it to a theory about the inexorable slide of the universe into utter randomness. It was a disorderly "gadgeteer's paradise," as Thorp later described it, packed with electronic and mechanical contraptions. Shannon was obsessed with automatons, machines that mimic human behavior, and he was especially fond of creating mechanical juggling dolls and coin tossers. He was a notorious unicyclist and impressed visitors by navigating a long tightrope stretched across his yard. One visitor was astounded by Shannon's daughter, who could ride a unicycle and skip rope at the same time. Shannon for a time was obsessed with trying to calculate how small one could make a unicycle and still ride it.

Science fiction writer Arthur C. Clarke visited Shannon's house a number of times. A device Shannon called the "ultimate machine" left him unnerved. "Nothing could be simpler," Clarke later wrote. "It is merely a small wooden casket, the size and shape of a cigar box, with a single switch on one face. When you throw the switch, there is an angry, purposeful buzzing. The lid slowly rises, and from beneath it emerges a hand. The hand reaches down, turns the switch off and retreats into the box. With the finality of a closing coffin, the lid snaps shut, the buzzing ceases and peace reigns once more. The psychological effect, if you do not know what to expect, is devastating. There is something unspeakably sinister about a machine that does nothing—absolutely nothing—except switch itself off."

Thorp and Shannon ordered a regulation roulette wheel from Reno for $1,500 and put it on a dusty slate billiard table. To parse its motion, they clocked it to the hypnotic pulse of a flashing strobe light. To time the ball, they would depress a switch each time it made one revolution around the wheel. The switch also triggered the strobe, marking where the ball stood at the moment the switch was hit. This let Thorp and Shannon gauge how well they were timing the ball, since it showed them how early or late they were in hitting the switch.

The results were ingenious, and perhaps doomed to fail. After much trial and error, Thorp and Shannon calculated a method to predict, with favorable odds, which octant of the roulette wheel the ball would tumble into. The wheel contained eight octants—six octants with five pockets each and two with four, making up the thirty-eight pockets on the wheel. If they could predict the octant, that tipped the odds sharply in their favor. If they bet on all four or five numbers in the predicted octant and their method proved accurate, winning would be guaranteed. It would be cheating, of course, and if they were caught, there was a predictably high chance that large, thick-necked casino bouncers with hairy knuckles would exact a price. But that was a concern for another day.

Thorp and Shannon designed a computer the size of a cigarette pack and embedded it in a pair of shoes. It had two switches: one switch turned on the computer, and the other timed the spinning of the rotor (one toe click when the wheel started and another when it made a single revolution). The computer calculated the results and transmitted which octant to bet on in eight tones to another person wearing a primitive sort of headphone in one ear. In all probability it was the world's first wearable computer.

However, technical problems doomed the project. The headphone wires often broke. One time Thorp, who generally wore the headphone and placed the bets, noticed a woman staring at him with horror. He promptly headed for the bathroom. In a mirror he saw the speaker jutting from his ear like an alien insect.

Though Shannon didn't lead Thorp to riches at the roulette wheel, the professor did make a key contribution to his younger colleague's blackjack strategy. While Thorp had devised a winning approach to blackjack, a key unanswered question remained: how much should a bettor wager if he doesn't want to risk financial ruin? Shannon told Thorp that the answer could be found in a 1956 paper by John Kelly Jr., a physics researcher at Bell Laboratories in Murray Hill, New Jersey. The paper described how much a gambler with inside information about the winner of a series of baseball games between two equally matched teams should wager if there is a certain amount of noise (and hence a possibility that the information could be faulty) in the channel communicating that information.

Thorp realized he could use Kelly's betting system to optimally regulate how much he wagered on various scenarios in blackjack. In simplest terms, when his odds of winning rose, he tossed more chips on the table. When his odds got worse, he backed off.

A good way to size up Kelly's system is by comparison with another gambling strategy: doubling down. Say you bet $10 on a hand of blackjack and you lose. If you bet $20 on the next hand and win, you're up again. But you could lose that, of course. Bet $40, win, and you're back ahead. Doubling down, also known as martingale betting, has been a time-honored strategy practiced by gambling legends such as Casanova. But there's an obvious flaw in the strategy: gambler's ruin. Eventually the martingale gambler will run out of money. The odds of this happening, if the gambler keeps playing, are 100 percent.

Kelly, however, limited the amount from a player's billfold that could be placed on any bet. The only time a player would go all in would be when the odds of winning are 100 percent, a very rare event that almost never happens in a casino—although Thorp would discover such opportunities on Wall Street several years later.

The mathematics of Kelly told him exactly how much to add or subtract, based on the amount in his billfold, in order to achieve the maximum gains. The formula described, in the words of Kelly, how a gambler could "cause his money to grow exponentially," while at the same time avoiding the curse of gambler's ruin.

In January 1961, Thorp presented his blackjack paper to the American Mathematical Society. Since the AMS wasn't as conservative as the National Academy, which had already received the paper, Thorp provocatively titled it "Fortune's Formula: A Winning Strategy for Blackjack." A reporter for the Associated Press picked up on the paper and wrote a story about a brilliant math professor who'd cracked blackjack. The story appeared in newspapers nationwide. Suddenly Ed Thorp was famous.

The article also caught the eye of a number of enterprising

gamblers always on the make for a new system. Thorp fielded a flood of requests about the nature of his system, as well as offers to back him. One of the most generous came from a New York businessman who promised to pony up $100,000. Thorp was eager to test his theory, but he didn't think he needed that much cash. He decided to accept $10,000 and promptly headed for Reno.

The same day Thorp beat the dealer in that ratty Reno casino at five in the morning, he awoke in the afternoon eager to continue his experiment. After a hearty meal, he met with one of his financial backers, known as the mysterious "Mr. X" in the book he would later write detailing his system, *Beat the Dealer*. Later that day, a "Mr. Y" arrived.

Mr. X was, in fact, a New York businessman with connections to organized crime. His name was Emmanuel "Manny" Kimmel, a short, white-haired racketeer with his fingers in everything from numbers games in Newark, New Jersey, to East Coast horse tracks. He was also part owner of a company called Kinney Parking, which owned sixty-four parking lots in New York City. A 1965 FBI memo on Kimmel said he was "a lifetime associate of several internationally known hoodlums." Mr. Y was Eddie Hand, a car-shipping magnate and Kimmel's regular high-stakes gambling pal.

After Hand arrived, they went to Harold's Club, a famous casino located in an enormous building in the center of downtown Reno. It was a significant step up from the second-rate casino Thorp had played in the night before, and it would represent an even more rigorous test of his system.

They sat down at the $500-maximum tables, the highest amount possible. Within fifteen minutes they'd won $500, playing hands ranging from $25 to $250.

The dealer hit a concealed button with her foot. Thorp watched as the casino's owner, Harold Smith, marched toward them across the casino's floor.

"Good evening, gentlemen," Smith said, all smiles and glad-handing. Thorp wasn't fooled for a second. *He's out to stop me.*

After a few more hands, the deck had about fifteen cards left. Typically, dealers play out a deck until only a few cards are left. One way to trip up card counters is to shuffle the deck early.

"Shuffle," Smith said to the dealer. With the newly shuffled deck, Thorp and Kimmel kept winning, since the tens strategy can start paying off after only four cards are dealt, though the odds remain relatively slim, mandating careful bets. As the next deck was about halfway through, Smith nodded at the dealer.

"Shuffle."

Thorp's system still kept picking up favorable odds after several hands. The dealer started shuffling after dealing only two hands. While the system still worked, the repeated shuffling significantly curbed favorable opportunities. Thorp and Kimmel finally left, but they'd already pocketed several thousand dollars.

The combination of Thorp's winning blackjack model and Kelly's optimal betting system was powerful. Thorp and Kimmel continued to beat the dealer, despite a number of hurdles thrown their way. After several days, they had more than doubled their initial $10,000 stake.

Soon after Thorp announced his results in Washington, D.C., he was watching a TV program about gambling. A reporter asked a casino owner whether gambling ever paid off.

"When a lamb goes to the slaughter, the lamb might kill the butcher," the owner said. "But we always bet on the butcher."

Thorp smiled. He knew that he'd beaten the butcher. As he would later write: "The day of the lamb had come."

After his first excursion to Vegas, Thorp began work on *Beat the Dealer*. Published in 1962, the book quickly became a *New York Times* bestseller—and struck terror into the heart of casino bigwigs everywhere.

Thorp continued to rack up gains at blackjack tables on several return trips to Las Vegas. Dealers were on the lookout for the gambling professor. He began wearing disguises, well aware of stories about card counters getting hauled into side alleys or casino basements for brutal beatings.

One day in 1964, when he was playing at a baccarat table in Las Vegas, he was offered a cup of coffee with cream and sugar. He took a few sips, then started feeling odd.

A friend who'd traveled to Las Vegas with Thorp and his wife happened to be a nurse. She peered into his eyes and recognized the look of drugged-out patients who landed in the emergency room. He walked it off, but the episode unnerved him. He decided he needed to find a fresh venue to test his strategies.

Thorp immediately set his sights on the biggest casino of all: Wall Street.

BEAT THE MARKET

On a typical day of desert sun and dry heat in Albuquerque, New Mexico, in the summer of 1965, Thorp settled into a lawn chair to read about an obscure corner of Wall Street: stock warrants.

Warrants are basically long-term contracts, much like a call option, that investors can convert into common stock. (A call option that gives an investor the right to purchase a stock at a future date is mathematically identical to a warrant.) At the time, warrants were thinly traded and generally considered the province of gamblers and bucket shops, the shadowy realm of off-exchange trading—not the typical domain of mathematically inclined professors. No one had figured out how to accurately price them.

In this obscure world, Thorp saw a vision of millions. Methods he'd used to win at blackjack, he realized, could be used to discern the value of warrants.

Soon after discovering this hidden gold mine, Thorp, who'd been teaching at New Mexico State, took a job at the University of California, Irvine. After arriving on campus, he heard about a finance professor at the university named Sheen Kassouf, a New York native of Lebanese descent, who'd also been plugging away at the problem of how to price warrants.

Kassouf had been dabbling in warrants since the early 1960s. He hadn't cracked the code for how to price the securities, but he had a strong grasp of how they worked. The two professors began meeting several times a week and eventually devised one of the first truly rigorous quantitative investing strategies—what they called "a scientific stock market system."

Their system enabled them to accurately price convertible bonds, which are a hybrid security made up of a bond, which spits out a regular interest payment, and those thinly traded warrants, which give the owner the right to convert the security to stock (hence the name of the bonds). Pricing a warrant was a difficult task, since its value depends on divining the likely price of the underlying stock at some future date. The system Thorp and Kassouf devised helped them make predictions about the future course of stock prices, allowing them to discover which convertible bonds were mispriced.

A key part of the answer, Thorp discovered, was found in a book he'd picked up after he'd switched his attention from blackjack to Wall Street. It was called *The Random Character of Stock Market Prices*, a collection of essays published in 1964, most of which argued that the market followed a so-called random walk. Essentially, that meant the future direction of the market as a whole, or any individual stock or bond, was a coin flip: there was a 50–50 chance that it could rise or fall.

The idea that the market moved in this fashion had been gaining ground since the mid-1950s, although the conceptual tool kit had been in the making for more than a century—all the way back, in fact, to June 1827 and a Scottish botanist and his love of flowers.

The botanist, Robert Brown, had been studying a species of pollen, called pinkfairies, through the lens of a brass microscope. The magnified pollen grains, he observed, jiggled incessantly, like thousands of tiny Ping-Pong balls moving in a frenetic dance.

Brown couldn't figure out what was causing the motion. After testing a range of other plant specimens, even the ground dust of rocks, and observing similar herky-jerky motion, he concluded that he was observing a phenomenon that was completely and mysteriously random. (The mystery remained unsolved for decades, until Albert Einstein, in 1905, discovered that the strange movement, by then known as Brownian motion, was the result of millions of microscopic particles buzzing around in a frantic dance of energy.)

The connection between Brownian motion and market prices was made in 1900 by a student at the University of Paris named Louis Bachelier. That year, he'd written a dissertation called "The Theory of Speculation," an attempt to create a formula that would capture the movement of bonds on the Paris stock exchange. The first English translation of the essay, which had lapsed into obscurity until it resurfaced again in the 1950s, had been included in the book about the market's randomness that Thorp had read in New Mexico.

The key to Bachelier's analysis was his observation that bond prices move in a way identical to the phenomenon first discovered by Brown in 1827. Bonds trading on the Paris stock exchange followed a pattern that, mathematically, moved just like those randomly oscillating pollen particles. Like the jiggling pollen grains, the minute-by-minute movement of the price of bonds appeared to be completely random, pushed up, down, and sideways by thousands of investors trying to guess where the market was going next. According to Bachelier's thinking, their guesses were futile. There was no way to know where the market would move next.

Bachelier's formula describing this phenomenon showed that the future course of the market is essentially a coin flip—a bond is as likely to rise as it is to fall, just as a coin is as likely to land on heads as tails, or a grain of pollen quivering in a mass of liquid is as likely to zig left as right. With bond prices, that's because the current price is "the true price: if the market judged otherwise, it would quote not this price, but another price higher or lower," Bachelier wrote.

This discovery came to be called the *random walk*. It's also called the *drunkard's walk*. Imagine it's late at night, and you're walking home through a thick fog—let's say a 1900 Parisian fog. You notice a drunk leaning against a lamppost in the bohemian quarter of Montmartre—perhaps some unknown artist celebrating a break-through. He's had too much absinthe and is wavering as he tries to decide which direction home lies. Is it east, north, west, south? Suddenly he lurches from the pole in a southward direction with great conviction, stumbling that way for the next five seconds. Then he changes his mind. He has every right—he's an artist in Paris, after all. Home, of course, lies to the west. Five seconds later, he changes his mind again—south. And so on.

According to Bachelier, the odds that the drunk will stagger five feet east, or five feet west, are the same, just as the odds that a 100-franc bond will rise 1 franc or fall 1 franc in a given time period are identical.

Visually, a chart of the various outcomes of a random walk is known as a *bell curve*, sloping gently upward to a rounded peak before sloping downward at the same rate. It's much more likely that the confused drunkard will sway randomly in many directions as the night progresses (samples that would fall in the middle of the curve) than that he will move continuously in a straight line, or spin in a circle (samples that would fall in the ends of the curve, commonly known as the tails of the distribution). In a thousand coin flips, it's more likely that the sample will contain roughly five hundred heads and five hundred tails (falling in the curve's middle) than nine hundred heads and one hundred tails (outer edge of the curve).

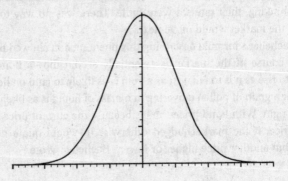

Thorp, already well aware of Einstein's 1905 discovery, was familiar with Brownian motion and rapidly grasped the connection between bonds and warrants. Indeed, it was in a way the same statistical rule that had helped Thorp win at blackjack: the law of large numbers (the more observations, the more coin flips, the greater the certainty of prediction). While he could never know if he'd win every hand at blackjack, he knew that over time he'd come out on top if he followed his card-counting strategy. Likewise, while he'd never know whether a stock would move up or down in the next week, he could determine how likely it was that the stock would rise or fall by, say, 2, 5, or 10 percent.

Thorp applied the formula to warrants. The future movement of a stock—a variable known to quants as *volatility*—is random, and therefore quantifiable. And if the warrant is priced in a way that underestimates, or overestimates, its likely volatility, money can be made.

Discovering how to price volatility was the key to unlocking the stock warrant treasure trove. Say you own a warrant for IBM. The current value of IBM's stock is $100. The warrant, which expires in twelve months, will be valuable only if IBM is worth $110 at some point during that twelve-month period. If you can determine how volatile IBM's stock is—how likely it is that it will hit $110 during that time period—you then know how much the warrant is worth. Thorp discovered that by plugging in the formula for Brownian motion, the random walk model, in addition to an extra variable for whether the stock itself tends to rise more or less than other stocks, he could know better than almost anyone else in the market what the IBM warrant was worth.

Gamblers make such time-dependent bets all the time. The time to expiration of the warrant is similar to the four quarters of a football game, baseball's nine innings, or a lap around the racetrack. Investors are wagering on a certain outcome within a predefined time frame. Thorp simply used his math skills and his well-honed gambling instincts to quantify the problem.

But to the conservative crowd—think investors in Treasuries and blue chips—all of this seemed a sort of crystal ball divination of the future, an approach better left to hucksters and charlatans. A trained physicist such as Thorp, however, saw that it was simply a matter of assigning a certain probability to a future outcome based on fixed parameters—a practice physicists and engineers engage in on a daily basis.

Using their models and their ability to predict volatility, Thorp and Kassouf realized there were a number of warrants that appeared to be mispriced. Some were too expensive, while others were cheap. The two professors collaborated on a 1967 book that described their findings. It was called *Beat the Market: A Scientific Stock Market System*. A quant touchstone, it soon became one of the most influential how-to books on investing ever written.

It also flew in the face of an increasingly popular theory in academia that it was impossible to consistently beat the market. Spearheaded by University of Chicago finance professor Eugene Fama in the late 1960s, this theory was known as the efficient-market hypothesis (EMH). At bottom, EMH was based on the idea, as Bachelier had argued, that the market moves in a random fashion and that current prices reflect all known information about the market. That being the case, it's impossible to know whether the market, or an individual stock, currency, bond, or commodity, will rise or fall in the future—the future is random, a coin flip. It's a fancy way of saying there's no free lunch. This idea eventually spawned the megabillion-dollar index fund industry, based on the notion that if active managers can't consistently put up better returns than the rest of the market, why not simply invest in the entire market itself, such as the S&P 500, for a much lower fee?

While Thorp fully understood the notion of random walks, which he'd used to price warrants, he thought EMH was academic hot air, the stuff of cloistered professors spinning airy fantasies of high-order math and fuzzy logic. Standard thinking had once been that it was also impossible to beat the dealer, and he'd proven the doubters wrong. He was convinced he could accomplish the same feats in the stock market.

He and Kassouf were soon investing in all kinds of warrants using their scientific system, and raking in piles of cash. Other faculty members who'd heard of Thorp and Kassouf's winning streak began asking to get in on the action. In short order, they were managing accounts for more than ten people, approaching the limit where they'd have to start filing with the government as investment advisors. It occurred to Thorp that the best way to invest for a number of people would be to create a single pool of assets, but he wasn't sure how to go about it.

The solution came from a man quickly gaining a reputation as one of the savviest investors in the world: Warren Buffett.

In the summer of 1968, Thorp drove from Irvine to Buffett's house in Laguna Beach, where Buffett often vacationed when he wasn't accumulating millions from his office in Omaha, Nebraska. Buffett was in the process of winding down his investing pool, Buffett Limited Partnerships, and distributing its assets to his investors—including shares of a New England textile factory called Berkshire Hathaway. In the coming years, Buffett would transform Berkshire into a cash-generating powerhouse that would turn the legendary investor who came to be known as the "Oracle of Omaha" into the richest man in the world.

At the time, however, Buffett wasn't very enthusiastic. Market conditions were unfavorable, he'd decided, and it was time to call it quits. One of his investors was Ralph Gerard, dean of the University of California, Irvine, where Thorp taught. Gerard was looking for a new place to invest his money and was considering Thorp. He'd asked Buffett if he would size up the hotshot math professor who was making a killing on stock warrants.

Buffett told Thorp about his partnership, which used a legal structure similar to the one created by his mentor, Benjamin Graham, author of *The Intelligent Investor* and father of value investing. The structure was also used by a former writer for *Fortune* magazine named Alfred Winslow Jones.

It was called a hedge fund.

In 1940, the U.S. Congress had passed the Investment Company Act, which was designed to protect small investors from devious mutual fund managers. But Congress made an exception. If a fund manager limited himself to no more than ninety-nine wealthy investors with assets of $1 million or more and didn't advertise, he could do pretty much whatever he liked.

Graham had been seared by brutal losses during the Great Depression and was a notoriously conservative investor who put his money only in companies he believed had a Grand Canyon–like "margin of safety." Jones, an Australian native who had worked as a writer and editor for Time Inc., was much more of a quick-fire trader, apt to bet on short-term swings in stocks or make speculative bets that a stock would plunge. In 1949, he founded A. W. Jones & Co. It was the first true hedge fund, with $100,000 in capital—$40,000 of it his own.

To further sidestep government oversight, A. W. Jones was domiciled offshore. Jones charged a 20 percent annual performance fee. To lessen the volatility of his fund, he'd sell certain stocks short, hoping to profit from a decline, while at the same time going long on certain stocks, benefiting from rising prices. In theory, this would boost returns during good times and bad. The short positions hedged his long portfolio, hence the name *hedge fund*, though the term didn't come into common parlance until the 1960s. His fund's eye-popping gains— 670 percent over the prior ten-year period, far better than the 358 percent return sported by the top mutual fund of that era—spawned a generation of copycats.

Jones may have been a reporter, but he was also a primitive quant, deploying statistical analysis to better manage his fund's risk. To amplify returns, he used leverage, or borrowed money. Leverage can be highly beneficial for funds that are properly positioned, but it can also be disastrous if prices move in the wrong direction.

As the go-go sixties bull market roared to life, other rock star hedge fund managers, such as the Hungarian savant George Soros, appeared on the scene. By 1968, there were 140 hedge funds in operation in the United States, according to a survey by the Securities and Exchange Commission. Ed Thorp was about to add to that growing list.

His chance came in August the following year, 1969. Hippies partied in Haight-Ashbury. The war in Vietnam raged. The New York Jets, led by "Broadway" Joe Namath, beat the Baltimore Colts to win the Super Bowl. But Ed Thorp focused like a laser on a single goal: making money.

That's when he happened to meet Jay Regan, a Dartmouth philosophy major working for a Philadelphia brokerage firm, Butcher &

Sherrerd. A full decade younger than Thorp, Regan had read *Beat the Market* and was blown away by the book's revolutionary trading strategy. Convinced the nerdy West Coast professors were onto something extremely lucrative, he called up Thorp and asked for a meeting.

Regan said he had contacts on the East Coast who could help seed a fund, with the kicker that the contacts were reliable sources of valuable market information. The idea appealed to Thorp, who didn't want to waste his time dealing with brokers and accountants.

They struck a deal: Thorp would stay in Newport Beach, continue teaching at UC Irvine, and work on the fund's investing strategies, while Regan would set up shop in Princeton, New Jersey, and keep tabs on Wall Street. Initially, the fund was called Convertible Hedge Associates. In 1975, they renamed it Princeton/Newport Partners.

In the meantime, Thorp continued to work on his formula for pricing warrants, always on the hunt for lucrative opportunities to apply his new scientific stock market system. Using his methodology to scan hundreds of warrants, he realized most were overpriced. For whatever reason, investors were too optimistic that the warrant would expire "in the money"—that the IBM stock would hit $110 in the next twelve months—much like starry-eyed gamblers wagering on their favorite team.

That opened up an exciting opportunity. Thorp could sell a presumably overpriced warrant short, borrowing it from a third party and selling it at the current price to another investor. His hope was that he could buy it back at a later date for a cheaper price, pocketing the difference. The risk was that the warrant would rise, possibly because the underlying stock gained in value. This could be crushing for a short seller, since there is theoretically no limit to how much a stock can increase in value.

But he had a safety net for that scenario: arbitrage, a practice that lies at the heart of how the modern-day financial industry operates—and a skeleton key to the quants' search for the Truth. Alfred Jones, with his long-short hedge strategy, had performed a primitive form of arbitrage, although it was the stuff of children compared to the quantitative method Thorp was devising.

True arbitrage is virtually a sure thing. It involves buying an asset in one market and almost simultaneously selling that asset, or its near equivalent, in another. Say gold is trading for $1,000 in New York and $1,050 in London. A fleet-footed arbitrageur will buy that New York gold and sell it in London (instantaneously), pocketing the $50 difference. While this was difficult when traders were swapping stocks beneath a buttonwood tree on Wall Street in the eighteenth century, the invention of the telegraph—and the telephone, the high-speed modem, and a grid of orbiting satellites—has made it much easier to accomplish in modern times.

Such obvious discrepancies in practice are rare and are often hidden in the depths of the financial markets like gold nuggets in a block of ore. That's where the quants, the math whizzes, step in.

Behind the practice of arbitrage is the law of one price (LOP), which states that a single price should apply to gold in New York as in London, or anywhere else for that matter. A barrel of light, sweet crude in Houston should cost the same as a barrel of crude in Tokyo (minus factors such as shipping costs and variable tax rates). But flaws in the information certain market players may have, technical factors that lead to brief discrepancies in prices, or any number of other market-fouling factors can trigger deviations from the LOP.

In the shadowy world of warrants, Thorp and Kassouf had stumbled upon a gold mine full of arbitrage opportunities. They could short the overpriced warrants and buy an equivalent chunk of stock to hedge their bet. If the stock started to rise unexpectedly, their downside would be covered by the stock. The formula also gave them a method to calculate how much stock they needed to hold in order to hedge their position. In the best of all worlds, the warrant price would decline and the stock would rise, closing out the inefficiency and providing a gain on each side of the trade.

This strategy came to be known as convertible bond arbitrage. It has become one of the most successful and lucrative trading strategies ever devised, helping launch thousands of hedge funds, including Citadel Investment Group, the mammoth Chicago powerhouse run by Ken Griffin.

Forms of this kind of arbitrage had been in practice on Wall Street for ages. Thorp and Kassouf, however, were the first to devise a precise, quantitative method to discover valuation metrics for warrants, as well as correlations between how much stock investors should hold to hedge their position in those warrants. In time, every Wall Street bank and most hedge funds would practice this kind of arbitrage, which would become known as delta hedging (*delta* is a Greek term that essentially captures the change in the relationship between the stock and the warrant or option).

Thorp understood the risks his strategy posed. And that meant he could calculate how much he was likely to win or lose from each bet. From there, he would determine how much he should wager on these trades using his old blackjack formula, the Kelly criterion. That allowed him to be aggressive when he saw opportunities, but it also kept him from betting too much. When the opportunities were good, like a deck full of face cards, Thorp would load the boat and get aggressive. But when the odds weren't in his favor, he would play it safe and make sure he had lots of extra cash on hand if the trade moved against him.

Thorp was also cautious almost to the point of paranoia. He was always concerned about out-of-the-blue events that could turn against him: an earthquake hitting Tokyo, a nuclear bomb in New York City, a meteor smashing Washington, D.C.

But it worked. Thorp's obsessive risk management strategy was at the heart of his long-term success. It meant he could maximize his returns when the deck was stacked in his favor. More important, it meant he would pull his chips off the table if he felt a chill wind blowing—a lesson the quants of another generation seemed to have missed.

After launching in late 1969, Thorp and Regan's fund was an almost immediate hit, gaining 3 percent in 1970 compared with a 5 percent decline by the S&P 500, which is a commonly used proxy for the market as a whole. In 1971, their fund was up 13.5 percent, next to a 4 percent advance by the broader market, and it gained 26 percent in 1972, compared with a 14.3 percent rise by the index. Thorp programmed formulas for tracking and pricing warrants into a Hewlett-Packard

9830A he'd installed in his office in Newport Beach, keeping tabs on Wall Street thousands of miles away from the edge of the Pacific Ocean.

In 1973, Thorp received a letter from Fischer Black, an eccentric economist then teaching at the University of Chicago. The letter contained a draft of a paper that Black had written with another Chicago economist, Myron Scholes, about a formula for pricing stock options. It would become one of the most famous papers in the history of finance, though few people, including its authors, had any idea how important it would be.

Black was aware of Thorp and Kassouf's delta hedging strategy, which was described in *Beat the Market*. Black and Scholes made use of a similar method to discover the value of the option, which came to be known as the Black-Scholes option-pricing formula. Thorp scanned the paper. He programmed the formula into his HP computer, and it quickly produced a graph showing the price of a stock option that closely matched the price spat out by his own formula.

The Black-Scholes formula was destined to revolutionize Wall Street and usher in a wave of quants who would change the way the financial system worked forever. Just as Einstein's discovery of relativity theory in 1905 would lead to a new way of understanding the universe, as well as the creation of the atomic bomb, the Black-Scholes formula dramatically altered the way people would view the vast world of money and investing. It would also give birth to its own destructive forces and pave the way to a series of financial catastrophes, culminating in an earthshaking collapse that erupted in August 2007.

Like Thorp's methodology for pricing warrants, an essential component of the Black-Scholes formula was the assumption that stocks moved in a random walk. Stocks, in other words, are assumed to move in antlike zigzag patterns just like the pollen particles observed by Brown in 1827. In their 1973 paper, Black and Scholes wrote that they assumed that the "stock price follows a random walk in continuous time." Just as Thorp had already discovered, this allowed investors to determine the relevant probabilities for volatility—how high or low a stock or option would move in a certain time frame.

Hence, the theory that had begun with Robert Brown's scrutiny of plants, then led to Bachelier's observations about bond prices, finally reached a most pragmatic conclusion—a formula that Wall Street would use to trade billions of dollars' worth of stock and options.

But a central feature of the option-pricing formula would come back to bite the quants years later. Practically stated, the use of Brownian motion to price the volatility of options meant that traders looked at the most likely moves a stock could make—the ones that lay toward the center of the bell curve. By definition, the method largely ignored big jumps in price. Those sorts of movements were seen as unlikely as the drunk wandering across Paris suddenly hopping from the cathedral of Notre Dame to the Sorbonne across the river Seine in the blink of an eye. But the physical world and the financial world—as much as they seem to have in common—aren't always in sync. The exclusion of big jumps left out a key reality about the behavior of market prices, which can make huge leaps in the blink of an eye. There was a failure to factor in the human element—a major scandal, a drug that doesn't pan out, a tainted product, or a panicked flight for the exits caused by all-too-common investor hysteria. History shows that investors often tend to act like sheep, following one another in bleating herds, sometimes all the way over a cliff.

Huge, sudden leaps were a contingency no one bothered to consider. Experienced traders such as Thorp understood this and made adjustments accordingly—his paranoid hand-wringing about distant earthquakes or nuclear bomb attacks, as well as his constant attention to the real odds of winning essential for his Kelly calculations, kept him from relying too much on the model. Other quantitative traders, less seasoned, perhaps less worldly, came to see the model as a reflection of how the market actually worked. The model soon became so ubiquitous that, hall-of-mirrors-like, it became difficult to tell the difference between the model and the market itself.

In the early seventies, however, the appearance of the Black-Scholes model seemed propitious. A group of economists at the University of Chicago, led by free market guru Milton Friedman, were trying to establish an options exchange in the city. The breakthrough formula for pricing options spurred on their plans. On April 26, 1973, one month before the Black-Scholes paper appeared in print, the Chicago Board Options Exchange opened for business. And soon after, Texas Instruments introduced a handheld calculator that could price options using the Black-Scholes formula.

With the creation and rapid adoption of the formula on Wall Street, the quant revolution had officially begun. Years later, Scholes and Robert Merton, an MIT professor whose ingenious use of sto-chastic calculus had further validated the Black-Scholes model, would win the Nobel Prize for their work on option pricing. (Black had passed away a few years before, excluding him from Nobel considera-tion.) Thorp never received any formal recognition for devising essen-tially the same formula, which hadn't fully published. He did, however, make hundreds of millions of dollars using it.

Princeton/Newport Partners had garnered so much attention by 1974 that the *Wall Street Journal* ran a front-page article on the fund: "Playing the Odds: Computer Formulas Are One Man's Secret to Suc-cess in the Market."

"Reliable brokerage-house sources close to the funds say they have averaged better than 20 percent a year in net asset growth," the article said. More remarkable, such gains came at a time when the market was experiencing its worst decline since the Great Depres-sion, rocked by high inflation and the Watergate scandal. In 1974, a year that saw the S&P 500 tumble 26 percent, Thorp's fund gained 9.7 percent.

The article went on to describe one of the world's most sophisti-cated investing operations—and the germ for the quant revolution to come. Thorp, it said, "relies on proprietary mathematical formulas programmed into computers to help spot anomalies between options and other convertibles and their common stock.... Mr. Thorp's funds are an example of an incipient but growing switch in money manage-ment to a quantitative, mechanistic approach, involving heavy use of the computer."

Starting in the mid-1970s, Princeton/Newport went on a hot streak, posting double-digit returns for eleven straight years (after the 20 percent incentive fees Thorp and Regan charged clients, typical for hedge funds). In fact, from its inception, the fund never had a down year or a down quarter. In 1982, Thorp quit his teaching job at UC Irvine and started working full-time managing money.

The gains kept coming, even in down years. In the twelve months through November 1985, Princeton/Newport was up 12 percent, compared with a 20 percent decline by the S&P 500. By then, Thorp and Regan were managing about $130 million, a heady increase from the $10,000 stake Thorp had received from Manny Kimmel for his first blackjack escapade in 1961. (In 1969, when the fund opened its doors for business, it had a stake of $1.4 million.)

But Thorp wasn't resting on his laurels. He was always on the lookout for new talent. In 1985, he ran across a hotshot trader named Gerry Bamberger who'd just abandoned a post at Morgan Stanley. Bamberger had created a brilliant stock trading strategy that came to be known as statistical arbitrage, or stat arb—one of the most powerful trading strategies ever devised, a nearly flawless moneymaking system that could post profits no matter what direction the market was moving.

It was right up Thorp's alley.

Gerry Bamberger discovered stat arb almost by accident. A tall, quick-witted Orthodox Jew from Long Island, he'd joined Morgan Stanley in 1980 after earning a degree in computer science at Columbia University. At Morgan, he was part of a group that provided analytical and technical support for the bank's stock trading operations.

In this capacity, Bamberger wrote software for Morgan's block trading desk, which shuffled blocks of ten thousand or more shares at a time for institutional clients such as mutual funds. The block traders also used a "pairs strategy" to minimize losses. If the desk held a block of General Motors stock, it would sell short a chunk of Ford that would pay off if the GM stock took a hit. Bamberger's software provided traders up-to-date information on the relative positions of the pairs.

Bamberger noticed that large block trades would often cause the price of the stock to move significantly. The price of the other stock in the pair, meanwhile, barely moved. This pushed the typical gap between the two stock prices, the "spread," temporarily out of whack.

Suppose GM typically traded for $10 and Ford for $5. A large buy order for GM could cause the price to rise temporarily to $10.50. Ford, meanwhile, would stay at $5. The "spread" between the two stocks had widened.

By tracking the historical patterns and moving with cheetah-quick speed, Bamberger realized he could take advantage of these temporary blips. He could short a stock that had moved upward in relation to its pair, profiting when the stocks returned to their original spread. He could also take a long (or short) position in the stock that hadn't moved, which would protect him in case the other stock failed to shift back to its original price—if the historical spread remained, the long position would eventually rise.

Much like Thorp's delta hedging strategy, it was the old game of buy low, sell high, with a quant twist.

After describing his ideas to his superiors, Bamberger was set up on Morgan's equity desk in early 1983 with $500,000 and a small group of traders. He started making buckets of cash right out of the gate. By September, his group had $4 million worth of long and short positions. In early 1984, it had $10 million. The stake rose to $15 million in October. By 1985, the group was running a $30 million book.

But almost as fast as Bamberger scaled the heights, he came crashing down. Morgan's higher-ups, reluctant to leave such a money machine in the hands of a programmer, turned it over to a hired gun named Nunzio Tartaglia. Bamberger, outraged, quit the firm.

The Brooklyn-born Tartaglia was a mass of contradictions. He'd earned a master's degree in physics from Yale University in the early 1960s, then promptly joined the Jesuits. After five years, he left the seminary to earn a Ph.D. in astrophysics from the University of Pittsburgh. By the early 1970s, Tartaglia found himself working on Wall Street as a retail broker at Merrill Lynch. After Merrill, the peripatetic Tartaglia went to five other firms before landing at Morgan in 1984.

He renamed the group he'd taken over Automated Proprietary Trading, or APT, and moved it to a single forty-foot-long room on the nineteenth floor in Morgan's Exxon Building headquarters in midtown Manhattan. Tartaglia added more automation to the system, linking the desk to the New York Stock Exchange's Super Designated

Order Turnaround System, or SuperDOT, which facilitated computerized trades. APT was soon trading so much that at times it accounted for 5 percent of the daily trading volume on the NYSE. The stat arb strategy earned $6 million in the first year Tartaglia ran the group. In 1986, it pulled in an eye-popping $40 million, then $50 million in 1987. The group started to gain legendary status on Wall Street, in part due to its CIA-like secrecy.

In 1986, Tartaglia hired David Shaw, a computer whiz teaching at Columbia University, to head APT's technology unit. The Stanford-educated Shaw was an expert in a hot new field called parallel processing, in which two or more mainframe computers crunched numbers on the same problem to ramp up speed and efficiency. Shaw had virtually no trading experience, but he was a quick learner, and soon became interested in the group's unique trading strategies. His colleagues found him shy, nervous around women, and self-conscious about his looks. Tall, thin as a spider, Shaw was a classic quant.

Morgan had hired Shaw with the promise that he'd be able to develop his own trading strategies, where the real money was to be made. But as Tartaglia steadily took over the group, making every effort to keep the lucrative trading platform to a chosen few, Shaw realized that he wouldn't have the opportunity to trade.

He decided to take matters into his own hands. One day in September 1987, the group was giving a presentation about its business model and trading strategies to senior management. Shaw's presentation on parallel processing and high-speed algorithms was proceeding normally. Suddenly, he started to expound on complex mathematical bond-arbitrage strategies. As the meeting ended, APT's traders and researchers sat fuming in their chairs. Shaw had crossed the line. Programmers weren't supposed to trade, or even think about trading. Back then, the line between programmer and trading strategist remained firmly in place, a boundary that steadily dissolved as trading became more and more computerized.

For his part, Shaw had hoped that Morgan's higher-ups would see the value of his ideas. He'd also approached upper management on his own about creating an entirely new research unit, a scientific laboratory for research on quantitative and computational finance.

But his ideas fell on deaf ears, and Tartaglia wasn't giving any ground. The weekend after the presentation, Shaw decided to quit, informing Tartaglia of his decision the following Monday. Tartaglia, possibly perceiving Shaw as a threat, was happy to see him go.

It may have been one of the most significant losses of talent in the history of Morgan Stanley.

Shaw landed on his feet, starting up his own investment firm with $28 million in capital and naming his fund D. E. Shaw. It soon became one of the most successful hedge funds in the world. Its core strategy: statistical arbitrage.

Tartaglia, meanwhile, hit a rough patch, and in 1988, Morgan's higher-ups slashed APT's capital to $300 million from $900 million. Tartaglia amped up the leverage, eventually pushing the leverage-to-capital ratio to 8 to 1 (it invested $8 for each $1 it actually had in its coffers). By 1989, APT had started to lose money. The worse things got, the more frantic Tartaglia became. Eventually he was forced out. Shortly after, APT itself was shut down.

In the meantime, Bamberger had found a new home. One day after he'd left Morgan, he got a call from Fred Taylor, a former Morgan colleague who'd joined a hedge fund that specialized in quantitative investing.

"What's it called?" Bamberger asked.

"Princeton/Newport Partners," Taylor told him. "Run by a guy named Ed Thorp."

Thorp, Taylor explained, was always interested in new strategies and was interested in looking at stat arb. Taylor introduced Bamberger to Jay Regan, and the two hit it off. Thorp and Regan agreed to back a fund called BOSS Partners, an acronym for Bamberger and Oakley Sutton Securities (Oakley and Sutton are Thorp and Regan's middle names, respectively). Bamberger set up shop in a 120-square-foot twelfth-floor office on West 57th Street in New York. With $5 million in capital, he hit the ground running, cranking out an annualized return of about 30 percent his first year in operation. By 1988, BOSS was running about $100 million in assets and generating consistent double-digit returns.

BOSS, like APT, hit a dry spell in early 1988. Toward the end of the year, Bamberger decided he'd had enough of Wall Street. He wound down BOSS and moved upstate to teach finance and law at the State University of New York at Buffalo. He never again traded stocks on a large scale.

But his strategy lived on, and not just at Princeton/Newport. Traders who'd worked for Bamberger and Tartaglia fanned out across Wall Street, bringing stat arb to hedge funds and investment banks such as Goldman Sachs. As D. E. Shaw raked in profits, other funds started trying to copy its superfast trading style. Robert Frey, who'd worked as an APT researcher, took stat arb to Jim Simons's fund, Renaissance Technologies, in the early 1990s. Peter Muller, the singing quant who triumphed at Wall Street Poker Night in 2006, appeared on the scene at Morgan a few years after Tartaglia was ousted and started up his own stat-arb money machine, one that proved far more robust. Ken Griffin, who kept a keen eye on everything Thorp was doing, adopted the strategy at Citadel. Stat arb soon became one of the most popular and consistent ways to make money on Wall Street—too popular, in fact, as its practitioners would discover in August 2007.

Ed Thorp's influence was spreading across the financial universe in other ways as well. At MIT, a team of blackjack card counters sprung up, the group that would eventually inspire the bestselling book *Bringing Down the House*. An early member of the group was a young math hotshot named Blair Hull, who'd read *Beat the Dealer* in the early 1970s. By the end of the decade, he'd parlayed $25,000 in winnings to jump-start a trading career in the Chicago options trading pits, having also read *Beat the Market*. In 1985, he founded Hull Trading, which specialized in using quantitative models and computers to price options on a rapid-fire basis. Hull eventually became one of the most advanced trading operations in the world, a quant mecca that transformed the options world. In 1999, Goldman Sachs shelled out $531 million for Hull, which it developed into one of Wall Street's premier high-frequency trading outfits.

For Thorp and Regan, meanwhile, everything had been running smoothly. The fund had posted solid gains in 1986 and was surging ahead in the first half of 1987, helped by BOSS's gains. Then stocks started to wobble. By early October, cracks were forming in the market that would turn into a full-blown earthquake. At the heart of the disaster: the quants and the Black-Scholes option-pricing formula.

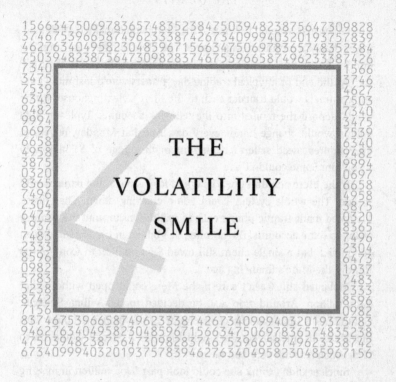

THE
VOLATILITY
SMILE

Sometime around midnight, October 19, 1987, Leo Melamed reached out a sweaty-palmed hand, picked up the phone in his nineteenth-floor office at the Chicago Mercantile Exchange, and dialed Alan Greenspan. The newly appointed chairman of the Federal Reserve, Greenspan was staying at the upscale Adolphus Hotel in Dallas to address the American Bankers Association's annual convention the next day. It was to be his first major speech as chairman of the central bank.

The speech would never happen. The Dow industrials had crashed, losing 23 percent in a single day. Other exchanges, including the Merc, were in chaos. Many players in the market were bankrupt and couldn't settle their bills. Greenspan had been fielding calls from executives at nearly every major bank and exchange in the country. His single goal: make sure the markets were up and running Tuesday morning.

Greenspan wanted to know if the Merc would make it. Melamed, the exchange's president, wasn't sure. The Merc had become a trading hub for a new financial product, futures contracts linked to the S&P 500. At the end of a typical trading day, traders who'd lost money on any contracts would transfer cash to the Merc's clearinghouse, which would deposit the money into the winners' accounts. Typically $120 million would change hands every day. But that Monday, buyers of S&P futures owed sellers an amount in the range of $2 billion to $3 billion. Some couldn't pay.

If the Merc couldn't open its doors for business, the panic would spread. The whole system could come crashing down. That night, Melamed made frantic phone calls to institutions around the country trying to settle accounts. By morning, $2.1 billion in transfers had been completed, but a single client still owed $400 million to Continental Illinois, the Merc's financing agent.

Melamed still wasn't sure if the Merc could open without that $400 million. Around 7:00 A.M. he decided to call Wilma Smelcer, Continental's financial officer in charge of the bank's account with the Merc. If Smelcer couldn't help him, his next call would be to Greenspan . . . with very bad news.

Smelcer didn't think she could look past $400 million in missing funds. It was a deal killer. "Wilma, I am certain your customer is good for it," Melamed pleaded. "You're not going to let a stinking couple of hundred million dollars cause the Merc to go down the tubes, are you?"

"Leo, my hands are tied."

"Please listen, Wilma. You have to take it upon yourself to guarantee the balance, because if you don't, I've got to call Alan Greenspan, and we're going to cause the next depression."

After a few moments of tense silence, Smelcer said, "Hold it a minute, Leo. Tom Theobald just walked in." Theobald was chairman of Continental.

After a few minutes, Smelcer was back. "Leo, we're okay. Tom said go ahead. You've got your money."

It was 7:17 A.M., three minutes before the opening of the Merc's currency markets. The world had little idea how close the financial system had come to a catastrophic seizure.

■   ■   ■

One of the critical factors behind the crash of Black Monday on October 19, 1987, can be traced to a restless finance professor's sleepless night more than a decade earlier. The result of that night would be a feat of financial engineering called portfolio insurance. Based on the Black-Scholes formula, portfolio insurance would scramble the inner workings of the stock market and set the stage for the single largest one-day market collapse in history.

On the evening of September 11, 1976, Hayne Leland, a thirty-five-year-old professor at the University of California at Berkeley, was having trouble sleeping. He'd recently returned from a trip to France. A weak dollar had made the trip excessively pricey. Stagflation, a crippling mix of high inflation and slow growth, was rampant. The economy and the stock market were in the tank. California governor Ronald Reagan was threatening cutbacks in the salaries of academics such as Leland, who worried that the prosperous American lifestyle of his parents' generation was in danger.

As he pondered this bleak reality, Leland recalled a conversation he'd had with his brother, John, who worked at an investment management company in San Francisco. Stocks had cratered in 1973, and pension funds had pulled out en masse, missing out on a bounce that followed. "If only insurance were available," John had said, "those funds could be attracted back to the market."

Leland was familiar with the Black-Scholes formula and knew that options behaved in ways like insurance. A put option, which pays off if a stock drops, is akin to an insurance policy on a stock. He thought of it step by step. *Say I own IBM at $50 and am worried about it losing value. I can buy a put for $3 that pays off if IBM falls to $45 (allowing me to unload it for $50), essentially insuring myself against the decline for a premium of $3.*

Leland realized his brother had been describing a put option on an entire portfolio of stocks. He sat down at his desk and started to scribble out the implications of his revelation. If the risk of an entire portfolio of stocks declining could be quantified, and if insurance could cover it, then risk would be controlled and managed, if not effectively eliminated. Thus portfolio insurance was born. No more sleepless nights for jittery professors.

Over the next few years, Leland and a team of financial engineers, including Mark Rubinstein and John O'Brien, created a product that would provide insurance for large portfolios of stocks, with the Black-Scholes formula as a guidepost. In 1981, they formed Leland O'Brien Rubinstein Associates Inc., later known simply as LOR. By 1984, business was booming. The product grew even more popular after the Chicago Mercantile Exchange started trading futures contracts tied to the S&P 500 index in April 1982. The financial wizards at LOR could replicate their portfolio insurance product by shorting S&P index futures. If stocks fell, they would short more futures contracts. Easy, simple, and sweet. And enormously profitable.

By the autumn of 1987, the company's portfolio insurance protected $50 billion in assets held by institutional investors, mostly pension funds. Add in LOR copycats and the total amount of equity backed by portfolio insurance was roughly $100 billion.

The Dow industrials had soared through the first half of 1987, gaining more than 40 percent by late August. The so-called Reagan Revolution had restored confidence in America. Inflation was in retreat. Japanese investors were flooding the United States with yen. New Agers around the country discovered the healing power of crystals. A new, young Fed chairman was in town. The New York Mets were the Cinderella world champions of baseball, having won the 1986 World Series in seven games, led by a young power hitter named Darryl Strawberry and a dazzling pitcher named Dwight Gooden. What could go wrong?

Plenty. By mid-October, the market had been knocked for a loop, tumbling 15 percent in just a few months. The block trading desk at Shearson Lehman Brothers installed a metal sign with an arrow that read: "To the Lifeboats."

The mood was grim. Traders talked of chain reaction declines triggered by mysterious computer-assisted trading strategies in stocks and futures markets. As trading wound down on Friday, October 16, a trader in stock index options on the floor of the American Stock Exchange shrieked, "It's the end of the world!"

Early on Monday, October 19, investors in New York were brac-
ing for an onslaught well before trading began. Over in the Windy
City, it was eerily quiet in the stock index futures pit at the Chicago
Mercantile Exchange as traders waited for the action to begin. All
eyes were on Chicago's "shadow markets," whose futures anticipate
the behavior of actual prices. Seconds after the open at the Merc—
fifteen minutes ahead of trading in New York—S&P 500 index futures
dropped 14 points, indicating a 70-point slump in the Dow industrials.

Over the next fifteen minutes before trading began on the
NYSE, massive pressure built up on index futures, almost entirely
from portfolio insurance firms. The big drop by index futures triggered a signal for another new breed of trader: index arbitrageurs,
investors taking advantage of small discrepancies between indexes
and underlying stocks. When trading opened in New York, a brick
wall of short selling slammed the market. As stocks tumbled, pressure increased on portfolio insurers to sell futures, racing to keep up
with the widely gapping market in a devastating feedback loop. The
arbs scrambled to put on their trades but were overwhelmed: futures
and stocks were falling in unison. Chaos ruled.

Fischer Black watched the disaster with fascination from his
perch at Goldman Sachs in New York, where he'd taken a job managing quantitative trading strategies. Robert Jones, a Goldman trader,
dashed into Black's office to report on the carnage. "I put in an order
to sell at market and it never filled," he said, describing a frightening
scenario in which prices are falling so fast there seems to be no set
point where a trade can be executed. "Wow, really?" Black said, clap-
ping his hands in amazement. "This is history in the making!"

In the final seventy-five minutes of trading on October 19, the decline hit full throttle as portfolio insurance sellers dumped futures and
sell orders flowed in from brokerage accounts around the country.
The Dow snapped, sliding 300 points, triple the amount it had ever
dropped in a single day in history and roughly the equivalent of a
1,500-point drop in today's market. The blue chip average finished the
day at 1738.74, having dropped 508 points.

In the new globally interlaced electronic marketplace, the devas-
tation wound around the globe like a poisonous serpent Monday

night, hitting markets in Tokyo, Hong Kong, Paris, Zurich, and London, then making its way back to New York. Early Tuesday, during a brief, gut-wrenching moment, the market would lurch even deeper into turmoil than Black Monday. The blue-chip average opened down more than 30 percent. Stocks, options, and futures trading froze. It was an all-out meltdown.

Over in Newport Beach, Thorp's team was scrambling. Thorp had watched in dismay Monday as the market fell apart. By the time he got back from a hastily snatched lunch, it had lost 23 percent. Trading was closed, and Thorp had a severe case of heartburn. But he quickly figured out that portfolio insurance was behind the market meltdown.

As trading opened Tuesday, a huge gap between S&P futures and the corresponding cash market opened up. Normally, that meant a great trading opportunity for arbs, including Thorp, always attracted to quantitative strategies. The massive gap between futures contracts, created by the heavy selling by portfolio insurers, and their underlying stocks was a sign to buy futures and short stocks.

By Tuesday, most of the arbs were terrified, having been crushed on Black Monday by the plummeting market. But Thorp was determined. His plan was to short the stocks in the index and buy the futures, gobbling up the big spread between the two.

The trouble was getting the orders through in the fast-moving market. As soon as a buy or sell order was placed, it was left behind as the market continued to tumble. In the heat of the crisis, Thorp got Princeton/Newport's head trader on the phone: "Buy $5 million worth of index futures at the market and short $10 million worth of stocks."

His best guess was that only half of the stock orders would be filled anyway because, due to technical reasons, it was hard to short stocks in the free-falling market.

At first his trader balked. "Can't, the market's frozen."

Thorp threw the hammer down. "If you don't fill these orders I'm going to do them in my own personal account. I'm going to hang you out to dry," Thorp shouted, clearly implying that the trader's firm wouldn't share any of the profits.

The trader reluctantly agreed to comply but was only able to make about 60 percent of the short sales Thorp had ordered up due to the volatility. Soon after, he did the trade again, pocketing more than $1 million in profits.

Thorp's calm leap into the chaos wasn't the norm. Most market players were in a this-is-the-big-one hand-wringing frenzy.

Then it stopped. Sometime Tuesday afternoon, the market landed on its feet. It started to climb as the Federal Reserve pumped massive sums of money into the system. The Dow finished the day up 102 points. The next day, it soared 186.84 points, its biggest one-day point advance in history at the time.

But the damage had been done. The mood around the country turned decidedly anti–Wall Street as the junk bond scandals hit the front pages of newspapers. An October 1987 *Newsweek* cover queried, "Is the Party Over? A Jolt for Wall Street's Whiz Kids." In December 1987, audiences in movie theaters listened to Gordon Gekko, the slimy takeover artist played by Michael Douglas, proclaim the mantra for the decade in Oliver Stone's *Wall Street*: "Greed is good." A series of popular books reflecting the anti–Wall Street sentiment hit the presses: *Bonfire of the Vanities* by Tom Wolfe, *Barbarians at the Gate* by *Wall Street Journal* reporters Bryan Burrough and John Helyar, *The Predators' Ball* by Connie Bruck, *Liar's Poker* by Michael Lewis.

The quants were licking their wounds. Their wondrous invention, portfolio insurance, was roundly blamed for the meltdown. Fama's efficient-market theory was instantly called into question. How could the market be "right" one day, then suffer a 23 percent collapse on virtually no new information the next day, then be fine the day after?

The now-you-see-it-now-you-don't math wizards had a unique retort: Black Monday never happened. Jens Carsten Jackwerth, a postdoctoral visiting scholar at the University of California at Berkeley, and Mark Rubinstein, coinventor of portfolio insurance, offered incontrovertible proof that October 19, 1987, was statistically impossible. According to their probability formula, published in 1995, the likelihood of the crash was a "27-standard-deviation event," with a probability of 10 to the 160th power: "Even if one were to have lived through the entire 20 billion year life of the universe and experienced this 20 billion times (20 billion big bangs), that such a decline could have happened even once in this period is a virtual impossibility."

Still, the very real crash on Black Monday left very real scars on the psyches of the traders who witnessed it, from the trading pits of Chicago to the exchange floors of lower Manhattan. Meltdowns of such magnitude and ferocity were not supposed to happen in the world's most advanced and sophisticated financial marketplace.

They especially weren't supposed to happen in a randomized, Brownian motion world in which the market obeyed neat statistical rules. A 27-standard-deviation event was tantamount to flipping a coin a hundred times and getting ninety-nine straight heads.

Was there a worm in the apple, a fatal flaw in the quants' theory? This haunting fear, brought on by Black Monday, would hover over them like a bad dream time and time again, from the meltdown in October 1987 until the financial catastrophe that erupted in August 2007.

The flaw had already been identified decades earlier by one of the most brilliant mathematicians in the world: Benoit Mandelbrot.

When German tanks rumbled into France in 1940, Benoit Mandelbrot was sixteen years old. His family, Lithuanian Jews, had lived in Warsaw before moving to Paris in 1936 amid a spreading economic depression. Mandelbrot's uncle, Szolem Mandelbrojt, had moved to Paris in 1929 and quickly rose to prominence among the city's mathematical elite. Young Mandelbrot studied under his uncle and entered a French secondary school. But his life was upended when the Nazis invaded.

As the Germans closed in, the Mandelbrot family fled to the small hill town of Tulle in southwest France, where they had friends. Benoit enrolled in the local school, where there was little competition. The freedom from the fierce head-to-head pressure of Paris nurtured his creative side. He soon developed the unique ability to picture complex geometric images in his mind and make intuitive leaps about how to solve difficult equations.

Mandelbrot's father, a clothing wholesaler, had no job, and the family was destitute. He knew a shopkeeper who had a bundle of coats from before the war with a strange Scottish design. The coats were so hideous that the shopkeeper had trouble giving them away. The senior Mandelbrot took one for his son, who welcomed it.

One day a group of French partisans blew up a nearby German outpost. A witness noticed that one of the attackers wore a strange-looking jacket with a Scottish design—the same jacket young Mandelbrot wore around the town. When a villager denounced him, he went into hiding, joined by his brother. During the next year, Mandelbrot, innocent of the attack, managed to avoid the German patrols. By the time Allied troops liberated Paris in 1944, he was twenty years old.

Those nomadic years spent in the countryside of France were crucial in the development of Mandelbrot's approach to mathematics. The absence of strict guidelines and competition from peers created an environment in which his mind could freely explore the outer limits of mathematical territories most students his age could never dream of.

He took the entrance examination for Paris's elite institutions of higher education, the École Normale Supérieure and the École Polytechnique. With no time to prepare, he took it cold. The mathematical section of the test was a complex riddle involving algebra and geometry in which the result (after a great deal of calculation) comes out to zero. Mandelbrot landed the highest score in the country, earning him a ticket to either school. He completed his Ph.D. in 1952.

After graduating, Mandelbrot entered a period of professional limbo, working for a time with the French psychologist Jean Piaget before spending a year at Princeton's Institute for Advanced Study in 1953.

In 1958, he took a job at IBM's Thomas J. Watson Research Center, the company's primary laboratory north of Manhattan. By then, his work on issues such as income distributions in various societies had captured the attention of economists outside the cloistered IBM research lab, and in 1961 he went to give a talk at Harvard. When he arrived on campus, he made a beeline to the office of his host for the event, the economics professor Hendrik Houthakker. Soon after entering, he was stunned by a strange diagram on the professor's blackboard, a convex V that opened out to the right. Mandelbrot sat down.

The image on the blackboard loomed over Houthakker's shoulder. Mandelbrot couldn't keep his eyes off it.

"I'm sorry," he said after a few minutes' chitchat. "I keep looking at your blackboard because this is a strange situation. You have on your blackboard a diagram from my lecture."

Houthakker turned and gazed at the diagram. "What do you mean?" he said. "I have no idea what you're going to talk about."

The diagram came from a student's research project on the behavior of cotton prices, an obsession of Houthakker's. The student was trying to discern how the patterns in cotton prices fit into the standard Brownian motion models that dominated financial theory. But to his great frustration, nothing worked. The data didn't fit the theory or the bell curve. Prices flitted about too erratically. The stunning coincidence for Mandelbrot was that the diagram of cotton prices on Houthakker's chalkboard exactly matched the diagram of income distributions Mandelbrot had prepared for his talk.

The bizarre leaps and plunges in cotton prices had proved too wild for Houthakker. Either the data were bad—unlikely, as there were a lot of data, going back more than a century from records kept by the New York Cotton Exchange—or the models were faulty. Either way, he was on the verge of giving up.

"I've had enough," he told Mandelbrot. "I've done everything I could to make sense of these cotton prices. I try to measure the volatility. It changes all the time. Everything changes. Nothing is constant. It's a mess of the worst kind."

Mandelbrot saw an opportunity. There might be a hidden relationship between his own analysis of income distributions—which also displayed wild, disparate leaps that didn't fall within the normal bell curve—and these unruly cotton prices that had driven Houthakker to his wits' end. Houthakker happily handed over a cardboard box full of computer punch cards containing data on cotton prices.

"Good luck if you can make any sense of these."

Upon returning to IBM's research center in Yorktown Heights, Mandelbrot began running the data through IBM's supercomputers.

He gathered prices from dust-ridden books at the National Bureau of Economic Research in Manhattan and from the U.S. Agriculture Department in Washington. He looked into wheat prices, railroad stocks, and interest rates. Everywhere he looked he saw the same thing: huge leaps where they didn't belong—on the outer edges of the bell curve.

After combing through the data, Mandelbrot wrote a paper detailing his findings, "The Variation of Certain Speculative Prices." Published as an internal research report at IBM, it was a direct attack on the normal distributions used to model the market. While praising Louis Bachelier, a personal hero of Mandelbrot's, the mathematician asserted that "the empirical distributions of price changes are usually too 'peaked' relative to samples" from standard distributions.

The reason: "Large price changes are much more frequent than predicted."

Mandelbrot proposed an alternative method to measure the erratic behavior of prices, one that borrows a mathematical technique devised by the French mathematician Paul Lévy, whom he'd studied under in Paris. Lévy investigated distributions in which a single sample radically changes the curve. The average of the heights of 1,000 people won't change very much as a result of the height of the 1,001st person. But a so-called Lévy distribution can be thrown off by a single wild shift in the sample. Mandelbrot uses the example of a blindfolded archer: 1,000 shots may fall close to the target, but the 1,001st shot, by happenstance, may fall very wide of the mark, radically changing the overall distribution. It was an entirely different way of looking at statistical patterns—all previous results could be overturned by one single dramatic shift in the trend, such as a 23 percent drop in the stock market in a single day. Lévy's formulas gave Mandelbrot the mathematical key to analyzing the wild moves in cotton prices that had befuddled Houthakker.

When plotted on a chart, these wild, unexpected moves looked nothing like the standard bell curve. Instead, the curve bubbled out on both ends, the "tails" of the distribution. The bubbles came to be known as "fat tails."

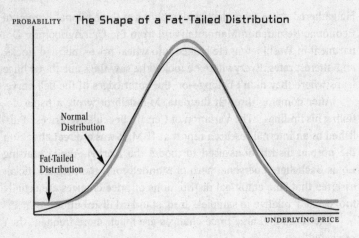

Word of Mandelbrot's paper spread through the academic community. In late 1963, he got a call from Paul Cootner, an MIT finance professor. Cootner was putting together a book of published material on recent mathematical insights into the workings of the market, including a translation of Bachelier's thesis on Brownian motion. He wanted to include Mandelbrot's paper. He called the book *The Random Character of Stock Market Prices*. It was the same book Ed Thorp read a year later when he was trying to figure out a formula to price warrants.

In the book, Cootner attacked Mandelbrot's submission in a strident five-page critique. Mandelbrot "promises us not utopia but blood, sweat, toil, and tears." The wild gyrating mess of Lévy's formulas, the sudden leaps in prices, simply wouldn't do. The result would be chaos. While several economists briefly glommed on to Mandelbrot's analysis, it soon fell out of favor. Some said the approach was too simplistic. Others simply found the method too inconvenient, incapable of predicting prices, as if one were trying to forecast the direction of a Mexican jumping bean. Critics said that while it may work for brief time periods when price action can be erratic, over longer time periods, prices appear to move in a more orderly Brownian fashion. An eyeball test of long-term trends in the stock market shows that prices of an entire market do tend to move in more regular, less erratic patterns.

Dow Jones Industrials 1995-2008

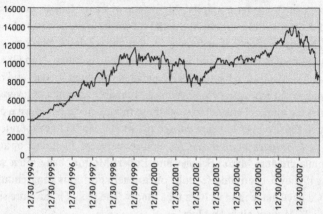

Mandelbrot agreed that over long periods, equilibrium tends to rule the day. But that misses the point. Prices can gyrate wildly over *short* periods of time—wildly enough to cause massive, potentially crippling losses to investors who've made large, leveraged wagers.

As Nassim Nicholas Taleb, a critic of quant models, later argued in several books, investors who believe the market moves according to a random walk are "fooled by randomness" (the title of one of his books). Taleb famously dubbed the wild unexpected swings in markets, and in life itself, "black swans," evoking the belief long held in the West that all swans are white, a notion exploded when sailors discovered black swans in Australia. Taleb argued that there are far more black swans in the world than many people believe, and that models based on historical trends and expectations of a random walk are bound to lead their users to destruction.

Mandelbrot's theories were shelved by the financial engineers who didn't want to deal with the messy, chaotic world they evoked. But they always loomed like a bad memory in the back of their minds, and were from time to time thrust to the forefront during wild periods of volatility such as Black Monday, only to be forgotten again when the markets eventually calmed down, as they always seemed to do.

Inevitably, though, the deadly volatility returns. About a decade after

Black Monday, the math geniuses behind a massive quant hedge fund known as Long-Term Capital Management came face-to-face with Mandelbrot's wild markets. In a matter of weeks in the summer of 1998, LTCM lost billions, threatening to destabilize global markets and prompting a massive bailout organized by Fed chairman Alan Greenspan. LTCM's trades, based on sophisticated computer models and risk management strategies, employed unfathomable amounts of leverage. When the market behaved in ways those models never could have predicted, the layers of leverage caused the fund's capital to evaporate.

The traders behind LTCM, whose partners included option-formula creators Myron Scholes and Robert Merton, have often said that if they'd been able to hold on to their positions long enough, they'd have made money. It's a nice theory. The reality is far more simple. LTCM went all in and lost.

Black Monday left an indelible stamp on the very fabric of the market's structure. Soon after the crash, options traders started to notice a strange pattern on charts of stock-option prices. Prices for deep out-of-the-money puts—long-shot bets on huge price declines—were unusually high, compared with prices for puts closer to the current price of the stock. Graphs of these prices displayed a curvy kink around such options that, according to the prevailing theory, shouldn't exist. Traders soon came up with a name for this phenomenon: the "volatility smile." It was the grim memory of Black Monday grinning sinisterly from within the very prices that underpinned the market.

The volatility smile disobeyed the orderly world of "no arbitrage" laid out by Black-Scholes and modern portfolio theory, since it implied that traders could make a lot of money by selling these out-of-the-money puts. If the puts were too expensive for the risk they carried (according to the formula), the smart move would be to sell them hand over fist. Eventually that would drive the price down to where it should be. But, oddly, traders weren't doing that. They were presumably frightened that another crash like Black Monday could wipe them out. They never got over the fear. The volatility smile persists to this day.

The volatility smile perplexed Wall Street's quants. For one thing, it made a hash of their carefully calibrated hedging strategies. It also raised questions about the underlying theory itself.

"I realized that the existence of the smile was completely at odds with Black and Scholes's 20-year-old foundation of options theory," wrote Emanuel Derman, a longtime financial engineer who worked alongside Fischer Black at Goldman Sachs, in his book *My Life as a Quant*. "And, if the Black-Scholes formula was wrong, then so was the predicted sensitivity of an option's price to movements in its underlying index. . . . The smile, therefore, poked a small hole deep into the dike of theory that sheltered options trading."

Black Monday did more than that. It poked a hole not only in the Black-Scholes formula but in the foundations underlying the quantitative revolution itself. Stocks didn't move in the tiny incremental ticks predicted by Brownian motion and the random walk theory. They leapt around like Mexican jumping beans. Investors weren't rational, as quant theory assumed they were; they panicked like rats on a sinking ship.

Worse, the engine behind the crash, portfolio insurance, was the spawn of the quants, a product designed to *protect* investors from big losses. Instead, it created the very losses it was meant to avoid.

Not everyone suffered catastrophic losses on Black Monday. Princeton/Newport Partners, due to Thorp's fancy footwork, lost only a few million dollars that day. After the crash, Thorp's models, scanning the marketplace like heat-seeking missiles, sought out numerous good deals. The fund closed the month flat. For the year, the fund earned a 27 percent return, compared with a 5 percent gain by the S&P 500.

Thorp had managed to survive the most devastating drawdown in the history of the stock market. Everything was looking up. Then, out of the blue, disaster struck Princeton/Newport Partners. It was Ed Thorp's black swan.

In mid-December 1987, an army of vans pulled up in front of a nondescript office complex in the heart of sleepy Princeton. A squad of fifty armed federal marshals clad in bulletproof vests burst from the vans and rushed into the office of Princeton/Newport Partners, which was perched in a small space over a Häagen-Dazs shop.

They were searching for documents related to the fund's dealings with Michael Milken's junk bond empire at Drexel Burnham Lambert. The man in charge of the case was Rudolph Giuliani, the U.S. attorney for the Southern District of New York. He was trying to build more evidence for the government's case against Drexel and was hoping employees of the hedge fund, threatened with stiff fines and possible prison terms, would turn against Milken.

It didn't work. In August 1989, a Manhattan jury convicted five Princeton/Newport executives—including Regan—of sixty-three felony counts related to illegal stock trading plots. Thorp, more than two thousand miles away at the Newport Beach office and oblivious to the alleged dark dealings in the fund's Princeton headquarters, was never charged. But Regan and the other convicted partners at Princeton/Newport refused to testify against Milken or acknowledge wrongdoing. Instead, they fought the government's charges—and won. In June 1991, a federal appeals court tossed out the racketeering convictions in the government's fraud case. Early the following year, prosecutors dropped the case. Not a single employee of Princeton/Newport spent a day in prison.

The biggest casualty of the government's assault was Princeton/Newport. It became impossible for Thorp to keep the ship steady amid all the controversy, and his associates in Princeton were obviously distracted dealing with the charges against them. Worried investors pulled out of the fund.

Thorp decided to simplify his life. He took a brief break from managing money for others, though he continued to invest his own sizable funds in the market.

He also worked as a consultant for pension funds and endowments. In 1991, a company asked Thorp to look over its investment portfolio. As he combed through the various holdings, he noticed one particular investment vehicle that had produced stunning returns throughout the 1980s. Every single year, it put up returns of 20 percent or more, far outpacing anything Thorp had ever seen—even Princeton/

Newport. Intrigued, and a bit dubious, he delved further into the fund's strategies, requesting documents that listed its trading activities. The fund, based in New York's famed Lipstick Building on Third Avenue, supposedly traded stock options on a rapid-fire basis, benefiting from a secret formula that allowed it to buy low and sell high. The trading record the fund sent Thorp listed the trades—how many options it bought, which companies, how much money it made or lost on the trades.

It took Thorp about a day to realize the fund was a fraud. The number of options it reported having bought and sold far outpaced the total number traded on public exchanges. For instance, on April 16, 1991, the firm reported that it had purchased 123 call options on Procter & Gamble stock. But only 20 P&G options *in total* had changed hands that day (this was well before the explosion in options trading that occurred over the following decade). Similar discrepancies appeared for trades on IBM, Disney, and Merck options, among others, Thorp's research revealed. He told the firm that had made the investment to pull its money out of the fund, which was called Bernard L. Madoff Investment Securities.

In late 2008, the fund, run by New York financier Bernard Madoff, was revealed as the greatest Ponzi scheme of all time, a massive fraud that had bilked investors out of tens of billions. Regulators had been repeatedly warned about the fund, but they never could determine whether its trading strategies were legitimate.

While Thorp was taking a break from the investing game, the stage for the amazing rise of the quants had been set. Peter Muller, working at a quant factory in California, was itching to branch out and start trading serious money. Cliff Asness was entering an elite finance program at the University of Chicago. Boaz Weinstein was still in high school but already had his eyes trained on Wall Street's action-packed trading floors.

As Thorp wound down Princeton/Newport Partners, he handed off his hedge fund baton to a twenty-two-year-old prodigy who would go on to become one of the most powerful hedge fund managers in the world—and who would become a key player during the market meltdown that began in August 2007.

FOUR OF A KIND

5

■ GRIFFIN ■

In 1990, Ed Thorp took a call from one of his longtime investors, a reclusive financier named Frank Meyer with a gimlet eye for talent. Meyer had a special request. "I've got a great prospect," Meyer told Thorp, his gruff, no-nonsense voice booming over the line. He sounded as excited as a college football coach who'd just spotted the next Heisman Trophy winner. "One of the savviest guys I've ever met. Traded convertible bonds out of his dorm room on his grandmother's bank account."

"Who is he?"

"A whip-smart Harvard grad named Ken Griffin. Reminds me of you, Ed."

"Harvard?" the MIT–educated Thorp snorted. "How old?"

"Twenty-one."

"Wow, that is young. What do you want from me?"

"Docs."

Hoping to save money, Meyer wanted to use Princeton/Newport's offering documents as a template for a hedge fund he was setting up for Griffin, a lanky, six-foot math whiz with a singular focus on making money. Thorp agreed and shipped a copy of PNP's legal papers (Thorp had renamed the fund Sierra Partners after the Giuliani debacle) to Meyer's office. At the time, it typically cost roughly $100,000 to draft the papers needed to set up a hedge fund. Using the shortcut—Meyer's lawyers essentially changed names on the partnership papers—it cost less than $10,000. The joke around Meyer's office was that they used the law firm of Cookie & Cutter to launch Griffin's fund. It would eventually be called Citadel Investment Group, a name designed to evoke the image of high ramparts that could withstand the most awesome financial onslaughts imaginable.

Meyer ran a "fund of hedge funds" in Chicago called Glenwood Capital Management. A fund of funds invests in batches of other hedge funds, passing the gains on to clients while taking a cut for themselves, typically around 10¢ on the dollar. The fund of funds industry is massive today, with hundreds of billions of dollars under management (though it shrank like a punctured balloon after the credit crisis). When Meyer launched Glenwood in 1987, the industry was practically nonexistent.

Indeed, when Princeton/Newport Partners had closed its doors in the late 1980s, hedge funds were still an obscure backwater in the rapidly expanding global financial ecosystem, a Wild West full of quick-draw gunslingers such as Paul Tudor Jones and George Soros willing to heave millions in a single bet based on gut instincts. Other upstarts included an obscure group of market wizards in Princeton, New Jersey, called Commodity Corp., a cutting-edge fund that largely dabbled in commodity futures. Commodity Corp. spawned legendary traders such as Louis Moore Bacon (who went on to manage the $10 billion fund Moore Capital Management) and Bruce Kovner (manager of Caxton Associates, with $6 billion). In New York, an aggressive and cerebral trader named Julian Robertson was in the process of turning a start-up stash of $8 million into more than $20 billion at Tiger Management. In West Palm Beach, a group of traders at a fund called Illinois Income Investors, better known as III or Triple I, was launching innovative strategies in mortgage-backed securities, currencies, and derivatives.

But trading was becoming increasingly quantitative, and more and more mathematicians were migrating to Wall Street, inspired by Thorp and fresh waves of research sprouting from academia. Jim Simons's firm Renaissance Technologies was launching its soon-to-be-legendary Medallion Fund. David Shaw was setting up shop over a communist bookstore in Greenwich Village with his stat arb white lightning. Investors in Thorp's fund, after losing their golden goose, were on the hunt for new talent. For many, Ken Griffin fit the bill.

Thorp also handed over a gold mine to Meyer and Griffin: cartons of prospectuses for convertible securities and warrants, many of which could no longer be obtained due to the passage of time. It was an incomparable archive of information about the industry, a skeleton key to unlock millions in riches from the market. By scanning the kinds of deals Thorp had invested in, Griffin learned how to hunt down similar deals on his own.

The information helped Griffin better discern what kind of trades were possible in the convertible bond market. While Thorp's records didn't provide every nugget of every trade, they did provide something of a treasure map. With the records in hand, Griffin had a much better notion for which parts of the market he should focus on, and he quickly developed strategies that were in many ways similar to those Thorp had pioneered decades before.

To learn more, Griffin flew out to Newport Beach for a meeting with Thorp, hoping to study at the feet of the master. Thorp walked Griffin through a series of bond-arbitrage trades and passed on priceless know-how gathered in more than two decades of trading experience. Griffin, an eager apprentice, gobbled it all up.

Thorp also described for Griffin Princeton/Newport's business model, which involved "profit centers" that would evolve over time depending on how successful they were, a concept Citadel copied in the following years. Griffin adopted Thorp's management fee structure, in which investors would pay for the fund's expenses rather than pay the flat management fee most hedge fund managers charged, usually around 2 percent of assets.

Meyer promised to back Griffin under one condition: he had to set up Citadel in Chicago. Griffin, a Florida native, agreed. In November 1990, he started trading with $4.6 million using a single, esoteric strategy: convertible bond arbitrage, the very same strategy Ed Thorp had used.

The son of a project manager for General Electric, Griffin had a high-tech mechanical bent and was always interested in figuring out how things worked. Known for his unblinking, blue-eyed stare, Griffin always seemed to be able to peer deeply into complex issues and take away more than anyone else, a skill that would serve him well in the chaotic world of finance.

As a student at the Boca Raton Community High School, he'd dabbled in computer programming and got a job designing computer codes for IBM. His mother would ferry him to the local Computerland, where he would spend hours chatting up the salespeople about new gizmos and software. In 1986, when Griffin was not yet eighteen, he came up with the idea of selling educational software to schools, teaming up with some of his pals from Computerland to launch a company called Diskovery Educational Systems. Griffin sold out a few years later, but the company is still in business in West Palm Beach.

During his first year at Harvard, after reading a *Forbes* magazine article arguing that shares of Home Shopping Network were overpriced, he purchased put options on the stock, hoping to profit from a decline. The bet was a good one, earning a few thousand dollars, but it didn't pay off as much as Griffin had hoped: commissions and transaction costs from the market maker, a Philadelphia securities firm called Susquehanna International Group, cut into his winnings. He realized the investing game was more complex than he'd thought, and started reading as many books about financial markets as he could get his hands on. Eventually, he came upon a textbook about convertible bonds—the favored investment vehicles of Ed Thorp. By then, Thorp's ideas, laid out in *Beat the Market*, had filtered into academia and were being taught in finance classrooms across the country. Of course, Griffin eventually went to the source, devouring *Beat the Market* as well.

Like Thorp, Griffin quickly discovered that a number of convertible bonds were mispriced. His computer skills came into play as he wrote a software program to flag mispriced bonds. Hungry for up-to-the-minute information from the market, he wired up his third-floor dorm room in Harvard's ivy-draped Cabot House with a satellite dish—planting the dish on top of the dorm and running a cable through the building's fourth-floor window and down another floor through the elevator shaft—so he could download real-time stock quotes. The only problem with the scheme: the fourth-floor window could never be completely shut, even in the frigid Cambridge winters.

During his summer vacation in 1987, between his freshman and sophomore years, he frequently visited a friend who worked at the First National Bank of Palm Beach. One day, he was describing his ideas about convertible bonds and hedging. A retiree named Saul Golkin happened to step into the office. After listening to Griffin's spiel for twenty minutes, Golkin said, "I've got to run to lunch, I'm in for fifty."

At first, Griffin didn't understand, until his friend explained that Golkin had just forked over fifty grand to the young whiz kid from Harvard.

Eager to raise more funds from friends and relatives, including his mother and grandmother, he eventually stockpiled $265,000 for a limited partnership, which he called Convertible Hedge Fund #1 (strikingly close to Thorp's original fund, Convertible Hedge Associates). After returning to Harvard in the fall, he started to invest the cash, mostly buying underpriced warrants and hedging the position by shorting the stock (Thorp's delta hedging strategy).

His timing proved auspicious. On October 19, the stock market crashed, and Griffin's short positions hit the jackpot, tumbling much further than the warrants.

Having weathered the storm, he quickly raised $750,000 for another fund, which he called Convertible Hedge Fund #2.

Griffin's ability to ride through Black Monday unscathed—and even with a tidy profit—was something of a revelation. The pros on Wall Street had been clobbered, while the whiz kid trading out of his Harvard dorm using satellites, computers, and a complex investing strategy had come out on top. It was his first inkling of the incredible possibilities that lay ahead.

But there was much more work to do. He needed access to more securities. And that meant an institutional trading account—the kind of account used by professional traders such as mutual funds and hedge funds. In 1989, Griffin, just nineteen years old, approached a Merrill Lynch convertible bond expert in Boston named Terrence O'Connor and presented what must have seemed like an insane plan: *Give me, Ken Griffin, a nineteen-year-old college kid, access to your most sophisticated trading platform, which will allow me to dabble in nearly every instrument known to God.*

Somehow he pulled it off, wowing the bond expert with his technical know-how. O'Connor agreed to bring Griffin on, despite the fact that the average institutional account ran around $100 *million* at the time.

Griffin started trading, and calling everyone on Wall Street who would speak with him. A typical reaction: "You're running two hundred grand out of your dorm room? Don't ever call me again." *Slam*.

But some were intrigued by the young Harvard phenom and would explain certain trades they were engaged in—arbitrage trades, why hedge funds were doing them, why the bank itself was involved. Griffin started making trips to New York and sitting at the feet of seasoned traders, sucking up knowledge. He was particularly interested in stock-loan desks, which gave him a peek at which funds the bank was lending shares to—and why.

Shortly before Griffin graduated from Harvard with a degree in economics, he met Justin Adams, a manager for Triple I. The two met over breakfast in a restaurant in West Palm Beach and discussed the market. Over a steaming omelet, Griffin explained how he'd devel-

oped contacts with traders at brokerage firms across Wall Street and
had learned many of the inner secrets of the trading world.

A former member of the Army's Special Forces who'd served in
Vietnam before venturing into the world of high finance, Adams was
agog. Griffin was smart and focused, and he asked penetrating and coherent questions about the market—questions that were so pointed
they made Adams stop and search for a coherent answer.

Adams arranged a meeting in New York between Griffin and
Frank Meyer, an investor in Triple I as well as Princeton/Newport.
Meyer too was floored by Griffin's broad understanding of technical
aspects of investing, as well as his computer expertise, an important
skill as trading became more mechanized and electronic. But it was
his market savvy that impressed Meyer most. "If you're a kid managing a few hundred thousand, it's very hard to borrow stock for short
selling," Meyer recalled. "He went around to every major stock loan
company and ingratiated himself, and because he was so unusual they
gave him good rates."

Griffin set up shop in Chicago in late 1989 with his $1 million in
play dough, and was quickly making money hand over fist trading
convertibles with his handcrafted software program. In his first year of
trading, Griffin posted a whopping 70 percent return. Impressed,
Meyer decided to help Griffin launch his own fund. He thought about
other funds with similar strategies, and that's when Ed Thorp came to
mind.

Griffin had his office. He had his seed money. He hired a small
group of traders, some of whom must have been shocked to be working for a kid who still smelled like a dorm room. The only thing he
needed was a name. Griffin and several of his new employees wrote
down their nominations on a list, then voted on their favorites.

The winner was Citadel. By 1990, the start of a decade that would
see phenomenal growth in the hedge fund industry, Griffin's fortress
of money was ready for battle and on its way to becoming one of the
most feared money machines in all of finance.

▪ MULLER ▪

When he was ten years old, Peter Muller went on a tour of Europe with his family. After visiting several countries, he noticed something strange: exchange rates for the dollar varied in different countries. He asked his father, a chemical engineer, whether he could buy deutschmarks in London and make a profit by exchanging them for dollars in Germany.

The young Muller had intuitively grasped the concept of arbitrage.

Born in 1963 in Philadelphia, Muller grew up in Wayne, New Jersey, a half hour's drive west of Manhattan. He showed an early aptitude for math and loved to play all kinds of games, from Scrabble to chess to backgammon. As a senior at Wayne Valley High School, Muller mixed his obsession with games with another growing interest, computer programming, and designed a program that could play backgammon. It was so effective his math teacher claimed the program cheated.

At Princeton, he studied theoretical mathematics, fascinated by the crystalline beauty of complex structures and by the universal patterns that abound in the more esoteric realms of number theory. Muller also grew interested in music, taking classes and playing piano for a jazz band that performed at student functions and college clubs.

After graduating in 1985, he drove across the country to California. A job in New York at a German software company called Nixdorf was waiting for him, but he kept putting off his starting date for various reasons. He wasn't sure he wanted to go back to the East Coast anyway. Muller had fallen in love with California.

He soon found himself in a gymnasium playing an electric piano as several tightly muscled women danced balletically in leotards while twirling plastic hoops and tossing around brightly colored rubber balls. He was trying, somewhat desperately, to pursue his music career and had landed a job playing background tunes for a rhythmic gymnastics team.

Apparently the job as a rhythmic gymnastics maestro didn't pull down enough for food and shelter, including the $200-a-month rent Muller was paying to stay at a friend of a friend's house. There was also the annoying habit of a roommate who liked to blast off random shotgun rounds in the backyard when he got the blues.

One day, Muller saw an ad from a small financial engineering outfit in Berkeley called BARRA Inc. for a programmer who knew Fortran, a computer language commonly used for statistical problems.
Muller didn't know Fortran (though he had little doubt that he could
learn it quickly) and had never heard of BARRA. But he applied for the
job anyway, interviewing for it at BARRA's Berkeley office.

Muller strolled into BARRA's office confident, his mind crackling
with the theoretical mathematics he'd learned at Princeton. But he was
completely unfamiliar with the quantitative financial world he was
stepping into, having never taken a finance course. He even considered
himself something of a socialist and had needled his girlfriend, a part-
timer at the *Wall Street Journal*'s San Francisco bureau, about being a
capitalist shill. But he was theoretically intrigued by how money
worked. More than anything, he wanted to start making some of it, too.

Before the interview, Muller made a pit stop in the men's bathroom and was horrified by what he saw: a cigarette butt. A compulsive
neat freak and health nut, Muller despised cigarettes. The butt was
nearly a deal killer. He thought about canceling the interview. There
was simply no way he would work in an office where people smoked.
Reluctantly he went ahead with the interview and learned that
BARRA didn't allow smoking in the office. The butt must have been
left by a visitor.

After a string of interviews, he was offered the job, and accepted.
Muller didn't know it at the time, but he had just stepped into the
world of the quants.

By 1985, BARRA was the West Coast *axis mundi* of the quant universe. The company was founded in 1974 by an iconoclastic Berkeley
economics professor, Barr Rosenberg, one of the pioneers of the
movement to apply the ivory tower lessons of modern portfolio theory
to the real-world construction of portfolios. A tall, lanky man with a
wavy mop of hair, he was also a longtime Buddhist. Rosenberg had always defied rigid categorization. In the 1960s, he'd studied how groups
of patients reacted in different ways to the same medication. At the
same time, he'd been collecting data on stocks, an interest that developed into an obsession. He noticed that just as patients' reactions to

drugs differed, stocks exhibited strange, seemingly inexplicable behavior over time. There must be a logical way to find order beneath the chaos, he thought.

One way to understand how stocks tick is to break down the factors that push and pull them up and down. General Motors is a medley of several distinct factors in the economy and the market: the automobile industry, large-capitalization stocks, U.S. stocks, oil prices, consumer confidence, interest rates, and so forth. Microsoft is a mix of large-cap, technology, and consumer factors, among others.

In the early 1970s, working long hours in his Berkeley basement, Rosenberg had cooked up quantitative models to track factors on thousands of stocks, then programmed them into a computer. Eventually Rosenberg started to sell his models to money management firms that were increasingly dabbling in quantitative strategies (though few were as yet remotely as sophisticated as the high-powered hedge fund Ed Thorp was running out of Newport Beach). In 1974, he started up a firm called Barr Rosenberg Associates, which eventually turned into BARRA.

In just a few years, BARRA developed a cultlike following. Rosenberg scored a hit with the company's Fundamental Risk Management Service, a computerized program that could forecast a stock's behavior based on categories such as earnings, industry, market capitalization, and trading activity.

By the time Muller arrived at BARRA, thousands of managers were running money using the newfangled quantitative strategies. Rosenberg himself left BARRA in 1985, soon after Muller was hired, with a small group of colleagues, to start his own money management firm, Rosenberg Institutional Equity Management, in Orinda, California. Within a few years it was managing several billion dollars in markets around the world. (More recently, Rosenberg has drifted away from the worldly pursuit of riches and has been teaching courses on Buddhism for the Nyingma Institute in Berkeley.)

One of the first projects Muller worked on at BARRA concerned an analysis of the various components of stock returns, the bread and butter of BARRA's factor models. Just before he left, Rosenberg took a look at Muller's work and demonstrated his ability to see the push and pull of economic forces at work in the market.

"This factor must be oil prices," he said. "Look at the spike during the energy crisis. . . . And this one must be related to interest rates."

One problem: Muller had screwed up the math and the data were bunk. He reworked the analysis and sheepishly showed the results to Rosenberg.

"This makes much more sense," Rosenberg said. "This factor must be the oil factor. . . . And here's where the Fed came in and tightened."

While this showed that Rosenberg could quickly convert math and models into real-world events, it also demonstrated that the models could fool the best in the business. Even with all the high-powered math, there always seemed to be a bit of the witch doctor in Rosenberg and the quant methods he spawned. The constant search for hidden factors in market prices could turn into a voodoolike hunt for prophecies in chicken entrails, dark portents in cloud shapes.

The relaxing, sun-splashed atmosphere of BARRA was something of a revelation to Muller after the do-nothing burbs of Jersey and the cloistered corridors of Princeton. It was the mid-1980s. Nostalgia for the sixties was on the rise. And there were few better places to catch that wave than Berkeley, a short hop to the surfer hangouts at Half Moon Bay and the hippie haven of Haight-Ashbury. Of course, working for a financial research outfit didn't exactly fit the classic hippie mold, but Muller was fine with that. He'd had enough of scrounging for money, playing music for peanuts. The $33,000-a-year salary he was making at BARRA was a boon, and there was certainly more to come. Most of all, he was determined that however much money he made, he wouldn't turn into Ebenezer Scrooge. Rosenberg had already set an example that one could make buckets of money and still retain a sense of spirituality.

And life was good at BARRA. The casual atmosphere. The go-easy dress code. The only guy seen in a suit was the company's marketing chief. Employees would take long lunches to talk about academic theory, politics, world events. Muller had a girlfriend and was playing part-time in a jazz band. Once a month, a group of employees would take late-night runs under a full moon, followed by a trip to a bar or, even better, an ice cream parlor.

Muller quickly learned Fortran and worked on fixing code for the company, but he was itching to learn more about the real work going on at BARRA: financial modeling. He put aside his music and buried himself in the literature of modern portfolio theory: Eugene Fama, Fischer Black, Robert Merton, the classics.

He was also becoming drawn into a new hobby: poker. He started haunting the Oaks Card Room in Emeryville, a twenty-minute ride from BARRA's office. He devoured poker strategy books and was soon cleaning up at the Oaks' high-stakes tables.

Gambling turned into an obsession. Muller would spend ten to fifteen hours a week playing cards at the Oaks. Sometimes he dove into marathon sessions that tested his endurance. Once he started playing at 6:00 P.M. after work on a Friday and didn't stop until 10:00 A.M. that Sunday. Driving home, he was so exhausted that he fell asleep at a stoplight.

In 1989, Muller got an assignment to do some work for a new BARRA client, a hedge fund operator called Renaissance Technologies. Jim Simons was looking for expert help to solve a thorny problem he faced with one of his funds named Medallion.

The problem involved the most efficient use of Medallion's spare cash. Muller's solution was so clever that Renaissance offered him a job. But he was skeptical and turned down the offer. Still under the spell of academia, he believed in Fama's efficient-markets hypothesis and the mounds of research that claimed it's not possible to beat the market over the long haul.

He soon changed his mind about that.

By 1991, Muller was pulling down a hundred grand a year. He lived in a beautiful house in the Berkeley Hills with his girlfriend and had a great job with enough spare time for his jazz band, gobs of poker, and surfing on the side. But he wanted more.

That year, BARRA went public. To Muller, the company seemed different after the IPO, less hungry, less energetic, less creative. A number of employees, good ones, left for other companies or to work on their own projects. Muller had an idea he thought could breathe new life into BARRA: use the quantitative models it developed for clients to manage its own money. In other words, set up an internal BARRA hedge fund. He had just the right people to run it, too: his poker buddies from the Oaks, all BARRA employees.

The firm's higher-ups scotched the plan. It wasn't a good idea to launch a risky operation so soon after the IPO, they said. Andrew Rudd, BARRA's CEO, suggested Muller create new models to forecast returns for stocks and sell them to clients. It wasn't quite what Muller had in mind, but he agreed. In short order, he helped design BARRA's best-selling Alphabuilder system, a PC-based software program that could analyze expected returns for stock portfolios.

Then he quit.

"Who the fuck are you, and why the fuck do you get an office?"

"I'm fucking Peter Muller, and I'm fucking pleased to meet you."

Muller stared bullets at the wiseass Morgan Stanley salesman who'd barged into his office as though he owned it. Muller had only recently begun setting up a quantitative trading group at Morgan, and this was the reception he got?

It had been like this since the day he arrived at the bank. After accepting a job at Morgan, and with it an incredible increase in pay, he'd given notice at BARRA and taken six weeks of R&R, spending most of it in Kauai, the lush, westernmost island of Hawaii. The transition from the placid green gardens of Kauai to the rock-'em-sock-'em trading floor of Morgan Stanley in midtown Manhattan had been a rude shock. Muller had been promised his own office and a battery of data sources before his arrival, but on his first day at the bank he saw that none of his requests had been met.

Until the promised office arrived, he'd found a seat at a desk in the middle of Morgan's football field of a trading floor and called a former BARRA colleague, Tom Cooper, who was working at a hedge fund in Boston.

"How can you work in an environment like this?" he asked.

Suddenly a woman sitting next to him grabbed the receiver from his hand. "I need that phone!"

Muller stared back in shock as she barked out trades that involved markets in Chicago and Tokyo. Politeness wasn't an option when money was on the line, Muller was learning. BARRA and its quaint quant models suddenly seemed a world away.

A friend sent Muller congratulatory flowers for his new job. The bouquet was delivered to his desk on the trading floor. It was raw meat to the grizzled traders around him: *Look at the California quant boy and his pretty flowers*. What had he gotten into? Muller wondered. The energy was maddening. Everyone was packed like sardines, shouting, sweating—and wearing suits!

This wasn't California. This certainly wasn't Berkeley. This was New York fucking City, this was Morgan fucking Stanley, one of the biggest, most aggressive investment banks in the world, and Muller was right in the boiling heart of it.

■ ASNESS ■

The muscular professor strode to the podium and faced yet another roomful of bright-eyed students eager to learn the secrets of how the stock market really worked. The professor, Eugene Fama, had been teaching at the University of Chicago since the early 1960s. Now, in September 1989, he was universally acknowledged as one of the brightest thinkers about financial markets and economics on the planet. Fama ran a hand across his balding head and squinted at the gangly sprawl of twentysomethings before him.

One trait about Fama that immediately jumped out to new students was his forehead. It was unusually large, high, and wide, traced with a stack of deep-cut lines that undulated like waves as he barked out wisdom about the markets in his Boston brogue as if agitated by the powerful thoughts percolating in his basketball-sized cranium. Clad in a loose-fitting blue cotton button-down shirt and tan chinos, he seemed more a refugee from the school's philosophy department than a tough-minded guru of the money set.

His first words came as a shock to the students in the room.

"Everything I'm about to say isn't true," said Fama in a gruff voice tinged with the accent of his Boston youth.

He walked to his chalkboard and wrote the following: *Efficient-market hypothesis.*

"The market is efficient," Fama said. "What do I mean by that? It means that at any given moment, stock prices incorporate all known information about them. If lots of people are drinking Coca-Cola, its stock is going to go up as soon as that information is available."

Students scribbled on their notepads, taking it all in.

The efficient-market hypothesis, perhaps the most famous and long-lasting concept about how the market behaved in the past half century, was Fama's baby. It had grown so influential, and had become so widely accepted, that it was less a hypothesis than a commandment from God in heaven passed down through his economic prophet of the Windy City.

"There are a number of consequences to market efficiency," Fama said, facing the classroom. "One of the most important is that it's statistically impossible to know where the market is going next. This is known as the random walk theory, which means that the future course of the market is like a coin toss. It either goes up or down, fifty-fifty, no one knows which."

A student near the front row raised a tentative hand.

"What about all the guys who get paid to pick stocks? They must get paid for a reason. It can't be all luck."

"The evidence shows that trying to pick stocks is a complete waste of time," Fama said flatly. "And money. Wall Street is full of salesmen trying to convince people to give them a buck. But there's never been a study in history showing active managers consistently beat the market. It's just not in the data. Managers have good runs, but it usually does just come down to dumb luck."

"Why do people pay these money managers so much money?"

"Hope? Stupidity? It's hard to say."

"What about Warren Buffett?"

Fama sighed. *That Buffett again*. Increasingly, students were obsessed with the track record of this hick investor from Omaha, whose company, Berkshire Hathaway, had beaten the S&P 500 for two decades in a row and counting.

"There do seem to be a few outliers that are impossible to explain. In every science there are freaks that seem to defy all the rules. Buffett, as well as Peter Lynch at Fidelity's Magellan fund, have had consistent returns over the years. I'm not aware of anyone else. These freak geniuses may be out there, but I don't know who they are. Who knows," he said with a shrug and a smile, "maybe they'll lose it all next year."

The math showed it was inevitable that a few traders would stand out, but that didn't mean they had skill. Give ten thousand people a quarter. Tell them to flip. Each round, eliminate the ones who flipped heads. After ten rounds, maybe a hundred will be left. After twenty, maybe three or four will still be in the game. If they were on Wall Street, they'd be hailed as expert coin flippers, coin flippers drenched in alpha. Buffett, according to Fama, was in all probability a lucky coin flipper.

Another student raised a hand. "But you said everything you're going to tell us isn't true. So does that mean that markets really aren't efficient?"

"That's right," Fama said. "None of what I'm telling you is one hundred percent true. These are mathematical models. We look at statistics, historical data, trends, and extrapolate what we can from them. This isn't physics. In physics, you can build the space shuttle, launch it into orbit, and watch it land at Cape Canaveral a week later. The market is far more unstable and unpredictable. What we know about it are approximations about reality based on models. The efficient-market hypothesis is just that, a hypothesis based on decades of research and a large amount of data. There's always the chance we're wrong."

He paused. "Although I'm virtually certain that we're right. God knows the market is efficient."

The classroom laughed nervously. Fama was an intimidating presence, radiating a cool disdain for those unable to keep up. Cliff Asness, a twenty-three-year-old Ph.D. student, nodded and scribbled Fama's words in his notebook: *freak geniuses . . . mathematical models* . . . None of this was new to him; he'd taken finance classes under some of the top finance thinkers in the world at the University of Pennsylvania's Wharton School. But he knew that Fama was the man, the top of the heap in academic finance.

But still, he couldn't help wondering. Indeed, Fama's words were almost a challenge: *Could I do it? Could I beat the market?*

As a child, Clifford Scott Asness gave no sign of his future as a Wall Street tycoon. He was born in October 1966 in Queens, New York. When he was four, his family moved to the leafy, suburban environs of Roslyn Heights on Long Island. In school Asness received good grades, but his interest in Wall Street didn't extend beyond the dark towers of Gotham in the pages of *Batman*. Obsessed with little besides girls and comic books, Asness was listless as a teenager, without direction and somewhat overweight. At times he showed signs of a violent temper that would erupt years later when he sat at the helm of his own hedge fund. Once a chess team rival taunted him in the school's parking lot about a recent match. Enraged, Asness seized his tormentor and tossed him into a nearby van, over and over again.

As an undergraduate at the University of Pennsylvania's Wharton School, Asness assumed he'd follow in the footsteps of his father, a trial lawyer. He wasn't sure *why* he wanted to become a lawyer, aside from that it seemed a family tradition. His father, however, was mystified by his son's plans.

"Why would you want to be a lawyer when you're good with numbers?" he said.

Asness took his father's words seriously. Open to new fields, he delved into the arcane world of portfolio theory as a research assistant for Wharton professor Andrew Lo, who later moved to MIT. To his surprise, he found the subject fascinating. He switched his focus to finance, picking up a degree in computer science along the way—a crackerjack quant combo.

As Asness neared graduation, he canceled his appointment to take the Law School Admission Test, the LSAT, and instead signed up for the Graduate Management Admission Test, or GMAT. With a solid score in hand, he was accepted by several business programs. His favorites were Stanford and Chicago. Decisively, Chicago offered to fly out the cash-poor Asness for a visit, while Stanford didn't. He arrived on a beautiful spring day—perhaps the most fortuitous sunny day of his life. It was the ultimate bait and switch, Asness would later say, joking that he must be the only person who ever chose the University of Chicago over Stanford based on weather.

Asness entered Chicago when Eugene Fama and his colleague, Kenneth French, were working on landmark research that would shake the foundations of business schools around the country. Their research would draw on the most important ideas in modern finance and push them into entirely new realms of theory and application.

Fama was the star of the duo. Born near the end of the Great Depression and raised around the rugged shipyards of Boston's Charlestown neighborhood, Fama was one of the first economists to work intensively with computers. As a student at the University of Chicago in the early 1960s, he also had access to one of the world's largest databases of stock market data, Chicago's Center for Research in Security Prices, otherwise known as CRSP (pronounced "crisp").

Fishing for subjects to teach, Fama realized that the university didn't offer any courses on Harry Markowitz, a former Chicago student who used quantitative methods to show how investors can maximize their returns and lower their risk profiles by diversifying their portfolios—quant-speak for the old saw "Don't put all of your eggs in one basket."

Fama started teaching Markowitz's theories in 1963. He soon added the works of William Sharpe, a Markowitz protégé who'd done pioneering work on the concept of beta, a measure of a stock's sensitivity to the broader volatility in the market. A stock that had a higher beta than the rest of the market was considered more risky, while a stock with a low beta was a safer play. The more risk, the more potential reward—and also the more pain. A stock with a beta of 1 has the same volatility as the rest of the market. Ho-hum blue chips such as AT&T typically have low betas. A beta of 2 is a highly volatile stock—often technology jumping beans such as Apple or Intel. If you know a stock's beta, you know something about how risky it is.

The result of Fama's efforts was the first course on modern finance at Chicago, called Portfolio Theory and Capital Markets (which Fama teaches to this day). In his research, he made extensive use of the university's database of stocks as well as its computers, running test after test and looking for hidden patterns in the data. By 1969, Fama distilled the collected ideas of this class, and years of computerized number crunching, into the first fully formed articulation of a cornerstone of modern portfolio theory: the efficient-market hypothesis, or EMH.

While many thinkers over the years had written about market efficiency, Fama's was the most coherent and concise statement of the idea that the market is unbeatable. The fundamental idea behind EMH is that all relevant new information about a stock is instantly priced into the stock, making it "efficient." Fama envisioned a large, well-developed market with many players constantly on the hunt for the latest news about companies. The process of injecting new information—a lousy earnings report, the departure of a CEO, a big new contract—is like tossing a juicy piece of fresh meat into a tank of piranhas. Before you know it, the meat has been devoured.

Since all current information is built into the stock's price and future information is essentially unknowable, it is impossible to predict whether a stock will rise or fall. The future, therefore, is random, a Brownian motion coin flip, a drunkard's walk through the Parisian night.

The groundwork for the efficient-market hypothesis had begun in the 1950s with the work of Markowitz and Sharpe, who eventually won the Nobel Prize for economics (together with Merton Miller) in 1990 for their work.

Another key player was Louis Bachelier, the obscure French mathematician who argued that bond prices move according to a random walk.

In 1954, MIT economist Paul Samuelson—another future Nobel laureate—received a postcard from Leonard "Jimmie" Savage, a statistician at Chicago. Savage had been searching through stacks at a library and stumbled across the work of Bachelier, which had largely been forgotten in the half century since it had been written. Savage wanted to know if Samuelson had ever heard of the obscure Frenchman. He said he had, though he'd never read his thesis. Samuelson promptly hunted it down and became enthralled with its arguments.

Since the future course of the market is essentially a 50–50 random coin flip, Bachelier had written, "The mathematical expectation of the speculator is zero." Samuelson had already started thinking about financial markets. His interest had been piqued by a controversial speech given in 1952 by Maurice Kendall, a statistician at the London School of Economics. Kendall had analyzed a variety of market data, including stock market indexes, wheat prices, and cotton prices, looking for some kind of pattern that would show whether price movements were predictable. Kendall found no such patterns and concluded that the data series looked "like a wandering one, almost as if once a week the Demon of Chance drew a random number from a symmetrical population." Kendall said this appeared to be "a kind of economic Brownian motion."

Samuelson realized this was a bombshell. He made the leap embedded in Bachelier's original paper: investors are wasting their time. Mathematically, there is no way to beat the market. The Thorps of the world should put away their computers and formulas and take up a more productive profession, such as dentistry or plumbing. "It is not easy to get rich in Las Vegas, at Churchill Downs, or at the local Merrill Lynch office," he wrote.

At the time, Samuelson was becoming an éminence grise of the economic community. If he thought the market followed a random walk, that meant everyone had to get on board or have a damn good reason not to. Most agreed, including one of Samuelson's star students, Robert Merton, one of the co-creators of the Black-Scholes option-pricing formula. Another acolyte was Burton Malkiel, who went on to write *A Random Walk Down Wall Street*.

It was Fama, however, who connected all of the dots and put the efficient-market hypothesis on the map as a central feature of modern portfolio theory.

The idea that the market is an efficient, randomly churning price-processing machine has many odd consequences. Fama postulates a vast, swarming world of investors constantly searching for inefficiencies—those hungry piranhas circling in wait of fresh meat. Without the hungry piranhas gobbling up juicy fleeting inefficiencies, the market would never become efficient. Would the piranhas exist without the fresh meat? No fresh meat, no piranhas. No piranhas, no market efficiency. It's a paradox that continues to baffle EMH acolytes.

Another offshoot of market efficiency is that, if true, it effectively makes it impossible to argue that a market is mispriced—*ever*. When the Nasdaq was hovering above 5,000 in early 2000, it was impossible to argue at the time that it was in a bubble, according to EMH. The housing market in 2005, when prices for many homes in the United States had doubled or tripled in a matter of a few years? No bubble.

Despite such mind-bending conundrums, the EMH became the dominant paradigm in academia as Fama spread the gospel. It was a frontal assault on the money management industry, which was built on the idea that certain people with the right methods and tools can beat the market.

The quants viewed EMH as a key weapon in their arsenal: The probabilities of various movements of an efficient market could be understood through the math spawned by Brownian motion. The most likely moves were those found near the middle of the bell curve, which could be used to make forecasts about the probable future volatility of the market over the course of a month, a year, or a decade. In the financial planning community, so-called Monte Carlo simulations, which can forecast everyday investors' portfolio growth over time, used the idea that the market moves according to a random walk. Thus, an annual gain or loss of 5 percent a year is far more likely, since it falls near the center of the bell curve. A gain or loss of 50 percent, such as the stock market crash seen in the credit crisis of 2008 (or the 23 percent single-day plunge seen on Black Monday, for that matter) was so unlikely as to be a virtual impossibility—in the models, at least. Today, nearly all large financial services firms, such as Fidelity Investments and T. Rowe Price, offer Monte Carlo simulations to investors. Thus, the insights of Bachelier more than a century earlier and prodded on by Fama had reached into the very nuts and bolts of how Americans prepare for retirement. It had also blinded them to the chance that the market could make extreme moves. Such ugly phenomena simply didn't fit within the elegant models spawned by the quants.

EMH was in many ways a double-edged sword. On one hand, it argued that the market was impossible to beat. Most quants, however—

especially those who migrated from academia to Wall Street—believed the market is only *partly* efficient. Fischer Black, co-creator of the Black-Scholes option-pricing formula, once said the market is more efficient on the banks of the Charles River than the banks of the Hudson—conveniently, after he'd joined forces with Goldman Sachs.

By this view, the market was like a coin with a small flaw that makes it slightly more likely to come up heads than tails (or tails than heads). Out of a hundred flips, it was likely to come up heads fifty-two times, rather than fifty. The key to success was discovering those hidden flaws, as many as possible. The law of large numbers that Thorp had used to beat the dealer and then earn a fortune on Wall Street dictated that such flaws, exploited in hundreds if not thousands of securities, could yield vast riches.

Implicitly, EMH also showed that there is a mechanism in the market making prices efficient: Fama's piranhas. The goal was to become a piranha, gobbling up the fleeting inefficiencies, the hidden discrepancies, as quickly as possible. The quants with the best models and fastest computers win the game.

Crucially, EMH gave the quants a touchstone for what the market should look like if it were perfectly efficient, constantly gravitating toward equilibrium. In other words, it gave them a reflection of the Truth, the holy grail of quantitative finance, explaining how the market worked and how to measure it. Every time prices in the market deviated from the Truth, computerized quant piranhas would detect the error, swoop in, and restore order—collecting a healthy profit along the way. Their high-powered computers would comb through global markets like Truth-seeking radar, searching for opportunities. The quants' models could discover when prices deviated from equilibrium. Of course, they weren't always right. But if they were right often enough, a fortune could be made.

This was one of the major lessons Cliff Asness learned studying at the University of Chicago. But there was more.

Fama, a bulldog with research, hadn't rested on his efficient-market laurels over the years. He continued to churn out libraries of papers, leveraging the power of computers and a stream of bright young students eager to learn from the guru of efficient markets. In 1992, soon after Asness arrived on the scene, Fama and French published their most important breakthrough yet, a paper that stands as arguably the most important academic finance research of the last two decades. And the ambition behind it was immense: to overturn the bedrock theory of finance itself, the capital asset pricing model, otherwise known as CAPM.

Before Fama and French, CAPM was the closest approximation to the Truth in quantitative finance. According to the grandfather of CAPM, William Sharpe, the most important element in determining a stock's potential future return is its beta, a measure of how volatile the stock is compared with the rest of the market. And according to CAPM, the riskier the stock, the higher the potential reward. The upshot: long-term investments in risky stocks tended to pay off more than investments in the ho-hum blue chips.

Fama and French cranked up their Chicago supercomputers and ran a series of tests on an extensive database of stock market returns to determine how much impact the all-important beta actually had on stock returns. Their conclusion: none.

Such a finding was nothing short of lobbing a blazing Molotov cocktail into the most sacred tent of modern portfolio theory. Decades of research were flat-out wrong, the two professors alleged. Perhaps even more surprising were Fama and French's findings about the market forces that did, in fact, drive stock returns. They found two factors that determined how well a stock performed during their sample period for 1963 to 1990: value and size.

There are a number of ways to gauge a company's size. It's generally measured by how much the Street values a company through its share price, a metric known as market capitalization (the price of a company's shares times the number of shares). IBM is big: it has a market cap of about $150 billion. Krispy Kreme Doughnuts is small, with a market cap of about $150 million. Other factors, such as how many employees a company has and how profitable it is, also matter.

Value is generally determined by comparing a company's share price to its book value, a measure of a firm's net worth (assets, such as the buildings and/or machines it owns, minus liabilities, or debts).

Price-to-book is the favored metric of old-school investors such as Warren Buffett. The quants, however, use it in ways the Buffetts of the world never dreamed of (and would never have wanted to), plugging decades of data from the CRSP database into computers, pumping it through complex algorithms, and combing through the results like gold miners sifting for gleaming nuggets—flawed coins with hidden discrepancies.

Fama and French unearthed one of the biggest, shiniest nuggets of all. The family tree of "value" has two primary offspring: growth stocks and value stocks. Growth stocks are relatively pricey, indicating that investors love the company and have driven the shares higher. Value stocks have a low price-to-book value, indicating that they are relatively unloved on Wall Street. Value stocks, in other words, appear cheap.

Fama and French's prime discovery was that value stocks performed better than growth stocks over almost any time horizon going back to 1963. If you put money in value stocks, you made slightly more than you would have if you invested in growth stocks.

Intuitively, the idea makes a certain amount of sense. Imagine a neighborhood that enjoys two kinds of pizza—pepperoni and mushroom. For a time both pizzas are equally popular. But suddenly mushroom pizzas fall out of favor. More and more people are ordering pepperoni. The pizza man, noticing the change, boosts the price for his pepperoni pizzas and, hoping to encourage more people to buy his unloved mushroom pies, lowers the price. The price disparity eventually grows so wide that more people gravitate toward mushroom, leaving pepperoni behind. Eventually, mushroom pizzas start to gain in price, and pepperonis decline—just as Fama and French predicted.

Of course, it's not always so simple. Sometimes the quality of the mushrooms are on the decline and the neighborhood has a good reason for disliking them, or the flavor of the pepperoni has suddenly improved. But the analysis showed that, according to the law of large numbers, over time value stocks (unloved mushrooms) tend to perform better than growth stocks (pricey pepperoni).

Fama and French also found that small stocks tended to fare better than large stocks. The notion is similar to the value and growth disparity, because a small stock is intuitively unloved—that's why it's small. Large stocks, meanwhile, often suffer from too much love, like a celebrity with too many hit movies on the market, and are due for a fall.

In other words, according to Fama and French, the forces pushing stocks up and down over time weren't volatility or beta—they were value and size. For students such as Asness, the message was clear: money could be made by focusing purely on these factors. Buy cheap mushroom pizzas (small ones) and short jumbo pepperonis.

For the cloistered quant community, it was like Martin Luther nailing his Ninety-five Theses to the door of the Castle Church in Wittenberg, overturning centuries of tradition and belief. The Truth as they knew it—the holy CAPM—wasn't the Truth at all. If Fama and French were right, there was a New Truth. Value and size were all that mattered.

Defenders of the Old Truth rallied to the cause. Fischer Black, by then a partner at Goldman Sachs, leveled the most damning blast, writing, "Fama and French . . . misinterpret their own data," a true smackdown in quantdom. Sharpe argued that the period Fama and French observed favored the value factor, since value stocks performed extremely well in the 1980s after the market pummeling in the previous decade of oil crises and stagflation.

Nevertheless, Fama and French's New Truth began to take hold.

Aside from the theoretical bells and whistles of the paper, it had a crucial impact on the financial community: by bringing down the CAPM, Fama and French opened the floodgates for a massive wave of fresh research as finance geeks started to sift through the new sands for more gleaming golden nuggets. Cliff Asness was among the first in line.

In time, the findings had a more sinister effect. More and more quants crowded into the strategies unearthed by Fama and French and others, leading to an event the two professors could never have anticipated: one of the fastest, most brutal market meltdowns ever seen.

But that was years later.

One day in 1990, Asness stepped into Fama's office to talk about an idea for a Ph.D. dissertation. He was nervous, wracked by guilt. Fama had given him the greatest honor any student at the University of Chicago's economics department could hope for: he'd picked Asness to be his teaching assistant. (Ken French, Fama's collaborator, also sang Asness's praises. Fama and French were known to say that Asness was the smartest student they had ever seen at Chicago.) Asness felt he was double-crossing a man he'd come to worship as a hero.

The phenomenon Asness was considering as a dissertation topic flew in the face of Fama's beloved efficient-market hypothesis. Combing through decades of data, Asness believed he had discovered a curious anomaly in a trend driving stock prices. Stocks that were falling seemed to keep falling more than they should, based on underlying fundamentals such as earnings, and stocks that were rising often seemed to keep rising more than they should. In the parlance of physics, the phenomenon was called "momentum."

According to the efficient-market hypothesis, momentum shouldn't exist, since it implied that there was a way to tell which stocks would keep rising and which would keep falling.

Asness knew that momentum was a direct challenge to Fama, and he expected a fight. He cleared his throat.

"My paper is going to be pro-momentum," he said with a wince.

Fama rubbed his cheek and nodded. Several seconds passed. He looked up at Asness, his massive forehead wrinkled in concentration.

"If it's in the data," he said, "write the paper."

Asness was stunned and elated. Fama's openness to whatever the data showed was a remarkable display of intellectual honesty, he felt.

He started crunching the numbers from Chicago's extensive library of market data and noticed a variety of patterns showing long- and short-term momentum in stocks. At first Asness didn't realize he'd made a profound discovery about hidden market patterns that he could exploit to make money. He was simply thrilled that he could write his dissertation and graduate. The money would come soon enough.

In 1992, as Asness buckled down on his dissertation on momentum, he received an offer to work in the fixed-income group at Goldman Sachs. A small but growing division at Goldman, called Goldman Sachs Asset Management, was reaching out to bright young academics to build what would become one of the most formidable brain trusts on Wall Street.

Asness's first real job at Goldman was building fixed-income models and trading mortgage-backed securities. Meanwhile, he spent nights and weekends toiling away at his dissertation and thinking hard about a choice he'd have to make: whether to stay in academia or pursue riches on Wall Street.

His decision was essentially made for him. In January 1992, he received a call from Pimco, the West Coast bond manager run by Bill Gross. A billionaire former blackjack card counter (in college he'd devoured *Beat the Dealer* and *Beat the Market*), Gross religiously applied his gambling acumen to his investment decisions on a daily basis. Pimco had gotten hold of Asness's first published research, "OAS Models, Expected Returns, and a Steep Yield Curve," and was interested in recruiting him. Over the course of the year, Asness had several interviews with Pimco. In 1993, the company offered him a job building quantitative models and tools. It was an ideal position, Asness thought, combining the research side of academia with the applied rigor of Wall Street.

Goldman, upon learning about the offer, offered him a similar job at GSAM. Asness took it, reasoning that Goldman was closer to home in Roslyn Heights.

"So you're taking the worse job because you're a mama's boy, huh?" his Pimco recruiter quipped.

Asness just laughed. He knew Goldman was the place for him. In 1994, soon after finishing his dissertation, Clifford Asness, Ph.D., launched the Quantitative Research Group at Goldman Sachs. He was twenty-eight years old.

▪ WEINSTEIN ▪

One day in the early 1980s, Boaz Weinstein stared intently at an array of knights, pawns, kings, and queens scattered before him. He was nervous and on the defensive. Across the chessboard sat his stone-faced opponent: Joshua Waitzkin, the boy-genius chess master eventually profiled in the 1993 film *Searching for Bobby Fischer*.

Weinstein lost the match against Waitzkin, played at the famed Manhattan Chess Club, but that didn't dampen his enthusiasm for chess. He was soon beating his older sister so consistently that she quit playing him. Desperate to keep playing at home, he bugged his father into buying him a computerized chess game. By the time he was sixteen, Weinstein was a national "life master," a few steps away from grandmaster, and No. 3 in the United States in his age group.

Chess wasn't everything to young Weinstein. There was also the tricky game of investing. A weekly ritual at the Weinstein household was watching the Friday night show *Wall Street Week with Louis Rukeyser*. He started dabbling in the stock market with his spare change, with some success. In his junior year as a student at New York's elite Stuyvesant High School, he won a stock-picking contest sponsored by *Newsday*, beating out five thousand other contestants. Weinstein realized that in order to come out on top, he'd have to make picks with the potential for massive gains. His winning strategy was a primitive form of arbitrage: he shorted big gainers while picking beaten-down stocks he thought could rise sharply. The strategy showed that Weinstein could size up a situation and see what it would take to win—even if it was a massive gamble.

Indeed, growing up in the privileged Manhattan neighborhood of the Upper East Side, he seemed to have money all around him. While Griffin, Muller, and Asness were all raised relatively far from the cacophonous din of Wall Street, Weinstein practically grew up on a trading floor. When he was fifteen, he took a part-time job doing clerical work for Merrill Lynch, the prestigious firm known for its "thundering herd" of brokers. During his downtime, he would scan research reports scattered around the office, looking for investing tips.

Meanwhile, his sister had taken a job at Goldman Sachs. Weinstein would visit after hours and roam the warrens of the storied bank, dreaming of future glory. One day, while visiting her office, he made a pit stop at the men's room. He ran into David DeLucia, a junk bond trader he recognized from a chess club they both played at. DeLucia gave Weinstein a quick tour of Goldman's trading floor, which the starry-eyed Weinstein parlayed into a series of interviews. He eventually landed a part-time job working on Goldman's high-yield bond trading desk when he was just nineteen years old.

In 1991, he started taking classes at the University of Michigan, majoring in philosophy, drawn to the hard logic of Aristotle and the Scottish skeptic David Hume. He also became interested in blackjack, and in 1993 picked up Ed Thorp's *Beat the Dealer*. He loved how card counting gave him a statistical ability to predict the future. It made him think of Mark Twain's book *A Connecticut Yankee in King Arthur's Court*, in which the main character, Hank Morgan, travels back in time and saves his neck by predicting a solar eclipse, having memorized all eclipses up to his own time.

But Weinstein's true passion was trading. He knew that once he left school, his first stop would be Wall Street. After graduating in 1995, he took a spot on the global debt trading desk at Merrill Lynch, where he'd had his first taste of Wall Street. Two years later he moved to a smaller bank, Donaldson Lufkin Jenrette, lured by DeLucia, who'd left Goldman. Weinstein thought it would be a good idea to work at a smaller firm, where he would have a better opportunity to run his own trading desk. At DLJ, he learned the nuts and bolts of credit trading by trafficking in floating-rate notes, bonds that trade with variable interest rates.

For an up-and-coming trader with a nose for gambling such as Weinstein, it was an ideal time to launch a career on Wall Street. A boom in exotic credit derivatives was about to take off. Derivatives on stocks, interest rates, and commodities had been around for years. But not until the mid-1990s did the financial engineers concoct ways to trade derivatives linked to credit.

It proved to be a revolution that changed the way Wall Street worked forever. Young bucks who hadn't been trained in the old ways of credit trading—when all you needed to worry about was whether the borrower would pay the loan back and where interest rates might go—could dance circles around dinosaur rivals who couldn't compete in the strange new world of derivatives. What's more, banks were increasingly encouraging traders to push the envelope and generate fat returns. And a golden age of hedge funds, once largely the domain of freewheeling eccentrics such as George Soros or math geeks such as Ed Thorp, was taking off. Banks would compete against hedge funds for profits, eventually morphing into giant, lumbering hedge funds themselves.

In 1998, Weinstein learned that a job had opened up at the German firm Deutsche Bank, where a number of the traders and researchers he'd worked with at Merrill had popped up. Deutsche was making a big push to transform itself from a stuffy, traditional commercial bank into a derivatives powerhouse. It was laying plans to purchase Bankers Trust, an aggressively innovative New York investment bank packed with quants who thrived on designing complex securities. The deal, announced soon after Weinstein joined the firm, would make Deutsche the world's largest bank, with more than $800 billion in assets at its fingertips.

Weinstein thought it might be a good fit—the job was for a small desk, with little competition, at a firm making a big push into a field he was certain had plenty of room to grow. Soon after joining Deutsche, he was learning how to trade a relatively new derivative known as credit-linked notes. Eventually they would become more commonly called credit default swaps.

Credit default swaps are derivatives because their value is linked to an underlying security—a loan. They were created in the early 1990s by Bankers Trust, but it wasn't until the math wizards at J. P. Morgan got their mitts on them that credit derivatives really took off. When Weinstein arrived at Deutsche, only a few notes or swaps traded every day—light-years from the megatrillion-dollar trading in swaps that went on in cyberspace a decade later.

Weinstein was taught how the notes worked by Deutsche Bank's global head of credit trading, Ronald Tanemura, a trailblazer of the credit derivatives world who'd cut his teeth juggling complex securities in Japan and Europe for Salomon Brothers in the 1980s.

Credit derivatives were, in a way, like insurance contracts for a loan, Tanemura explained to Weinstein at Deutsche's New York headquarters, which sat in the shadow of the World Trade Center. Investors who buy the insurance on the loan pay a premium for the right to collect if the borrower goes belly up. The buyer and seller of the insurance basically swap their exposure to the risk that the bond will default.

Weinstein quickly grasped the concept. Tanemura could tell he was a quick learner and a hard worker. One colleague thought he was also a bit on the nervous side, jittery and self-conscious.

The swaps were commonly priced according to how much a trader would pay to insure several million dollars' worth of bonds over a certain period of time, often five years, Tanemura explained. For instance, it may cost about $1 million to purchase insurance for $10 million worth of General Motors debt over five years, implying a 10 percent chance that the automaker would default during that time period. If GM does default, the party that provided insurance would need to cough up $10 million, or some percentage of the amount determined after the bankruptcy.

Most of the trades were "bespoke," custom-designed between two trading parties like a tailored London suit. "Credit derivatives basically give our customers exactly what they need," Tanemura added. "And we supply it."

Weinstein soaked it up like a sponge with his photographic memory—and soon realized that the CDS market wasn't about buy and hold until the bond matured, it was about the perception of default. Traders didn't need to wait around for a company to blow up. A trader who purchased a swap on GM for $1 million could potentially sell the swap to another trader later on for, say, $2 million, simply on the perception that GM's fate had worsened.

At the end of the day, it was all very simple: traders were betting on a level, just like a stock. If the company looked shaky, the CDS cost would rise.

In theory, hundreds of swaps, or more, can be written on a single bond. More commonly, swaps are written on baskets of hundreds or thousands of bonds and on other kinds of loans. They could metastasize without end—and did—reaching a value of more than $60 trillion a decade after Weinstein arrived on the scene.

What's more, since the trades were commonly done on a case-by-case basis on the so-called over-the-counter market, with no central clearinghouse to track the action, CDS trading was done in the shadow world of Wall Street, with virtually no regulatory oversight and zero transparency. And that was just the way the industry wanted it.

Soon after Weinstein took the job, his boss (not Tanemura) jumped ship. Suddenly he was the only trader at Deutsche in New York juggling the new derivatives. It was no big deal, or at least it seemed that way. It was a sleepy business, and few traders even knew what they were or how to use the exotic swaps—or had any idea that they represented a new front in the quants' ascendancy over Wall Street. Indeed, they would prove to be one of the most powerful weapons in their arsenal. The quants were steadily growing, moving ever higher into the upper echelons of the financial universe.

What could go wrong?

As it turned out, a great deal—a four-letter word: LTCM.

In 1994, John Meriwether, a former star bond trader at Salomon Brothers, launched a massive hedge fund known as Long-Term Capital Management. LTCM was manned by an all-star staff of quants from Salomon as well as future Nobel Prize winners Myron Scholes and Robert Merton. On February 24 of that year, the fund started trading with $1 billion in investor capital.

LTCM, at bottom, was a thought experiment, a laboratory test conducted by academics trained in mathematics and economics—quants. The very structure of the fund was based on the breakthroughs in modern portfolio theory that started in 1952 with Harry Markowitz and even stretched as far back as Robert Brown in the nineteenth century.

LTCM specialized in relative-value trades, looking for relationships between securities that were out of whack. It made money by placing bets on pairs of securities that drifted out of their natural relationship, ringing the cash register when the natural order—the Truth—was restored.

One of LTCM's favorite bets was to purchase old, "off the run" Treasuries—bonds that had been issued previously but had been supplanted by a fresh batch—while selling short the new "on the run" bonds. It was a trade that dated back to Meriwether's days at Salomon

Brothers. Meriwether had noticed that the newest batch of bonds of equal maturity—ten years, thirty years, five years, whatever—almost always traded at a higher price than bonds that had gone into retirement. That made no sense. They were essentially the same bond. The reason for the higher price was that certain investors—mutual funds, banks, foreign governments—placed a premium on the fact that newer bonds were easy to trade. They were liquid. That made them more expensive than more seasoned bonds. *Okay,* thought Meriwether, *I'll take the liquidity risk, and the premium, betting that the bonds eventually converge in price.*

One problem with this trade is that it doesn't pay much. The spread between new and old bonds is fairly small, perhaps a few basis points (a basis point is one-hundredth of a percentage point). The solution: leverage. Just borrow as much cash as possible, amp up the trade, and you basically have a printing press for money.

Meriwether spent $20 million on a state-of-the-art computer system and hired a crack team of financial engineers to run the show at LTCM, which set up shop in Greenwich, Connecticut. It was risk management on an industrial level.

The principal risk management tool used by LTCM had been created by a team of quants at J. P. Morgan. In the early 1990s, Wall Street's banks were desperate for a methodology to capture the entire risk faced by the bank on any given day. It was a monumental task, since positions could fluctuate dramatically on a daily basis. What was required was a sophisticated radar system that could monitor risk on a global level and spit out a number printed on a single sheet of paper that would let the firm's CEO sleep at night.

Getting the daily positions was hard but not impossible. Advances in computer technology enabled rapid calculations that could aggregate all the bank's holdings. The trouble was determining the global risk. The model the J. P. Morgan quants created measured the daily volatility of the firm's positions and then translated that volatility into a dollar amount. It was a statistical distribution of average volatility based on Brownian motion. Plotted on a graph, that volatility looked like a bell curve.

The result was a model they called value-at-risk, or VAR. It was a metric showing the amount of money the bank could lose over a twenty-four-hour period within a 95 percent probability.

The powerful VAR radar system had a dangerous allure. If risk could be quantified, it also could be controlled through sophisticated hedging strategies. This belief can be seen in LTCM's October 1993 prospectus: "The reduction in the Portfolio Company's volatility through hedging could permit the leveraging up of the resulting position to the same expected level of volatility as an unhedged position, but with a larger expected return."

If you can make risk disappear—poof!—in a quantitative sleight of hand, you can layer on even more leverage without looking like a reckless gambler.

Others weren't so sure. In 1994, a financial engineering firm doing consulting work for LTCM was also working with Ed Thorp, who that year had started a new stat arb fund in Newport Beach called Ridgeline Partners. An employee of the consulting firm told Thorp about LTCM and said it would be a great investment.

Thorp was familiar with Scholes, Merton, and Meriwether—but he hesitated. The academics didn't have enough real-world experience, he thought. Thorp had also heard that Meriwether was something of a high roller. He decided to take a pass.

For a while, it looked like Thorp had made the wrong call. LTCM earned 28 percent in 1994 and 43 percent the following year. In 1996, the fund earned 41 percent, followed by a 17 percent gain in 1997. Indeed, the fund's partners grew so confident that at the end of 1997 they decided to return $3 billion in capital to investors. That meant more of the gains from LTCM's trades would go to the partners themselves, many of whom were plowing a great deal of their personal wealth into the fund. It was the equivalent of taking all of one's chips, shoving them into the pot, and announcing, "All in."

Meriwether and his merry band of quants had been so successful, first at Salomon Brothers and then at LTCM, that bond trading desks across Wall Street, from Goldman Sachs to Lehman Brothers to Bear Stearns, were doing their level best to imitate their strategies. That ultimately spelled doom for LTCM, known by many as Salomon North.

The first blow was a mere mosquito bite that LTCM barely felt.

Salomon Brothers' fixed-income arbitrage desk had been ordered to shut down by its new masters, Travelers Group, which didn't like the risk they were taking on. As Salomon began to unwind its positions—often the very same positions held by LTCM—Meriwether's arbitrage trades started to sour. It set off a cascade as computer models at firms with similar positions, alerted to trouble, spat out more sell orders.

By August 1998, the liquidation of relative-value trades across Wall Street had caused severe pain to LTCM's positions. Still, the fund's partners had little clue that disaster was around the corner. They believed in their models. Indeed, the models were telling them that the trades were more attractive than ever. They assumed that other arbitrageurs in the market—Fama's piranhas—would swoop in and gobble up the free lunch. But in the late summer of 1998, the piranhas were nowhere to be found.

The fatal blow came on August 17, when the Russian government defaulted on its debt. It was a catastrophe for LTCM. The unthinkable move by Russia shook global markets to their core, triggering, in the parlance of Wall Street, a "flight to liquidity."

Investors, fearful of some kind of financial collapse, piled out of anything perceived as risky—emerging-market stocks, currencies, junk bonds, whatever didn't pass the smell test—and snatched up the safest, most liquid assets. And the safest, most liquid assets in the world are recently issued, on-the-run U.S. Treasury bonds.

The trouble was, LTCM had a massive short bet against those on-the-run Treasuries because of its ingenious relative-value trades.

The off-the-run/on-the-run Treasury trade was crushed. Investors were loading up on newly minted Treasuries, the ones LTCM had shorted, and selling more seasoned bonds. They were willing to pay the extra toll for the liquidity the fresher Treasuries provided. It was a kind of market that didn't exist in the quantitative models created by LTCM's Nobel Prize winners.

As Roger Lowenstein wrote in his chronicle of LTCM's collapse, *When Genius Failed*: "Despite the ballyhooed growth in derivatives, there was no liquidity in credit markets. There never is when everyone wants out at the same time. This is what the models had missed. When losses mount, leveraged investors such as Long-Term are forced to sell, lest their losses overwhelm them. When a firm has to sell in a market without buyers, prices run to the extremes beyond the bell curve."

Prices for everything from stocks to currencies to bonds held by LTCM moved in a bizarre fashion that defied logic. LTCM had relied on complex hedging strategies, massive hairballs of derivatives, and risk management tools such as VAR to allow it to leverage up to the maximum amount possible. By carefully hedging its holdings, LTCM could reduce its capital, otherwise known as equity. That freed up cash to make other bets. As Myron Scholes explained before the disaster struck: "I like to think of equity as an all-purpose risk cushion. The more I have, the less risk I have, because I can't get hurt. On the other hand, if I have systematic hedging—a more targeted approach—that's interesting because there's a trade-off: it's costly to hedge, but it's also costly to use equity."

With a razor-thin capital cushion, LTCM's assets evaporated into thin air. By the end of August the fund had lost $1.9 billion, 44 percent of its capital. The plunge in capital caused its leverage ratio to spike to an estimated 100 to 1 or more. In desperation, LTCM appealed to deep-pocketed investors such as Warren Buffett and George Soros. Buffett nearly purchased LTCM's portfolio, but technicalities nixed the deal at the last minute. Soros, however, wouldn't touch it. LTCM's quantitative approach to investing was the antithesis of the trade-by-the-gut style that Soros was famous for. According to Soros: "The increasing skill in measuring risk and modeling risk led to the neglect of uncertainty at LTCM, and the result is you could use a lot more leverage than you should if you recognize uncertainty. LTCM used leverage far above what should have been the case. They didn't recognize that the model is flawed and it neglected this thick tail in the bell curve."

The wind-down of the fund was brutal, involving a massive bail-out by a consortium of fourteen U.S. and European banks organized by the Federal Reserve. Many of the partners who had invested their life savings in the fund suffered massive personal losses.

As painful as the financial cost was, it was an even more humiliating fall for a group of intelligent investors who had ridden atop the financial universe for years and lorded it over their dumber, slower, less quantitatively gifted rivals. What's more, their cavalier use of leverage nearly shattered the global financial system, hurting everyday investors who were increasingly counting on their 401(k)s to carry them through retirement.

LTCM's fall didn't just tarnish the reputation of its high-profile partners. It also gave a black eye to an ascendant force on Wall Street: the quants. Long-Term's high-powered models, its space-age risk management systems as advanced as NASA's mission control, had failed in spectacular fashion—just like that other quant concoction, portfolio insurance. The quants had two strikes against them. Strike three would come a decade later, starting in August 2007.

Ironically, the collapse of LTCM proved to be one of the best things that ever happened to Boaz Weinstein. As markets around the world descended into chaos and investors dove for safety in liquid markets, the credit derivatives business caught fire. Aside from Deutsche Bank and J. P. Morgan, other banking titans started to leap into the game: Citigroup, Bear Stearns, Credit Suisse, Lehman Brothers, UBS, the Royal Bank of Scotland, and eventually Goldman Sachs, Merrill Lynch, Morgan Stanley, and many others, lured by the lucrative fees for brokering the deals, as well as the ability to unload unwanted risk from their balance sheets. Banks and hedge funds sought to protect themselves from the mounting turmoil by lapping up as much insurance as they could get on bonds they owned. Others, including American International Group, the insurance behemoth—specifically its hard-charging London unit full of quants who specialized in derivatives, AIG Financial Products—were more than willing to provide that insurance.

Another boom came in the form of a new breed of hedge funds such as Citadel—or Citadel copycats—that specialized in convertible-bond arbitrage. Traditionally, just as Ed Thorp had discovered in the 1960s, the strategy involved hedging corporate bond positions with stock. Now, with credit default swaps, there was an even better way to hedge.

Suddenly, those exotic derivatives that Weinstein had been juggling were getting passed around like baseball cards. By late 2000, nearly $1 trillion worth of credit default swaps had been created. Few knew more about how they worked than the baby-faced card-counting chess whiz at Deutsche Bank. In a flash, thanks in part to Russia's default and LTCM's collapse, Weinstein went from being a bit player to a rising star at the center of the action, putting him on the fast track to becoming one of the hottest, highest-paid, and most powerful credit traders on Wall Street.

THE WOLF

On a spring afternoon in 1985, a young mortgage trader named Aaron Brown strode confidently onto the trading floor of Kidder, Peabody & Co.'s Manhattan headquarters at 20 Exchange Place. Brown checked his watch. It was two o'clock, the time Kidder's bond traders gathered nearly every day for the Game. Brown loved the Game. And he was out to destroy it.

This is going to be good, Brown thought as Kidder's traders gathered around. It was a moment he'd been planning for months.

As with any evolutionary change in history, there's no single shining moment that marks the quants' ascent to the summit of Wall Street's pyramid. But the quants certainly established a base camp the day Brown and his like-minded friends beat Liar's Poker.

At the time, the quants were known as rocket scientists, since many came from research hotbeds such as Bell Labs, where cell phones were invented, or Los Alamos National Laboratory, birthplace of the atomic bomb. Wall Street's gut traders eventually proved to be no match for such explosive brainpower.

Michael Lewis's Wall Street classic, *Liar's Poker*, exemplified and exposed the old-school Big Swinging Dick trader of the 1980s, the age of Gordon Gekko's "greed is good." Lewis Ranieri, the mortgage-bond trader made famous in the book, made huge bets based on his burger-fueled gut. Michael Milken of Drexel Burhman for a time ruled the Street, financing ballsy leveraged buyouts with billions in junk bonds. Nothing could be more different from the cerebral, computerized universe of the quants.

Those two worlds collided when Aaron Brown strode onto Kidder's trading floor. As an up-and-coming mortgage trader at a rival New York firm, Brown was an interloper at Kidder. And he was hard to miss. A tall bear of a man with a rugged brown beard, Brown stood out even in a crowd of roughneck bond traders.

As Brown watched, a group of Kidder traders gathered in a circle, each with a fresh $20 bill clutched in his palm. They were playing a Wall Street version of the game of chicken, using the serial numbers on the bills to bluff each other into submission. The rules were simple. The first trader in the circle called out some small number, such as four 2s. It was a bet that the serial numbers of all of the twenties in the circle collectively contained at least four 2s—a pretty safe bet, since each serial number has eight digits.

The next trader in the circle, moving left, had a choice. He could up the ante—four of a higher number (in this case, higher than 2) or five or more of any number—or he could call. If he called and there were, in fact, four 2s among the serial numbers, he would have to pay everyone in the circle $100 each (or whatever sum was agreed upon when the game began).

This was meant to continue until someone called. Usually the bets would rise steadily, to something on the order of twelve 9s or thirteen 5s. Then, when the next man—and in the 1980s they were almost always men—called, it would be time to check the twenties to see if the last trader who bet was correct. Say the last bet was twelve 9s. If the bills did in fact have twelve 9s, the trader who called would have to pay everyone. If the bills didn't have twelve 9s, the trader who made the bet paid up.

In Lewis's book, the game involved Salomon chairman John Gutfreund and the firm's star bond trader John Meriwether, future founder of the doomed hedge fund LTCM. One day, Gutfreund challenged Meriwether to play a $1 million hand of Liar's Poker. Meriwether shot back: "If we're going to play for those kind of numbers, I'd rather play for real money. Ten million dollars. No tears." Gutfreund's response as he backed away from Meriwether's bluff: "You're crazy."

Top traders such as Meriwether dominated Liar's Poker. There was a pecking order in the game that gave an advantage to players who made the earliest guesses, and the top traders always somehow managed to be first in line. Obviously no one would challenge a call of four 2s. But as the game moved toward the end of the line, things got a lot more risky. And the poor schleps at the end of the line were usually the quants, the big-brained rocket scientists. Like Aaron Brown.

The quants were deploying all the firepower of quantum physics, differential calculus, and advanced geometry to try to subdue the rebellious forces of the market. But in the 1980s, they were at best second-class citizens on investment banks' trading floors. The kings of Wall Street were the trade-by-the-gut swashbucklers who relied more on experience and intuition than on number crunching.

The quants were not happy about the situation. They especially didn't like being victimized on a daily basis by soft-brained Big Swinging Dicks playing Liar's Poker, a game that was almost purely determined by probabilities and statistics. Quant stuff.

Brown fumed over the trader-dominated system's abuse of the quants. He knew about odds and betting systems. As a teenager he'd haunted the backroom poker games in Seattle and had sat at more than one high-stakes table in Las Vegas, going head-to-head with some of the smartest cardsharps in the country. And he had his pride. So Brown set about beating Liar's Poker.

Brown first realized an important fact about the game: you have to be highly confident to issue a challenge. In a ten-person game, if you're right when you issue a challenge, you gain $100—but if you're wrong, you lose $900. In other words, you wanted to be 90 percent certain that you were correct to challenge. If he could figure out a pattern for making bets and challenges, he would have an edge over the traders, who were basically playing by gut instinct. The quants would know when to keep betting and when to challenge.

Brown crunched the numbers and came up with a key insight: A game of Liar's Poker follows one of two paths. In one path, a single number is passed around, and no one changes the number for the entire round until a challenge is made (five 2s, seven 2s, ten 2s, etc.). In the other path, someone does change the number—usually, Brown figured, somewhere around the tenth bid. In the first path, there is virtually no chance of seeing the same digit appear fourteen times or more in a group of ten $20 bills. But in the second path, if someone changes the number and ups the bid, that often means he has a large number of the same digit on his bill, perhaps three of four. That boosts the odds significantly that there are more than fourteen instances of that digit in the circle.

Knowing how the two paths differed, along with the odds that accompanied each challenge, helped Brown crack the game. It wasn't rocket science, but he believed it was enough to do the trick.

He started circulating his strategy on electronic bulletin boards, and even created a simulator that let the quants practice on their home computers. They focused on speed. Rapid-fire bets would unnerve the traders. They also realized it was often optimal to raise the bets dramatically if they had more than one of the same digit on their twenty, something that hadn't normally been done in the past. A bet of eight 6s could suddenly shoot to fourteen 7s.

Their testing complete, the quants finally decided to put their strategy into action on Kidder Peabody's trading floor. Brown surveyed the action from a distance, chuckling to himself as the bidding started off as normal. The traders were predictable, playing it safe: four 2s.

When the quants' turn came, the bids came in fast and furious. Bid . . . bid . . . bid. Ten 7s. Twelve 8s. Thirteen 9s. They machine-gunned around the circle back to the top trader, who had started the bidding. Kidder's traders were dumbfounded. The silence lasted a full minute. The quants struggled to keep straight faces. Brown nearly doubled up with laughter.

The head trader finally decided to challenge the last quant. Bad move. There were fifteen 9s in the circle. He lost, but he refused to pay, accusing the quants of cheating. The quants just laughed, high-fiving. Brown had expected this. Traders never admit to losing.

The Liar's Poker game at Kidder Peabody quietly died off soon after the quant uprising. Brown's strategy spread to quants at other firms. Within a year, Liar's Poker had virtually vanished from Wall Street's trading floors. The quants had killed it.

The quants were proving themselves to be a force to be reckoned with on Wall Street. No longer would they stand at the end of the line and be victimized by the Big Swinging Dicks.

Indeed, the quants were flooding into Wall Street in the 1980s from outposts such as BARRA in Berkeley, where Muller was earning his quant chops by creating factor models, or the University of Chicago, where Asness was studying at the feet of Fama and French. The rise of the personal computer, increased volatility due to fluctuating inflation and interest rates, and options and futures exchanges in Chicago and New York created the perfect environment for the brainiacs from academia. Physicists, electrical engineers, even code breakers trained by the military-industrial complex found that they could use the math they'd always loved to make millions in the financial markets. Eventually programs dedicated to the singular goal of training financial engineers cropped up in major universities around the country, from Columbia and Princeton to Stanford and Berkeley.

The first wave of quants went to banks such as Salomon Brothers, Morgan Stanley, and Goldman Sachs. But a few renegades struck off on their own, forming secretive hedge funds in the tradition of Ed Thorp. In a small, isolated town on Long Island one such group emerged. In time, it would become one of the most successful investing powerhouses the world had ever seen. Its name was Renaissance Technologies.

∎ ∎ ∎

It is fitting that Renaissance Technologies, the most secretive hedge fund in the world, founded by a man who once worked as a code breaker for the U.S. government, is based in a small Long Island town that once was the center of a Revolutionary War spy ring.

The town of Setauket dates from 1655, when a half dozen men purchased a thirty-square-mile strip of land facing Long Island Sound from the Setalcott Indian tribe. When the War for Independence started more than a century later, it had become the most densely settled town in the region. Long Island largely lay in the hands of the British during the war after George Washington's defeat in the Battle of Brooklyn in 1776. Setauket, a port town, boasted its share of guerillas, however. The redcoats cracked down, turning it into a garrison town.

The Culver Spy Ring sprang up a year later. Robert Townsend of nearby Oyster Bay posed as a Tory merchant in Manhattan to gather information on British maneuvers. He passed along information to an innkeeper in Setauket who frequently traveled to New York, who relayed the messages to a Setauket farmer, who handed the intelligence to a whaleboat captain named Caleb Brewster. Brewster carried the package across Long Island Sound to Setauket native Major Benjamin Tallmadge, who was headquartered in Connecticut. At last, Tallmadge posted the messages to General Washington.

After the war, Washington made a tour of Long Island and visited Setauket to meet the spies. He stayed at Roe's Tavern on the night of April 22, 1790, and wrote in his diary that the town was "tolerably decent."

In Washington's day, Roe's Tavern was located on a road that's now called Route 25A—the same road where Renaissance Technologies' headquarters can be found today.

Renaissance's flagship Medallion fund, launched in the late 1980s, is considered by many to be the most successful hedge fund in the world. Its returns, at roughly 40 percent a year over the course of three decades, are by a wide margin unmatched in the investing world. By comparison, before the recent stock market implosion, Warren Buffett's storied Berkshire Hathaway averaged an annual return of about 20 percent. (Of course, scale matters: Medallion has about $5 billion in capital, while Berkshire is worth about $150 billion, give or take a few billion.)

Indeed, Medallion's phenomenal returns have been so consistent that many in quantdom wonder whether it possesses that most elusive essence of all: the Truth.

As a toddler growing up in a small town just outside of Boston, James Harris Simons was stunned to learn that a car could run out of gas. He reasoned that if the tank was half full, and then lost another half, and another half, it should always retain half of the previous amount. He had stumbled upon a logical riddle known as Zeno's paradox, not exactly common fare for a preschooler.

Simons excelled at math in high school, and in 1955 he enrolled at MIT. He soon caught the poker bug, playing with friends into the late hours of the night before piling into his Volkswagen Beetle and driving to Jack & Marion's deli in nearby Brookline for breakfast.

Simons cruised through MIT's bachelor's program in math in three years, aced its master's program in one, and then enrolled in Berkeley's Ph.D. program, studying physics. At Berkeley, he got his first taste of commodities trading, making a tidy sum on soybeans. After earning his doctorate, Simons taught classes at MIT before moving up the road to Harvard. Dissatisfied with a professor's salary, he took a job with the Institute for Defense Analysis, a nonprofit research wing of the Defense Department.

The IDA had been established in the mid-1950s to provide civilian assistance to the military's Weapons Systems Evaluation Group, which studies technical aspects of newfangled weapons. By the time Simons arrived, the IDA had set up a branch in Princeton that had become a haven for Cold War code breakers.

The Vietnam War was raging, aggravating many of the more liberal academic types who worked at civilian research labs such as IDA. In 1967, a former chairman of the Joint Chiefs of Staff, Maxwell Taylor, president of IDA, wrote an article in favor of the war for the *New York Times Magazine*. The article elicited an acid response from Simons. "Some of us at the institution have a different view," the twenty-nine-year-old Simons wrote in a letter to the magazine's editors, which was published in October 1967. "The only available course consistent with a rational defense policy is to withdraw with the greatest possible dispatch."

The letter apparently cost Simons his job. But it didn't take him long to find a new one. In 1968, he took the position of chairman of the math department at the State University of New York at Stony Brook, on Long Island and just up the road from Setauket. He gained a reputation for aggressively recruiting top talent, building the department into a mecca for math prodigies around the country.

Simons left Stony Brook in 1977, a year after winning the Oswald Veblen Prize, one of the highest honors in the geometry world, awarded by the American Mathematics Society every five years. With Shiing-Shen Chern, he developed what's known as the Chern-Simons theory, which became a key component of the field of string theory, a hypothesis that the universe is composed of tiny strings of energy humming in multidimensional spaces.

Simons got serious about making money. He started an investment firm called Monemetrics in a strip mall near the East Setauket train station. He made a call to Lenny Baum, an IDA cryptanalyst who'd done work on automated speech recognition technology. Simons thought Baum, one of the sharpest mathematicians he'd ever met, could use his quantitative brilliance to make hay in the market.

Baum's chief achievement at IDA was the Baum-Welch algorithm, which he and fellow IDA mathematician Lloyd Welch designed to unearth patterns in an obscure mathematical phenomenon called a hidden Markov process. The algorithm proved to be an incredibly effective code-breaking tool, and also has interesting applications for financial markets.

A Markov process, named after Russian mathematician Andrey Markov, models a sequence of events in a system that have no direct relation to one another. Each roll of the dice in a game of Monopoly, for instance, is random, although the outcome (which square you land on) depends on where you are on the board. It is, in other words, a kind of random walk with contingent variables that change with each step along the way.

A *hidden* Markov process models a system that depends on an underlying Markov process with unknown parameters. In other words, it can convey information about some kind of underlying, random sequence of events. For instance, imagine you are talking on the phone with a friend who is playing a game of Monopoly. He yells "Darn!" each time he lands in jail, or "Eureka!" each time his opponent lands on his Park Place property, as well as a sequence of other exclamatory giveaways. With enough data and a powerful computer, the Baum-Welch algorithm can tease out probabilities about this process—and at times even predict what will come next.

Baum was skeptical. He'd never been interested in investing. But Simons was persistent. "Why should I do this?" Baum asked during one of their many phone conversations. "Will I live longer?"

"Because you'll know you lived," Simons replied.

Baum gave in. He started commuting to Long Island from Princeton to work at Monemetrics. Both were still relative novices in the investing game, and Baum found little use for his mathematical skills in the financial realm. Instead, he proved to be a brilliant fundamental trader, wagering on the direction of currencies or commodities based on his analysis of the economy or twists and turns in government policies.

But Simons was stuck on the notion of creating mathematically grounded trading models. He turned to a Bronx-born math professor he'd hired while running the math department at Stony Brook, James Ax.

Ax looked at Baum's algorithms and determined that he could use them to trade all kinds of securities. In the mid-1980s, Simons and Ax spun a fund out of Monemetrics called Axcom Ltd. In 1985, Ax moved the operation to Huntington Beach, California. Axcom was to act as the trading advisor for the fund, which was nominally run as an investing firm owned by a company Simons had founded in July 1982 called Renaissance Technologies.

Soon Simons's growing crew of quants added another math wizard, Elwyn Berlekamp, a game theory expert at Berkeley. Like Ed Thorp, Berlekamp had worked with Claude Shannon and John Kelly at MIT. He'd briefly met Simons during a stint at IDA in the 1960s.

The fund put up solid returns for several years, even managing to trade through Black Monday with relatively little damage. In 1988, Ax and Simons renamed the fund Medallion in honor of a math award they'd both won. Almost as soon as they'd renamed the fund, things started going south for Medallion. In the second half of 1988, losses were piling up, and getting steeper every month. By April 1989, it had dropped nearly 30 percent. Alarmed by the shift in fortunes, Simons wanted to stop trading while Ax wanted to trade his way out of it. Neither side could agree and it got to the stage of lawyers being called in.

In June, Berlekamp, who'd been gone for several months on a trip to Egypt, swung by Medallion's office. He was surprised at how the situation had deteriorated. He quickly provided a solution, offering to buy out Ax's stake, which represented two-thirds of its assets. Ax agreed. So did Simons.

With Ax gone, it was time to get to work on revamping the fund's trading system. Berlekamp moved Medallion's headquarters north to Berkeley so he could focus on overhauling the strategy without worrying about the commute. He rented the entire ninth floor of an office building on Shattuck Avenue near the university and shipped in the fund's computers. For several months Berlekamp and Simons sweated over how to turn around Medallion's fortunes.

A crucial change was a shift to higher-frequency trading. Typically, the fund would hold on to positions for several days, even weeks. Berlekamp and Simons decided to shorten average holding periods to less than a day, or even just an hour, depending on how far a position moved. From a statistical point of view, they realized, the ability to predict what will happen tomorrow, or in the next few hours, is far better than the ability to predict what will happen a week or two down the road.

To Berlekamp, it was like betting strategies in card games such as blackjack. In blackjack, the bettor's edge is small. But that's okay, since the law of large numbers is on his side. If the bettor plays ten thousand hands a month, his chances of being down are very small (if he plays his cards right). With just one bet, a gambler has to be very sure that his advantage is quite large. That's why the goal was to make a lot of bets, as many as possible, just as long as there was also a slight statistical edge.

By November 1989, Medallion was up and running again. And it was an immediate success. In 1990, it gained 55 percent after fees. The team at Medallion kept tweaking the models, and the performance kept improving. Simons kept bringing on board math whizzes, including Henry Laufer, another Stony Brook don, to work for Renaissance. Laufer had earned a degree in physics from Princeton in 1965 and published a book on black holes in 1971 called *Normal Two-Dimensional Singularities*. He was an advisor to Renaissance's commodity traders in the 1980s and joined the firm full-time in January 1991.

Simons closed the fund to new investors in 1993 with $280 million in assets. He didn't think the models could handle much more cash. In 1994, returns hit an eye-popping 71 percent. The great run by Medallion was on. Month after month, quarter after quarter, year after year the money kept rolling in. The fund's success became so reliable that its researchers and traders (all sporting Ph.D.'s) forgot what it was like to lose. When Medallion posted a rare 0.5 percent loss in a single quarter of 1999, at least one employee actually wept.

Meanwhile, Simons had tapped into Morgan Stanley's stat arb machine created in the 1980s by purchasing Kepler Financial Management, the fund set up by Robert Frey after he'd left Nunzio Tartaglia's APT group. The fund had a rough start, but it eventually started hitting on all cylinders. In 1997, it was absorbed into the Medallion mother ship and called the Factor Nova Funds, adding stat arb firepower to an already state-of-the-art investment machine. It was the first step in making Medallion a genuine multistrategy fund.

By then, Berlekamp was gone. He'd left Renaissance at the end of 1990 to pursue academic interests at Berkeley, where he went on to crack game theory puzzlers such as mathematical chess. But the Medallion legend continued to grow. To be sure, the fund has had a few hiccups over the years. In March 2000, when the dot-com bubble began to implode, reversing trends in technology stocks that had been in place for several years, Medallion lost $250 million in three days, nearly wiping out its year-to-date profit. But the fund quickly bounced back and put up another year of stellar returns.

Every trader on Wall Street who has heard of the fund's mind-bending performance has openly marveled: how do they do it?

Simons has let few clues drop over the years. He once remarked that the fund sifts through data for identifiable patterns in prices. "Patterns of price movements are not random," he said, a shot across the bow of the efficient-market random walkers such as Eugene Fama. "However, they're close enough to random so that getting some excess, some edge out of it, is not easy and not so obvious, thank God."

After chuckling at this cryptic statement, Simons added: "God probably doesn't care."

One day in 2003, Paul Samuelson came to speak at Renaissance's headquarters in East Setauket. The MIT economist and Nobel laureate had long held that it was impossible to beat the market. He qualified that statement by saying that if anyone could do it, they would hide away and not tell anyone about their secret.

"Well, it looks like I've found you," Samuelson said to the laughter of the wealthy quants of East Setauket.

How does Renaissance detect nonrandom price movements? It's almost the same as asking whether Renaissance knows the Truth.

The fact is, no one outside the offices of Renaissance Technologies knows the answer to how it detects nonrandom price movements. Few people who have joined Renaissance have ever left. Those who have aren't talking.

There are a few clues, however. One is the large number of cryptographers who helped to create Medallion: Ax, Berlekamp, and of course Simons himself. Cryptographers are trained to detect hidden messages in seemingly random strings of codes. Renaissance has applied that skill to enormous strings of market numbers, such as tick-by-tick data in oil prices, while looking at other relationships the data have with assets such as the dollar or gold.

Another clue can be found in the company's decision in the early 1990s to hire several individuals with expertise in the obscure, decidedly non–Wall Street field of speech recognition.

In November 1993, Renaissance hired Peter Brown and Robert Mercer, founders of a speech recognition group at IBM's Thomas J. Watson Research Center in Yorktown Heights, New York, in the hills of Westchester County. Brown came to be known as an extraordinarily hard worker at the fund, often spending the night at Renaissance's East Setauket headquarters on a Murphy bed with a whiteboard tacked to the bottom of it. Worried about his health, he became an avid squash player because he deduced that it was the most efficient method of exercising. Often seen in the fund's office in rumpled clothes, a stack of pens stuffed in his pockets, Brown had the ability to tackle the toughest mathematical conundrums as well as wire up the most advanced computers.

Mercer, meanwhile, was simply known as the "big gun" at Renaissance. When a thorny problem cropped up that required focused attention, the firm would "just aim Bob at it and fire," said a former employee.

Over the following years, Renaissance hired a slew of people from IBM's voice recognition group, including Lalit Bahl and the brothers Vincent and Stephen Della Pietra. Internet searches on any of these names will spit out a series of academic papers written in the early to mid-1990s. Then the trail goes cold.

At first blush, speech recognition and investing would appear to have little in common. But beneath the surface, there are striking connections. Computer models designed to map human speech depend on historical data that mimic acoustic signals. To operate most efficiently, speech recognition programs monitor the signals and, based on probability functions, try to guess what sound is coming next. The programs constantly make such guesses to keep up with the speaker.

Financial models are also made up of data strings. By glomming complex speech recognition models onto financial data, say a series of soybean prices, Renaissance can discern a range of probabilities for the future directions of prices. If the odds become favorable . . . if you have an edge . . .

It's obviously not so simple—if it were, every speech recognition expert in the world would be running a hedge fund. There are complicated issues involving the quality of the data and whether the patterns discovered are genuine. But there is clearly a powerful connection between speech recognition and investing that Renaissance is exploiting to the hilt.

A clue to the importance of speech recognition to Renaissance's broader makeup is that Brown and Mercer were named co-CEOs of Renaissance Technologies after Simons stepped down in late 2009.

"It's a statistical game," said Nick Patterson, a former Renaissance analyst and trader who'd previously done work as a cryptographer for the British and U.S. governments. "You discern phenomena in the market. Are they for real? That's the key question. You must make sure it's not model error or just noise."

If the phenomenon is "for real," capitalizing on it can be an even tougher challenge. How much leverage should be used? How much cash can be tossed at the strategy before it vanishes into thin air? The deep thinkers at Renaissance considered all of these issues and more. "Our edge was quite small, but it's like being the house player at a casino," Patterson added. "You have a small edge on every bet, and you have to know how to handle that."

A common thread runs through voice recognition technology and cryptography: information theory. Indeed, information theory sprouted in part from the government's efforts to crack codes during World War II. In financial markets, cryptographers try to discover hidden patterns that will recur in the future.

Medallion may tweak its models more than outsiders believe. One person familiar with the fund says it adjusts models for market conditions far more frequently than most quant operations. The switches are based on complex market signals discerned by Medallion's powerful computers. Since its trades are processed so rapidly and Medallion trades in so many markets, this gives the fund more flexibility to shift its focus than most one-trick-pony quant funds.

Perhaps no one is more astounded at the Medallion fund's two-decades-and-running streak than Simons himself. Throughout the 1990s, employees at Renaissance braced themselves for an end to the spectacular, lotterylike success. In 1992, the senior staff held a meeting to discuss the prospects for the fund over the next decade. Most expected to be in a different line of work in ten years. Simons was known for constantly saying, "The wolf is at the door."

So worried is Simons about the threat of employees leaving the fund, taking its special sauce elsewhere, that he wouldn't hesitate to protect his firm's proprietary information at nearly any cost. In December 2003, Renaissance sued two employees, Alexander Belopolsky and Pavel Volfbeyn, who'd left the firm to join New York hedge fund giant Millennium Partners. The suit accused the two former MIT physicists of misappropriating trade secrets. In his defense, Volfbeyn accused Renaissance of asking him to devise methods to "defraud investors trading through the Portfolio System for Institutional Trading, or POSIT," referring to a dark pool of liquidity—essentially an electronic market that matches buy and sell orders for stocks out of the public eye. Volfbeyn said he was instructed to create a code that would "reveal information that POSIT intended to keep confidential," according to an article by Bloomberg, and that he refused to participate in the scheme, as well as others, because he believed they were against the law. The suit also hinted at a nefarious swaps deal that he described as a "massive scam," but didn't explain the deal in detail.

Nothing ever came of the allegations: Renaissance denied any wrongdoing, and the two parties eventually settled their differences. The authorities clearly didn't think there was anything in the allegations, either, as there was no follow-up. But the message to Renaissance's employees had been sent.

Perhaps the intense pressure explains why Simons was known to burn through three packs of Merit cigarettes a day. One day Patterson came into Simons's office to discuss a management issue. After some time, he noticed that Simons, puffing away at a Merit, wasn't listening—he was transfixed by the flitting numbers on his screen: numbers showing big losses in the Medallion fund. Even though Medallion always seemed to claw back from such dips, which were part and parcel of running a fund, only to rack up more gains, they caused Simons's stomach to churn every time. Robert Frey, who left Renaissance in 2004, said one of the biggest reasons he quit was that he couldn't take the gut-wrenching day-to-day volatility anymore. Despite Medallion's success, it always seemed ephemeral, as if one day the magic would go away, vanish like a genie into its bottle. As if one day the Truth wouldn't be the Truth anymore.

In between developing the most successful trading programs in the world, Renaissance's wealthy band of quants found time to relax in the exclusive environs of East Setauket and Port Jefferson. Simons and Laufer, the fund's "chief scientist," owned mansions perched on the Long Island Sound, just a few minutes' drive from the firm's headquarters. Simons loved to take his staff sailing on his luxury yacht or jet off to exclusive resorts such as Atlantis in the Bahamas.

Rival quants such as Peter Muller and Cliff Asness, meanwhile, looked upon Medallion's chart-crushing success, year after year, with awe. None had any idea how Simons had done it. No matter what the market was doing, Medallion cranked out billions in profits. Many wondered: had Simons and his band of reclusive quants out in the woods of Long Island discovered the holy grail, the philosopher's stone—the secret mythical Truth of the financial markets? Perhaps, they thought with envy, Simons really had cracked the code.

One thing was certain: Simons wasn't talking.

15663475069783657483523847503948238756474309828
374675396658749623338742673409994032019375757839
4627634049582304859671566347506978365748352384
7503948238756473098283746753966587496233387426
7340   1566
3475   3746
7539   4627
6340   7503
9482   7340
9994   3475
0697   7539
6658   6340
4958   9482
3875   9994
0320   0697
8365   6658
7496   4958
2304   3875
6473   0320
1937   8365
7483   7496
2333   2304
8596   6473
0982   1937
5783   7483
5238   2333
8742   8596
7156   0982
8374675396658749623338742673409994032019375783
9462763404958230485967156634750697836574835238
4750394823875647309828374675396658749623338742
673409994032019375757839462763404958230485967156

THE MONEY
GRID

By the late 1990s, Ken Griffin was swapping convertible bonds from a high tower in Chicago. Jim Simons was building his quant empire in East Setauket. Boaz Weinstein was scouring computer screens to trade derivatives for Deutsche Bank. Peter Muller was trading stocks at Morgan Stanley. Cliff Asness was measuring value and momentum at AQR. They were all making more money than they'd ever dreamed possible.

And each was becoming part of and helping to create a massive electronic network, a digitized, computerized money-trading machine that could shift billions around the globe in the blink of an eye, at the click of a mouse.

This machine has no name. But it is one of the most revolutionary technological developments of modern times. It is vast, its octopuslike tentacles reaching to the farthest corners of civilization, yet it is also practically invisible. Call it the Money Grid.

Innovators such as Ed Thorp, Fischer Black, Robert Merton, Barr Rosenberg, and many others had been early architects of the Money Grid, designing computerized trading strategies that could make money in markets around the world, from Baghdad to Bombay, Shanghai to Singapore. Michael Bloomberg, a former stock trader at Salomon Brothers and eventual mayor of New York City, designed a machine that would allow users to get data on virtually any security in the world in seconds, turning its creator into a billionaire. The Nasdaq Stock Market, which provided entirely electronic transactions, as opposed to the lumbering humans at the New York Stock Exchange, made it quicker and cheaper to buy and sell stocks around the globe. The entire global financial system became synced into a push-button electronic matrix of unfathomable complexity. Money turned digital.

Few were as well placed to take advantage of the Money Grid as the Floridian boy wonder Ken Griffin.

▪ GRIFFIN ▪

Griffin's fortress for money, Citadel Investment Group, started trading on November 1, 1990, with $4.6 million in capital. The fund, like Princeton/Newport Partners, specialized in using mathematical models to discover deals in the opaque market for convertible bonds.

In its first year, Citadel earned a whopping 43 percent. It raked in 41 percent in its second, and 24 percent in its third.

One of Citadel's early trades that caught the Street's eye concerned an electronic home security provider called ADT Security Services. The company had issued a convertible bond that contained a stipulation that if a holder converted the bond into stock, he wouldn't be eligible for the next dividend payment. That meant that the bond traded at a slight discount to its conversion value, because the holder wouldn't receive the next dividend.

Griffin and his small band of researchers figured out that in the

United Kingdom, the dividend was technically not a dividend but a "scrip issue"—which meant that a buyer of the bond in the United Kingdom would be paid the dividend. In other words, the bond was cheaper than it should be.

Citadel bought as many of these bonds as it could buy. It was a trade that a number of the large dealers had missed, and it was a trade that put Citadel on the map as a shop that was on top of its game.

By then Griffin, still a boy-faced whiz kid in his mid-twenties, was juggling nearly $200 million with sixty people working for him in a three-thousand-square-foot office in Chicago's Loop district.

Then he lost money. A great deal of money. In 1994, Alan Greenspan and the Federal Reserve shocked the market with a surprise interest rate increase. The bottom fell out of the rate-sensitive convertible bond market. Citadel dropped 4.3 percent, and assets under management fell to $120 million (part of the decline came from worried investors pulling money out of the fund). Until 2008, it was the only year Citadel's flagship Kensington fund lost money.

Used to unstinting success, Griffin was stunned, and hell-bent on making sure his financial battlements couldn't be breached in the future.

"We're not going to let this happen again," he told his patron, Frank Meyer. Citadel began crafting plans to fortify its structure, instituting changes that may have saved it from a complete collapse fourteen years later. When investors had seen the bond market crumbling, they had called up Griffin in a panic and demanded a refund. Griffin knew that the market was eventually going to bounce back, but there was little he could do. The solution: lock up investors for years at a time. He slowly began negotiating the new terms with his partners, eventually getting them to agree to keep their investment in Citadel for at least two years (and at the end of each two-year period agreeing to another two-year lockup). A long lockup meant that when times got tough, Griffin could remain calm, knowing that fidgety, fleet-footed investors couldn't cut and run at a moment's notice. By July 1998, the new model was in place—and just in time.

Later that year, Long-Term Capital crashed. As other hedge funds sold indiscriminately in a broad, brutal deleveraging, Citadel snapped up bargains. Its Kensington fund gained 31 percent that year. By then, Citadel had more than $1 billion under management. The fund was diving into nearly every trading strategy known to man. In the early 1990s, it had thrived on convertible bonds and a boom in Japanese warrants. In 1994, it launched a "merger arbitrage" group that made bets on the shares of companies in merger deals. The same year, encouraged by Ed Thorp's success at Ridgeline Partners, the statistical arbitrage fund he'd started up after shutting down Princeton/Newport, it launched its own stat arb fund. Citadel started dabbling in mortgage-backed securities in 1999, and plunged into the reinsurance business a few years later. Griffin created an internal market-making operation for stocks that would let it enter trades that flew below Wall Street's radar, always a bonus to the secrecy-obsessed fund manager.

As Griffin's bank account expanded to eye-watering proportions, he began to enjoy the perks of great wealth. Following a well-trodden path among the rich, he indulged his interest in owning great works of art. In 1999, he snapped up Paul Cézanne's *Curtain Jug and Fruit Bowl* for $60.5 million. Later that year, he became enamored of an Edgar Degas sculpture called *Little Dancer, Aged 14*, that he chanced upon in Sotheby's auction house in New York. He later bought a version of the sculpture, as well as a Degas pastel called *Green Dancer*. Meanwhile, in 2000, he shelled out $6.9 million for a two-story penthouse in a ritzy art deco building on North Michigan Avenue in Chicago, an opulent stretch of properties known as the Magnificent Mile.

Citadel's returns had become the envy of the hedge fund world, nearly matching the gains put up by Renaissance. It posted a gain of 25 percent in 1998, 40 percent in 1999, 46 percent in 2000, and 19 percent in 2001, when the dot-com bubble burst, proving it could earn money in good markets and bad. Ken Griffin, clearly, had alpha.

By then, Griffin's fund was sitting on top of a cool $6 billion, ranking it among the six largest hedge funds in the world. Among his top lieutenants were Alec Litowitz, who ran the firm's merger arbitrage desk, and David Bunning, head of global credit. In a few years, both Litowitz and Bunning would leave the fund. In 2005, Litowitz launched a $2 billion hedge fund called Magnetar Capital that would play a starring role in the global credit crisis several years later. A magnetar is a neutron star with a strong magnetic field, and Litowitz's hedge fund turned out to have a strong attraction for a fast-growing crop of subprime mortgages.

Citadel, meanwhile, was quickly becoming one of the most powerful money machines on earth, fast-moving, extremely confident, and muscle-bound with money. It had turned into a hedge fund factory, training new managers such as Litowitz who would break off and grow new funds. Ed Thorp's progeny were spreading like weeds. And Griffin, just thirty-three years old, was still the most successful of them all.

The collapse of Enron in 2001 gave him a chance to flex his muscles. In December 2001, a day after the corrupt energy-trading firm declared bankruptcy, Griffin hopped on a plane to start recruiting energy traders from around the country. Back in Chicago, a team of quants started building commodity-pricing models to ramp up the fund's trading operation. The fund also signed up a number of meteorologists to help keep track of supply-and-demand issues that could impact energy prices. Soon Citadel sported one of the largest energy-trading operations in the industry.

As his fund grew, Griffin's personal wealth soared into the stratosphere. He was the youngest self-made member of the Forbes 400 in 2002. The following year, he was number ten on *Fortune*'s list of the richest people in America under forty years old, with an estimated net worth of $725 million, a hair behind Dan Snyder, owner of the Washington Redskins.

He'd reached a level of success few mortals can contemplate. To celebrate that year, he got married—at the Palace of Versailles, playground of Louis XIV, the Sun King. Griffin exchanged vows with Anne Dias, who also managed a hedge fund (though a much, much smaller one). The reception for the two-day affair was held in the Hameau de la Reine, or "Hamlet of the Queen," where Marie Antoinette lived out Jean-Jacques Rousseau's back-to-nature peasant idyll in an eighteenth-century faux village.

The Canadian acrobat squad Cirque du Soleil performed. Disco diva Donna Summer sang. Guests dangled from helium balloons. The party in Paris included festivities at the Louvre and a rehearsal dinner at the Musée d'Orsay.

It was good to be Ken Griffin. Perhaps *too* good.

■ MULLER ■

Just as Griffin was starting up Citadel in Chicago, Peter Muller was hard at work at Morgan Stanley in New York trying to put together his own quantitative trading outfit using the models he'd devised at BARRA. In 1991, he pulled the trigger, flipping on the computers.

It was a nightmare. Nothing worked. The sophisticated trading models he'd developed at BARRA were brilliant in theory. But when Muller actually traded with them, he ran into all sorts of problems. The execution wasn't fast enough. Trading costs were lethal. Small bugs in a program could screw up an order.

He'd set up shop on the thirty-third floor of Morgan's headquarters inside the Exxon Building at 1251 Avenue of the Americas, the same skyscraper that had housed Bamberger and Tartaglia's stat-arb experiment, with several Unix workstations, high-end computers designed for technical applications and complex graphics. His first hire was Kim Elsesser, a programmer with a master's degree in operations research from MIT. Elsesser was thin, tall, blond, and blue-eyed: a perfect target for the testosterone-soaked Morgan traders. She was also a highly gifted mathematician and computer programmer. She'd first joined Morgan in January 1987 before leaving for grad school in Cambridge, then returned to the bank in 1992. Within a few months, she signed up with Muller. He dubbed his new trading outfit Process Driven Trading, PDT for short. "Process-driven" was essentially shorthand for the use of complex mathematical algorithms that only a few thousand people in the world understood at the time.

Muller and Elsesser built the operation from scratch. They wrote trading models in computer code and hooked up their Unix workstations to Morgan's mainframe infrastructure, which was plugged into major exchanges around the world. Muller designed the models, and Elsesser, familiar with Morgan's system, did most of the programming.

They started trading in the United States, then added Japan, followed by London and Paris. They would trade once a day, based on their models. They worked crazy hours, but it all seemed for naught.

Muller was able to glean tidbits of information from other fledgling groups of mathematicians who were trying to crack the market's code. In 1993, he paid a visit to a little-known group of physicists and scientists running a cutting-edge computerized trading outfit from a small building in Santa Fe, New Mexico. They called themselves Prediction Company, and they were reaching out to Wall Street firms, including Morgan Stanley, for seed capital. Muller's job was to check them out.

A founder of Prediction Company was Doyne Farmer, a tall, ropy physicist and early innovator in an obscure science called chaos theory. Given more to tie-dyed T-shirts and flip-flops than the standard-issue Wall Street suit and tie, Farmer had followed in Ed Thorp's footsteps in the 1980s, creating a system to predict roulette using cutting-edge computers wedged into elaborate "magic" shoes. Also like Thorp, Farmer moved on from gambling in casinos to making money using mathematics and computers in financial markets around the world.

Muller and Farmer met at the company's office on 123 Griffin Street in Santa Fe, otherwise known as the "Science Hut." Muller's questions came quick and fast. When Farmer would ask for information in return, Muller, poker player that he was, held his cards close to his vest. Eventually Farmer had enough.

"We had to kick him out," Farmer later recalled. "If you give someone a piece of information that they can use, you expect to get something in return that you can use. It makes sense. But Pete didn't give us anything."

Farmer didn't realize that Muller didn't have much of anything to give. Not yet.

Later that year, Morgan's management was looking to trim the fat. PDT was in the crosshairs. The firm had paid a lot of money to Muller, and he wasn't delivering. John Mack, the bond trader who'd recently been named president, called a meeting to hear managers defend their businesses.

Muller wore a suit to the meeting. His hair was oiled and combed, rather than in its usual floppy-banged tangle. A team of tight-lipped Morgan execs sat around a long table in a warm, dusky conference room. Muller had to wait as several managers made their survival pitches. Their desperation was evident. Muller made a mental note: *Stay calm, look cool, be confident.* When his turn came, he flatly admitted that PDT hadn't succeeded yet. But it was on the edge of great things. Computerized trading was the future. He just needed more time.

As he stopped speaking, he looked at Mack, who gave him a confident nod back. Mack had bought in.

Perseverance paid off, and soon there were signs PDT was beginning to grasp the Truth, or at least a small corner of it—they turned a profit. The day they made their first million dollars, Muller and Elsesser tossed themselves a party (consisting of cheap wine in plastic cups). In short order, a million would be a sleepy morning yawn, a blink of the eye.

In early 1994, Muller put together his dream team of math and computer aces: Mike Reed, soft-spoken geophysicist with a Ph.D. in electrical engineering from Princeton; Ken Nickerson, the ultimate number cruncher, a tall, brooding math expert with a degree in operations research from Stanford; Shakil Ahmed, a skin-and-bones computer programming whiz from Yale; and Amy Wong, who sported a master's in electrical engineering from MIT. This small group would form the core of what soon became one of the most profitable, and little known, trading operations in the world.

Aside from deep pockets, Muller had another advantage in working for a giant investment bank. Other trading outfits, such as hedge funds, funneled their trades to exchanges such as the NYSE through regulated broker dealers, including Morgan. One hedge fund that used Morgan as its brokerage for stocks was a trading group at Renaissance Technologies called Nova, run by Robert Frey, the mathematician who'd worked under Nunzio Tartaglia at Morgan Stanley.

In the mid 1990s, the Nova fund had a bad stretch. PDT took the positions off Renaissance's hands and folded them into its own fund. It worked out quite well, as the positions eventually became profitable and also gave Muller a rare glimpse inside Renaissance's secret architecture. Renaissance, for its part, retooled Nova into a profit-generating machine.

■ ■ ■

By 1994, the stage was set. Muller had the money and the talent to go to work. They didn't have much time. Mack would slam the door shut in a heartbeat if he thought the group wasn't delivering.

Working late hours and weekends, PDT's dream team built an automatic trading machine, a robot for making money. They called their robot Midas—as if everything it touched would turn to gold. Nickerson and Ahmed did the fine-grained number crunching, searching for hidden signals in the market that would tell the computer which stocks to buy and sell. Nickerson focused on the U.S. market, Ahmed overseas. Reed built up the supercomputer infrastructure, mainlining it into financial markets around the world. The strategy was statistical arbitrage—the same strategy Bamberger had devised at Morgan Stanley in the 1980s. PDT's quants had largely discovered how to implement the strategy on their own, but there's little question that by the time Midas was up and running, the idea of stat arb was in the air. Doyne Farmer's Prediction Company was running a stat arb book in Sante Fe, as were D. E. Shaw, Renaissance, and a number of other funds. Over the years, however, few stat arb funds would do nearly as well as PDT, which in time became the most successful proprietary trading desk on Wall Street in terms of consistency, longevity, and profitability.

Midas focused on specific industries: oil drillers such as Exxon and Chevron, or airline stocks such as American Airlines and United. If four airline companies were going up and three were going down, Midas would short the stocks going up and buy the stocks going down, exiting the position in a matter of days or even hours. The tricky part was determining exactly when to buy and when to sell. Midas could do these trades automatically and continuously throughout the day. Better yet, Midas didn't ask for a fat bonus at year's end.

By the fourth quarter of 1994, the money started piling up. Midas was king. Just flip on the switch and *zzip-zip-zip . . . zap . . . zap . . . zooing . . . bapbapbapbap . . . zing . . . zing . . . zap!* The digitized computerized trades popped off like firecrackers, an electronic gold mine captured in upward-flying digits on PDT's computer screens as the money rolled in like magic.

It was amazing, exhilarating, and at times terrifying. One night Elsesser was riding home in a taxicab, exhausted after a long day's work. The buildings and lights of the city flashed by in a blue blur. The driver's radio was an annoying fuzz in the background. A piece of news broke through the static: a radio announcer was describing unusual trading activity that was wreaking havoc in Tokyo's markets.

Elsesser's ears pricked up. *Could that be us? Shit.*

Frantic, she ordered the taxi to take her back to Morgan's headquarters. She was always worried that some glitch in their computer program could unleash tsunamis of buy or sell orders. You never knew if the system would go haywire like some kind of computerized Frankenstein. PDT wasn't responsible for the chaos in Tokyo that day, but the possibility always lurked in the background. It could be hard to sleep at night with the computers whirring away.

But those were worries for another day. PDT's performance was so incredible, it matched and at times even outpaced Renaissance's Medallion fund. In 1997, however, Medallion's returns leapt to a new dimension. The gains were unbelievable. Jim Simons had left everyone behind, and no one knew how he'd done it. Eventually, Renaissance stopped trading through Morgan, concerned that Muller's operation was eyeballing its strategies. True to the spymaster culture they'd come from, the quants on Long Island were becoming increasingly paranoid, worried that rivals such as Muller would steal their special sauce. Likewise, Muller grew increasingly nervous about spies inside Morgan Stanley. PDT's own traders were kept in silos, familiar only with their own positions and in the dark about the rest of PDT's growing strategies.

Even as he reveled in PDT's success, Muller was wary of overconfidence. "Keep your emotions in check," Muller said to his traders over and over again. He knew from experience. After he and Elsesser first started trading in the early 1990s, they made several snap decisions to bypass the computer models. An unexpected economic report or surprise move by the Fed would send the market into chaos. Better to override the models, they thought, or simply shut everything down.

But they quickly concluded that the computers were more reliable than people. Every time they tried to outsmart the computer, it turned out to be a bad move. "Always trust the machine" was the mantra.

One day in 1994, Muller came across some old records from a quantitative trading group at Morgan Stanley that had briefly shot the moon in the 1980s. He'd heard stories about the group, trading-floor legends about a wild Italian quant named Nunzio Tartaglia, the astrophysicist and onetime Jesuit seminarian. Much of the history of the group had been lost. The rising young quants at PDT had little idea that the group was the originator of stat arb. While Muller and his team had developed the strategy on their own and had added their own unique bells and whistles to it, the earlier Morgan group was the first to discover it. By the 1990s, the strategy was spreading rapidly, and quants such as Muller and Farmer were trying to crack its code.

Knowing about stat arb and actually applying it were two different propositions, however. PDT had pulled it off.

The records from APT also taught Muller a valuable lesson. APT had piled up huge returns for a few years. Then, suddenly, the music stopped. It meant he could never let his guard down; he had to always keep moving, improving, fine-tuning the system.

In 1995, a young quant named Jaipal Tuttle arrived at PDT. Tuttle, who sported a Ph.D. in physics from the University of California at Santa Cruz, had been trading Japanese warrants in Morgan's London offices for the previous few years. But Japan's stock market and economy collapsed in the early 1990s, and so did the Japanese warrant business.

Tuttle's physics background gave him the tools to understand many of the complex trades PDT executed. But since he didn't have any computer programming skills, it limited his ability to design and implement models. Instead, he became PDT's "human trader." At the time, there were still certain markets, such as stock index futures, that weren't fully automatic. Trades spat out by PDT's models had to be called in over the telephone to other desks at Morgan. That was Tuttle's job.

The automated trading system didn't always go smoothly. Once

PDT mistakenly sold roughly $80 million worth of stock in about fifteen minutes due to a bug in the system. Another time Reed, who was running the Japanese stock system at the time, asked another trader to cover for him. "Just hit *Y* every time it signals a trade," he said. He failed to mention the need to also hit enter. None of the trades went through properly.

PDT often hired outside consultants to work for the group temporarily, typically academics out to make an extra buck in between teaching gigs. One day a consultant named Matt was implementing an arbitrage strategy on S&P 500 index options. The trade involved selling an option tied to the S&P 500 for one month, such as May, and buying an option for another month, such as June, to capitalize on an inefficiency between the two options. Tuttle had to process the trades over the phone. The consultant was in another room in PDT's office, methodically reading trade orders to Tuttle. It was a large order, in the tens of millions of dollars.

Tuttle suddenly heard a faint scream somewhere in the office. He looked up and saw the consultant racing down the hall, flailing his arms in the air and screeching, "Stop! *Stooooppp!* Don't buy, sell, *seeeellll*!"

The consultant had crossed his orders: what he'd meant to sell, he'd bought, and what he'd meant to buy, he'd sold. Tuttle unwound the trade, but it was a lesson learned: humans are flawed; it's best to let the computer run the show.

The year Tuttle arrived, PDT moved to Morgan's new headquarters at 1585 Broadway, a hulking skyscraper just north of Times Square. They set up shop in better digs in a corner of the sixth floor of the building, one floor above Morgan's main trading floor. As their track record improved, so did their space.

They started expanding the quant approach into more and more markets. "I want lots of systems," demanded Vikram Pandit, who oversaw the group. (Pandit went on to become CEO of Citigroup in late 2007.) The group started trading Eurodollar futures, a relatively young market based on the price of dollars in overseas bank accounts. Soon, PDT was expanding into energy futures, bonds, options—whatever they could model, they would trade.

The group started getting rich as Midas grew and grew, especially Muller. He bought a beachfront cottage in Westport, Connecticut, and an expansive apartment in Tribeca, a chic Manhattan neighborhood known for its celebrity denizens such as Robert De Niro, Gwyneth Paltrow, and Meryl Streep. He took well to a life of luxury and started picking up quirky habits. He told his housecleaner to iron his sheets as soon as they emerged from the dryer because he didn't like wrinkles. He'd arrange for an assistant to buy groceries in Manhattan and drive them to his Westport cottage, rather than go to the local grocery store down the street. "He was in a kind of different zone in terms of what was rational," said one person who knew Muller at the time. As one of his many, ever-mushrooming sideline avocations, Muller wrote crossword puzzles, and several were published in the *New York Times*.

The group started taking trips to exotic locales around the world: Jamaica, Grenada, the Turks and Caicos. They'd go on ski trips in Vermont and rafting jaunts in Maine, with paintball games on the weekends they stayed in town. They'd eat lunch together at a table in the office's common area, sharing their crunchy salmon rolls from the local sushi shop. It was a long stretch from the onion-burger-pounding orgies of Salomon's mortgage bond traders in the 1980s.

There was something New Agey about it all to the few Morgan traders who knew about the group, something so San Francisco, flower children on the trading floor—the horror! the horror!—but it was all designed to bond the group, and it worked for the most part. Over the years, very few of the original PDT team had left, an extremely unusual record in an industry known for high turnover and stress-shortened careers.

Elsesser was one of the first to hit the road, moving on to study gender issues in the workplace at UCLA. She'd grown sick of Morgan's Big Swinging Dick, macho culture, even though she was relatively isolated from the worst behavior under PDT's protective bubble. Traders often treated her as if she were Muller's secretary. One time soon after they'd launched PDT, Elsesser was trading futures contracts electronically. A man walked into PDT's office, stared at Elsesser, looked around, left. He came again, looked, and left. The next time he came, looking around in confusion, scratching his crotch, Elsesser finally asked, "Can I help you?"

"They keep telling me some quant trader is in here trading futures and I keep telling them there's nobody back here."

After a furious pause, Elsesser said, "That's me."

The guy stood staring at her slack-jawed, then left again without saying a word.

A number of oddballs passed through PDT's offices over the years. One trader grew frantic about the glare off his computer screen. He duct-taped a ruler to the top of his monitor, then attached a slab of cardboard to the ruler to block the light. Visitors walking by peering into the trading room through the glass partition would see a hunched quant typing beneath a jagged cardboard canopy. A Morgan bigwig with an office across the hall was outraged. "You can't have this contraption!" he said one day, barging into the office. "I meet with high-profile CEOs. It's embarrassing!"

Another quant liked to work in the dark, late at night. The trading room's lighting system was equipped with motion sensors that would go off with the slightest twitch. He taped slices of paper across the sensors so he could type away happily in his dark room.

Interview sessions could be harrowing, at times bizarre. Muller liked to ask job applicants to guess, within a range, how much money he had in his wallet with a 95 percent confidence level.

"I don't know. Between ten and one hundred dollars."

Muller would pull out a $100 bill and put it on his desk.

"Between one and two hundred."

Muller would pull out $200.

"Five?"

Muller, smiling and shaking his head, would pull out $500. It was a trick question. Muller might have a wallet full of cash for a late-night poker game. Or he might not have anything. The applicant obviously had no idea. A guess with a 95 percent confidence level should encompass a very wide range, between zero and a few thousand. More often than not, the question simply made the interviewee angry: Who is this freaking guy?

Muller also liked to interview top professional poker players, to the exasperation of his colleagues. *Sure, these guys are good at poker, but can they trade? Can they program a computer? Do they know anything about factor modeling?* None of the poker players panned out. One guy, it turned out, had a rap sheet for sports betting.

Headhunters caught the whiff of money and were continually pushing new candidates at Muller. Office secretaries fielded frantic phone calls from headhunters desperate to get a client a shot at the hot new Morgan hedge fund. "Get Muller on the phone right now!" they'd scream. "If you don't put him on the phone right now, I'm going to lose millions!"

Everyone suddenly wanted a piece of Peter Muller. The success led to even more unconventional behavior. Muller started skipping the firm's early-morning meetings and would drop by the office around 11:00 A.M. or later—if he showed up at all. Tuttle wore torn Clash T-shirts and flashy earrings, a bizarre sight at buttoned-down Morgan Stanley. The group would celebrate days when they'd earned $10 million with rounds of wine in plastic cups. As time went on, there were more and more plastic-cup wine days.

On one occasion, Muller decided he needed the calming burble of trickling water in his office. He purchased a giant stone waterfall called Niagara. It was shipped into PDT's office in a massive crate. The building's office personnel went ballistic—the waterfall was so heavy it could collapse into the floor below, Morgan Stanley's main trading floor. Not good. The box sat in the office for weeks. One wag scratched out the *N* in the waterfall's name and replaced it with a *V*, suggesting that Muller had taken delivery of a massive box full of erectile dysfunction medication.

Another time, Muller told Elsesser he wanted to install a revolving door between their offices to make it easier to go back and forth and exchange ideas. Muller meant it as a joke. Elsesser, spooked by the idea of Muller rotating in and out of her office all day, didn't think it was so funny.

The top brass at Morgan couldn't care less about the bizarre behavior of their secretive sixth-floor quants. The money they were kicking out was a miracle. Morgan Stanley won't reveal precisely how much money PDT made over the years, but former employees commonly characterize its profitability as off the charts. For the ten years through 2006, PDT churned out an estimated $4 billion in profits, after shaving 20 percent off the top, which the company paid to members of PDT. That means the small group of traders during that time took home roughly $1 billion. The salaries of the top brains at PDT such as Muller, Nickerson, and Ahmed in some years vastly exceeded the take-home pay of top executives in the firm, including the CEO. In certain years—especially during the late 1990s and early 2000s—PDT accounted for one-quarter of Morgan Stanley's net income.

"I would describe it as a superhumanly large amount, a staggeringly large amount. It was beyond belief how large it was. It was an exceptionally well-functioning machine," said Tuttle, who left the firm in 2001 to follow his dream of competitive windsurfing.

"PDT keeps the lights running at Morgan Stanley," Vikram Pandit liked to say.

In 1999, Muller bought Nickerson an expensive bottle of single-malt scotch to reward him for his work on Midas. In the five years since it had been up and running, Midas had delivered $1 billion in net income to Morgan, in the process making everyone at PDT rich beyond their wildest dreams. In the coming years, it would only get better, making everyone even richer. Especially Peter Muller.

∎ ASNESS ∎

When Cliff Asness took a full-time job at Goldman in late 1994, he wasn't sure what his job was supposed to be. He was given the task of building quantitative models to forecast returns on multiple asset classes, a broad mandate. Essentially, Goldman was taking a gamble on the young phenom from Chicago, trying to see if his ivory tower schooling would pay off in the real world. Goldman had made one of its first wagers on book smarts with Fischer Black in the 1980s. By the early 1990s, it was the go-to bank for bright mathletes from universities around the country.

Asness called his fledgling operation Quantitative Research

Group. To beef up QRG's brainpower, he recruited several of the smartest people he'd come across at the University of Chicago, including Ross Stevens, Robert Krail, Brian Hurst, and John Liew. Krail and Liew had spent time working at Trout Trading, the money management firm started by trading legend Monroe Trout Jr. Liew, the son of an economics professor at Oklahoma University, had planned to follow in his father's footsteps and pursue a career in academia. But his time at Trout, where he worked building quantitative trading models, changed his mind. One day he was talking to Krail about their work at Trout Trading. "This actually isn't that bad; this is kind of fun," he said. Liew had always expected to hate work. He was surprised to find that he was actually enjoying himself.

"Don't think of this as a job," Krail said. And it paid well, too.

At first Asness's group didn't directly manage money. Its initial task was to act as a sort of quant prosthesis for a group of fundamental stock pickers who'd run into trouble trying to pick stocks outside the United States. Was there a way to use quantitative techniques to guide investment decisions on a country-by-country level? This was not a problem Asness or anyone on his team had previously considered. It had never come up in the classroom or in the stacks of textbooks they'd memorized.

Asness's reply: "Of course!"

They put their heads together. Was there any similarity between the strategies they'd learned at Chicago and the task of assessing the health of an entire country? The surprising answer, they discovered, was yes. The value and momentum anomalies in stocks they'd studied in academia could actually work for entire countries.

It was a monumental leap. They would measure a country's stock market, divide that by the sum of the book value of each company in that market, and get a price-to-book value for the entire country. If Japan had a price-to-book value of 1.0 and France had a price-to-book of 2.0, that meant Japan was cheap relative to France. The investing process from there was fairly easy: long Japan, short France.

The applications of this insight were virtually endless. Just as it didn't matter whether a company made widgets or tanks, or whether its leaders were visionaries or buffoons, the specifics of a country's

politics, leadership, or natural resources had only a tangential bearing on the view from a quant trader's desk. A quantitative approach
could be applied not only to a country's stocks and bonds but also
to its currencies, commodities, derivatives, whatever. In short order,
Asness's team designed models that looked for cheap-versus-expensive
opportunities around the globe. Momentum strategies quickly followed. Goldman's higher-ups were impressed with their bright young
quants. In 1995, they agreed to seed a small internal hedge fund with
$10 million.

It would be called Global Alpha, a group that would go on to become one of the elite trading operations on all of Wall Street. Global
Alpha would also become a primary catalyst for the quant meltdown
of August 2007.

During his first few years at Goldman, Asness frequently came in
contact with one of the chief architects of the Money Grid, Fischer
Black.

Along with Thorp, Black was one of the most crucial links between post–World War II advances in academia and innovations on
Wall Street that led to the quantitative revolution. Unlike the practical-
minded Thorp, Black was much more of a theorist and even something of a philosopher. Among his many quirks, Black was known for
his conversational sinkholes, extended periods of awkward silence
that left his companions off-guard and confused. Asness had his fill of
these experiences at Goldman. He would step into Black's office, just
off Goldman's trading floor, to answer a question from the great man
about some market phenomenon. Asness would quickly spit out his
thoughts, only to be met by Black's blank stare. Black would swivel
his chair around, facing his blinking computer screen, and sit thinking, sometimes minutes at a time. Then, after a crushingly long silence,
he would swivel back and say something along the lines of "You may
be right."

"It was like the air coming out of the *Hindenburg*," Asness recalled.

Black believed in rationality above all else. But he was also a man
awash in contradictions. A central figure in quantitative finance, he

never took a course in finance or economics. He was a trained mathematician and astrophysicist, as risk-averse as a NASA launch director, with a childlike wonder about the inner workings of stars and planets. He soaked his cereal in orange juice instead of milk, and in his later years confined his lunch to broiled fish and a butterless baked potato. Worried about a family history of cancer, the disease that eventually took his life, Black scanned his workplaces with a radiation meter and bought long cords for his computer keyboard to distance himself from the monitor. But he also had a rebellious streak. He dabbled in psychedelic drugs as a young man and trolled through pages of classified ads seeking companionship, suggesting to his estranged wife at the time that she do the same.

As a teenager growing up in Bronxville, New York, in the 1950s, Black loved to play the role of devil's advocate, extolling communism to his conservative father and expressing admiration for Greenwich Village's bohemians to his religious mother. He started a neighborhood group called the American Society of Creators, Apostles, and Prophets, which would gather to discuss topics such as Aldous Huxley's experimentation with mind-altering drugs. He attended Harvard, grew fascinated with computers, and eventually gravitated toward finance after working for a management-consulting firm near Boston called Arthur D. Little.

In the fall of 1968, he met Myron Scholes, a young MIT economist from Canada. Scholes had recently started thinking about a tough problem: how to price stock warrants. Black had been mulling over the same puzzle. The pair teamed up with Robert Merton and several years later published their groundbreaking research, with a little help from Thorp, on how to price stock options.

In the early 1970s, Black took a job teaching finance at the University of Chicago. His third-floor office in Rosenwald Hall was sandwiched between the offices of Myron Scholes and Eugene Fama. He then took a job teaching at MIT for the following nine years.

But he was getting restless, stymied by the slow pace of academia. Robert Merton, meanwhile, had been working as a consultant for Goldman Sachs. He'd once suggested to Robert Rubin, then head of the firm's equities division and future Treasury secretary under Bill Clinton, that Goldman should consider creating a high-level position for a financial academic.

One day Merton asked Black if he knew anyone who fit the bill.

"Bob, I'd be interested in that job," Black replied. In December 1983, he took a trip to New York to discuss the job with Rubin. In early 1984, Black was hired as head of Goldman's Quantitative Strategies Group.

One story—perhaps apocryphal—goes that soon after taking the job, Black was getting the grand tour of Goldman's trading floor in downtown Manhattan. The noise on the floor was deafening. Traders shouted buy and sell orders at the top of their voices. Harried men ran to and fro. It was a bizarre scene to the middle-aged Black, more used to the cloistered halls of universities where he had spent most of his career.

Black was eventually brought to the firm's options desk to meet the head of trading. "So you're Fischer Black," the trader said, reaching out a hand to greet the legend. "Nice to meet you. Let me tell you something: you don't know shit about options."

Welcome to Wall Street, Mr. Black.

Black's office was on the twenty-ninth floor of Goldman's main building at 85 Broad Street, a few blocks from the New York Stock Exchange. Hanging on the wall of his office, situated next to the firm's trading floor, was a poster of a man jogging along a dirt road that read: "The race is not always to the swift but to those who keep running." He could often be seen typing away on his Compaq Deskpro 386 computer, obsessively entering notes into a program called Think Tank as he swigged bottle after bottle of water kept in an office credenza.

His job was simple: figure out how to turn his quantitative theories into cold hard cash for Goldman. There was something of a problem, however. Black hewed to the Chicago School notion that markets are efficient and impossible to beat. In one of his first attempts to trade, he lost half a million for the firm. But he soon realized, watching Goldman's traders make millions of dollars from an endless cycle of inefficiencies, that the market might not be quite the perfect humming machine he'd thought back in his ivory towers in Cambridge and Chicago.

Slowly but surely, Black was turning into one of Fama's piranhas. Always attuned to the power of the microprocessor, he became an innovator in transforming trading into a highly automated man-machine symbiosis. Goldman's edge, he foresaw, would be the powerful mix of financial theory and computer technology.

It was only the beginning of a dramatic change on Wall Street, the creation of the Money Grid, made up of satellites, fiber-optic cables, and computer chips, all of it tamed and fed by complex financial theories and streams of electricity. Like a spider in its web, Black was at the center of it all in his dark office at Goldman Sachs, pecking away at his computer and torturing subordinates such as Cliff Asness with his deafening silences and oracular comments about the market.

Quants make their living juggling odds, searching for certainty, shimmering probabilities always receding into the edge of randomness. Yet for Cliff Asness, there seems to be one single factor in his success that he almost obsessively returns to: luck.

Asness readily admits that luck is not the only factor in success or failure. Being prepared and working hard puts a person in position to capitalize on that lucky chance when it comes around the corner. But luck is without question a major force in Asness's world.

After flipping the switch on Global Alpha in 1995 in Goldman's office at One New York Plaza, the fund promptly proceeded to lose money for eight straight days. Then its luck changed. Massively. After the initial downtrend, Global Alpha didn't lose money for a very long time. It gained a whopping 93 percent in its first year, 35 percent in its second. A very auspicious, and lucky, start.

To show their appreciation for all the money Asness's group started bringing in, Goldman's bigwigs arranged a meeting with one of the biggest wigs of them all, the firm's chief operating officer, Henry Paulson (who went on to become CEO of Goldman and then Treasury secretary in the second term of the George W. Bush administration).

Asness could have thought of better ways for Goldman's brass to express their appreciation, but he didn't object. He slapped together a

PowerPoint presentation to explain to Paulson exactly what he was doing.

The big day came. As Asness went to meet the firm's notoriously prickly and long-jawed COO, he thought back to the day he'd gone to tell Fama about his research on momentum. Asness respected Fama far more than Paulson, whom he barely knew. So why was he so nervous?

The presentation involved, among other things, the various markets Global Alpha traded in. Asness rattled off a string of regions and countries: North America, Southeast Asia, Brazil, Japan.

"We trade in all of the countries in the EAFE index," Asness added.

Paulson had been silent throughout the presentation. So he shocked Asness when he suddenly blurted out, "Hold it."

Asness froze.

"How many countries are in that index?"

"Well," Asness said, "it comprises Europe, Australasia, the Far East—"

"That's not what I asked," Paulson said curtly. "How many countries?"

"I believe twenty-one," Asness said.

"Name 'em."

Asness looked at Paulson in shock. *Name them? Is this guy screwing with me?*

Paulson wasn't laughing. Asness swallowed hard and started to tick off the names. France, Germany, Denmark, Australia, Japan, Singapore . . . He listed every country in the EAFE index. His broad forehead had sprouted a dew of sweat. Paulson sat there coolly watching Asness with his steely eyes, clenching his massive mandible. There was an awkward silence.

"That's eighteen," Paulsen said.

He'd been counting the names. And Asness had come up short—or so Paulson was implying. There was little Asness could say. He fumbled through the rest of the presentation and left in confusion.

Great way to show your appreciation for my hard work, he thought.

■   ■   ■

As Global Alpha continued to churn out awe-inspiring returns, Gold-man poured in billions. By late 1997, the Quantitative Research Group was managing $5 billion in a long-only portfolio and nearly $1 billion in Global Alpha (which could also take short positions). Barely a month went by in which they didn't put up eye-popping gains. Asness kept pulling in new talent, hiring Ray Iwanowski and Mark Carhart, alums of Chicago's Ph.D. program in finance.

He also started teaching classes from time to time as a guest lec-turer at New York University's Courant Institute, a rising quant factory. Universities throughout the country were adding financial engineering courses. Carnegie Mellon, Columbia University, and Berkeley, as well as the stalwarts at MIT and the University of Chicago, were hatching a whole new generation of quants. The Courant Institute, a short hop from Wall Street in Greenwich Village, was gaining a reputation as a top quant farm. It was at Courant in the late 1990s that Asness met a young quant from Morgan Stanley named Peter Muller, as well as Neil Chriss. Several years later, he became a regular at the quant poker game.

Meanwhile, the success of Global Alpha was making Asness and his Chicago all-star team wealthy. In retrospect, Asness would realize he and his cohorts had been especially lucky to start investing during a period that was very good for both value and momentum strategies. At the time, however, luck didn't seem to have much to do with Global Alpha's success. Asness got cocky and restless. When he'd come to Goldman in 1994, he'd hoped to combine the brainy environ-ment of academia with the moneymaking prospects of Wall Street, a kind of intellectual's nirvana where he'd get richly rewarded for cook-ing up new ideas. Trouble was, he didn't have time to do as much re-search as he would have liked. Goldman was constantly shuttling him around the world to meet new clients in Europe or Japan or to counsel employees. Then there were all the office politics, plus nuts like Paul-son. He started thinking the unthinkable: leave the mother ship.

It wasn't an easy decision. Goldman had given Asness his start, shown faith in his abilities, and provided him the freedom to implement his ideas and hire his own people. It seemed like a betrayal. The more Asness thought about it, the more it seemed like a bad idea. Then he met a man with the ideal set of skills to help launch a hedge fund: David Kabiller.

David Kabiller had been something of a wanderer among Goldman's ranks since he'd joined the bank in a summer training program in 1986. He'd worked in fixed income, equities, and pension services. He first met Asness as a liaison between institutional investors and GSAM, which managed money for outside clients in addition to running proprietary funds for Goldman itself.

Kabiller was quick to notice that Global Alpha was raking in money. Global Alpha had a live, second-by-second computerized tabulation of its profit and loss. One day Kabiller was watching the ticking numbers fly across the screen. It was increasing, he saw with a gasp, by millions of dollars *every second*.

Something very special was going on with these nerdy quants from Chicago, he realized. They weren't like the other people at Goldman. Not only were they smart, they were intellectually honest. They were on a quest—a quest for the Truth. He didn't quite understand all the mumbo jumbo, but he did know that he wanted to be part of it.

Asness and a select group from Global Alpha, as well as Kabiller, started meeting at Rungsit, a Thai restaurant on the East Side of Manhattan. Over steaming bowls of tom yum soup and satay chicken they weighed the pluses and minuses of striking out on their own. Goldman paid well and offered long-term security. Asness had recently been made a partner. There were rumors of an IPO on the horizon, and all the money that would mean. But it still wouldn't be their company.

At the end of the day, it seemed the choice was clear. Much of the conversation centered on what to call the new firm: Greek god? Mythical beast? True to their nerd roots, they settled on a name more blandly descriptive than colorful: Applied Quantitative Research Capital Management, AQR for short.

For a brief period Asness got cold feet. Goldman's bigwigs were pressing him to stay. Goldman was his home. Kabiller was crushed, but there was nothing he could do to change Asness's mind.

Then, one night in late 1997, Kabiller got a phone call.

"It's Cliff."

Kabiller knew something was up. Asness never made personal phone calls.

"How you doing?" Kabiller asked. He was smiling so hard his face hurt. There was a long pause. Kabiller could hear Asness breathing on the other end of the line. "You ready to do this now?"

"Yeah," Asness said.

And that was it. In December 1997, just a few days after the bank handed out its bonuses, Cliff Asness, Robert Krail, David Kabiller, and John Liew turned in their resignations to Goldman's management. Asness listened to the soundtrack from the Broadway play *Les Misérables* to psych himself up for the task. He didn't want to change his mind again.

Less than a year later, on August 3, 1998, AQR was up and running with $1 billion in start-up capital—one of the largest hedge fund launches on record at that point, and three times as much as they'd originally projected they could raise. Indeed, Asness and company turned down more than $1 billion in *extra* cash because they weren't sure their strategies could handle so much capital. Investors were desperate to get in. The charismatic French fund of funds manager Arpad "Arki" Busson, future beau of the supermodel Elle Macpherson and the actress Uma Thurman, wanted in. AQR turned him down flat.

Indeed, AQR had the ideal hedge fund pedigree: University of Chicago quant geniuses, a plethora of pension fund and endowment clients through Kabiller, sterling Goldman Sachs credentials, mind-boggling returns . . .

"It was a total labor of love," recalled Kabiller. "We knew our shit, we were prepared. We had the right blend of skills, we were the real deal."

In its first month, AQR Capital, once described as a dream-team blend of Long-Term Capital Management and Julian Robertson's Tiger Management, scored a small gain. From there, it fell off a cliff. It was a disaster. The reason for AQR's downturn was in many ways more unlikely than the chain of events that destroyed LTCM.

Luck, it seemed, had abandoned Cliff Asness.

▪ WEINSTEIN ▪

A pair of black limos raced out of Las Vegas into the desert night. It was the fall of 2003, and Boaz Weinstein's credit traders were celebrating at an off-site bonding session. The plan was to discuss the changing landscape of the credit markets, but this was Vegas. Weinstein's traders were itching to cut loose.

"It was a lot of betting, a lot of drinking, a lot of blackjack," said a former Deutsche Bank trader who worked under Weinstein.

After hitting the blackjack tables, where Weinstein won over and over again using the card-counting techniques he'd learned from *Beat the Dealer*, and playing hand after hand of high-stakes poker and roulette, they piled into rented stretch limos, popped open bottles of chilled champagne, and told the drivers to step on it. Their destination: that classic quant pastime, paintball.

At the paintball facility outside the city, the teams squared off. "Prop" traders, the gunslingers who did nothing but trade all day to earn money for the bank (and themselves), faced the "flow" traders, who had the less glamorous job of acting as go-betweens for clients of Deutsche Bank, matching up buy and sell orders that "flowed" through the firm. Flow traders were allowed to make side bets, making their lives somewhat worth living, but they were never able to put the real money on the line, the colossal billion-dollar balls-to-the-walls positions that could make a year or break it.

Weinstein led the prop paintballers. One of his top lieutenants, Chip Stevens, led the flow squad. Clad in T-shirts that read "Credit Derivatives Offsite Las Vegas 2003," the Deutsche Bank credit quants donned their goggles and fanned out across the paintball obstacle course.

Naturally, the gunslingers were victorious. But it was all in good fun. Everyone piled back into their limos, guzzled more champagne, and convened at Weinstein's huge luxury suite at the Wynn Las Vegas, where the festivities—including a magician and mentalist recommended by Bear Stearns chairman Ace Greenberg—really began. If there was one thing Weinstein's credit traders knew, it was that they understood how the game was played—and they played it better than anybody else. Blackjack was a joke. The real casino, the biggest in the world, was the booming global credit derivatives market. And they were playing it like a fiddle. The money was huge and everyone was brilliant and inside the secret. Deutsche Bank had just been named Derivatives House of the Year by *Risk* magazine, topping the previous champ, J. P. Morgan, which started referring to Deutsche as "enemy number one."

To Weinstein, ascending to the top wasn't a surprise. They had developed an aggressive, no-holds-barred approach that the rest of the Street couldn't match. And that was the real point of the Vegas trips, some of those attending thought. At Deutsche Bank, risk wasn't fuck-ing *managed*. Risk was bitch-slapped, risk was tamed and told what to do.

The traders lapped it up.

It was all happening. Weinstein's dream of becoming an elite Wall Street trader, nurtured ever since he watched Louis Rukeyser on TV as a precocious chess prodigy on the Upper East Side, was coming true.

And it had been so very easy.

Just as AQR was starting to trade in 1998, Weinstein had set up shop at Deutsche Bank's fledgling credit derivatives desk. A mere twenty-four years old, he seemed nervous and a bit frightened by the frantic action of a trading floor. But he absorbed knowledge like a sponge and was soon able to spit out information about all kinds of stocks and bonds at will from his steel-trap photographic memory.

Weinstein's expertise at his previous job had been in trading float-ing rate notes, bonds that trade with variable interest rates. It wasn't much of a leap from there to credit default swaps, which act much like bonds with interest rates that swing up and down.

As Ron Tanemura had explained to Weinstein, traders can use the swap to essentially bet on whether a company is going to default or not. Thus, an entirely new dimension had been introduced into the vast world of credit: the ability to short a loan or a bond. Buying protection on a bond through a credit default swap was, in essence, a short position. In a flash, the sleepy bond market became the hottest casino in the world—and Weinstein was right at home.

Because the derivative was so new, few other banks were trading it in heavy volume. To help gin up volume, Weinstein started to make trips to other trading outfits across Wall Street, such as the giant money manager BlackRock, talking up the remarkable traits of the credit default swap.

In 1998, he was essentially shorting the credit market, buying insurance on all kinds of bonds through swaps. Because he was buying insurance—which would pay off if investors started worrying about the creditworthiness of the bond issuers—he was in a perfect position to capitalize on the turmoil that shot through the market after Russia defaulted on its debt and LTCM collapsed. He made a nice profit for Deutsche Bank, catapulting his career.

In 1999, Deutsche Bank promoted him to vice president. In 2001, he was named a managing director at the age of twenty-seven, one of the youngest to reach the title in the history of the German bank.

Weinstein and his fellow derivatives dealers got help from regulators, who were rapidly *de*regulating. In November 1999, the Glass-Steagall Act of 1933, which had cleaved the investment banking and commercial banking industry in two—separating the risk-taking side of banks from the deposit side—was repealed. Giant banks such as Citigroup had argued that the act put them at a disadvantage compared to overseas banks that didn't have such restrictions. For Wall Street's growing legions of proprietary traders, it meant access to more cash; also, those juicy deposits could be used as fodder for prop desk exploits. Then, in December 2000, the government passed legislation exempting derivatives from more intense federal scrutiny. The way had been cleared for the great derivatives boom of the 2000s.

A big test of the credit default swap market came in 2000, when the California utilities crisis struck and prices soared due to rampant shortages. Suddenly there was the real possibility that a number of large power companies could default. The implosion of Enron in late

2001 was another test of the market, which demonstrated that the credit derivatives market could withstand the default of a major corporation. The telecom meltdown and the collapse of WorldCom was another trial by fire.

The new credit derivatives market had shown that it could function properly, even under stress. Trades were settled relatively quickly. Skeptics were proven wrong. The credit default swap market would soon be one of the hottest, fastest-growing markets in the world. Few traders would be as well versed at it as Weinstein, who began putting together one of the most successful and powerful credit derivatives trading outfits on Wall Street.

By 2002, the economy was in a ditch. With formerly blue chip companies such as Enron and WorldCom unraveling, the worry was that anything could happen. Investors started feeling anxious about the largest media company in the world at the time, AOL Time Warner. Debt holders, especially, were panicking, while the stock was down less than 20 percent.

One day Weinstein was strolling past AOL's headquarters near Rockefeller Center. Thinking several steps into the future, much like a chess player plotting his strategy multiple moves in advance, he realized that while the stock had fallen about 20 percent, the collapse in its bond prices was far too severe, as if the company were on the verge of bankruptcy. Such a catastrophe was unlikely for a company with so many long-standing, relatively profitable businesses, including the television networks CNN and HBO. Deciding that the company had a good chance of surviving the turmoil, he purchased AOL bonds while shorting the stock to hedge the position. The bet turned into a huge home run as the bond market, and AOL (now simply Time Warner), recovered.

Gambling became a way of life for Weinstein's crew. One of his first hires was Bing Wang, who went on to finish in thirty-fourth place in the World Series of Poker in 2005. Weinstein learned that several traders at Deutsche were members of MIT's secretive blackjack team. He was soon joining them a few times a year to hit the blackjack tables in Las Vegas, deploying the skills he'd learned reading Thorp's *Beat the Dealer* in college. People who know Weinstein say his name is on more than one Vegas casino's list of players banned for card counting.

In their downtime, Weinstein's traders would randomly bet on just about anything in sight: a hundred on the flip of a coin, whether it would rain in the next hour, whether the Dow would close up or down. A weekly poker game with a $100 buy-in started up off Deutsche Bank's trading floor. Every Friday after the closing bell struck, Weinstein's traders would gather in a conference room and face off against one another for hours.

Deutsche's top managers either didn't know about the poker game or simply winked at it. It hardly mattered. Since Deutsche was a German company, most of its upper management was based in London or Frankfurt, Germany's financial hub. Weinstein became the seniormost member of the fixed-income side of the bank in New York. His traders had the run of the bank's headquarters on 60 Wall Street and by many accounts were running amok. With a young, freewheeling boss who liked to gamble, and billions in funds at the tips of their fingers, Deutsche's New York trading operation became one of the most aggressive trading outfits on the Street, the shimmering essence of cowboy capitalism.

Weinstein was also honing his poker skills. In 2004, he attended the second annual Wall Street Poker Night at the St. Regis Hotel. He'd heard about a private poker game run by several of Wall Street's top quant traders and hedge fund managers, including Peter Muller, Cliff Asness, and a rising star named Neil Chriss. A veteran of Goldman Sachs Asset Management, Chriss at the time was working at SAC Capital Advisors, a giant hedge fund in Stamford, Connecticut.

At the St. Regis, Weinstein approached Chriss. He mentioned that he'd heard about the game, and that he'd love to sit in on a few hands. Chriss hesitated. There was no official "membership" in the quant poker game, but there was little doubt that the game was highly exclusive. It was a high-stakes game, with pots in the tens of thousands. One of the key qualifications for players was that losing couldn't matter financially. Egos might be bruised. Self-esteem might slip a notch. But the hit to the wallet needed to be trivial. That required an epic bank account, eight digits minimum. Players had to be able to walk away ten, twenty grand short, and not care. Did Weinstein have the financial chops? Chriss decided to invite him, test him out—and the boy-faced Deutsche Bank credit-default-swap whiz turned out to be an instant hit. Not only was he an ace cardsharp, he was also one of the savviest investors Chriss, Muller, and Asness had ever met. Soon Weinstein was a permanent member of the quant poker group, part of the inner circle.

All the practice paid off. In 2005, Weinstein's boss, Anshu Jain, flew to meet with Berkshire Hathaway chairman Warren Buffett in Omaha, Nebraska, to discuss a number of the bank's high-profile trades, including Weinstein's. The two moguls were chatting about one of their favorite pastimes, bridge, and the conversation eventually switched to poker. Jain mentioned that Weinstein was Deutsche Bank's poker ace. Intrigued, Buffett invited Weinstein to an upcoming poker tournament in Las Vegas run by NetJets, the private-jet company owned by Berkshire.

Weinstein made his boss proud, winning the tournament's grand prize: a spanking new Maserati. Still, gambling was just a pastime, a mental curiosity or warm-up for the real deal. Weinstein's main focus, his obsession, remained trading—winning, crushing his opponents, and making money, huge money. He loved it. Soon he started expanding his operation into all kinds of markets, including stocks, currencies, and commodities—much as Ken Griffin was creating a diversified multistrategy fund at Citadel (Weinstein seemed to be modeling his group after Citadel). His signature trade was a strategy called "capital structure arbitrage," based on gaps in pricing between various securities of a single company. For instance, if he thought its bonds were undervalued relative to its stock, he might take bullish positions on the bonds and simultaneously bet against the stock, waiting for the disparity to shrink or vanish. If his long position on the debt fell through, he'd be compensated on the other side of the trade when the stock collapsed.

Weinstein was looking for inefficiencies in firms' capital structures, their blend of debt and stock, and used credit default swaps in creative ways to arb the inefficiencies. It was the old relative-value arbitrage trade, much like that crafted by Ed Thorp in the 1960s, wrapped in fancy new derivative clothes. But it worked like clockwork. Weinstein's group was racking up millions.

Then it all nearly fell apart in 2005 when the market didn't behave exactly as Weinstein's models had predicted.

It was May 2005. Weinstein stared in disbelief at one of several computer screens in his third-floor office. A trade was moving against him, badly.

Weinstein had recently entered one of his signature capital structure arbitrage trades on General Motors. GM's shares had tumbled in late 2004 and early 2005 as investors worried about a possible bankruptcy and the auto giant hemorrhaged cash. GM's debt was also getting crushed—too much, Weinstein thought. GM's debt had been pummeled so much that it seemed as though investors thought the automaker would go bankrupt. Weinstein knew that even if the company declared bankruptcy, debt holders would still receive at least 40¢ on the dollar, likely a lot more. The shares, however, would be worthless.

So he decided to sell protection on GM's debt through a credit default swap, collecting a steady fee to insure the bonds. If GM did declare bankruptcy, Deutsche Bank would be on the hook. To hedge against such a possibility, Weinstein shorted GM's stock, which was trading for about $25 to $30 a share.

But now, in a flash, the trade was looking like a disaster. The reason: a billionaire investor named Kirk Kerkorian had made a surprise tender offer for twenty-eight million GM shares through his investment company, Tracinda Corp., causing the stock to surge—and crushing short sellers such as Weinstein.

If that weren't enough, several days later, the rating agencies Standard & Poor's and Moody's downgraded GM's debt to junk, forcing a number of investors to sell it.

That meant both sides of Weinstein's trade were going against him, hard. The debt was plunging and the stock was soaring. It was incredible, and it wasn't how the market was supposed to work. There was little he could do about it except wait. *The market is irrational*, he thought, *and Kerkorian is nuts. Eventually things will move back into line. The Truth will be restored.* In the meantime, Weinstein needed to figure out what to do.

Weinstein and his traders huddled at the New York apartment of one of his top lieutenants. On the table: what to do about the GM trade. Some in the room argued that it was too risky and that they should take the loss and get out. If the position kept moving against them, the losses could become unsustainable. The bank's risk managers would only allow things to go so far.

Others took the other side. Bing Wang, the poker expert, said that the trade was more attractive than ever. "Load the boat," Wang said, trader lingo for doubling down.

Weinstein decided to play it safe at first, but over the following months the group kept adding to the GM trade, expecting things to eventually move back into line.

And they did. By the end of 2005, Weinstein's GM trade had paid off. It did even better in 2006. GM's stock fell back to earth, and the debt recovered much of the ground it lost in the wake of the rating agency's downgrade.

It was a lesson Weinstein wouldn't soon forget. While his arbitrage trades were incredibly clever, they could spin out of control due to chance outside events. But if he could hold on long enough, they'd pay off. They had to. The market couldn't avoid the Truth.

Or so he thought.

LIVING THE
DREAM

By the early 2000s, the hedge fund industry was poised for a phenomenal run that would radically change the investment landscape around the world. Pension funds and endowments were diving in, and investment banks were expanding their proprietary trading operations such as Global Alpha at Goldman Sachs, PDT at Morgan Stanley, and Boaz Weinstein's credit-trading shop at Deutsche Bank. Hundreds of billions poured into the gunslinging trading operations that benefited from an age of easy money, globally interconnected markets on the Money Grid, and the complex quantitative strategies that had first been deployed by innovators such as Ed Thorp more than three decades before.

Thorp, however, saw the explosion of hedge funds as a dark omen. So much money was flooding into the field that it was becoming impossible to put up solid returns without taking on too much risk.

Copycats were operating everywhere in a field he'd once dominated. In October 2002, he closed shop, shutting down his stat arb fund, Ridge-line Partners.

Other traders weren't so inclined—especially Ken Griffin, whose Citadel Investment Group, the fund Thorp had helped start more than a decade before, was quickly becoming one of the most powerful and feared hedge funds in the world.

▪ GRIFFIN ▪

As Ken Griffin settled down into married life, Citadel kept growing like a very complex, digitized weed. The Chicago hedge fund had become one of the most technologically advanced trading machines on the street, hooked into the Money Grid, with offices in Chicago, San Francisco, New York, London, Tokyo, and Hong Kong and more than a thousand employees. It had its own generator on the roof of 131 South Dearborn Street, the skyscraper it occupied, to ensure its computer systems could function in a blackout. The primary computer room was equipped with a system that could drain the room of oxygen in seconds in case of fire. Some thirty miles from the office, in a secret location in the town of Downers Grove, a redundant computer system hummed quietly. Every personal computer in the office—each one top of the line—had been partially walled off so that it could be accessible to a systemwide program that crunched the numbers of the fund's massive mortgage positions, creating a virtual "cloud" computer that churned in cyberspace twenty-four hours a day.

Griffin was quietly building a high-frequency trading machine that would one day become one of Citadel's crown jewels and a rival to PDT and Renaissance's Medallion fund. In 2003, he'd hired a Russian math genius named Misha Malyshev to work on a secretive stat arb project. At first, the going was tough, and profits were hard to come by. But on July 25, 2004, the operation, which came to be named Tactical Trading, kicked into gear, posting gains that went up all day. After that, it almost never stopped going up, spitting out consistent returns with very little volatility. Malyshev focused on speed, leveraging Citadel's peerless computer power to beat competitors to the punch in the race to capture fleeting arbitrage opportunities in the stock market.

The same year that Tactical started turning a profit, Griffin hired Matthew Andresen, a whiz kid who'd launched an electronic trading platform called Island ECN, to turbocharge Citadel's technology and trading systems. Under Andresen, the hedge fund's options market–making business, known as Citadel Derivatives Group Investors, would soon become a cash cow, the largest listed options dealer in the world.

Griffin was steadily turning Citadel into far more than a hedge fund—it was becoming a sprawling financial juggernaut controlling the flow of billions in securities. Griffin's ambitions were expanding right along with Citadel's assets, which had neared $15 billion.

Like any power broker, Griffin was making his share of enemies. Citadel was scooping up more and more talented traders and researchers from other hedge funds. That infuriated one notoriously testy and outspoken competitor, Daniel Loeb, manager of Third Point Partners, a New York hedge fund. In 2005, Citadel hired Andrew Rechtschaffen, a star researcher for Greenlight Capital, the fast-rising fund managed by David Einhorn, one of the regulars, along with Griffin, at the Wall Street Poker Night. Loeb, a friend of Einhorn's, shot off an email to Griffin packed with a seething rage that indicated more was going on than just the filching of a star researcher.

"I find the disconnect between your self-proclaimed 'good to great, Jim Collins–esque' organization and the reality of the gulag you created quite laughable," Loeb wrote, referring to the popular management guru. "You are surrounded by sycophants, but even you must know that the people who work for you despise and resent you. I assume you know this because I have read the employment agreements that you make people sign."

Griffin was unfazed and did not respond to the attack. Great men were bound to make enemies. Why sweat it?

But was there a cutting edge of truth to Loeb's attack? Turnover at Citadel was high. The pressure to succeed was intense, the consequences of failure dramatic. Departures from the fund were sometimes bitter, dripping with bad blood.

Worse, returns for the fund weren't what they used to be. In 2002, Citadel's flagship Kensington Fund gained 13 percent, and annual gains slipped below 10 percent the next three years. Part of the reason, Griffin suspected, was an explosion of money flowing into hedge fund strategies—the same strategies Citadel used. Indeed, it was that very factor that had influenced Ed Thorp's decision to close up shop. Imitation may be the sincerest form of flattery, but it doesn't do much for the bottom line in hedge fund land.

That's not to say that work at Citadel turned into a life sentence in a gulag, as Loeb would have it (though some ex-employees might dispute that). The fund tossed lavish parties. A movie buff, Griffin frequently rented out theaters at Chicago's AMC River 24 for premieres of films such as *The Dark Knight* and *Star Wars Episode III: Revenge of the Sith*. The money was head-spinning. Employees may have left Citadel bitter; they also left rich.

Concern was also mounting about an issue far more serious than interindustry squabbles: whether Citadel posed a risk to the financial system. Researchers at a firm called Dresdner Kleinwort wrote a report posing questions about the elephantine growth of Citadel and arguing that its heavy-handed use of leverage could destabilize the system. "At face value, and without being able to look into the black box, the balance sheet of today's Citadel hedge fund looks quite similar to LTCM," the report stated ominously.

Citadel's leverage, however, which was at roughly 8 to 1 around 2006—though some estimate it rose as high as 16 to 1—didn't approach that of LTCM, which hovered around 30 to 1 and topped 100 to 1 during its 1998 meltdown. But Citadel was quickly becoming far bigger than the infamous hedge fund from Greenwich in terms of assets under management, turning into a multiheaded leviathan of money almost entirely unregulated by the government—exactly as Griffin liked it.

In March 2006, Griffin attended the Wall Street Poker Night, hooting down Peter Muller as the Morgan Stanley quant faced off against Cliff Asness. Several months later, in September 2006, he made one of his biggest coups yet.

A $10 billion hedge fund called Amaranth Advisors was on the verge of collapse after making a horrifically bad bet on natural gas prices. A lanky, thirty-two-year-old Canadian energy trader and Deutsche Bank alum named Brian Hunter had lost a whopping $5 billion in the course of a single week, triggering the biggest hedge fund blowup of all time, outpacing even the collapse of LTCM.

Amaranth, which had originally specialized in convertible bonds, had built up its energy-trading desk after the collapse of Enron in 2001. It brought Hunter on board soon after the trader left Deutsche Bank amid a dispute over his pay package. Hunter proved so successful at trading natural gas that the fund let him work from Calgary, where he zipped to and from work in a gray Ferrari. Hunter had a reputation as a gunslinger, doubling down on trades if they moved against him. He was preternaturally confident that he would make money on them in the long run, so why not?

But Hunter's approach to trading got him in trouble when natural gas prices turned highly volatile late in the summer of 2006, after Hurricane Katrina plowed into the energy-rich Gulf Coast. Hunter was deploying complex spread trades that exploited the difference between the prices of contracts for delivery in the future. He was also buying options on gas prices that were far "out of the money" but would pay off in the event of big moves. In early September, Hunter's trades started turning south after reports showed that a natural-gas storage glut had been building up. Hunter believed prices would rebound, and boosted his positions. As he did so, prices continued to fall, and his losses piled up—soon reaching several billion. Eventually the pain proved too much and Amaranth started to implode from within.

Griffin smelled an opportunity. Citadel's energy experts, including a few of his own Enron alumni wizards, started poring over Amaranth's books. They were looking to see if there was a chance that Hunter's bets would, in fact, eventually pay off. While the short-term losses could prove painful, Citadel's vast reserves would let it ride out the storm. Griffin called Amaranth's chief operating officer, Charlie Winkler, and started to work out a deal. Within days, Citadel agreed to take half of Amaranth's energy book. JP Morgan took the other half.

Critics scoffed that Citadel had made a stupid move. They were wrong. The fund gained 30 percent that year.

The gutsy deal further cemented Citadel's reputation as one of the most powerful and aggressive hedge funds in the world. The speed and size of the deal and the decisiveness, not to mention its success, reminded experts of similar quick-fire exploits pulled off by none other than Warren Buffett, the "Oracle of Omaha." Buffett was always near the top of the list of deep-pocketed investors whom distressed sellers would speed-dial when things turned south. Now Ken Griffin, the boy-faced hedge fund titan of Chicago, had joined that list.

He continued to snatch up artwork at jaw-dropping prices. In October 2006, he purchased *False Start* by Jasper Johns, a rainbow-colored pastiche of oils stenciled with the names of various colors—"red," "orange," "gray," "yellow," and so on. The seller: Hollywood mogul David Geffen. The price: $80 million, making it the most expensive painting by a living artist ever sold. It was also a fair indicator of the boom in art prices—fueled in large part by hedge fund billionaires—having been sold to publishing magnate S. I. Newhouse less than twenty years earlier for $17 million. (Newhouse sold it to Geffen in the 1990s for an undisclosed price.) Shortly before buying the painting, Griffin and his wife donated $19 million to the Art Institute of Chicago to finance a 264,000-square-foot wing to house modern art.

The Griffins ate well, dining regularly at the ritzy Japanese mecca NoMi, which was located in the Park Hyatt Chicago building where they lived and boasted $50 plates of sushi. Griffin was also known for his junk food obsessions, wolfing down buttered popcorn on the trading floor or ordering Big Macs from the local McDonald's on business trips.

He also indulged his passion for cars. Citadel's garage was often filled with about half a dozen of Griffin's Ferraris, each constantly monitored on screens inside the hedge fund's office.

Griffin's ambitions were becoming painfully evident to those around him. He was known to say that he wanted to turn Citadel into the next Goldman Sachs, a startling goal for a hedge fund. A catchphrase he seized upon: Citadel would be an "enduring financial institution," one that could last beyond even its mercurial leader. Rumors percolated that Citadel was mulling an initial public offering, a deal that would reap billions in personal wealth for Griffin. As a mark of its sky's-the-limit aspirations, Citadel sold $2 billion worth of high-grade bonds in late 2006, becoming the first hedge fund to raise money on the bond market. It was widely seen as a move to lay the groundwork for an IPO.

A few other funds beat Griffin to the IPO punch bowl in early 2007. First, there was Fortress Investment Group, a New York private equity and hedge fund operator with $30 billion under management. Fortress, whose name echoed Citadel's, stunned Wall Street in February 2007 when it floated shares at $18.50 each. On the first day of trading, the stock shot up to $35 and finished the day at $31. The five Wall Street veterans who'd created Fortress reaped an instant gain of more than $10 billion from the deal.

Private equity firms are akin to hedge funds in that they are largely unregulated and cater to wealthy investors and large institutions. They wield war chests of cash raised from deep-pocketed investors to take over stumbling companies, which they revamp, strip down, and sell back to the public for a tidy profit.

They also like to party. The Tuesday after the Fortress IPO, Stephen Schwarzman, cofounder and chief executive of private equity powerhouse Blackstone Group, threw himself a lavish sixtieth-birthday bash in midtown Manhattan. Blackstone had just completed its $39 billion buyout of Equity Office Properties, the largest leveraged buyout in history, and Schwarzman was in a festive mood. The celebrity-studded, paparazzi-thick blowout smacked of the grandiose robber baron excesses of the Gilded Age, and it marked the crest of a decades-long boom of vast riches on Wall Street—though few knew it at the time.

The location was the Seventh Regiment Armory on Park Avenue. New York police closed part of the fabled boulevard for the event. The five-foot-six Schwarzman didn't need to travel far for the festivities. The elite gathering was held near his thirty-five-room Park Avenue co-op, once owned by oil tycoon John D. Rockefeller. He'd reportedly paid $37 million for the spacious pad in May 2000. (Schwarzman had also purchased a home in the Hamptons on Long Island, previously owned by the Vanderbilts, for $34 million, and a thirteen-thousand-square-foot mansion in Florida called Four Winds, originally built for the financial advisor E. F. Hutton in 1937, which ran $21 million. He later decided the house was too small and had it wrecked and reconstructed from scratch.)

The guest list at Schwarzman's fete included Colin Powell and New York mayor Michael Bloomberg, along with Barbara Walters and Donald Trump. Upon entering the orchid-festooned armory to a march played by a brass band, ushered by smiling children in military garb, visitors were treated to a full-length portrait of their host by the British painter Andrew Festing, president of the Royal Society of Portrait Painters. The dinner included lobster, filet mignon, and baked Alaska, topped off with potables such as a 2004 Louis Jadot Chassagne-Montrachet. Comedian Martin Short emceed. Rod Stewart performed. Patti LaBelle and the Abyssinian Baptist Church choir sang Schwarzman's praises, along with "Happy Birthday." On its cover, *Fortune* magazine declared Schwarzman "Wall Street's Man of the Moment."

High-society tongues were still wagging about the party a few months later, when Schwarzman gave himself another eye-popping gift. In June, Blackstone raised $4.6 billion in an IPO that valued the company's stock at $31 a share. Schwarzman, who was known to shell out $3,000 a weekend on meals, including $400 on stone crabs ($40 per claw), personally pocketed nearly $1 billion. At the time of the offering, his stake in the firm was valued at $7.8 billion.

None of this was lost on Griffin. He was biding his time, waiting for the right moment to strike with his own IPO and his dream of rising to challenge Goldman Sachs.

As spring turned to summer, the subprime crisis was heating up. Griffin had been planning for this moment for years, having girded Citadel for hard times with provisions such as those long lockups for investors to keep them from bolting for the exits during market panics. With billions at his fingertips, Griffin could sense a golden opportunity was presenting itself. Weak hands would be flushed out of the market, leaving the pickings for muscle-bound powerhouses such as

Citadel. It had about thirteen hundred employees toiling away for Griffin in offices around the world. By comparison, AQR had about two hundred employees and Renaissance about ninety, almost all of them Ph.D.'s.

In July 2007, Griffin got his first chance to strike. Sowood Capital Management, a $3 billion hedge fund based in Boston run by Jeffrey Larson, a former star of Harvard University's endowment management, was on the ropes. Earlier in the year, Larson had started to grow worried about the state of the economy and realized that a great deal of risky debt would lose value. To capitalize on those losses, he shorted a variety of junior debt that would take the first hits as other investors grew concerned. To hedge those positions, Larson purchased a chunk of higher-grade debt. Turbocharging the bets, Larson borrowed massive amounts of money, leveraging up the fund to maximize its returns.

The first losses hit Sowood in June, when its investments lost 5 percent. Larson stuck to his guns and even put $5.7 million of his own cash into the fund. Expecting his positions to rebound, he told his traders to add even more leverage to the bets, pushing the fund's leverage ratio to twelve times its capital (it had borrowed $12 for each $1 it owned).

Larson, without realizing it, had stepped into a snake pit of risk at the worst possible time. The subprime mortgage market was collapsing, triggering shock waves throughout the financial system. In June, the ratings agency Moody's downgraded the ratings of $5 billion worth of subprime mortgage bonds. On July 10, Standard & Poor's, another major ratings group, warned it might downgrade $12 billion of mortgage bonds backed by subprime mortgages, prompting many holders of the bonds to dump them as quickly as possible. A number of the bonds S&P was reviewing had been issued by New Century Financial, a subprime mortgage giant based in Southern California that had filed for bankruptcy protection in April. The subprime house of cards was crumbling fast.

Other hedge funds making bets similar to Sowood's were also under fire and started unloading everything they owned into the market, including supposedly safe high-grade bonds owned by Sowood. The trouble was, few other investors wanted to buy. Credit markets gummed up. "S&P's actions are going to force a lot more people to come to Jesus," Christopher Whalen, an analyst at Institutional Risk Analytics, told Bloomberg News. "This could be one of the triggers we've been waiting for."

It was the first hint of the great unwinding that would nearly destroy the global financial system in the following year. The value of Sowood's investments cratered, and Larson started selling to raise cash as its lenders demanded more collateral, adding to the distress that was roiling the market. Larson appealed to the executives of Harvard's endowment for more cash to carry him through what he believed was just a temporary, irrational hiccup in the market. Wisely, they turned him down.

The speed of the collapse of Sowood was stunning. On Friday, July 27, the fund was down 10 percent. By the end of the weekend, it was down 40 percent. Larson picked up the phone and called the one investor he knew who could bail him out: Ken Griffin.

Griffin, vacationing in France with his wife, called a team of thirty Citadel traders at their homes and ordered them into the office to begin poring over Sowood's books, sniffing for value. They liked what they saw. On Monday, Citadel purchased most of Sowood's remaining positions for $1.4 billion, more than half of what the fund had been worth a few months prior. In an email sent to clients the week before, Griffin had opined that the markets were acting irrationally and that the robust U.S. and global economy would soon soar to new heights. That meant it was time for some deal making to capitalize on all those foolish investors who couldn't see the rebound coming. Sowood fit the bill.

Citadel swept in on the distressed fund and picked it clean, profiting as many of the positions rebounded as Larson had expected. Just as he had done with Amaranth, Griffin had amazed Wall Street once again with his ability to make quick judgments and deploy billions in the blink of an eye. By the start of August 2007, Citadel seemed poised for even greater triumphs. It had $15.8 billion in assets, a huge leap from the $4.6 million Griffin had started with in 1990.

Little did he realize that a year later, Citadel itself would be teetering on the edge of collapse.

■ MULLER ■

Peter Muller, sweating hard, gazed down upon the expansive blue Pacific Ocean. Palm trees rippled in the warm breeze. He was standing high up on the winding Kalalau Trail, a rugged eleven-mile trek on the west coast of the lush island of Kauai in Hawaii.

Wall Street seemed so far way. In the late 1990s, Muller was running away from Wall Street. The Kalalau Trail, a place he'd visited repeatedly since working at BARRA years before, was about as far as he could get.

Muller was doing what he loved most: hiking. And not just hiking anywhere—he loved being on the Kalalau Trail, an ancient path that winds through five valleys and past high green waterfalls and overgrown terraces of taro along the steep Na Pali cliffs of the oldest Hawaiian island, ending at Kalalau Beach, a remote hangout for hippies and drifters, but not a typical haunt of megamillionaire Wall Street traders.

The hike, in and out, typically took at least two or three days. Once Muller and a few friends hiked the entire trail, start to finish, in a day.

He looked back from the ocean to the trail ahead, wiping the sweat from his brow, and pushed on, moving quickly out of the Hanakoa Valley into a dry, open stretch of land, tiring but lured on by a panoramic view of fluted cliffs and the coastline of the Kalalau Valley beyond.

Muller was living a life few people could imagine. With little need to work as his quant machine cranked out profits in New York, he was free to travel the world. He'd become interested in heli-skiing, jumping out of helicopters in high, off-trail locations. Among his favorite spots were the dizzy verticals of the Rocky Mountains near Jackson Hole, Wyoming, where he would stay at the expansive ranch of Ken Griffin's friend and longtime investor Justin Adams. He took kayaking trips to getaways as far afield as New Zealand and river trips in Arizona and Idaho.

At the same time, he was working on an album of songs. In 2004, he self-produced *More Than This*, a collection of sentimental, saccharine ballads, such as "In This World," that seemed a mix between Barry Manilow and Bruce Hornsby. He also started hosting a "songwriters' circle" on Tuesday nights from his Tribeca apartment, which featured a grand piano. He maintained a personal website, petemuller .com, featuring pictures of himself at his piano with his golden retriever, Mele. A press release about the album says: "Pete Muller woke up more than 6 years ago and realized that he could no longer find happiness in the corporate world. While he felt accomplished and satisfied, he couldn't find a new challenge, a goal to aspire to, and turned his attention wholly to his music."

Meanwhile, PDT continued to churn out hundreds of millions in yearly profits for Morgan Stanley. By the early 2000s, PDT had become so successful that it commanded the largest proprietary trading book in Morgan Stanley's mammoth equities division. Its traders were treated like hothouse flowers, allowed to ditch the standard attire of an investment banker—the bespoke suits, the polished Italian leather shoes, the watch worth more than a minivan. Traditional bankers at Morgan started sharing elevators with slacker nerds in ripped jeans, torn T-shirts, and tennis shoes. *Who the hell are these guys?* When queried, PDTers would respond vaguely, with a shrug. *We do technical stuff, you know, on computers. Quant stuff.*

"Whatever," the banker would say, adjusting his Hermès tie. Little did the banker realize that the nerdy slacker had made ten times his bonus the previous year.

Despite Muller's phenomenal success, he had kept PDT so secret that few employees at Morgan were even aware of the group's existence. That was fine with Muller, who had grown paranoid about outsiders copying PDT's strategies.

As PDT's success took off in the late 1990s, Muller's private life became more complicated. Elsesser had introduced him to a friend named Katie, a trim, dark-haired catalog designer for an antique restoration retailer called *Urban Archaeology*. The two hit it off. Katie seemed happy to wrap herself up in his life and Muller loved the attention. She helped him decorate his Tribeca apartment as well as his new beachfront cottage in Westport.

But Muller often seemed distracted. He'd disappear at work for days on end and didn't seem dedicated to the relationship. As PDT grew, generating huge profits, the pressure to keep delivering by Morgan's bigwigs began to ramp up. Muller was feeling the heat.

Out of the blue, Katie left Muller for a mutual friend who'd just been through a tough divorce.

Muller became an emotional wreck. He'd talked about ending the relationship himself to colleagues in the office, but he seemed unnerved by the idea that she would leave him. It seemed a matter of control, and he'd lost it.

He threw himself into his music, especially heartfelt ballads, and distributed the songs around a firm known for its rough-edged trading culture. Behind Muller's back, traders made cracks about the songs. His colleagues at PDT were mortified. One song was called "Plug and Play Girl," a tune only a brokenhearted quant could dream up:

I miss my plug and play, plug and play, plug and play girl

In the late 1990s, Muller went to a derivatives conference in Barcelona, attended by luminaries such as Myron Scholes of LTCM. After Muller gave his talk, he grabbed his five-pound electronic keyboard and took a cab to La Rambla, the city's funhouse pedestrian avenue that slopes down to the edge of the Mediterranean. He set up his keyboard in the midst of the milling crowd and lurched into song. It was the first time he'd sung in public.

It was just a warm-up for his next venue: the subway stations of New York City.

Soon after his Barcelona adventure, Muller packed up his electronic keyboard and walked outside his Tribeca apartment.

He was nervous. Still self-conscious about singing in public, he was trying to work out the jitters. He went to a nearby subway stop and briskly took the steps down into the underground station, plopping a token into the booth and moving through the turnstiles, lugging his keyboard case behind him.

The air was dry, and it stank. A few commuters lingered along the platform, glancing anxiously at their watches, reading books and newspapers. Muller took a breath and plunked down his case, snapped open the catches, and quickly set up the keyboard. He flipped on the switch and, beginning to sweat, tried a few notes. The commuters looked idly his way. Subway buskers were common in New York, a sideshow in the city's energetic bustle and flow. That was exactly what Muller was counting on.

He closed his eyes and started playing, a tune by one of his favorite lyricists, Harry Chapin, "Cat's in the Cradle."

My child arrived just the other day . . .

A few onlookers tossed some spare coins into the instrument's case splayed beside him—with no idea the sandy-haired singer was a hotshot trader for one of the most powerful Wall Street firms in the world.

Muller, who never actually *rode* the subway, didn't see many of his fellow investment bankers in the subway system. But one evening a colleague from Morgan walked by and glanced at Muller hunched over his keyboard.

He did a double take.

"Pete, what are you doing down here?" he said, shocked, looking Muller up and down. Recovering slightly, he added, "I guess you've done well enough—you can do whatever you want."

But he didn't toss any money in the piano case.

People began to wonder what Muller was up to. A man who made money controlling the chaotic flow of the market through mind-bending math was acting in an increasingly strange fashion. Eyebrows were raised, but who cared? Muller's group made money, buckets of money. That was all that mattered. *Let him behave like that. He deserves it.*

All the success seemed to weigh on Muller, who thought of himself as a carefree California child of the sun, a collector of crystals, singer of songs, lover of women and complex algorithms, not a ruthless, self-absorbed banker. He began to disappear from the office for weeks at a time, then months, only to pop up one day with a sweeping critique of PDT's operations before vanishing again just as abruptly. One PDT trader labeled it seagull management: swoop by every now and then, shit all over everything, and fly away.

Around 2000, Shakil Ahmed took over the reins. Muller became a paid advisor, though he remained a partner at Morgan. He traveled the world, visiting the most exotic locales he could find: Bhutan, New Zealand, Hawaii. He sang during regular gigs in Greenwich Village cabarets and grungy lounges such as the Cutting Room and Makor Cafe. Old colleagues from PDT would swing by for the performances from time to time and wonder: *What the hell happened to Pete?*

Muller stayed in touch with his fellow quants, however, and often spoke at industry events. In May 2002, he attended the wedding of Neil Chriss, one of his poker buddies whom he'd met at Morgan Stanley in the 1990s. One of the most respected mathematical minds in quantdom, Chriss was marrying a stunning, tall blonde named Natasha Herron, who was on the verge of completing a medical degree in psychology at Cornell University. The wedding was held at Troutbeck, a tony, aging resort in the Berkshire foothills that in its heyday had seen guests from Ernest Hemingway to Teddy Roosevelt.

At the reception, Chriss's quant friends were seated together. They included John Liew of AQR, whom Chriss knew from his days at Chicago; Muller; and Nassim Nicholas Taleb, a New York University professor and hedge fund manager who'd just published a book, *Fooled by Randomness*, which claimed that nearly all successful investors were more lucky than skilled.

Stocky, balding, with a salt-and-pepper beard, Taleb had little patience for quants and their fine-tuned models. His peripatetic life had shown him that little was permanent in the affairs of men. Born in 1960 in Amioun, Lebanon, a Greek Orthodox town north of Beirut, Taleb first encountered extreme randomness in the mid-1970s with the outbreak of the fifteen-year-long Lebanese civil war. To escape the violence, he left Lebanon to attend the University of Paris, where he studied math and economics. He then moved to the United States, earning a master's in business administration from Wharton.

When he was twenty-eight, he joined the investment bank First Boston, working out of the bank's Park Avenue office in New York. He started accumulating a large position in out-of-the-money Eurodollar futures contracts, one of the largest, most liquid markets in the world. On October 19, 1987—Black Monday—stocks crashed. Panicky investors fled into the most liquid assets they could find, including Taleb's Eurodollars. The value of his position exploded, giving Taleb an estimated one-day profit of about $40 million. He was well aware that the gains had nothing to do with why he'd been investing in Eurodollars. He'd been very, very lucky, and he knew it.

Over the next decade, Taleb, wealthier than he'd ever dreamed he'd become, bounced from firm to firm, at the same time earning a Ph.D. from the University of Paris Dauphine, writing a textbook on option trading, and working as a pit trader at the Chicago Mercantile Exchange. In 1999, he started teaching graduate courses in finance at NYU, at the same time launching a hedge fund called Empirica for its focus on empirical knowledge.

By the time of Chriss's wedding, Taleb had gained a reputation as a gadfly of the quants, constantly questioning their ability to beat the market. Taleb didn't believe in the Truth. He certainly didn't believe it could be quantified.

Due in part to his experience on Black Monday, Taleb believed that markets tended to make moves that were much more extreme than had been factored into quantitative models. As a teacher of financial engineering at NYU, he was well aware of the proliferation of models that attempted to take account of extreme moves—the "jump diffusion" model that allowed for sudden leaps in price; the tongue-twisting "generalized autoregressive conditional heteroscedasticity model," or GARCH, which doesn't look at prices as a coin flip but rather takes into account the immediate past, and allows for feedback processes that can result in sudden jumps that create fat tails (Brownian motion with a kick); and a number of others. Taleb argued that no matter what model the quants used—even those that factored in Mandelbrot's Lévy fat-tailed processes—the volatility in market events could be so extreme and unpredictable that no model could capture it.

The conversation at the table was cordial at first. Then people started noticing Taleb getting agitated. His voice was rising, and he was pounding the table. "It is impossible," he shouted at Muller. "You will be wiped out, I swear it!"

"I don't think so," Muller said. The normally calm and collected Muller was sweating, his face flushed. "We've proven we can beat the market year after year."

"There is no free lunch," Taleb boomed in his thick Levant accent, his forefinger wagging in Muller's face. "If ten thousand people flip a coin, after ten flips the odds are there will be someone who has turned up heads every time. People will hail this man as a genius, with a natural ability to flip heads. Some idiots will actually give him money. This is exactly what happened to LTCM. But it's obvious that LTCM didn't know shit about risk control. They were all charlatans."

Muller knew when he was being insulted. LTCM? Hardly. PDT could *never* melt down. Taleb didn't know what he was talking about.

At the end of the day, he didn't care about Taleb. He knew he had alpha. He knew the Truth, or a respectable slice of it. But he still didn't want to trade every day. There was more to life than making money, and he'd already proven he could do that in spades. He became more serious about his music and about poker.

In 2004, Muller pocketed $98,000 in a tournament on the World Poker Tour, often bringing his golden retriever to the table as a tail-wagging good-luck charm. When he won the Wall Street Poker Night challenge in March 2006, beating Cliff Asness in the final round, he didn't collect any money, but he did gain a healthy dose of bragging rights over his fellow poker-playing quants.

Once or twice a month, Muller, Weinstein, Asness, and Chriss, among other top-tier quants and hedge fund managers, would meet in ritzy New York hotels for private poker games. The buy-in was $10,000, but the pots were often much higher.

The money was chump change to all of them. It was all about the game: who knew when to raise, when to fold, when to bluff like there was no tomorrow. Asness loved playing, and he hated it. He couldn't stand folding, taking the small, incremental losses so essential to success at poker. He was too competitive, too aggressive. But he knew that the only way to win was to fold until he had a hand he could really believe in, until the odds shifted in his favor. But it seemed like he never got that hand.

Muller, however, had mastered the art of knowing exactly when to fold, when to raise, when to go all in. He never lost his cool, even when he was down. He knew it was only a matter of time before he was back on top. The quant poker games lasted late into the night, at times stretching into the following morning.

In 2006, Muller took the PDTers on a ski trip to an exclusive ski resort out west, flying the gang on a NetJets private plane. His treat. It would be one of the last few such trips they would make in years. A credit crisis brewing on Wall Street would put an end to such carefree jaunts. But that was a worry for another day.

Muller, meanwhile, was getting restless. Playing endless rounds of poker, hiking exotic trails in Hawaii, kayaking in Peru, shooting off on private jets to the Caribbean, dating models—it was all fun, but something was missing: trading, making millions in the blink of an eye, watching the winnings tick up like a rocket. He had to admit it. He missed it.

Muller decided he wanted back in. He had a steady girlfriend once again and was thinking about settling down. Plus PDT's returns weren't what they used to be. It had put up just single-digit gains in 2006 as a flood of copycats plowed into stat arb strategies, making it harder to discover untapped opportunities. Morgan's higher-ups wanted more. Muller said he could deliver.

A power struggle over control of PDT ensued. Shakil Ahmed, who'd been running PDT for the past seven years, quit the firm, outraged that Morgan would hand over the reins to their absentee leader. He soon took a job as head of quant strategies and electronic trading at Citigroup. Vikram Pandit, his former boss, had recently taken charge at Citi after Chuck Prince left in disgrace amid massive subprime losses. Pandit was quick to hire Ahmed, long considered one of the secret geniuses behind PDT.

Back at Morgan, Muller was on top again at his old trading outfit. He had bold plans to expand the operation and increase its profits. Part of his plans included juicing returns by taking on bigger positions. One portfolio at PDT with the capacity to take more risk was the quant fundamental book, longer-term trades based on a stock's value, momentum—AQR's bread and butter—or other metrics used to judge whether a stock will go up or down. Such positions were typically held for several weeks or months, rather than the superfast Midas trades that usually lasted a day or less.

"They skewed the book much more toward quant fundamental," said a onetime PDTer. "They basically turned a large part of PDT into AQR." The size of the book grew from about $2 billion to more than $5 billion, according to traders familiar with the position.

Ken Griffin, who ran strategies similar to PDT's, wasn't overjoyed by Muller's return. He was overheard telling Muller that he was sorry to hear he'd come back—a typical double-edged dig by Griffin. Muller took it as a compliment. He was eager to get back in the mix of things, eager to start making money. Big money.

He wouldn't have much time to enjoy himself. Just months after he returned, Muller would face the biggest test of his career: a brutal meltdown that nearly destroyed PDT.

● ASNESS ●

On November 13, 1998, shares of a little-known company called Theglobe.com Inc. debuted on the Nasdaq Stock Market at $9 apiece. Founders of the Web-based social networking site were expecting a strong reaction.

The frenzy that greeted the IPO defied all expectations and common sense. The stock surged like a freight train, hitting $97 at one point that day. Theglobe.com, formed by Cornell students Stephan Paternot and Todd Krizelman, was, for a brief moment, the most successful IPO in history.

A few days earlier, EarthWeb Inc., perhaps feeling the force of gravity, merely tripled in its IPO. Investors gobbled up EarthWeb's shares despite the following warning in its prospectus: "The company anticipates that it will continue to incur net losses for the foreseeable future."

A few months before the dot-com IPO frenzy began, LTCM had collapsed. Alan Greenspan and the Federal Reserve swept in, orchestrating a bailout. Greenspan also slashed interest rates to salve the wounds to the financial system left by LTCM's implosion and flood the system with liquidity. The easy money added fuel to the smoldering Internet fires, which were soon raging and pushing the tech-laden Nasdaq to all-time highs on an almost daily basis.

While minting instant millionaires among dot-com pioneers, this series of unlikely events proved a disaster for AQR, which had started trading in August 1998. Asness's strategy involved investing in cheap companies with a low price-to-book-value ratio, while betting against companies his models deemed expensive. In 1999, this was the worst possible strategy in the world. Expensive stocks—dot-com babies with no earnings and lots of hot air—surged insanely. Cheap stocks, sleepy financial companies such as Bank of America, and steady-as-she-goes automakers such as Ford and GM were stuck, left in the blazing wake of their futuristic New Economy betters.

AQR and its Goldman golden boys were hammered mercilessly, losing 35 percent in their first twenty months. In August 1999, in the middle of the free fall, Asness married Laurel Fraser, whom he'd met at Goldman, where she was an administrative assistant in the bond division. As AQR's fortunes plummeted, he complained bitterly to her about the insanity of the market. *What is wrong with these people? They are so monumentally stupid. Their stupidity is killing me.*

Asness believed his strategy worked because people made mistakes about value and momentum. Eventually they wised up, pushing markets back into equilibrium—the Truth was restored. He made money on the gap between their irrationality and the time it took them to wise up.

Now investors were acting far more stupidly and self-destructively than he could possibly have imagined.

"I thought you made money because people make mistakes," his wife chided him. "But when the mistakes are too big, your strategy doesn't work. You want this Goldilocks story of just the right irrationality."

Asness realized she was right. His Chicago School training about efficient markets had blinded him to the wilder side of human behavior. It was a lesson he'd remember in the future: People could act far more irrationally than he'd realized, and he had better be ready for it. Of course, it's impossible to prepare for every kind of irrationality, and it's always the kind you don't see coming that gets you in the end.

By early 2000, AQR was on life support. It was a matter of months before it would have been forced to shut its doors. Asness and company had coughed up $600 million of its $1 billion seed capital, in part due to investors pulling out of the fund. Only a few loyal investors remained. It was a brutally humbling experience for Goldman's wonderquant.

Adding to the misery for AQR's leading lights was Goldman's highly lucrative initial public offering. It was too easy for Asness to do the math in his head. By leaving when he had, he'd missed out on a fortune. His hedge fund was on the brink of disaster. Worthless dotcom stocks were sucking in obscene sums. The world had gone mad.

His response? Like any good academic, he wrote a paper.

"Bubble Logic: Or, How to Learn to Stop Worrying and Love the Bull" is a quant's cri de coeur, Asness's protest against the insanity of prices ascribed to dot-com stocks such as Theglobe.

The stock market's price-to-earnings ratio hit 44 in June 2000—more than doubling in just five years and triple the long-term average. The title's nod to Stanley Kubrick's black-humor satire of the Cold War, *Dr. Strangelove, or, How I Learned to Stop Worrying and Love the Bomb*, gives a clue to Asness's dark mood as he banged away at "Bubble Logic" late at night from the confines of AQR's offices near Rockefeller Center (the fund later moved to Greenwich, Connecticut). The bubble was about as welcome to Asness as an atomic bomb. AQR has "had our assets handed to us," he writes in the introduction. "Have pity on a partially gored bear."

"Bubble Logic" began by making a rather startling argument: the market of early 2000 was not like the market of the past. Of course, that was exactly what the dot-com cheerleaders were claiming. The economy was different. Inflation was low. Productivity had surged thanks to new advances in technology, such as laptops, cell phones, and the Internet. Stocks should be given higher values in such an environment, because companies would spit out more cash.

Asness, however, was turning this argument on its head. Yes, things were different this time, in a bad way. History has shown that the stock market has almost always been a good investment over the long run. Asness trotted out numbers showing that stocks beat inflation in every twenty-year period since 1926. Stocks beat bonds, and stocks beat cash. So investors should always invest in stocks, right?

Wrong. Stocks generally perform better than most other investments "not because of magic, but largely because throughout the period we study they were generally priced reasonably, or even cheaply vs. their earnings and dividends prospects," Asness wrote. "That is not necessarily the case anymore."

As a sample case, Asness examined the New Economy darling, Cisco Systems, which makes Internet routers. He systematically demolished the case for investing in Cisco by showing that there was no possible way that the company's earnings prospects could match its valuation. And yet, despite the obviousness of the case, he noted, "Cisco is on almost every 'must own' recommended list I see. Go figure."

In the paper's conclusion, the agitated hedge fund manager made an argument that flew in the face of Fama's efficient-market hypothesis. According to the EMH, it's impossible to know when a bubble is occurring, since current prices reflect all publicly known available information. Only in retrospect, when the bubble has popped (on new information about how crappy those companies were, or how little those new homeowners could actually pay), is it clear that prices were overinflated. Asness, however, wrote that the case was already clear: the market was in a bubble. "Unless we see 20-year growth for the S&P far, far in excess of anything ever seen for 125 years starting from similar good times, long-term S&P returns become quite ugly," he wrote.

Such a negative outcome seemed impossible to investors experiencing dot-com dipsomania in late 1999 and early 2000. Of course, Asness was right all along.

"Bubble Logic" was never published. By the time Asness finished writing it, in mid-2000, the dot-com bubble was imploding in spectac-ular, horrific fashion. The Nasdaq peaked in March 2000 at more than 5,000. By October 2002, it had crumbled to 1,114.

Time, and reality, had overtaken stupidity. And AQR rebounded magnificently. Investors who'd ridden out the storm were rewarded for their patience as value stocks gained a new lease on life. AQR's flagship Absolute Return Fund would gain roughly 180 percent in the three years following its low point.

Asness would wear AQR's horrific performance during the dot-com bubble as a bloodied badge of courage, a clear sign that supports the fund's claims that it is completely "market neutral." When the market crashed, AQR was still standing. Hedge funds that had plowed into Internet stocks crashed and burned.

Still, other quantitative funds such as Renaissance Technologies, D. E. Shaw, and PDT soared through the Internet bubble largely un-scathed. Their models weren't as exposed to the destruction of value stocks as were AQR's. What's more, their trading strategies were based on capturing extremely short-term changes in market prices and benefited from the volatility as the bubble expanded, then burst. Losses could also be limited, since such "high-frequency" funds, as they're called, could dump assets that moved against them in rapid order. AQR's strategies were focused on price changes that take place over the course of weeks or even months, rather than over the course of an afternoon. That meant that when the fund's models were wrong, the pain was more intense. When the models were right, of course, the gains were massive.

The dot-com flameout was a watershed event for the hedge fund industry. Sophisticated investors started to buy into the case Asness made in "Bubble Logic" that stocks aren't necessarily a one-way road to riches. Rock-bottom interest rates forced pension funds and en-dowments to find new areas to invest in. Assets under management by hedge funds surged, rising to $2 trillion by early 2007 from about $100 billion two decades earlier.

At the head of the pack were the quants. It all seemed so perfect. Their quantitative models worked. The theories describing how the market behaved had been tested and appeared to be accurate. They knew the Truth! The computers were faster, more powerful than ever. A river of money flowed in until it became a torrent, making many who bathed in it rich beyond their wildest dreams. In 2002, Asness personally pulled down $37 million. The following year, he raked in $50 million.

Helping to drive the returns at quant funds such as AQR was a highly lucrative tactic known as the carry trade. The trade had its roots in Japan, where interest rates had been lowered to below 1 percent to help pull the country out of a debilitating deflationary spiral. A bank account in Japan would yield about half a percent a year, compared with about 5 percent in the United States or 10 percent or more in some other countries.

This dynamic meant firms with the know-how and financial dexterity could borrow yen in Japan—practically for free—and invest it in other assets with higher interest rates, such as bonds, commodities, or other currencies. And the extra cash that kicked out could be deployed into even more investments, such as commodities or subprime mortgages. Add a healthy dose of leverage, and you have a perfect recipe for a worldwide speculative binge.

Indeed, by early 2007, about $1 trillion was staked on the carry trade, according to *The Economist*. The tactic was especially popular at Asness's old quant shop, Goldman's Global Alpha fund.

The trouble was, nearly all the investors in the trade, mostly hedge funds but also banks and some mutual funds, were putting their money in similar corners of the market, including high-yielding currencies such as the Australian and New Zealand dollars. Traders talked nonstop about tidal waves of "liquidity sloshing around," pushing up the price of stocks, gold, real estate, and oil.

But who cared? The trade was so perfect, so incredibly profitable— about as close to a free lunch in the market as possible—that there was no stopping it.

Asness, meanwhile, had been running AQR from cramped Manhattan offices, boxes full of files and computer equipment spilling out of spare rooms and lining the hallways. As the firm grew, and the partners married and started to raise families, he decided it was time for a change. He scoped out several locations in Greenwich and finally decided on Two Greenwich Plaza, a squat office building next to the town's train station, allowing easy access to the Big City for the fund's growing legions of twentysomething quants.

One day in 2004, he rented out a car on the Metro North railway and took AQR's staff on a field trip to the new digs. Later that year, the move was complete. Flush with hedge fund riches, Asness purchased a 12,500-square-foot mansion on North Street in Greenwich for $9.6 million. In 2005, he was the subject of an extended article in the *New York Times Magazine*. When the article's author asked him what it was like to be incredibly rich, Asness quoted Dudley Moore's character from the movie *Arthur*: "It doesn't suck."

As his imperial ambitions soared, so did his lifestyle. The firm bought a fractional share in NetJets, giving its partners access to a fleet of private jets at their beck and call. Asness decided the North Street mansion was too constricting and purchased a twenty-two-acre property in Greenwich's swank Conyers Farm community. A team of architects would visit Asness at AQR's headquarters and lay out their plans for a sprawling new mansion. Estimates of the cost of the project ran as high as $30 million.

Asness and company started to think about the next big step for AQR. The IPOs of Fortress and Blackstone hadn't gone unnoticed at Two Greenwich Plaza. Asness's friend Ken Griffin was also mulling over an IPO at Citadel.

So was AQR. By late July 2007, the papers were drawn up. The IPO was essentially a done deal. All AQR needed to do was mail the documents to the Securities and Exchange Commission and wait for the money to roll in.

The billions.

▪ WEINSTEIN ▪

One day in 2005, Boaz Weinstein was patrolling the endless, computer-swathed tables of Deutsche Bank's fixed-income flow desk. A Russian trader on the desk had heard that Weinstein was known for his chess skills. As Weinstein paused by his terminal, the Russian said, "I hear you play a mean game of chess."

"I suppose," Weinstein said.

"I too play chess." The Russian smiled. "We play, you and I."

"Let's go," Weinstein responded without skipping a beat.

Flustered, perhaps, by Weinstein's calm retort, the Russian trader made a strange demand: he'd play only if Weinstein was "blindfolded." Weinstein knew what that meant. He didn't actually need to wear a blindfold, but he did have to sit with his back to the chessboard. Weinstein agreed.

After the closing bell, Weinstein and the Russian met in a conference room. Word about the match started to spread, and a few traders gathered to watch. As the match wore on, more and more Deutsche employees showed up. Soon there were hundreds, cheering on every move as Weinstein and the Russian went head-to-head—and making side bets on who would win. The match lasted two hours. By the time it was over, Weinstein was victorious.

Those were heady days for Weinstein. The money was rolling in. He was dating beautiful women. And it was only the beginning. As his success grew at Deutsche Bank, he started thinking about making the very same step Cliff Asness had made at Goldman Sachs in 1998: breaking away from the mother ship and launching a hedge fund.

The credit trading operation he'd created at Deutsche had become one of the elite outfits on Wall Street. Top traders would ring Weinstein on the phone to pick his brains on the latest action in credit default swaps, bonds, stocks, you name it. His group had become a true multistrategy hedge fund inside the bank, trading every kind of security imaginable and juggling upward of $30 billion in positions.

Weinstein was gaining a reputation as a multitalented savant, a Renaissance man of Wall Street. His prop trading team was also becoming known as a force to be reckoned with. Like PDT, they were also developing their own odd rituals, testing one another's mental skills in ways only a nerdy band of hothouse quants could dream up.

Take the Maptest ritual. The Maptest website shows a layout of all fifty states in America. The trick: the states are unlabeled. Columns arrayed below the map include the state names. The task is to drag the names onto the appropriate state within a certain time. Players receive a score for how quickly the task is completed. To spice things up, the veterans, including Weinstein, would place bets on the newbies' scores. "Look at the tiny size of his cranium," a Deutsche Bank trader might crack as a new recruit feverishly dragged state names across the computer screen. "Bet a hundred he doesn't know where Wyoming is."

"You're on."

Weinstein tried to tone down the group's overtly nerdy side and often claimed that he wasn't *really* a quant, downplaying the complexity of his trades. His emails contained the quip "It's not rocket surgery," deliberately conflating the clichés of the rocket scientist quant practicing brain surgery with complex derivatives.

Quants were too careful, too worried about risk management; they had no feel for the market. No risk, no reward. But an aggressive approach holds its dangers. Deutsche Bank had its own cautionary tale in the person of Brian Hunter, who'd worked on Deutsche's energy desk before moving on to Amaranth. Hunter had generated millions of dollars for the bank trading natural gas in the early 2000s, until losing $51 million in a single week in 2003. Hunter blamed Deutsche's faulty software. Deutsche blamed Hunter, and the two parted ways.

Some worried that Weinstein was getting in over his head. He also helped run Deutsche Bank's U.S. "flow" desk, which facilitated trades with clients such as hedge funds or the bond giant Pimco. The job put Weinstein atop the so-called Chinese wall that separates a bank's trading operations from its client-facing side. There were never any allegations that Weinstein abused his position. But the fact that Deutsche Bank gave Weinstein such power was testimony to its desperation to keep him at the switch, pulling in hundreds of millions in profits. The high-stakes race for profits was transforming once-staid banks into hot-rod hedge funds fueled by leverage, derivatives, and young traders willing to risk it all to make their fortunes. Weinstein was at the center of the shift.

He didn't let Deutsche down. Weinstein and his prop desk gunslingers continued to ring the cash register. The prop group pulled in $900 million in 2006, earning Weinstein a paycheck of about $30 million.

Most of his attention was focused on his prop desk, however, alienating his underlings on flow, who didn't think they were getting enough recognition. In 2005, he'd hired Derek Smith, a star trader at Goldman Sachs, to run the flow desk, angering a number of traders who felt they deserved to run the show. The number of Weinstein's enemies within Deutsche started to grow.

"Why do we need an outsider?" they grumbled.

Weinstein's monetary incentives from the bank were skewed heavily toward the prop desk side. While his compensation for his flow desk job was a discretionary bonus, his prop desk business rewarded him with a healthy percentage of the profits.

Also, there was a good reason for Weinstein's tunnel vision: his eyes were squarely focused on launching his own hedge fund in the next few years following the tradition set by Cliff Asness years ago when he'd broken away from Goldman Sachs to launch AQR. In early 2007, Weinstein renamed his prop-trading group Saba. It encompassed about sixty people working in offices in New York, London, and Hong Kong.

The name would brand the group on the Street, making it immediately recognizable once it broke away from Deutsche Bank. Saba was increasingly known and feared as a major force with massive financial ammunition, a major player nearing the level of bond-trading powerhouses such as Citadel and Goldman Sachs.

Weinstein reveled in his success. Now a wealthy playboy, every summer he would rent a different vacation home in the Hamptons. He continued to gamble, playing high-stakes games alongside celebrities such as Matt Damon.

He also continued to gamble with his fellow quants in New York. The game, of course, was poker.

Boaz Weinstein dealt crisply, talking a blue streak. There was no smoke in the room as the cards fell about the table. Peter Muller, the compulsive health nut who nearly passed on the BARRA job due to his discovery of a single cigarette butt in the company's bathroom, didn't allow smoking

Muller's rule didn't bother the quants. Neither Cliff Asness nor

Weinstein smoked. But every now and then, a seasoned poker professional who couldn't fathom the notion of poker separated from an endless chain of cigarettes would sit in on the quants' game and be forced to clock an excruciating night of nicotine-free, high-stakes gambling.

On this particular night in late 2006, it was just the quants going head-to-head. Weinstein was regaling the table with tales of "correlation," a technical term from credit trading that he was explaining in detail to his poker buddies.

"The assumptions are crazy," he said, placing the deck on the table and picking up his hand. "The correlations are ridiculous."

It all had to do with the explosion in housing prices. The housing market had been booming for years and looked to be losing steam in overheated regions such as southern California and Florida. Home prices had more than doubled nationwide in a matter of five years, helping prop up the economy but leading to an unsustainable bubble. A growing number of investors, including Weinstein, thought it was about to pop like an infected boil.

Weinstein had a unique view into Wall Street's end of the bubble. Deutsche Bank was heavily involved in mortgage lending—some of it on the subprime side. In 2006, it had purchased Chapel Funding, a mortgage originator, and had teamed up with the Hispanic National Mortgage Association to make loans to Hispanic and immigrant borrowers.

Deutsche Bank was also a big player in the securitization market, buying mortgage loans from lenders, packaging those loans into securities, then slicing and dicing them into different pieces to peddle to investors around the world.

One reason why banks engage in securitization is to spread around risk like jelly on toast. Instead of lumping the jelly on one small piece of the toast, leaving all the reward (or risk that it falls off the toast) for one bite, it's evenly distributed, making for lots more tasty bites—and, through the quant magic of diversification (spreading the jelly), less risk.

If an investor buys a single subprime mortgage worth $250,000, that investor bears the entire risk if that mortgage goes into default, certainly possible given the fact that subprime mortgages usually go to the least creditworthy borrowers. But if a thousand subprime mortgages, each worth about $250,000, were pooled together and turned into a single security with a collective value of $250 million, the security could be divided into some number of shares. The potential loss caused by any one mortgage going into default would be offset by the fact that it represented only a tiny portion of the security's total value.

Parts of the securities, in many cases the lowest on the food chain, were often bundled into even more esoteric monstrosities known as collateralized debt obligations, which took into account the fact that some of the underlying mortgages were more likely than others to default. The more-likely-to-default bundles obviously carried greater risk, though along with that came its corollary, greater potential reward. Between 2004 and 2007, billions in subprime home loans were stuffed into these so-called CDOs. The CDOs were then sliced into tranches. There were high-quality slices, stamped AAA by rating agencies such as Standard & Poor's, and there were poor-quality slices, some of which were so low in quality they didn't even get a rating.

Bizarrely, the ratings weren't based on the relative quality of the underlying loans. The AAA tranches could hold loans of the same value and quality as those in the lowest-rated tranches. The ratings, rather, were based on who got paid first in the stack of loans. The owners of AAA tranches had the first dibs on payments. When borrowers started to default, the owners of the lowest-tier tranches got whacked first. If enough borrowers defaulted, higher-rated tranches would start to suffer.

One of the problems with the Byzantine practice of carving up CDOs into all of these slices was figuring out how to price them. Sometime around 2000, the quants came up with an answer: correlation. By getting the price of one small part of the bundle of slices, quants could figure out the "right" prices of all the other slices by looking at how correlated they were with one another. If the pool of loans started experiencing, say, a 5 percent rate of defaults, the quants could calculate the impact on each of the slices through their computers and figure out the correlations between each slice of the pie, all the way up to the AAA slice.

It was assumed, of course, that the poor-quality slices and the AAA slices had very little in common in terms of the likelihood of defaults by the homeowners who received the original mortgages. Put another way, the correlation between them was extremely low, almost infinitesimal.

Weinstein and several other traders at Deutsche Bank (and a number of clever hedge funds) figured out that the correlations in most models were off by miles. When they peered into the underlying loans in the CDOs, they discovered that many of the loans were so shaky, and so similar, that when one slice of the pie started to go bad, that meant the entire pie would be rotten. So many low-quality loans had been stuffed into the CDOs that even owners of seemingly safe, high-rated tranches would suffer. In other words, the correlations were very *high*. But most people buying and selling the slices thought they were very *low*.

To Weinstein, that meant a trade. Through even more esoteric quant alchemy, there were ways to "short" CDO slices through Weinstein's favorite method: credit default swaps. By purchasing a swap, or a bunch of swaps bundled together, Weinstein would effectively take out an insurance policy on the underlying subprime loans. If those loans went belly up—which Weinstein thought most likely—the policy paid out. In simple terms, Weinstein was betting that the market was underestimating the toxicity of the subprime mortgage market.

Even better for Weinstein, most traders were so enthusiastic about the housing market and the CDOs bundling all those loans that the cost of shorting the market was extremely cheap. Weinstein saw this as an almost can't-lose bet. Huge profits could be made. And if he was wrong, he'd lose only the scant amount he'd paid for the insurance policy.

"We're putting on the trade at Deutsche," Weinstein said, gazing at his cards.

Asness and Muller nodded. It was typical quant shoptalk, one trader describing a clever new bet to his peers, but they were getting bored. It was time to get down to the business at hand. The only bet

on their minds at the moment involved a pile of chips worth several
thousand dollars in the center of the table.

Weinstein looked at his hand and grimaced. He had nothing and
folded.

"Raise a thousand," Asness said, tossing more chips on the pile.

Muller peered at Asness, who sat back in his chair and grinned
nervously, his face reddening. *Poor Cliff. It's so easy to tell when he's
bluffing. No poker face whatsoever on the man.*

"Call," Muller said, throwing down another winning hand to Asness's agonized groan. Muller was on a hot streak, and he laughed as
he swept the chips into the steadily rising pile in front of him.

"I KEEP MY FINGERS CROSSED FOR THE FUTURE"

Boaz Weinstein wasn't the only one worrying about the health of CDOs in 2007. Aaron Brown—the quant who'd beaten Liar's Poker in the 1980s—had gotten his hands dirty in the securitization industry almost since its inception. His career had provided him with a front-row seat on its evolution and cancerous growth throughout Wall Street. For years he had watched with increasing trepidation as the CDO industry grew larger and, at the same time, more divorced from reality. By 2007, Brown was working at Morgan Stanley as a risk manager and growing uncomfortable with Morgan's subprime exposure. He was ready to get out.

He'd already been in low-level discussions about a job with a hedge fund that was staffing up for an IPO: AQR. Cliff Asness's firm was looking for a risk management veteran to deal with thorny issues such as international risk regulations. Brown loved the idea. He'd never worked at a hedge fund and was eager to give it a shot. In June 2007, he signed on as AQR's chief risk officer.

Brown was well aware of AQR's reputation as a top-of-the-line quant shop that spoke his language. But he had little idea that AQR, like Morgan Stanley, was sitting on top of a bubbling cauldron of risk that was about to explode in spectacular fashion.

Growing up in Seattle, Brown had always been fascinated by numbers—baseball box scores, weather charts, stock pages. He couldn't have cared less about the events they denoted—the walk-off home runs, the hurricane-wrecked trailer parks, the mergers of corporate rivals. It was the rows of digits that caught Brown's fancy, the idea that there was some kind of secret knowledge behind the numbers. His love of mathematics eventually led him to one of the most influential books he would ever read: Ed Thorp's *Beat the Dealer*.

Brown devoured the book, mesmerized by the idea that he could use math to make money at a game as simple as blackjack. After mastering Thorp's card-counting method, he moved on to poker. At fourteen, he became a regular in Seattle's underground gambling halls. Seattle was a port town full of sailors, hard-luck transients, and been-around-the-world sharpies. Brown couldn't match them for machismo, but they couldn't touch his math or his intuition. He quickly realized that he was very good; he excelled not just at figuring the odds of each hand but at reading the poker faces of his opponents. He could sense a bluff a mile away.

In 1974, he graduated from high school with top grades, got perfect scores on his college board exams, and headed straight for Harvard. He studied under Harrison White, a sociologist who applied quantitative models to social networks, and also dove into Harvard's active poker scene, which included George W. Bush as a regular in Harvard Business School's poker circles. Indeed, Harvard's bumper crop of spoiled rich kids seemed eager to lose money to Brown, and he was happy to oblige. But the stakes were usually too low for his taste, or the games too unprofessional. He made his way to a game future Microsoft founder Bill Gates ran at Harvard's Currier House, but Brown found it too regimented and uptight. A bunch of tense nerds trying to act cool, he thought.

After graduating in 1978, Brown took a job at American Management Systems, a consulting firm in northern Virginia. The job was fine, but the D.C. poker circuit was a bigger draw. It was no trouble to get in on games with the odd congressman. Once he heard about a party that had a hot backroom game. He walked into an apartment and saw a heavyset man wearing a tight T-shirt, girls who looked like dolled-up secretaries hanging from each arm. It was none other than Texas congressman Charlie Wilson, future subject of the book and movie *Charlie Wilson's War*. Brown liked Wilson, thought he was a fun guy. Better yet, Wilson loved to play poker. He wasn't bad at it, either.

Brown wasn't satisfied with his job, though, and once again felt the tug of academia. In 1980, he started taking classes at the University of Chicago's graduate school in economics. In Chicago, Brown became enthralled with the mysterious world of stock options. He picked up Thorp's *Beat the Market* and quickly mastered the book's technique for pricing stock warrants and convertible bonds. In short order, he was doing so well trading options that he considered dropping out of school and pursuing a full-time trading career. Instead, he decided to see through his term at Chicago, while trading on the side.

Brown had no intention of becoming an academic, however. His experience trading options had given him a taste for the real thing. After years playing poker and blackjack in backroom card parlors around the country, he heard the siren song of the world's biggest casino: Wall Street. After graduating in 1982, he moved to New York. His first job was helping to manage the pension plans of large corporations for Prudential Insurance Company of America. A few years later, he took a job as head of mortgage research at Lepercq, de Neuflize & Co., a boutique investment advisor in New York.

With each move, Brown delved more deeply into quantdom. At the time, quants were seen as second-class citizens at most trading firms, computer nerds who didn't have the balls to take the kinds of risks that yielded the real money. Brown got sick of seeing the same rich kids he'd suckered at Harvard lord it over the quants in trading-floor games such as Liar's Poker. That's when he decided to bust up Liar's Poker with quant wizardry.

At Lepercq he picked up a new quant skill: the dark art of securitization. Securitization was a hot new business on Wall Street in the mid-1980s. Bankers would purchase loans such as mortgages from thrifts or commercial banks and bundle them up into securities (hence the name). They would slice those securities into tranches and sell off the pieces to investors such as pension funds and insurance companies. Brown quickly learned how to carve up mortgages into slices with all the dexterity of a professional chef.

Prior to the securitization boom, home loans were largely the province of community-based lenders who lived and died by the time-honored business of borrowing cheap and lending at higher rates. A loan was made by the bank and stayed with the bank until it was paid off. Think Jimmy Stewart and the Bailey Building & Loan Association of the Frank Capra classic *It's a Wonderful Life*. It was such a stolid business that local bankers lived by what some called the "rule of threes": borrow money at 3 percent, lend it to home buyers at three points higher, and be on the golf course by three.

But as baby boomers started buying new homes in the 1970s, Wall Street noticed an opportunity. Many savings and loans didn't have enough capital to satisfy the demand for new loans, especially in Sunbelt states such as California and Florida. Rust Belt thrifts, meanwhile, had too much capital and too little demand. A Salomon bond trader named Bob Dall saw an opening to bring the two together through the financial alchemy of securitization. Salomon would be the middle-man, shifting stagnant assets from the Rust Belt to the Sunbelt, plucking out a portion of the money for itself along the way. To trade the newly created bonds, he turned to Lewis Ranieri, a thirty-year-old trader from Brooklyn working on the bank's utility bond desk.

Over the next few years, Ranieri and colleagues fanned out across the United States, wooing bankers and lawmakers to their bold vision. Mortgage loans made by local banks and thrifts were purchased by Salomon, repackaged into tradable bonds, and sold around the globe. And everybody was happy. Homeowners had access to loans, often at a cheaper interest rate, since there was more demand for the loans from Wall Street. The S&Ls no longer had to worry about borrowers defaulting, because the default risk had been shifted to investors. The banks gobbled up a tidy chunk of middleman fees. And investors could get custom-made, relatively low-risk assets. It was quant heaven.

The Salomon wizards didn't stop there. Like car salesmen always looking to lure buyers and increase share with shiny new models, they began to concoct something called collateralized mortgage obligations, or CMOs, bondlike certificates built from different tranches of a pool of mortgage-backed securities. (A mortgage-backed security is a bunch of loans sliced into tranches; a CMO is a bunch of those tranches sliced into even more tranches.) The first CMO deal had four tranches worth about $20 million. The tranches were divided into various levels of quality and maturity that spit out different interest payments—as always, greater risk resulting in greater reward. An ancillary benefit, for the banks at least, was that investors who bought these CMOs took on the risk if the underlying loans defaulted or if borrowers refinanced their loans in the event interest rates shifted lower.

That's where quants such as Brown entered the scene. As Ranieri once said, "Mortgages are math." With the rising levels of complexity, all those tricky tranches (there would soon be CMOs with a hundred tranches, each one carrying a somewhat different mix of risk and reward), the devil was in figuring out how to price the assets. The quants pulled out their calculators, cracked open their calculus books, and came up with solutions.

With the math whizzes at the helm, it was a relatively safe business, give or take the odd, predictable blowup every few years. Brown ran Lepercq's securitization business with a steady hand. The bank had tight relationships with local bankers throughout the country. If Brown had questions about a loan he was packaging, he could call up the banker directly and ask about it. "Sure, I just drove by that house the other day, he's putting in a new garage," the banker might say.

But in the late 1980s, Lepercq's business was overwhelmed when Salomon massively ramped up its mortgage securitization business.

Salomon poured billions into the business, bidding for every loan it could get its hands on. A single deal by Salomon could match the entire year's product at Lepercq. Small dealers such as Lepercq couldn't compete. Salomon didn't just offer better deals for loans to the bankers Brown was dealing with—Salomon bought the bank. And it didn't stop at home mortgages. Securitization was the flavor of the financial future, and the future belonged to whoever controlled the supply.

Salomon was soon securitizing every kind of loan known to man: credit cards, car purchases, student loans, junk bonds. As profits kept increasing, so did its appetite and capacity for risk. In the 1990s, it started securitizing riskier loans to borderline borrowers who as a class came to be known as subprime.

Wall Street's securitization wizards also made use of a relatively new accounting trick called "off-balance-sheet accounting." Banks created trusts or shell companies in offshore tax havens such as the Cayman Islands or Dublin. The trusts would buy loans, stick them in a "warehouse," and package them up like Christmas presents with bows on top (all through the cybermagic of electronic transfers). The bank didn't need to set aside much capital on its balance sheet, since it didn't own the loans. It was simply acting as middleman, shuffling assets between buyers and sellers in the frictionless ether of securitization.

The system was extremely profitable due to all the sweet, sweet fees. Guys such as Aaron Brown either jumped on board or moved on to other things.

Brown moved on. Several top firms offered him jobs after he left Lepercq, but he turned them down, eager to get away from the Wall Street rat race. He started teaching finance and accounting courses at Fordham University and Yeshiva University in Manhattan while keeping his hand in the game by taking the odd consulting job. Consulting at J. P. Morgan, he helped design a revolutionary risk management system for a group that eventually became an independent company called RiskMetrics, a top risk management shop.

Securitization, meanwhile, took off like a freight train in the early 1990s after the savings and loan crisis, when the federal Resolution Trust Corporation took over defaulted savings and loans that once held more than $400 billion of assets. The RTC bundled up the high-yielding, risky loans and sold them in just a few years, whetting the investors' appetites for more.

In 1998, Brown took a consulting job with Rabobank, a staid Dutch firm that had started dabbling in credit derivatives. He was introduced to the exciting world of credit default swaps and created a number of trading systems for the new derivatives. It was still the Wild West of the swap market, and there was lots of low-hanging fruit to be had with creative trading.

Credit default swaps may sound fiendishly complex, but they're actually relatively simple instruments. Imagine a family—call it the Bonds family—moves into a beautiful new home worth $1 million recently built in your neighborhood. The local bank has given the Bondses a mortgage. Trouble is, the bank has too many loans on its books and would like to get some of them off its balance sheet. The bank approaches you and your neighbors and asks whether you would be interested in providing insurance against the chance that the Bonds family may one day default.

Of course, the bank will pay you a fee, but nothing extravagant. Mr. and Mrs. Bonds are hardworking. The economy is in solid shape. You think it's a good bet. The bank starts paying you $10,000 a year. If Mr. and Mrs. Bonds default, you owe $1 million. But as long as Mr. and Mrs. Bonds keep paying their mortgage, everything is fine. It's almost like free money. In essence, you've bought a credit default swap on Mr. and Mrs. Bonds's house.

One day you notice that Mr. Bonds didn't drive to work in the morning. Later you find out that he's lost his job. Suddenly you're worried that you may be on the hook for $1 million. But wait: another neighbor, who thinks he knows the family better than you, is confident that Mr. Bonds will get his job back soon. He's willing to take over the responsibility for that debt—for a price, of course. He wants $20,000 a year to insure the Bondses' mortgage. That's bad news for you, since you have to pay an extra $10,000 a year—but you think it's worth it because you really don't want to pay for that $1 million mortgage.

Welcome to the world of credit default swaps trading.

Many CDS traders, weren't really in the game to protect

themselves against a loss on a bond or mortgage. Often these investors never actually held the debt in the first place. Instead, they were gambling on the *perception* of whether a company would default or not.

If all of this weren't strange enough, things became truly surreal when the world of credit default swaps met the world of securitization. Brown had watched, with some horror, as banks started to bundle securitized loans into a product they called a collateralized debt obligation, or CDO. CDOs were similar to the CMOs (collateralized mortgage obligations) Brown had encountered in the 1980s. But they were more diverse and could be used to package any kind of debt, from mortgages to student loans to credit card debt. Some CDOs were made up of other pieces of CDOs, a Frankenstein-like beast known as CDO-squared. (Eventually there were even CDOs of CDOs of CDOs.)

Just when things seemingly couldn't get stranger, CDOs underwent a completely new twist when a team of J. P. Morgan quants created one of the most bizarre and ultimately destructive financial products ever designed: the "synthetic" CDO.

In the mid-1990s, a New York group of J. P. Morgan financial engineers began thinking about how to solve a problem that plagued the bank: a huge inventory of loans on the bank's balance sheet that was earning paltry returns. Because the bank was limited in how many loans it could make due to capital reserve requirements, those loans were holding it back. What if there was a way to make the risk of the loans disappear?

Enter the credit default swap. The bank came up with the novel idea of creating a synthetic CDO using swaps. The swaps were tied to the loans that had been sitting on J. P. Morgan's balance sheet, repackaged into a CDO. Investors, instead of buying an actual bundle of bonds—getting the yield on the bonds, but also assuming the risk of default—were instead agreeing to *insure* a bundle of bonds, getting paid by a premium to do so.

Imagine, in other words, thousands of swaps tied to bundles of mortgages (or other kinds of loans such as corporate and credit card debt) such as those owned by Mr. and Mrs. Bonds.

By selling slices of synthetic CDOs to investors, J. P. Morgan off-loaded the risk of the debt it held on its balance sheet. Since the bank was essentially insuring the loans, it didn't need to worry anymore about the risk the loan holder would default. With that—presto change-o—the bank could use more capital to make more loans . . . and book more fees.

It was brilliant, on paper. In December 1997, J. P. Morgan's New York derivatives desk unveiled its masterpiece of financial engineering. It was called Bistro, short for Broad Index Secured Trust Offering. Bistro was a high-powered vacuum cleaner for a bank's credit exposure, an industrialized risk management tool. The first Bistro deal allowed J. P. Morgan to unload nearly $1 billion in credit risk from its balance sheet on a portfolio of $10 billion in loans. The bank retained a certain part of the synthetic CDO in the form of a high-grade "super-senior" tranche, which had been deemed so safe that there was virtually no chance that it would ever see losses. This fizzing concoction would play a critical role in the credit meltdown of 2007 and 2008.

As time went on, more and more credit default swaps, or tranches of them, spread through the financial system. Traders scooped them up like racetrack gamblers betting on which horse would finish last. In certain ways, the whole increasingly complex derivatives fantasia harkened back to the block-trading desk at Morgan Stanley in the early 1980s when Gerry Bamberger came up with the idea of statistical arbitrage: an idea that started off as a risk management tool had turned into a casino. But Bamberger's creation was kid stuff compared to the industrial-strength mathematical nightmare cooked up in the quant labs of J. P. Morgan. Complexity built upon complexity. Soon it went viral.

In 1998, the Russian government defaulted on its bonds and Long-Term Capital Management collapsed. The resulting chaos helped to turbocharge the credit derivatives industry (helping set the stage for the rise of Boaz Weinstein). Everyone wanted a piece of these arcane swaps, since they provided a form of protection against the risk of default. J. P. Morgan pumped new products into the system as it Bistro'd up its balance sheet. Other banks quickly followed suit.

A robust secondary market for credit default swaps sprang up in which traders such as Weinstein made bets on whether they were mispriced.

Brown, meanwhile, went back to full-time work at Citigroup in 2000, working on a firmwide risk management system for the largest bank in the world. He found that Citi had much of its risk under control. But one corner of the bank bothered him: securitization. Since the bank's securitization activities took place "off balance sheet," in offshore accounts, Brown reckoned there was a disturbing lack of transparency. It was hard to know exactly what was going on, how much risk was being taken. There seemed little he could do about it, aside from complaining to management from time to time. But who would listen? The business was a profit juggernaut. Naysayers were ignored.

Brown watched as the relatively sedate financial system he'd joined in the 1980s turned into a derivatives-laden, debt-grinding monster. Banks were dabbling in the most exotic derivatives imaginable. Blowups were becoming more frequent, but they seemed dwarfed by the massive amounts of money coming in the door. The casino stayed open for business. Indeed, it started branching out, searching for more ways to pull in capital its traders could play around with. For instance, subprime mortgages.

Like most Wall Streeters, however, Aaron Brown was dazzled by the numbers, by the ingenious trading strategies that could arb out inefficiencies and deliver seemingly endless profits. Indeed, virtually the entire quant community, aside from a few random party-poopers, embraced the derivatives explosion wholeheartedly. The layered levels of complexity didn't bother them whatsoever. They loved it.

Perhaps the most egregious example of over-the-top quantitative creativity involved those synthetic CDOs such as J. P. Morgan's Bistro. Because of the complexity of all of their tangled and tranched swaps and bonds, it was very difficult to price all of the pieces. The biggest problem was the one Weinstein focused on years later: correlation. If loans in one piece of the CDO weaken, what are the odds that loans in other parts will see problems? It's the same problem as asking whether all the apples in a bag will start to rot if a few go bad.

Naturally, a quant was waiting in the wings with an elegant solution to it all—a solution that would help drive global credit markets into a ditch several years later.

That solution came from a Chinese-born quant named David X. Li, a financial engineer at the New York headquarters of the Canadian Imperial Bank of Commerce, or CIBC. Rather than try to model all of the fiendishly difficult factors that make the pricing of all the inter-related pieces so thorny, Li hit upon a quick fix that would immediately provide the data to price the hodgepodge of CDO tranches.

Li often discussed the problem with colleagues from academia who were experts in an actuarial science called survival analysis. One concept they studied was the fact that after the death of a spouse, people tend to die sooner than their demographic peers. In other words, they were measuring correlations between the deaths of spouses.

The link between dying spouses and credit default swaps was quant wizardry at its best—and its worst. Li showed how this model could assign correlations between tranches of CDOs by measuring the price of credit default swaps linked to the underlying debt. Credit default swaps supply a single variable that incorporates the market's assessment of how the loan will perform. The price of a CDS, after all, is simply a reflection of the view investors have on whether or not a borrower will default.

Li's model supplied a method to bundle the prices of many different credit default swaps in a CDO and spit out numbers showing the correlations between the tranches. In April 2000, having moved on to J. P. Morgan's credit department, he published his results in the *Journal of Fixed Income* in a paper called "On Default Correlation: A Copula Function Approach." The model's name was based in part on the statistical method he used to measure correlations: the Gaussian copula.

Copulas are mathematical functions that calculate the connections between two variables—in other words, how they "copulate." When X happens (such as a homeowner defaulting), there's a Y chance that

Z happens (a neighboring homeowner defaults). The specific copulas Li used were named after Carl Friedrich Gauss, the nineteenth-century German mathematician known for devising a method, based on the bell curve, to measure the motion of stars.

The correlations between the slices in a CDO were, therefore, based on the bell curve (a copula is essentially a multidimensional bell curve). Thousands of bonds (or the swaps linked to them) weren't expected to make big, sudden jumps; rather, they were generally expected to move from one point to another, up or down, in relatively predictable patterns. Extreme moves in a large number of underlying bonds weren't part of the model. It was the law of large numbers all over again, the same mathematical trick Ed Thorp used to beat black-jack in the 1960s and that Black and Scholes used to price options. Now, however, it was being applied on a scale so vast and complex that it approached the absurd. Undaunted, the quants lapped it up.

As the synthetic CDO market boomed, Wall Street and credit rating agencies adopted Li's model. "The Gaussian copula was the Black-Scholes for credit derivates," said Michel Crouhy, Li's boss at CIBC in the 1990s. So-called correlation traders sprang up at banks such as Goldman Sachs, Morgan Stanley, and Deutsche Bank, using the model to trade CDO tranches, and the underlying correlations between them, like baseball cards. The model seemed to work relatively well and was easy to use.

Crucially, and disastrously, the model was based on how *other investors* viewed the market through the lens of credit default swaps. If CDS traders thought few homeowners would default on their loans, Li's Gaussian copula priced the tranches accordingly. And since the CDO boom was occurring at the same time that a housing bubble was inflating—indeed, it helped inflate the bubble—most investors believed there was little chance that a large number of loans would default. What resulted was a vicious feedback loop—an echo chamber, one might say—in which enthusiastic investors snapped up tranches of CDOs, creating demand for more CDOs—and that created a demand for more mortgage loans. The CDOs were showing very little risk, according to Li's model. For some reason, nearly everyone, except for a few doubting Thomases in the wilderness, believed in it, even though the historical record of how mortgage loans behaved in a broad economic downturn was vanishingly slim.

Then, in 2004, to meet the insatiable demand, banks started packing CDOs with a type of loan Li hadn't considered when creating his model in the late 1990s: subprime mortgages. The CDO market went into hyperdrive.

Thanks to even more quant alchemy, certain tranches of subprime CDOs could earn AAA ratings from agencies such as Standard & Poor's, a stamp of approval that allowed regulated entities such as pension funds to gobble them up. Here's how it worked: Financial engineers would take lower-rated slices of a mortgage-backed security or other securitized bundle of loans such as credit card lines, and package them in a CDO. It would then slice the CDO into different pieces, based on priority—which slices had the right to the cash spit out by the loans first, second, third, and so on. A product that began as home loans to the riskiest kind of borrower went through the looking glass of quantdom and came out a gold-plated security, suitable for some of the most closely watched and regulated investors. In fact, they were only low-risk relative to other, even more volatile tranches, when viewed through the rose-colored glasses of boom-time investors.

In 2004, $157 billion in CDOs was issued, much of which contained subprime mortgages. The amount spiked to $273 billion in 2005 and a whopping $550 billion in 2006, its peak year.

The Gaussian copula was, in hindsight, a disaster. The simplicity of the model hypnotized traders into thinking that it was a reflection of reality. In fact, it turned out that the model was a jury-rigged formula based on the irrationally exuberant, self-reinforcing, and ultimately false wisdom of the crowd that assigned make-believe prices to an incredibly complex product. For a while it worked, and everyone was using it. But when the slightest bit of volatility hit in early 2007, the whole edifice fell apart. The prices didn't make sense anymore. Since nearly every CDO manager and trader used the same formula to price the fizzing bundles—yet another instance of crowding that results from popular quant methodologies—they all imploded at once.

Is it any wonder why? The complexity had become malevolent. The quants and correlation traders were modeling cash flows on tranches of credit default swaps tied to CDOs that were bundles of mortgage-backed securities, which in turn were tranched packages of opaque loans from homeowners around the country. The model created an illusion of order where none existed.

A key player in the CDO boom was a Citadel baby, a $5 billion hedge fund called Magnetar Capital run by one of Ken Griffin's star traders, Alec Litowitz. In 2006, *Total Securitization,* an industry news-letter, named Magnetar investor of the year. "Magnetar bought bespoke deals in massive size in 2006, investing in a series of CDOs—each over $1 billion," the newsletter said in March 2007.

Magnetar's presence in the CDO world can be found in Litowitz's seeming fascination with astronomy. A large number of toxic CDOs created at the height of the subprime frenzy had astronomical names, such as Orion, Aquarius, Scorpius, Carina, and Sagittarius. Magnetar was "their lynchpin investor," according to an investigation by the *Wall Street Journal.* But Magnetar, which gained 25 percent in 2007, was also taking the other side of slices of those CDOs, buying positions that would pay off when higher-rated slices turned sour.

Magnetar's trade was ingenious, and possibly diabolical. It would hold the riskiest slices of CDOs, known as the "equity"—those most vulnerable to defaults. But it also was buying protection on less-risky slices higher up the stack of the CDO's structure, essentially betting on a wave of defaults. The roughly 20 percent yield on the equity slices provided the cash to purchase the less-risky slices. If the equity im-ploded, as it did, the losses would mean little if the higher-quality slices also saw significant losses, which they did.

In hindsight, Magnetar turned out to be a facilitator of the CDO boom, because it gobbled up those equity slices when few other in-vestors wanted to buy them. Without a willing buyer of the junk slices, banks would have had a much harder time constructing the increas-ingly dicey CDOs hitting the market in 2006 and 2007. In all, Magne-tar was a key investor in roughly $30 billion of constellation CDOs issued from mid-2006 to mid-2007.

There's clear evidence that Wall Street's gluttonous demand for loans and all the fat fees they spit out was the key factor that allowed, and encouraged, brokers to concoct increasingly risky mortgages with toxic bells and whistles such as adjustable interest rates that shot higher a few years—or in some cases a few months—after the loan was made. Out of twenty-five of the top subprime mortgage lenders, twenty-one were either owned or financed by major Wall Street or European banks, according to a report by the Center for Public Integrity. Without the demand from the investment banks, the bad loans would never have been made.

As the CDO boom took off, so did home prices across the United States. From January 2000 through July 2006, the peak of the housing bubble, the average price of a home in the United States rose 106 percent, according to the S&P/Case-Shiller National Home Price Index. To models such as the Gaussian copula, the message was clear: the housing market was getting safer and safer. In fact, it was getting far more dangerous. In late 2006, the home price index started to move in the opposite direction, falling more than 30 percent three years later.

Some quants, including Brown himself, criticized the models that banks and credit rating agencies were using to price CDOs. He knew the correlations spat out by the Gaussian copula were a fantasy. But as long as the money was rolling in, no one wanted to hear it—not the correlation traders making fat bonuses, and definitely not the Wall Street CEOs making even fatter bonuses.

Like crack cocaine, it was addictive, and ultimately ruinous. While the boom lasted, securitization helped Wall Street become an increasingly powerful force in the U.S. economy. The financial sector's share of total U.S. corporate profits hit 35 percent in 2007, up from 10 percent in the early 1980s, when quants such as Brown started to arrive on the scene. Financial institutions made up one-fourth of the market cap of the S&P 500, far more than any other industry.

Helping to drive the surge in financial profits was that clever tactic favored by funds such as AQR, Global Alpha, Citadel, and Saba: the carry trade. By late 2006, more money than ever had been plowed into the trade, in which investors, usually banks and hedge funds, borrowed low-yielding currencies such as Japanese yen to buy higher-yielding currencies such as the New Zealand dollar or British pound. It was a frictionless digital push-button cash machine based on math and computers—a veritable quant fantasyland of riches.

The carry trade was fueling a worldwide liquidity boom, sparking a frenzy in everything from commodities to real estate—and subprime mortgages. "They can borrow at near zero interest rates in Japan . . . to relend anywhere in the world that offers higher yields, whether Argentine notes or U.S. mortgage securities," marveled the United Kingdom newspaper the *Telegraph*. "It has prolonged asset bubbles everywhere."

"The carry trade has pervaded every single instrument imaginable, credit spreads, bond spreads: everything is poisoned," HSBC currency analyst David Bloom told the paper.

Few, however, seemed to worry about what would happen if the trade suddenly fell apart. Every now and then, a hiccup foreshadowed the incredible turmoil to come. In February 2007, traders started getting nervous about whether stocks in China and other emerging markets had run up too far, too fast. As Chinese stocks started to fall, traders who'd plowed into the market using carry-trade rocket fuel started to panic, buying back their borrowed yen and causing the yen to spike.

At roughly the same time, the Bank of Japan voted to raise a benchmark interest rate, further causing the yen to rise. A dangerous self-reinforcing feedback loop began: As the yen kept rising, others in the trade were forced to buy back yen to stem the bleeding, since the longer they waited, the more money they could lose. That caused further appreciation in the yen. The Chinese market began to collapse, falling 10 percent in a single day and triggering a global stock market rout that saw the Dow Jones Industrial Average drop more than 500 points.

It was only a blip, though, and the global stock-market freight train took off again in the spring. But it was a warning that few heeded. As long as the trade kept churning out seemingly riskless profits, the music kept playing.

Then, in 2007, the music stopped. The carry trade blew up. The securitization machine collapsed as homeowners started defaulting on their loans in record numbers.

As a risk manager, Brown watched it all go down at Morgan Stanley, one of the biggest players in the CDO casino, which he'd joined in 2004 after leaving Citigroup.

■   ■   ■

Brown joined "Mother Morgan," as it was known, under the reign of Phil Purcell, who'd taken over several years earlier in a vicious power struggle with another Morgan kingpin, John Mack. Purcell had joined Morgan as part of a $10 billion merger in 1997 between the elite storied bank and Dean Witter Discover & Co., a brokerage that largely catered to middle-income customers. White-shoe Morganites were aghast. But Purcell, named CEO in the deal, proved a savvy rival to Mack, who'd been at Morgan since 1972, starting off as a bond trader. In 2001, Mack left the bank, realizing he couldn't unseat Purcell; he first worked at Credit Suisse First Boston before joining a hedge fund.

After Mack left, however, earnings at Morgan hadn't kept pace with those of its rivals, especially Goldman Sachs. Between Mack's departure and early 2005, the market value of the company had fallen nearly 40 percent, to $57 billion. While the value of competitors had also taken a hit, Morgan's drop was among the steepest on Wall Street. Underlings fumed at Purcell. They said he was too cautious. That he wasn't a real risk taker. That he didn't have the balls to make real money—like John Mack.

Brown thrived, however. He'd been hired to help the bank's credit system get up to speed with an arcane set of regulations known as the Basel Accord, an international standard designating how much capital banks needed to hold to guard against losses. Morgan's chief financial officer, Steve Crawford, a Purcell protégé, had hired Brown. He wanted him to accomplish the task—which had taken commercial banks such as Citigroup several years—in eighteen months or less.

"If you can do that, you can have any job at the bank you want," Crawford promised.

Brown was impressed by Morgan's higher-ups, who seemed to appreciate the oft-ignored quants and had encouraged a number of programs to gear up the firm's risk management capabilities. But in a palace coup, Purcell and his favorites, including Brown's benefactor, Crawford, were forced out in June 2005 by a band of high-powered shareholders. His replacement: John Mack.

Mack, a native of North Carolina and son of Lebanese immigrants, promised to bring back the old aggressive culture of Morgan. He found the performance of his beloved Morgan under Purcell unacceptable. Over all his years at the bank, he'd overseen the first stat arb operation under Nunzio Tartaglia in the 1980s, and had also helped manage Peter Muller's group. He had a taste for risk. Morgan, he believed, had lost it. Upon his return, Mack marched onto the Morgan trading floor like a triumphant general on the streets of ancient Rome. The financial news channel CNBC broadcast the event live. The bank's traders peeled their eyes away from their ubiquitous Bloomberg terminals to loudly cheer the second coming of "Mack the Knife," a nickname earned by his willingness to slash payrolls and cut costs.

Morgan had been left behind by fast movers such as Goldman Sachs and Lehman Brothers, Mack said, and its profits were suffering. The new paradigm for investment banks on Wall Street was risk taking. The ideal model was Henry Paulson's Goldman Sachs, with its hugely successful Global Alpha Fund and outsized profits in private equity.

Paulson himself had outlined the new paradigm in the bank's 2005 annual report. "Another key trend is the increasing demand from clients for investment banks to combine capital and advice," he wrote. "In other words, investment banks are expected to commit more of their own capital when executing transactions. . . . Investment banks are increasingly using their own balance sheets to extend credit to clients, to assume market risk on their behalf and sometimes co-invest alongside them."

Goldman's strategy reflected the shifts that had been going on at investment banks for more than a decade. Banks were in a life-and-death struggle to keep talented traders from jumping ship and starting hedge funds—as Cliff Asness had done in 1998. They were going head-to-head with the Greenwich gunslingers and losing. No bank saw this more clearly than Goldman. Others, such as Boaz Weinstein's Deutsche Bank and Peter Muller's Morgan Stanley, were close behind. The only way to compete would be to offer their best and brightest massive paychecks, and open the gates wide on risk taking and leverage. In short order, Wall Street's banks morphed into massive, risk-hungry hedge funds, Goldman leading the way and Morgan close behind.

Regulators lent a helping hand. On a spring afternoon in late April 2004, five members of the Securities and Exchange Commission gathered in a basement hearing room to meet a contingent of representatives from Wall Street's big investment banks to talk about risk. The banks had asked for an exemption for their brokerage units from a regulation that limited the amount of debt they could hold on their balance sheets. The rule required banks to hold a large reserve of cash as a cushion against big losses on those holdings. By loosening up these so-called capital reserve requirements, the banks could become more aggressive and deploy the extra cash in other, more lucrative areas—such as mortgage-backed securities and derivatives.

The SEC complied. It also decided to rely on the banks' own quantitative models to determine how risky their investments were. In essence, in a move that would come to haunt not just the agency but the entire economy, the SEC outsourced oversight of the nation's largest financial firms to the banks' quants.

"I'm happy to support it," said Roel Campos, an SEC commissioner. "And I keep my fingers crossed for the future."

Initially, Morgan wasn't eager to join the party. A mantra at Morgan before John Mack returned was that the bank "wouldn't be another Goldman," according to a person who worked at the bank. Morgan would exercise caution during boom times to be prepared for the inevitable bust when the music stopped.

Mack's return changed that. His solution was that the firm should take bigger, bolder gambles, and more of them, just like Goldman.

Looking on, Brown grew concerned as Morgan's risk appetite surged. The new regime seemed to act as if risk management were simply a matter of filling out the forms, dotting the *i*'s and crossing the *t*'s, but not a central part of the firm's ethos, which was to ring the cash register.

Brown also raised his eyebrows at one of Mack's themes. In meeting after meeting in conference rooms near the bank's executive offices, Mack said he wanted to double Morgan's revenues in five years and keep costs flat. *Nice idea*, Brown thought. *But how exactly are we going to do that?*

The answer, he feared, was simply to take more risk.

Among the ideas Mack's staff cooked up for reaching his goal: increase investments in the financial derivatives business, plow headlong into the booming field of residential mortgages, and take more risk with the firm's own capital on its proprietary trading desks such as Peter Muller's PDT.

Morgan quickly found a way to combine all three of those goals in one area: subprime mortgages. In August 2006, Morgan rolled out a plan to purchase subprime mortgage lender Saxon Capital for $706 million. The bank's perpetual-motion subprime machine was cranking up.

Brown could see it all happening before his eyes. His job as a risk manager for the bank's credit division gave him unique visibility into the positions on Morgan's fixed-income balance sheet. For the most part, it seemed under control. But there was one area that troubled him: securitization and all those subprime mortgages.

Subprime mortgages had become the new darlings of Wall Street. The more high-risk borrowers who could be enticed to take high-interest mortgages, the more high-risk/high-reward CDOs—and synthetic CDOs—could be created by and for Wall Street investors. As long as the carousel kept spinning, everyone would get a brass ring.

Brown, however, was growing increasingly concerned about Morgan's securitization merry-go-round. Just as it had at Citigroup, one of his biggest worries centered on the massive "warehouses" of subprime mortgages Morgan used to store the loans. Most banks, inspired by Salomon Brothers, had created off-balance-sheet vehicles that would temporarily house the loans as they were bundled, packaged, sliced, diced, and sold around the world. Such vehicles funded themselves using the commercial paper markets, short-term loans that constantly needed to be rolled over. Any hitch in the chain, Brown realized, could result in disaster. Still, he didn't think it represented a risk that could substantially damage the bank. Profits were through the roof. He also took consolation in Morgan Stanley's sky-high share price. If the bank suffered a huge hit, it could always raise cash on the open market with a share offering. He hadn't factored in the possibility that Morgan's share price would collapse in an industrywide meltdown.

By early 2007, Morgan Stanley was on one of the hottest streaks in its history. The bank was coming off its best quarter ever, and its best year ever, in profitability. One big success, Mack noted in the firm's April 2007 conference call, was the institutional securities group run by Morgan's high-flying co-president, Zoe Cruz. The group managed "a tremendous amount of risk in a very smart and disciplined way," Mack said.

Its leverage ratio, however—the amount of borrowed money it uses to trade every day—was a whopping 32 to 1. In other words, Morgan was borrowing $32 for every $1 it actually owned. Other investment banks, such as Bear Stearns, Lehman Brothers, and Goldman Sachs, also had sky-high leverage ratios.

One of Cruz's desks was a proprietary credit-trading group formed in April 2006. Howard Hubler, a managing director with years of experience trading complex securities at Morgan, was in charge of it. It was a hedge-fund-like trading outfit that would wager Morgan's own money in the credit markets, a bond-trading mirror image of PDT.

At first Hubler's group was a roaring success, netting the firm $1 billion by early 2007. Hubler was among Wall Street's new breed of correlation traders using David Li's Gaussian copula to measure the risks of defaults among various tranches of CDOs. His strategy involved shorting the lower rungs of subprime CDOs (or derivatives tied to them) while holding on to the higher-rated CDO tranches. By the quants' calculations, those high-quality CDO slices had little chance of losing value.

As subsequent events proved, correlation trading turned out to be a hornet's nest of risk. Hubler thought he was shorting subprime. But in a cruel twist, Hubler ended up long subprime. He got the correlations wrong.

Brown, meanwhile, had been growing more and more alarmed about the risks the firm was taking in the subprime mortgage market. The loans were fed into one end of Morgan's securitization machine by subprime lenders such as Countrywide and New Century Financial and pumped out the other end to investors around the world. Indeed, though few realized it at the time, Morgan was one of the biggest players during the peak years of subprime, 2005 and 2006, underwriting $74.3 billion in subprime mortgages, according to *Inside Mortgage*

Finance (Lehman was number one, with $106 billion in mortgages underwritten).

Morgan was also lending aggressively elsewhere, backing massive volumes of credit card debt and corporate loans. Brown realized it was an unsustainable process bound to come crashing down. "It all only made sense if the people we were lending to could pay us back," recalled Brown. "But it became clear that the only way they could pay us back was by borrowing more. There were all kinds of deals we were doing that only made sense if credit is good. We knew at some point that the musical chairs would stop, and we would own a lot of this stuff, and we wouldn't have the capital to pay for it."

Brown believed the quants who worked on the CDO models were often narrowly focused on the Byzantine details of the deals and rarely looked at the big picture—such as the looming bubble in the housing market. "They were showing zero risk," he recalled. It was the same mistake everyone made, from the rating agencies to the banks to the home builders to the buyers of those homes who expected to refinance their mortgages as soon as the payments shot up. On the surface there was little reason to think otherwise. Home prices had never declined on a national level since the Great Depression. Plus, everyone was happy. Some were getting filthy rich.

Despite his concerns, Brown didn't raise serious alarms at Morgan. He realized that the bank was going to take losses, large ones, once the credit cycle turned. But it wouldn't be fatal. Plus there was that sterling stock price.

Indeed, virtually no one on Wall Street had any notion of the massive implosion heading its way. The industry, fueled by greater and greater feats of financial engineering, seemed to be hitting on all cylinders. Huge profits were certainly rolling in at Morgan Stanley. Hubler's bet on subprime, initiated in December 2006, contributed significantly to Morgan's 70 percent increase in net income to a record $2.7 billion in its fiscal first quarter of 2007.

But problems in the complex bet sprouted in the spring of 2007 as homeowners started defaulting in huge numbers in states that had seen massive run-ups in prices, including California, Nevada, and Florida. The higher-rated subprime CDO tranches also started to quiver.

Cracks had first started to appear in February 2007, when HSBC Holdings, the third-largest bank in the world, boosted estimates of expected losses from subprime mortgages by 20 percent to $10.6 billion. Just four years earlier, HSBC had piled into the U.S. subprime market when it snapped up Household International Inc., which became HSBC Finance Corp. Household's chief executive at the time, William Aldinger, had boasted after the deal closed that the company employed 150 quants who were whizzes at modeling credit risk. Other firms, ranging from Seattle banking giant Washington Mutual to mortgage lenders such as New Century and IndyMac Bancorp, were also warning of large losses from subprime mortgage holdings.

Brown started to think of jumping ship, and that's when he began talking to AQR.

It seemed like propitious timing. This new Morgan, this subprime-fueled leverage-happy hot rod, wasn't a place he wanted to be a part of anymore. In late 2006, he'd taken a call from Michael Mendelson, a top researcher at AQR. Brown had recently published a book called *The Poker Face of Wall Street*, a mix of biographical reflections and philosophical ruminations about gambling and finance. The quants at AQR loved the book and thought Brown would be a good fit.

More important, AQR was considering an IPO and needed someone familiar with the nitty-gritty compliance details that went with becoming a public company. Disillusioned with Morgan and disappointed with a less-than-stellar bonus that spoke to the company's lack of appreciation for his talents, Brown was intrigued. He had several interviews with AQR and met Asness, who seemed to speak his language and clearly understood quantitative risk management (though in their first meeting they primarily compared notes on a shared passion: old movies). By June 2007, Brown was making the daily commute on the Metro-North Railroad from New York to AQR's Greenwich headquarters.

By then, serious trouble was erupting in subprime. The same month Brown joined AQR, news emerged that a pair of Bear Stearns hedge funds that had dabbled heavily in subprime CDOs—the mind-numbingly named Bear Stearns High Grade Structured Credit Strategies Master Fund and Bear Stearns High Grade Structured Credit Strategies Enhanced Leverage Master Fund—were suffering unexpected losses. Managed by a Bear Stearns hedge fund manager named Ralph Cioffi, the funds had invested heavily in subprime CDOs.

Broadly, Bear Stearns was optimistic that while the housing market was shaky, it wasn't poised for serious pain. A report issued on February 12, 2007, by Bear researcher Gyan Sinha argued that weakness in certain derivatives tied to subprime mortgages represented a buying opportunity. "While the subprime sector will experience some pain as it removes some of the froth created by excesses," he wrote, "an overreaction to headline risk will create opportunities for nimble investors."

Such thinking was a recipe for a blowup. Cioffi's Enhanced fund first started to lose money the same month Sinha wrote his report. The more sedate High Grade fund, which had posted positive returns for more than three years in a row, slipped 4 percent in March. The leveraged fund was on the cusp of imploding. In April, an internal Bear Stearns report on the CDO market revealed that huge losses could be on the way. Even those sterling AAA bonds could be in trouble. One of the Bear fund's managers, Matthew Tannin, wrote in an internal email that if the report was correct, "the entire subprime market is toast. . . . If AAA bonds are systematically downgraded then there is no way for us to make money—ever."

Spooked investors started to ask for their money back. Goldman Sachs, which acted as a trading partner for the Bear funds, said its own marks on the securities the funds held were much worse than Cioffi's marks. From there, it was only a matter of time. On June 15, Merrill Lynch, a creditor to the funds, seized about $800 million of their assets. The following week, Merrill started to sell off the assets in a series of auctions, triggering shock waves throughout the CDO market. The fire sale forced holders of similar CDOs to mark down the prices of their own securities.

Back at Morgan Stanley, Howie Hubler was beginning to sweat. The collapse of low-rated CDO tranches was exactly what he'd bet on. But weakness in the high-rated tranches, the AAAs, wasn't in his playbook. Hubler was short $2 billion worth of low-quality CDOs. Disastrously, he held $14 billion of high-rated "supersenior" CDOs—the kind that in theory could *never* suffer losses.

In July, panic set in. Credit markets began to quake as investors in subprime CDOs all tried to bail out at once. The commercial paper market, which had been used to fund the off-balance-sheet vehicles that were the engine of Wall Street's securitization machine, started to freeze up. With all the forced selling and few buyers, the losses proved far worse than anyone could have imagined.

The bad news came rapid-fire, one catastrophe after another. First, there were Ralph Cioffi's collapsing hedge funds at Bear Stearns. On July 30, the funds were instructed to file for bankruptcy. Soon after, Cioffi and Tannin were fired. In June 2008, the two were indicted for conspiring to mislead investors about the health of their funds. In late 2009, however, a jury ruled that both traders were innocent of any wrongdoing.

Illustrating the international nature of the crisis, an Australian hedge fund called Basis Capital Fund Management that had invested heavily in subprime securities collapsed. From there, the falling dominoes multiplied. Sowood, the hedge fund Ken Griffin had snapped up, fell by more than 50 percent in a matter of weeks. American Home Mortgage Investment, one of the nation's largest mortgage lenders, saw its stock plunge nearly 90 percent after it warned it was having trouble accessing cash from the capital markets and might have to shut down. A week later, American Home filed for Chapter 11 bankruptcy protection.

In early August, Countrywide Financial, the nation's largest mortgage lender, warned of "unprecedented disruptions" in the credit market. The company said that while it had "adequate funding liquidity . . . the situation is rapidly evolving and the impact on the company is unknown."

All the bad news made it clear that many CDOs were worth far less than most had thought. The losses proved jaw-droppingly large. Later that year, Morgan took a loss of $7.8 billion, much of it from Hubler's desk.

The losses in high-rated tranches of CDOs—the superseniors—

devastated the balance sheets of banks in the United States and overseas and were a primary cause of the credit meltdown that swept the financial system starting that summer. The CDO machine, and the highly leveraged house of cards built upon it, cascaded into a black hole. Trading dried up, and pricing for CDOs became nearly impossible due to the complex, misused models such as the Gaussian copula.

As the mortgage market imploded, quant funds such as AQR, Renaissance, PDT, Saba, and Citadel believed they were immune to the trouble. Renaissance and PDT, for instance, didn't dabble in subprime mortgages or credit default swaps. They mostly traded stocks, options, or futures contracts, which had little to do with subprime. Citadel, AQR, and Saba believed they were the smart guys in the room and had either hedged against losses or were on the right side of the trade and were poised to cash in.

Deutsche Bank, for example, was cashing in on Weinstein's bearish bet, which eventually made about $250 million for the bank. A thirty-six-year-old colleague named Greg Lippmann had also placed a huge bet against subprime that would earn the bank nearly $1 billion. Lippmann's colleagues could be seen wearing gray T-shirts around the trading floor that read "I Shorted Your House" in bold black letters.

Weinstein, poised to cash in on his bets, threw a party at his Southampton digs on July 28, a warm summer Saturday night. A row of tiki torches illuminated the unassuming front of Weinstein's two-story cottage. Guests lounged under a white tent in the expansive backyard as they sipped white wine from self-illuminated cocktail glasses. Weinstein, dressed in a jet-black button-down shirt, trim brown hair slicked back to reveal his pale, broad forehead, was relaxed and confident as he mingled with his well-heeled guests.

Two days later, the credit crisis that had been building for years would explode with full force. With Muller back from his self-imposed exile, Asness poised to make untold millions with AQR's IPO, Weinstein planning to break away from Deutsche to launch his own hedge fund powerhouse, and Griffin ready to vault into the highest pantheon of the investing universe, the stakes were as high as they'd ever been for the small band of quants.

THE AUGUST FACTOR

At the start of August 2007, the nation was treated to the typical mid-summer news lull. The junior senator from Illinois, Barack Obama, gave a speech in Washington declaring that the United States should shift its military focus away from the Iraq war to fight Islamic extremism. More than a dozen people drowned near Minneapolis after the Mississippi River flooded. Starbucks said its quarterly profits rose 9 percent and that it planned to open another 2,600 stores in fiscal 2008. Barbie and Hot Wheels maker Mattel said it was recalling one million toys made in China, including Elmo Tub Sub and Dora the Explorer figures, because they contained lead.

But beneath the calm surface, a cataclysm was building like magma bubbling to the surface of a volcano. All the leverage, all the trillions in derivatives and hedge funds, the carry-trade cocktails and other quant esoterica, were about to explode. Those close enough to the action could almost feel the fabric of the financial system tearing apart.

On the afternoon of August 3, a Friday, a torrential downpour hit New York City like a fist. As the rain fell, CNBC talk-show host and onetime hedge fund jockey Jim Cramer had a televised fit of hysteria in which he accused the Federal Reserve of being asleep at the switch. "These firms are going to go out of business! They're nuts, they're nuts! They know nothing!" he screamed into the stunned face of his colleague, Erin Burnett. Cramer raved about calls he'd been fielding from panicked CEOs. Firms were going to go bankrupt, he predicted. "We have Armageddon in the fixed-income markets!"

Viewers were stunned and unnerved, though most couldn't begin to fathom what he was raving about. One of the CEOs Cramer had been talking to was Angelo Mozilo, CEO of the mortgage giant Countrywide Financial. The Dow Jones Industrial Average gave up 281 points, most of which came after Cramer's outburst. Over a sultry August weekend, Wall Street's legions of traders, bankers, and hedge fund titans tried to relax, hopping in their Bentleys and BMWs, their Maseratis and Mercedeses, and retreating to the soft sands of the Hamptons beaches or jetting away for quick escapes to anywhere but New York City or Greenwich. They knew trouble was coming. It struck Monday with the force of a sledgehammer.

Cliff Asness walked to the glass partition of his corner office and frowned at the rows of cubicles that made up AQR's Global Asset Allocation group.

GAA was replete with hotshot traders and researchers who scoured the globe in search of quantitative riches in everything from commodity futures to currency derivatives. On the other side of the building, separated by a wall that ran down the middle of the office, AQR's Global Stock Selection team labored away. A job at GSS could be rough. It involved the grunt work of combing through reams of data about stock returns and the grueling task of hoping to find some pattern that the thousands of other Fama-bred quants hadn't found yet.

That Monday afternoon, August 6, 2007, something was going

wrong at GSS. The stocks its models picked to buy and sell were moving in strange directions—directions that meant huge losses to AQR.

Asness snapped shut the blinds on the glass partition and returned to his desk. He reached out and clicked his mouse, bringing his computer screen to life. There it was in bright red digits. The P&L for AQR's Absolute Return Fund. Sinking like a rock.

Throughout AQR, the hedge fund's legions of quants also were mesmerized by the sinking numbers. It was like watching a train wreck in slow motion. Work had ground to a halt that morning as everyone tried to assess the situation. Many of the fund's employees walked about the office in a confused daze, turning to one another in hope of answers.

"You know what's going on?"

The answer was always the same: "No. You?"

Rumors of corporate collapses were making the rounds. Banks and hedge funds were reeling from their exposure to toxic subprime mortgages. Countrywide Financial, some said, was imploding and looking in desperation for a white knight, such as Warren Buffett's Berkshire Hathaway or Bank of America. But no one wanted anything to do with the distressed mortgage lender.

Inside his office, Asness again stared grimly at his computer screen. Red numbers washed across it. He didn't know what to do. His greatest fear was that there was nothing he could do.

Outside, people noticed the closed blinds on the boss's office. It was unusual and a bit spooky. Asness always had an open-door policy, even if very few people used it. Employees presumed Asness couldn't stand the idea of his employees peeking in through the window to see how the big guy was taking it.

The registration statements for AQR's initial public offering were ready and waiting to be shipped off to the SEC. Indeed, Asness was set to make the big announcement about his plans later that month, making headlines in all the important papers. But now, the IPO and all the money it would have spun off were getting more distant by the second, a distance measured by the tick-by-tick decline of Absolute Return, as well as a number of other funds at AQR that were getting pounded by the mysterious downturn.

Several blocks away from AQR's office, Michael Mendelson, head of global trading, was in line at the local Greenwich Subway sandwich shop. He glanced at his BlackBerry, which came equipped with a real-time digital readout of all of AQR's funds. His jaw dropped. Something bad was happening. Something horrible.

A longtime Goldman Sachs veteran, mastermind of the bank's elite high-frequency trading outfit, Mendelson was one of the brightest thinkers at AQR, and one of the first people Asness would call when he needed answers about a trade going awry. He knew instantly that something needed to be done fast to stem the bleeding.

He raced back to AQR's office and huddled with several of AQR's top traders and researchers, including Jacques Friedman, Ronen Israel, and Lars Neilson. After determining that a huge deleveraging was taking place, directly impacting AQR's funds, they marched to Asness's office.

"It's bad, Cliff," Mendelson said, stepping into the room. Friedman, Israel, and Neilson followed close behind. "This has the feel of a liquidation."

"Who is it?" Asness said.

"We're not sure. Maybe Global Alpha."

"Oh God, no."

Since Asness had left Goldman in 1998, Global Alpha had been run by Mark Carhart and Ray Iwanowski, alums, like Asness, of the University of Chicago's finance program, and Fama protégés. Under their guidance, Global Alpha had expanded its reputation as one of the smartest investing outfits on Wall Street. It never had a losing year through 2005, when it posted an eye-popping return of 40 percent.

But Global Alpha had been slipping, losing money in 2006 and the first half of 2007. The worry: to reverse its fortunes, it was juicing up its leverage. And the more leverage, the more risk. Many feared that Global Alpha and its sister fund, Global Equity Opportunity—a stock-focused fund—were doubling down on bad trades with more and more borrowed money.

"They're one of the few funds big enough to leave such a big footprint." Mendelson hunched his shoulders in frustration.

"Have you talked to anyone over there?"

"No," Mendelson said. "I was going to ask you."

"I'll give it a shot."

There had been no small amount of bad blood between Asness and his old colleagues at Goldman, who were embittered after being left behind when Asness and the others bolted. Asness felt bad about it all, but he hadn't wanted to alienate the head honchos at Goldman by leading a mass exodus.

The tensions had cooled over the years. Global Alpha had developed into an elite trading outfit, with $12 billion in assets and a solid record—except for a severe misstep in 2006—that could go head-to-head with the best hedge funds in the business, including AQR.

Asness put in a few calls to Goldman, but no one was picking up the phone. That made him more worried than ever.

Boaz Weinstein was relaxed that Monday after the weekend bash at his house in the Southhamptons. But soon after lunch, he started to fret. Something was going wrong with Saba's quant equities desk, which he'd added to his operation to complement his bond-trading group. The news trickled in around two o'clock when Alan Benson, the trader who ran the desk, sent his second daily email with his desk's P&L.

Benson's first email, sent at 10:00 A.M., showed early signs of losses. But Weinstein had shrugged it off. Benson's desk, which managed $2 billion worth of positions in stocks and exchange-traded funds, could be highly volatile. Losses in the morning could easily turn into gains by the afternoon.

The 2:00 P.M. update showed the losses hadn't turned to gains. They'd gotten much worse. Benson was down tens of millions. Weinstein stood and walked one floor down to Saba's trading operation on the second floor. Benson looked tense and was sweating.

"What's up, Alan?" Weinstein said, outwardly calm as always. But there was tension in his voice caused by the startling sight of millions of dollars going up in smoke, just like the GM trade back in 2005.

"It's weird," Benson said. "Stocks that we're betting against are going up, a lot. Looks like short covering on a really big scale, across a lot of industries."

In a short sale, an investor borrows a stock and sells it, hoping to purchase it back at a lower price sometime in the future. Say IBM is trading at $100 a share and you expect it to decline to $90. You borrow a hundred shares from another investor through a prime broker and sell them to yet another investor for $10,000. If your crystal ball was correct and IBM does in fact fall to $90, you buy the stock back for $9,000, return the shares to the broker, and pocket the $1,000.

But what if, for instance, IBM starts to shoot higher? You're on the hook for those shares, and every dollar it goes up is a $100 loss. To minimize your losses, you buy the stock back. That can have the effect of pushing the stock even higher. If hundreds or thousands of short sellers are doing this at once, it turns into what's known as a short squeeze. That Monday, August 6, was beginning to look like possibly the biggest short squeeze in history.

"Has the feel of a big gorilla getting out of a lot of positions, fast," Benson added.

"Anything we can do about it?"

"Keep an eye on it. I doubt this will last much longer. The rate this guy is unwinding his trades, it can't go on for long. If it does . . ."

"What?"

"We'll have to start unwinding, too."

At PDT that same Monday, Peter Muller was absent, visiting a friend just outside Boston. Mike Reed and Amy Wong manned the helm, PDT veterans from the old days when the group was nothing more than a thought experiment, its traders a small band of young math whizzes tinkering with computers like brainy teenagers in a cluttered garage.

PDT was now a global powerhouse, with offices in London and Tokyo and about $6 billion in assets (the amount could change daily depending on how much money Morgan funneled its way). It was a well-oiled machine that did little but print money, day after day. That week, however, PDT wouldn't print money—it would destroy it like an industrial shredder.

The unusual behavior of stocks that PDT tracked had begun to slip sometime in mid-July and had gotten worse in the first days of August. The previous Friday, five of the biggest gainers on the Nasdaq were stocks that PDT had sold short, expecting them to decline, and five of the biggest losers were stocks PDT had bought, expecting them to rise. It was Bizarro World for quants. Up was down, down was up. The models were operating in reverse. The Truth wasn't the Truth anymore. It was the anti-Truth.

The losses were accelerating Monday and were especially bad in the roughly $5 billion quant fundamental book—the one PDT had increased in size after Muller returned in late 2006.

Wong and Reed knew that if the losses got much worse, they would need to start liquidating positions in the fundamental book to bring down PDT's leverage. Already the week before, the group had started to ease back on Midas's engine as the market's haphazard volatility picked up steam.

Midas was one thing. It was a high-frequency book that bought and sold securities at a rapid pace all the time. The fundamental book was different. The securities it held, often small-cap stocks that didn't trade very often, could be hard to get rid of, especially if a number of other traders who owned them were trying to dump them at the same time. The positions would need to be combed through and unwound piece by piece, block by block of unwanted stock. It would be hard, it would be time-consuming, and it would be very costly.

The market moves PDT and other quant funds started to see early that week defied logic. The fine-tuned models, the bell curves and random walks, the calibrated correlations—all the math and science that had propelled the quants to the pinnacle of Wall Street—couldn't capture what was happening. It was utter chaos driven by pure human fear, the kind that can't be captured in a computer model or complex algorithm. The wild, fat-tailed moves discovered by Benoit Mandelbrot in the 1950s seemed to be happening on an hourly basis. Nothing like it had ever been seen before. *This wasn't supposed to happen!*

The quants did their best to contain the damage, but they were like firefighters trying to douse a raging inferno with gasoline—the more they tried to fight the flames by selling, the worse the selling became. The downward-driving force of the deleveraging market seemed unstoppable.

Wong and Reed kept Muller posted on the situation through emails and phone calls. It would be Muller's decision whether to sell into the falling market to deleverage the fund, and by how much. Volatility in the market was surging, confusing PDT's risk models. Now Muller needed to decide whether to deleverage the fundamental book, which was taking the brunt of the damage. If the losses in that book continued much longer, PDT had little choice but to start selling. It would mean cutting off branches in the hope of saving the tree.

Quant funds everywhere were scrambling to figure out what was going on. Ken Griffin, on vacation in France, kept in touch with the traders at Citadel's Chicago headquarters. Renaissance was also taking big hits, as were D. E. Shaw, Barclays Global Investors in San Francisco, J. P. Morgan's quant powerhouse Highbridge Capital Management, and nearly every other quantitative fund in the world, including far-flung operations in London, Paris, and Tokyo.

Tuesday, the downturn accelerated. AQR booked rooms at the nearby Delamar on Greenwich Harbor, a luxury hotel, so they could be available around the clock for stressed-out sleep-deprived quants. Griffin hopped in his private plane and flew back to Chicago for crisis management, and to tie up loose ends on the Sowood deal.

Authorities had little idea about the massive losses taking place across Wall Street. That Tuesday afternoon, the Federal Reserve said it had decided to leave short-term interest rates alone at 5.25 percent. "Financial markets have been volatile in recent weeks, credit conditions have become tighter for some households and businesses, and the housing correction is ongoing," the Fed said in its policy statement. "Nevertheless, the economy seems likely to continue to expand at a moderate pace over coming quarters, supported by solid growth in employment and incomes and a robust global economy."

The crisis was mounting, and Washington's central bankers were completely out of touch. The losses on Monday and Tuesday were among the worst ever seen by quant hedge funds, with billions of dollars evaporating into thin air. Wednesday they got far worse.

At the headquarters of Goldman Sachs Asset Management in downtown New York, everyone was on red alert. One of the largest hedge fund managers in the world, with $30 billion in assets, GSAM was getting hit on all sides. It was seeing big losses in value, growth, small-cap stocks, mid-caps, currencies, commodities, *everything*. Global Alpha, the Global Equity Opportunity fund—every strategy was getting crushed. And like every other quant fund, its captains, Carhart and Iwanowski, had no idea why.

GSAM's risk models, highly sophisticated measures of volatility, had been spiking for all of July. It was a strange sight, because volatility had been declining for years. And the way GSAM's risk models worked, the decline in volatility meant that it had needed to take more risk, use more leverage, to make the same amount of money. Other quant funds had followed a similar course. Now volatility wasn't behaving anymore. Volatility was actually . . . *volatile*.

Another disturbing trend that Goldman's quants noticed was a rapid unwinding of the worldwide carry trade. Funds such as Global Alpha, AQR, Citadel, and others had been borrowing low-yielding yen on the cheap and investing it in higher-yielding assets, generating huge profits. The trade had been highly successful for years, helping fuel all kinds of speculative bets, but it depended on one trend remaining in place: cheap yen.

In early August 2007, the yen started to surge. Funds that had borrowed the yen, expecting to repay the loan at a later date, were scrambling to repay as the yen leapt in value against other currencies. That triggered a self-reinforcing feedback loop: As the yen kept rising, more funds were needed to repay the loans, pushing the yen up even more.

At GSAM, the sudden unwind meant a potential catastrophe. Many of its positions—bonds, currencies, even stocks—were based on the yen carry trade.

The collapse of the carry trade and the spike in volatility were potentially disastrous. The first major dislocation in the market, one not seen in years, had happened the previous Friday, August 3. The dislocation turned into an earthquake on Monday. By Tuesday, the situation was critical, and GSAM had to start selling hard.

Walking downtown on Broadway to Morgan Stanley's office through thick, sweaty crowds, Peter Muller was growing impatient. It was

Wednesday, August 8, and traffic in midtown Manhattan was jammed up like he'd never seen before. People swarmed the sidewalks, not just the usual tourists but businessmen in suits, nearly everyone jabbering frantically on their cell phones.

He'd just left his spacious apartment in the Time-Warner Center at Columbus Circle, located at the southwest corner of Central Park and fourteen blocks north of Morgan's headquarters. There was no time to waste. He checked his watch for the twentieth time. The market would be opening soon. And he was worried—worried the meltdown would continue. He checked his BlackBerry for news. Japan had gotten killed again. Christ. Muller didn't know why the meltdown had started. Worse, he didn't know when it would stop. It had to stop. If it didn't . . .

Muller elbowed through the buzzing throng in front of the old Ed Sullivan Theater in frustration. Even nature seemed to be conspiring against him. Earlier that morning, a tornado had struck the city, hitting land shortly before the morning commute in New York City began in earnest. Whipped up by winds as high as 135 miles per hour, the freak twister first hit Staten Island, then leapfrogged across the Narrows of New York Bay to Brooklyn, knocking down trees, ripping up rooftops, and damaging cars and buildings in Sunset Park and Bay Ridge. It was the first tornado to strike Brooklyn in more than fifty years, and only the sixth to strike New York City since 1950.

Major roadways flooded and subway tunnels were drenched, shutting down services across the city and freezing traffic. The chaos that ensued as stranded commuters took to the streets brought to more than a few minds the horrors of six years earlier, when terrorists struck the World Trade Center's Twin Towers on September 11.

As quickly as the storm had rushed in, it cleared away, swirling into the Atlantic. A boiling August sun emerged, baking the city in a steamy, humid soup. Wall Street's army of traders struggled to make it to the office before the start of trading at 9:30 A.M. Many were on edge, and that had nothing to do with the weather. The storm that was building in the world's financial markets was bursting forth in ways no one could have ever imagined. The first bands of the tempest had already hit, and Muller was in the center of it.

It had been a long, wild ride for Muller. PDT was an industrial electronic humming machine that spit out endless streams of money. But things had changed. It was so much more corporate now, regimented, controlled. Nothing like the group's glory days, a decade earlier, when the money seemed to fall from the sky like manna, surprising everyone.

There was that afternoon in—what was it, 1996, 1997?—when a band of PDTers were lounging on a beach in Grenada, the spice island. It was one of many trips to exotic ports around the world that the adventurous group of math wizards would take in those heyday years. As the tropical sunlight faded, and the warm breeze rolled off the blue waters of the Caribbean Sea, Muller decided to check in on the team back in New York. He pulled out his cell phone and hit the speed dial for PDT's trading desk, calling one of the few traders who'd stayed behind to man PDT's computers.

"What's the P&L?" he'd asked, using trader shorthand for profit and loss. Muller was in the habit of hearing a lot about the "P" side of the ledger. "L," not so much.

"Let's see," said a calm voice on the other end of the line. "Seventeen." As in $17 million.

"Beautiful," Muller said, and he meant it. Everything was beautiful. He smiled and flicked a lock of sandy-blond hair from his eyes, toasting another day's bonanza to the group of quants gathered around him in the golden Grenada sunset. Not bad for another day on the beach.

Muller pushed urgently toward Morgan Stanley's headquarters through the chaotic tangle of Times Square. He clenched his jaw and looked up. The storm was gone, the sun shining. The investment bank's impressive profile loomed against the slate-blue sky.

There it was: 1585 Broadway, world headquarters of Morgan Stanley. The skyscraper towered over Duffy Square in the heart of midtown Manhattan. Completed at the start of the go-go nineties, 1585 Broadway contained nearly 900,000 square feet of office space on forty-two floors. Several stories above a row of shops, three rows of streaming data fly across the east-facing side of the high tower. Stock prices, currencies, breaking news from around the world. The hulking skyscraper looked somewhat like a heavyset floor trader itching to bully the neon-glutted towers of Times Square cowering at its concrete feet.

At the sight of the building, Muller still felt the old thrill. He knew, more than most who worked there, the trading power housed inside the intimidating structure. Through miles of endlessly ramifying fiber-optic cables and an array of satellite dishes mushroomed about the building, the glass-windowed tower was plugged into financial markets around the globe, mainlined into the Money Grid.

Traders deep in the bowels of 1585 Broadway bought and sold options on Japanese corporate bonds, derivatives linked to European real estate and West Texas crude, billions in currencies from Canada to Zimbabwe to Peru, as well as the odd slice of subprime mortgage and mortgage derivatives. And, of course, stocks. Billions of dollars' worth of stocks.

Muller stepped briskly into Morgan's spacious air-conditioned lobby, escaping the mayhem outside, swiped his ID badge at the electric turnstile, and jumped onto an elevator that would take him to PDT's high-tech trading hub.

The elevator stopped on the sixth floor, and Muller flew into the lobby, sweeping his security pass before the locked doors of PDT's office. He rushed past the *Alphaville* poster that had hung in PDT's office for more than a decade and stepped into his private office. He flicked on his rank of computers and Bloomberg terminals with access to data on nearly every tradable security in the world. After a quick check of the market action, he checked PDT's P&L.

It was bad.

This was the most brutal market Muller had ever seen. Quant funds everywhere were getting crushed like bugs beneath a bulldozer. Muller had been swapping ideas about what was happening with other managers, ringing up Asness and grilling him about what was going on at AQR, trying to find out if anyone knew what was happening at Goldman Sachs. Everyone had theories. No one knew the answer. They all worried that it would be fatal if the unwind lasted much longer.

Rumors of a disaster were rife. The U.S. housing market was

melting down, causing huge losses at banks such as Bear Stearns and UBS and hedge funds around the world. Stock markets were in turmoil. Panic was spreading. The subprime catastrophe was mutating through the Money Grid like some strange electronic virus. The entire system started to seize up as the delicate, finely wrought creations of the quants spun out of control.

As the losses piled up, the root of the meltdown remained a mystery. Oddly enough, as much as the furor seized the world of finance, it went largely overlooked in the larger world beyond. Indeed, investors on Main Street had little idea that a historic blowup was occurring on Wall Street. Aaron Brown at AQR had to laugh watching commentators on CNBC discuss in bewilderment the strange moves stocks were making, with absolutely no idea about what was behind the volatility. Truth was, Brown realized, the quants themselves were still trying to figure it out.

Brown had been spending all his time trying to get up to speed on AQR's systems to help manage the fund's risk. He'd decided to stay in the office that Tuesday night and sleep on a small couch he kept near his desk. He wasn't the only one. Near midnight, he stepped out of his office, eyes bloodshot from peering at numbers on a computer screen for the past twenty hours. The office was buzzing with activity, dozens of haggard quants chugging coffee, iPods plugged into their ears as they punched frantically on keyboards, unwinding the fund's positions in markets around the globe. It was a strange sight. The office was nearly as busy as it was during the day, but it was pitch black outside.

And still, the outside world had no idea that a meltdown of such size was taking place. One of the first to spread word to the masses was an obscure quantitative researcher who worked at Lehman Brothers.

Matthew Rothman was still groggy from his red-eye flight into San Francisco the night before as he walked into the office of a potential client on Tuesday morning, August 7. The chief quantitative strategist for Lehman Brothers was on a West Coast road trip, pitching the models he'd spent the last year sweating over during late nights at the office and tedious weekends. This was payoff time.

As Rothman, a heavyset, middle-aged man with a moon face and curly brown hair, sat in the client's waiting room with his laptop and luggage—he hadn't had time to swing by the Four Seasons, where he was staying—he wondered about the odd activity in the market he'd seen the previous day. His quantitative models had been hit hard, and he didn't know why.

He bolted up from his chair, startled. The trader he was waiting to see rushed toward him, his face frantic. "Oh my God, Matthew," he said, pulling him toward his office. "Have you seen what's going on?"

He showed Rothman his portfolio. It was down sharply. Something terrible was happening, something never seen before. Rothman didn't have any answers.

The pitch was out the window. No one wanted to hear about his whiz-bang models. Rothman visited several more quant funds that day. It was a bloodbath.

And it made no sense. A true believer in market efficiency who'd studied under Eugene Fama at Chicago, Rothman expected the market to behave according to the strict quantitative patterns he lived to track. But the market was acting in a way that defied any pattern Rothman—or any other quant—had ever seen. Everything was losing money. Every strategy was falling apart. It was unfathomable, if not outright insane.

That evening, Rothman dined out with his friend Asriel Levin at a sushi restaurant in downtown San Francisco. Levin had once run the flagship quant fund 32 Capital inside Barclays Global Investors in San Francisco, the largest money manager in the world. In late 2006, he'd started up his own hedge fund, Menta Capital. "Uzi," as people called Levin, was one of the smartest quants Rothman knew. He felt lucky to be able to pick Levin's brain during such a critical time. Over sushi and wine, the two started hashing out their ideas about what had triggered the meltdown. By the time they were through—they closed the restaurant—they had a working hypothesis that would prove prescient.

A single, very large money manager had taken a serious hit from subprime assets, they theorized. That, in turn, would have triggered a margin call from its prime broker.

Margin call: two of the most frightening words in finance. Investors often borrow money from a prime broker to buy an asset, say a boatload of subprime mortgages. They do this through margin accounts. When the value of the asset declines, the prime broker calls up the investor and asks for additional cash in the margin account. If the investor doesn't have the cash, he needs to sell something to raise it, some liquid holding that he can get rid of quickly.

The most liquid assets tend to be stocks. Rothman and Levin figured the money manager in trouble was a multistrategy hedge fund, one that dabbled in every kind of investing strategy known to man, from futures to currencies to subprime mortgages.

The trigger, they realized, had to be the collapse in subprime. When Ralph Cioffi's Bear Stearns hedge funds started to melt down, the value of all subprime CDOs started to decline at once. Ratings agencies such as Moody's and Standard & Poor's were also downgrading large swaths of CDOs, pushing their value down even further and prompting more forced selling. Margin calls on funds with significant subprime holdings were rolling across Wall Street.

Funds that primarily owned mortgages were stranded, since the only way they could raise cash would be to dump the very assets that were plunging in value. Multistrat funds, however, had more options. At least one of these funds—there may have been several—had a large, highly liquid equity quant book, Rothman and Levin reasoned. The fund manager must have looked around for assets he could dump with the utmost speed to raise cash for the margin call, and quickly fingered the quant equity book.

The effects of that sell-off would have started to ripple through other funds with similar positions. The short positions were suddenly going up, and the longs were going down.

In other words, a large hedge fund, possibly several large hedge funds, was imploding under the weight of toxic subprime assets, taking down the others in the process, like a massive avalanche started by a single loose boulder. All the leverage that had piled up for years as quant managers crowded into trades that increasingly yielded lower and lower returns—requiring more and more leverage—was coming home to roost.

It was impossible to know how much money was in these trades, but by any estimate the figure was massive. Since 2003, assets in market-neutral hedge funds that made long and short bets, such as AQR's, had nearly tripled to about $225 billion by August 2007, according to the widely followed Lipper TASS Database of hedge funds. At the same time, profits in the strategies were dwindling as more and more funds divvied them up. Several quant funds were slouching toward gigantism, plowing cash into the sector. Renaissance's RIEF fund had added $12 billion in just the past year, bringing its assets under management to $26 billion. AQR had bulged to $40 billion. Other Wall Street operators were jumping on the quant bandwagon as well. Among the most popular trading strategies at the time were so-called 130/30 funds, which used the smoke and mirrors of leverage and quant wizardry to amp up their long positions to 130 percent of capital under management, while shorting stocks equal to another 30 percent of capital (RIEF was a 170/70 fund, indicating the use of even more leverage). By the summer of 2007, about $100 billion had been put in such strategies, many of which were based on quantitative metrics such as Fama's value and growth factors.

The carnage also revealed a dangerous lack of transparency in the market. No one—not Rothman, not Muller, not Asness—knew which fund was behind the meltdown. Nervous managers traded rumors over the phone and through emails in a frantic hunt for patient zero, the sickly hedge fund that had triggered the contagion in the first place. Many were fingering Goldman Sachs's Global Alpha. Others said it was Caxton Associates, a large New York hedge fund that had been suffering losses in July. More important, Caxton had a large quant equity portfolio called ART run by Aaron Sosnick.

Behind it all was leverage. Quant funds across Wall Street in the years leading up to 2007 had amped up their leverage, reaching for yield. Returns had dwindled in nearly all of their strategies as more and more money poured into the group. The fleeting inefficiencies that are the very air quants breathe—those golden opportunities that Fama's piranhas gobble up—had turned microscopically thin, as Fama and French's disciples spread the word about growth and value stocks and stat arb became a commoditized trade copied by guys with turbo-charged Macs in their garages.

The only way to squeeze more cash from the wafer-thin spreads was to leverage up—precisely what had happened in the 1990s to Long-Term Capital Management. By 1998, nearly every bond arbitrage desk and fixed-income hedge fund on Wall Street had copied LTCM's trades. The catastrophic results for quant funds a decade later were remarkably similar.

Indeed, the situation was the same across the entire financial system. Banks, hedge funds, consumers, and even countries had been leveraging up and doubling down for years. In August 2007, the global margin call began. Everyone was forced to sell until it became a devastating downward spiral.

Near midnight, Rothman, luggage still in tow, hopped in a cab and told the driver to take him to the Four Seasons. As he leaned back in the cab, exhausted, he pondered his next move. He was scheduled to fly to Los Angeles the next day to visit more investors. But what was the point? The models were toast. *Forget it*, he thought, deciding to cancel the L.A. trip. *I need to hammer out a call*.

As the losses piled up at AQR, Asness continued to put in frantic calls to Goldman Sachs Asset Management. But GSAM was in radio silence. At the height of the convulsions, Robert Jones, who ran Goldman's quantitative equities team, emailed Asness with a terse three-word note: "It's not me."

Asness wasn't so sure. He knew GSAM about as well as anybody outside of Goldman, having launched Global Alpha more than a decade before. And he knew Global Alpha had cranked up the leverage. He looked with horror at how big his creation had become, a lumbering monster of leverage. Asness knew that if GSAM imploded, it would be a disaster.

AQR traders were running low on fuel, high on adrenaline. It was something like the energy of a firefight, full of both fear and grim exhilaration, as if history was in the making.

Asness decided to give a pep talk to his bedraggled quants. Rumors that AQR was on the verge of melting down were spreading.

There was no central meeting area in the office, so employees huddled in a number of conference rooms and Asness addressed the troops over speakerphones from his office. Some of the traders thought the setup was strange. Why didn't Cliff address them directly, face-to-face? Instead, he was just a voice, like the Wizard of Oz behind his curtain. Beside him were partners such as John Liew and David Kabiller, as well as Aaron Brown.

He acknowledged that the fund was seeing unprecedented losses, but told his crew not to panic. "We're not in a crisis," he said. "We have enough money to keep the trades on. We can handle the situation."

He ended the call on an optimistic note, referring back to the dot-com bubble that had nearly crushed AQR. "The partners have been in this situation before. The system works. This is something that we'll get through, although I understand that it's difficult."

But there was one cruel fact Asness couldn't escape: AQR's IPO would have to be put on hold, he said. "And it may never come back."

At Saba, Alan Benson, the trader in charge of its quant fundamental book, was verging on collapse. He was putting in eighteen-hour days, trading in a frenzy. He and only a few other traders ran billions worth of assets, and it was impossible to keep track of it all. The fund had lost about $50 million or $60 million in two days alone, and Weinstein wasn't happy. He kept pressing Benson to sell and cut his losses as fast as possible.

The losses were brutal throughout quantdom. Tykhe Capital, a New York quant fund named after the Greek goddess of good luck, was in tatters, down more than 20 percent. In East Setauket, Renaissance's Medallion fund was getting pummeled, as was the Renaissance Institutional Equity Fund, the massive quant fundamental fund Jim Simons had once said could handle $100 billion in assets.

The losses in Medallion, however, were the most perplexing. Simons had never seen anything like it. Medallion's superfast trading strategy, which acts as a liquidity provider for the rest of the market, was buying up the assets from quant funds that were frantically trying to exit positions. Medallion's models predicted that the positions would move back into equilibrium. But the snapback didn't happen. The positions kept declining. There was no equilibrium. Medallion kept buying, until its portfolio was a near mirror image of the funds that were in a massive deleveraging. It was a recipe for disaster.

The losses were piling up so quickly, it was impossible to keep track of them. The Money Grid was on the precipice of disaster and no one knew when it would stop.

At PDT, Muller kept ringing up managers, trying to gauge who was selling and who wasn't. But few were talking. In ways, Muller thought, it was like poker. No one knew who was holding what. Some might be bluffing, putting on a brave face while massively dumping positions. Some might be holding out, hoping to ride through the storm. And the decision facing Muller was the same one he confronted all the time at the poker table, but on a much larger order of magnitude: whether to throw in more chips and hope for the best or to fold his hand and walk away.

Other managers were facing the same problem. "We were all freaking out," recalled AQR cofounder John Liew. "Quant managers tend to be kind of secretive; they don't reach out to each other. It was a little bit of a poker game. When you think about the universe of large quant managers, it's not that big. We all know each other. We were calling each other and saying, 'Are you selling?' 'Are you?'"

As conditions spun out of control, Muller was updating Morgan's top brass, including Zoe Cruz and John Mack. He wanted to know how much damage was acceptable. But his chiefs wouldn't give him a number. They didn't understand all of the nuts and bolts of how PDT worked. Muller had kept its positions and strategy so secret over the years that few people in the firm had any inkling about how PDT made money. Cruz and Mack knew it was profitable almost all the time. That was all that mattered.

That meant it was Muller's call. By Wednesday morning, August 8, he'd already decided. The previous day, he'd caught a flight out of Boston as it became clear that something serious had happened. At La Guardia Airport, he was picked up by his chauffeur, a retired police officer. Riding into the city in the backseat of his BMW 750Li, he placed a phone call to the office to gauge the damage.

The losses had been severe, twice as bad as on Monday. He knew something had to be done fast. There wasn't much time. It was already late in the day. A decision had to be made.

After stopping off at his Time-Warner apartment, he walked down to the office. It was about 7 P.M. He'd come into Morgan's office to meet Amy Wong, the trader in charge of the quant fundamental portfolio getting clobbered. They huddled in a conference room just off PDT's small trading floor, along with several other top PDT staffers. Wong tallied up the damage. The quant fundamental book had suffered a loss of about $100 million.

"What should we do?" Wong asked.

Muller shrugged and gave the order: sell.

By Wednesday morning, PDT was executing Muller's command, dumping positions aggressively. And it kept getting killed. Every other quant fund was selling in a panicked rush for the exits.

That Wednesday, what had started as a series of bizarre, unexplainable glitches in quant models turned into a catastrophic meltdown the likes of which had never been seen before in the history of financial markets. Nearly every single quantitative strategy, thought to be the most sophisticated investing ideas in the world, was shredded to pieces, leading to billions in losses. It was deleveraging gone supernova.

Oddly, the Bizarro World of quant trading largely masked the losses to the outside world at first. Since the stocks they'd shorted were rising rapidly, leading to the appearance of gains on the broader market, that balanced out the diving stocks the quants had expected to rise. Monday, the Dow industrials actually gained 287 points. It gained 36 more points Tuesday, and another 154 points Wednesday. Everyday investors had no insight into the carnage taking place beneath the surface, the billions in hedge fund money evaporating.

Of course, there was plenty of evidence that something was seriously amiss. Heavily shorted stocks were zooming higher for no logical reason. Vonage Holdings, a telecom stock that had dropped 85 percent in the previous year, shot up 10 percent in a single day on zero news. Online retailer Overstock.com; Taser International, maker of stun guns; the home building giant Beazer Homes USA; and Krispy Kreme Doughnuts—all favorites among short sellers—rose sharply even as the rest of the market tanked. From a fundamentals perspective, it made no sense. In an economic downturn, risky stocks such as Taser and Krispy Kreme would surely suffer. Beazer was obviously on the ropes due to the housing downturn. But a vicious marketwide short squeeze was causing the stocks to surge.

The huge gains in those shorted stocks created an optical illusion: the market seemed to be rising, even as its pillars were crumbling beneath it. Asness's beloved value stocks were spiraling lower. Stocks with low price-to-book ratios such as Walt Disney and Alcoa were getting hammered.

"A massive unwind is occurring," Tim Krochuk, managing director of Boston investment manager GRT Capital Partners, told the *Wall Street Journal*. Pissed-off plain-vanilla investors vented their rage on the quants as they saw their portfolios unravel. "You couldn't get a date in high school and now you're ruining my month," was one sneer Muller heard.

Amid the carnage, Mike Reed had an idea: stop selling for an hour to see if PDT itself was driving the action—a clear indication of how chaotic the market had become. No one knew who was causing what. But the desperate move didn't work. PDT continued to get crushed. There was a deceptive lull soon after lunchtime. But as the closing bell neared in the afternoon, the carnage resumed. Mom-and-pop investors watching the market make wild swings wondered what was going on. They had no way of knowing about the massive computer power and decades of quant strategies that were behind the chaos making a hash of their 401(k)s and mutual funds.

Reed's intuition that PDT's decision to sell was hurting the market wasn't completely wrongheaded. A source of the extreme damage Wednesday and the following day was the absence of high-frequency stat arb traders that act as liquidity providers for the market. Among the largest such funds were Renaissance's Medallion fund and D. E. Shaw. PDT had already significantly deleveraged its stat arb fund, Midas, the week before. Other stat arb funds were now following suit. As investors tried to unload their positions, the high-frequency funds weren't there to buy them—they were selling, too. The result was a black hole of no liquidity whatsoever. Prices collapsed.

By the end of the day on Wednesday, PDT had lost nearly $300 million—*just that day*. PDT was going up in smoke. Other funds were seeing even bigger losses. Goldman's Global Alpha was down nearly 16 percent for the month, a loss of about $1.5 billion. AQR had lost about $500 million that Wednesday alone, its biggest one-day loss ever. It was the fastest money meltdown Asness had ever seen. He was well aware that if it continued for much longer, AQR would be roadkill.

And there was nothing he could do to stop it. Except keep liquidating, liquidating, liquidating.

Inside GSAM, the grim realization was taking hold that a catastrophic meltdown would occur if all the furious liquidations weren't somehow stopped. Goldman's elite traders were running on fumes, staying at the office fifteen or twenty hours—some not leaving at all.

Carhart and Iwanowski, like every other quant manager, were feverishly trying to delever their funds, trying to get their volatility-based risk models back into alignment. But there was a problem: every time GSAM sold off positions, volatility spiked again—meaning it had to keep selling. Higher volatility readings automatically directed the fund to dump more positions and raise cash.

The upshot was terrifying: GSAM was trapped in a self-reinforcing feedback loop. More selling caused more volatility, causing more selling, causing more volatility. It was a trap that had snared every other quant fund.

They were trying to make sure that their positions were liquid, that they could exit them whenever necessary without major losses. But every time they deleveraged positions, they were back to square one. The GSAM team realized, with shock, that they might be trapped in a death spiral. Talk about an LTCM-like meltdown, one that didn't just take down one giant fund but dozens, started to make the rounds.

"There was a sense that this could be the end," said one GSAM trader.

And if it continued much longer, it would make LTCM's collapse in 1998 seem like a walk in the park.

What to do?

Matthew Rothman woke early on Wednesday, August 8, and walked to Lehman Brothers' San Francisco office on California Street, just around the corner from the Four Seasons. He sent a stream of emails to his quantitative research team back in New York with essentially a single order: get to work on a report explaining the quant meltdown.

But several members of his staff were having trouble making it to Lehman's midtown Manhattan office on Seventh Avenue. The massive storm had knocked out the city's subway system, and no one could find a cab. Rothman told them they had to find a way to get into the office, no matter what. Walk, run, ride a horse. Whatever. They had to get this call out.

Rothman, in constant contact with his research staff in New York, spent all day collecting data, working the Street for insight, writing, putting together complicated charts. By the time the note was finished, it was midnight local time, 3:00 A.M. Eastern. Rothman stumbled back to the Four Seasons, exhausted.

"Over the past few days, most quantitative fund managers have experienced significant abnormal performance in their returns," he wrote with classic Wall Street analyst understatement. "It is not just that most factors are not working but rather they are working in a perverse manner, in our view."

The report continued with the scenario Rothman had worked out over sushi with Levin: "It is impossible to know for sure what was the catalyst for this situation. In our opinion, the most reasonable scenario is that a few large multi-strategy quantitative managers may have experienced significant losses in their credit or fixed income portfolios. In an attempt to lower the risks in their portfolios and being afraid to 'mark to market' their illiquid credit portfolios, these managers probably sought to raise cash and de-lever in the most liquid market—the U.S. equity market."

The following pages of the report were a detailed examination of the specific trades that were blowing up. The oddest section, however, was its conclusion, a terse reiteration of the quant credo that at the end of the day, people—and investors—generally behave in a rational manner. The Truth, after all, is the Truth. Right?

"We like to believe in the rationality of human beings (and particularly quants) and place our faith in the strong forces and mutual incentives we all have for orderly functioning of the capital markets," Rothman wrote. "As drivers of cars down dark roads at night, we learn to have faith that the driver approaching on the other side of the road will not swerve into our lane to hit us. In fact, he is just as afraid of our swerving to hit him as we are of his swerving to hit us. We both exhale as we pass by each other headed into the night in our respective opposite directions, successfully avoiding both of our destructions."

The report, called "Turbulent Times in Quant Land," was posted on Lehman's servers early that morning. It quickly became the most highly distributed note in the history of Lehman Brothers.

As word of his report seeped out, he got a call from *Wall Street Journal* reporter Kaja Whitehouse. When asked to describe the severity of the meltdown, Rothman didn't mince words.

"Wednesday is the type of day people will remember in quant-land for a very long time," Rothman said. "Events that models only predicted would happen once in 10,000 years happened every day for three days."

He spoke as though the worst were over. It wasn't.

Early Thursday morning, August 9, PDT held a series of emergency meetings in Peter Muller's office. The situation was dire. If the fund lost much more money, it ran the risk of getting shut down by Morgan's risk managers—a disaster that could mean the group would have to liquidate its entire portfolio. Reed advocated even more aggressive selling. Muller agreed but wanted to wait one more day before ratcheting up. Meanwhile, the losses were piling up.

By then, the quant meltdown was affecting markets across the globe. The Dow Jones Industrial Average tumbled 387 points Thursday.

The Japanese yen, which quant funds liked to short due to extremely low interest rates in Japan, surged against the dollar and the euro—an example of more short covering by quant funds as the carry trade fell apart. But the dollar rose against most other currencies as investors snapped it up in a panicked flight to safe, liquid assets, just as they had during Black Monday in October 1987 and in August 1998 when LTCM imploded.

On Friday morning, Muller came into the office early. The plan was to deleverage like mad before everything was wiped out. But before he gave the thumbs-up on the plan, Muller wanted to see what happened at the opening bell. *You never know,* he thought. *Maybe we'll get a break.* But he wasn't counting on it.

There was plenty of bad news to worsen the mood. France's largest publicly traded bank, BNP Paribas, froze the assets of three of its funds worth a combined $2.2 billion. In a refrain that would echo across financial markets repeatedly in the coming year, BNP blamed the "complete evaporation of liquidity" in securitization markets related to U.S. housing loans, which had "made it impossible to value certain assets fairly regardless of their quality or credit rating."

Late Thursday, Jim Simons had issued a rare midmonth update on the state of one of his funds. The Renaissance Institutional Equities Fund, which managed about $26 billion in assets, was down 8.7 percent so far from the end of July—a loss of nearly $2 billion.

In a letter to investors, Simons attempted to explain what had gone wrong. "While we believe we have an excellent set of predictive signals, some of these are undoubtedly shared by a number of long/short hedge funds," wrote the white-bearded wizard of East Setauket. "For one reason or another many of these funds have not been doing well, and certain factors have caused them to liquidate positions. In addition to poor performance these factors may include losses in credit securities, excessive risk, margin calls and others."

The Medallion fund, however, was doing even worse than RIEF. It had dropped a whopping 17 percent for the month, a loss of roughly $1 billion. Like Muhammad Ali getting licked by Joe Frazier in Madison Square Garden in 1971, the greatest fund of all time was on the ropes, and seemed at risk of getting knocked out.

Over at AQR, the mood was even more grim. Its traders were tense and tired. The hard, round-the-clock work was completely atypical for quants used to the rigid, structured, predictable flow of markets. Complete chaos wasn't supposed to be part of the package.

The fun was over. AQR had reserved a movie theater that Thursday night for a showing of *The Simpsons Movie* as an employee event. The reservation was canceled.

Ken Griffin, meanwhile, sensed blood in the water. While the quantitative Tactical Trading fund run by Misha Malyshev was getting hammered, it represented only a fraction of Citadel's massive girth.

Late Thursday night, Griffin picked up the phone and called Cliff Asness. Griffin wasn't calling as a friend. He wanted to know if AQR needed help.

Asness knew what that meant. He was hearing from Griffin the grave dancer, the vulture investor of Amaranth and Sowood fame. It brought home how much trouble he was in. While the call was friendly, there was an air of tension between the two managers. "I looked up and saw the Valkyries coming and heard the Grim Reaper's scythe knocking on my door," Asness later joked about the call. But at the time, he wasn't laughing.

Friday morning at AQR, August 10. Asness glanced pensively at a candy-colored array of Marvel superhero figurines lined up along his east-facing window: Spider-Man, Captain America, the Hulk, Iron Man. Comic book heroes of his boyhood days on Long Island.

The fund manager wished he had some kind of superhuman power over the markets to make it all stop. *Make the bleeding stop.* AQR's Absolute Return Fund was down 13 percent for the month, its biggest drop in such a short stretch of time ever. *It doesn't make sense . . . it's perverse.* He walked to his desk and looked at the P&L on his computer screen, a red flash of negative numbers. The losses were astronomical. Billions gone.

Through the eastern window of his office, Asness could see the blue shimmer of the city's teeming marina beyond Steamboat Road. A decade earlier, a short drive down Steamboat had led directly to the headquarters of Long-Term Capital Management.

If the losses continued, AQR would be seen as just another LTCM, a quant disaster that wreaked havoc on the financial system, Wall Street's eggheads run amok all over again as their witchy black boxes turned into loose-cannon HAL 9000s destroying everything in sight.

He didn't want to let that happen. And he thought: *Maybe there's a way.*

Asness had been huddling with his top lieutenants in his office, including Mendelson, John Liew, and David Kabiller. They were getting ready to make a momentous decision. It wasn't easy. The fate of the hedge fund hung in the balance.

Throughout the week, AQR, like every quant fund, had been trying to figure out what was going on, searching for the elusive patient zero. By the end of Thursday, they had determined that almost every large quant hedge fund had taken down its leverage significantly. Every quant fund but one: GSAM.

AQR had been frantically trying to get information about what was going on inside Goldman. But Goldman wouldn't talk. Through careful analysis of the situation, AQR had determined that GSAM's Global Equity Opportunities fund hadn't completely deleveraged. That meant one of two things: either Goldman was going to inject a large amount of money into the fund to keep it afloat or it was about to implode in a vicious sell-off, causing the market to spiral even further out of control.

If the latter were the case, certain disaster would have been in store for AQR and every other quant fund, as well as the broader market. Goldman's GEO fund was massive, with roughly $10 billion in assets. If it had started selling on top of all the other losses quant funds had endured, a meltdown of epic proportions would have ensued, rocking investors everywhere.

Like PDT, the team at AQR had planned to shrink its book even further that day. But Asness made a gut decision, one of the most important of his trading career: *It's time to buy.*

If not now, when? he thought. Goldman, he decided, wouldn't let the system collapse if it had the wherewithal. Instead, the bank would do the smart thing, the rational thing: inject capital into the GEO fund. That would allow it to hold on to its positions. It wouldn't have to deleverage.

That meant it was time to get back in, throw more chips on the table. AQR put out the word to its traders and told them to be intentionally loud about the move. They wanted everyone to know that AQR, one of the big lumbering gorillas of quantdom, was back in action. *Maybe that will make the bleeding stop*, Asness thought.

It was like a poker game, the highest-stakes hand he'd ever played. This time, it wasn't just that wiseass Peter Muller who could call his bluff; it was the market itself that could ruin him. Asness was all in, and he knew it.

Back in New York, Muller sat poker-faced and pensive as strategies to cope with the chaos raced through his mind. As he waited for the market to open Friday morning, he knew PDT was on the edge. The group had lost an inconceivable $600 million. If the losses intensified much more, Morgan could decide to shut it down. The group's brilliant fourteen-year run, and possibly Muller's career, restarted only months earlier, could be over.

It didn't look good. European markets were still a basket case. So was Asia. The tension mounted as the 9:30 a.m. start of regular trading in the United States neared. Muller, Simons, Asness, Weinstein, Griffin, and nearly every other quant manager in the world were glued to their screens as the minutes ticked by, sweating, nervous, sick with dread.

Then something of a miracle happened. When U.S. trading began, quant strategies started to rally, hard. Muller gave the order: don't sell. Other quants followed suit. There was an initial lull, and then their positions took off in a rocket-mad surge. By the end of the day, the gains were so strong that many quant managers said it was one of their best days ever. Whether the rebound was a result of AQR's decision to leap back into the market is impossible to know for certain. But there's little doubt that it helped turn the tide.

Inside Goldman, rescue efforts had in fact been in full swing since Wednesday—a $3 billion infusion of cash that helped to stop the bleeding. The bailout, about $2 billion of which was Goldman's own money, was targeted at the GSAM's Global Equity Opportunities fund, which had also suffered a huge blow and had lost a stunning 30 percent, or $1.6 billion, for the month through August 9. Global Alpha and its North American Equity Opportunities fund were left to fend for themselves. By the end of August, Global Alpha's assets had plunged to $6 billion, down from $10 billion the previous year, an enormous 40 percent decline for one of Wall Street's elite trading groups.

"There is more money invested in quantitative strategies than we and many others appreciated," wrote Global Alpha's managers in a report to battered investors later that month. A staggering amount of that money was sitting at Goldman Sachs Asset Management. Including the GEO fund and Global Alpha, GSAM had about $250 billion in funds under management, of which about $150 billion was in hedge funds.

In a separate letter, Global Alpha's managers explained that a big driver of the losses was the carry trade. "In particular," they wrote, "we saw very poor performance in our currency selection strategies, both developed and emerging, as positions of ours that were aligned with carry traders were punished in the massive unwind of the worldwide carry trade."

They were chastened, but they still believed in their system. Acknowledging that the 23 percent decline that month had been "a very challenging time for our investors," they said they "still hold to our fundamental investment beliefs: that sound economic investment principles coupled with a disciplined quantitative approach can provide strong, uncorrelated returns over time."

Asness issued his own letter late Friday—and he pointed the finger at copycats riding his coattails. "Our stock selection investment process, a long-term winning strategy, has very recently been shockingly bad for us and for all of those pursuing similar strategies," he wrote. "We believe that this occurred as the very success of the strategy over time has drawn in too many investors."

When all of those copycats rushed for the exit at once, it led to "a deleveraging of historical proportions."

It was a black swan, something neither AQR nor any of the quants had planned for.

Matthew Rothman, meanwhile, was frazzled to the bone. He'd spent most of Thursday and Friday explaining the situation to investors, clients of Lehman, confused CEOs of companies whose stock was getting crushed by the quant meltdown ("You do *what* to stocks? Why?"). He'd barely slept for two days.

He called up a friend who lived in Napa Valley, an hour's drive from San Francisco. "I've had a crazy week," he said. "Mind if I stay at your place for the weekend?" Rothman spent the days visiting wineries and relaxing. It was one of the last moments he'd have for such a break in a very long time.

Over the weekend, Alan Benson came into Saba's office to go over his positions and bumped into Weinstein, who was trying to keep up to speed on the chaos that had enveloped the markets. Saba's quant equities desk had lost nearly $200 million. Weinstein was clearly upset and told Benson to keep selling. By the time Benson was done, his positions had been cut in half.

On Monday, Goldman Sachs held a conference call to discuss the meltdown and the $3 billion infusion into the GEO fund. "The developments of the last few days have been unprecedented and characterized by remarkable speed and intensity across global markets," said David Viniar, Goldman's chief financial officer. "We are seeing things that were 25-standard-deviation events, several days in a row."

It was the same out-of-this-world language the quants used to describe Black Monday. According to quant models, the meltdown of August 2007 was so unlikely that it could never have happened in the history of the human race.

The meltdown by the quant funds was over, at least for the moment. But it was only the first round of a collapse that would bring the financial system to its knees. The following week, the turmoil in the financial markets only worsened. A global margin call was under way, and spreading.

On Thursday morning, August 16, Countrywide Financial said it needed to tap $11.5 billion in bank credit lines, a sign that it couldn't raise money on the open market. About the same time, in London, about $46 billion in short-term IOUs issued outside the United States were maturing and had to be rolled over into new debt. Typically this happens almost automatically. But that morning, no one was buying. Only half of the debt was sold by the end of the day. The Money Grid was breaking down.

The yen continued to pop, surging 2 percent in a matter of minutes midday in New York that Thursday, a move that can crush a currency trader leaning the wrong direction. Treasuries were also soaring as panicked investors continued to buy the most liquid assets, a swing one trader at the time called "an extraordinarily violent move."

"These shocks reflected one of the most perilous days for global capital markets, the circulatory system of the international economy, since the 1997–98 crisis that began in Asia, spread to Russia and Brazil and eventually to the U.S.-based hedge fund Long-Term Capital Management," stated a front-page article in the *Wall Street Journal*.

Stock investors were pummeled by whiplash swings that saw the Dow industrials dip and surge by hundreds of points in the space of a few minutes. It was dizzying. The meltdown that had begun in subprime mortgages and spread to quant hedge funds was now visible to everyone—including the Federal Reserve.

Early that Friday morning, stock markets were in free fall. At one point, futures tied to the Dow industrials were indicating that the market would open more than 500 points lower.

Then, shortly after 8:00 A.M. Eastern time, the Fed lowered interest rates on its so-called discount window, through which it makes direct loans to banks, to 5.75 percent from 6.25 percent. The central bank hoped that by cutting rates through the window, it would encourage banks to make loans to customers that had previously been squeezed. Banks had been cutting off certain clients, such as hedge funds, that they feared held large portfolios of subprime mortgages. The fear about who was holding toxic assets was spreading. The Fed also signaled that it would likely lower the federal funds rate, the more important rate it charges banks for overnight loans, when it met again in September.

It was a highly unusual move, and it worked. Stock futures surged dramatically and markets opened sharply higher.

For the time being, the deleveraging appeared to have stopped. The quants had stared into the abyss. If the selling had continued— which likely would have happened if Goldman Sachs hadn't bailed out its GEO fund—the results could have been catastrophic, not only for the quants but for everyday investors, as the sell-off spilled into other sectors of the market. Just as the implosion of the mortgage market triggered a cascading meltdown in quant funds, the losses by imploded quant funds could have bled into other asset classes, a crazed rush to zero that could have put the entire financial system in peril.

The most terrifying aspect of the meltdown, however, was that it revealed hidden linkages in the Money Grid that no one had been aware of before. A collapse in the subprime mortgage market triggered margin calls in hedge funds, forcing them to unwind positions in stocks. The dominoes started falling, hitting other quant hedge funds and forcing them to unwind positions in everything from currencies to futures contracts to options in markets around the world. As the carry trade unraveled, assets that had benefited from all the cheap liquidity it had spun off began to lose their mooring.

A vicious feedback loop ensued, causing billions to evaporate in a matter of days. The selling cycle had stopped before major damage had been inflicted—but there was no telling what would happen the next time around, or what hidden damage lurked within the system's mostly invisible plumbing.

The unwind that week had been so unusual, so unexpected, that several of the rocket scientists at Renaissance Technologies gave it its own name: the August Factor. The August Factor represented a complete reversal of quant strategies, the Bizarro World in which up was down and down was up, bad assets rose and good assets fell, ignited by a mass deleveraging of funds with overlapping strategies. It was an entirely new factor, with strong statistical properties unlike any that had ever been seen in the past—and, hopefully, would never be seen again.

But there were new, far more destructive disruptions coming. Indeed, a financial storm of unprecedented fury was already under way. In the next two years, the relentless deleveraging that first hit obscure places such as PDT's New York office and AQR's Greenwich headquarters spread throughout the financial system like a mutating virus, pushing the financial system to the edge of a cliff. Trillions were lost, and giant banks failed.

Looking back, however, many quants would see the dramatic, domino-like meltdown of August 2007, one that scrambled the most sophisticated models in the world, as the strangest and most unexplainable event of the entire credit crisis.

"In ten years, people may remember August '07 more than they remember the subprime crisis," Aaron Brown observed. "It started a chain reaction. It's very interesting that there was this tremendous anomalous event before the great crisis."

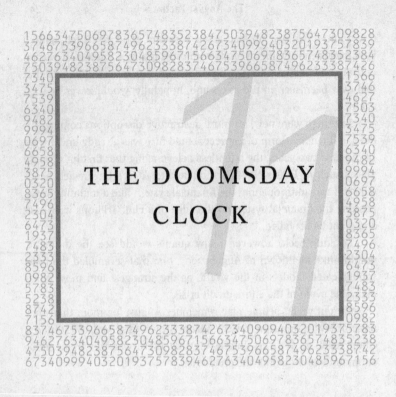

THE DOOMSDAY
CLOCK

Cliff Asness paced back and forth, alone in his corner office at AQR, wringing his hands. It was late November 2007, and AQR was on its heels all over again, suffering huge losses.

What had happened? The fund had ripped higher after the August meltdown, making back almost all the losses of that insane week. Everything looked fine. For a while he even dared to dream the IPO might be on the table again. September was okay, and so was October.

In November, the nightmare started all over again. AQR was slammed as a number of quant strategies were hit. The global margin call continued to batter the financial system. Subprime CDO assets continued to collapse, and investors were coming to realize that far more banks than they had imagined were holding toxic assets. Morgan Stanley fessed up to a $7.8 billion loss, assigning most of the blame to Howie Hubler's desk. Mortgage giant Freddie Mac revealed a $2 billion loss. HSBC, one of Europe's biggest banks, took $41 billion in assets it had held in special investment vehicles—those off-balance-sheet entities that ferried subprime mortgages through the securitization pipeline—onto its balance sheet, a symptom of the frozen credit markets. Citigroup, Merrill Lynch, Bear Stearns, and Lehman Brothers also started to show even more severe strains from the crisis.

AQR was getting hit on all sides. Asness's precious value stocks were plunging. Currencies and interest rates were all over the map. A big bet he'd made on commercial real estate turned south in dramatic fashion, losing hundreds of millions in the course of a few weeks.

Less than three years earlier, back in the golden days of the Wall Street Poker Night at the St. Regis, the quants had been one of the most powerful forces in the market, the Nerd Kings of Wall Street. Asness and Muller had stood shoulder to shoulder, the poker trophies in their hands like symbols of their shared ability to make the right calculations to collect pots of money. Now it seemed to have been only act two of a three-act Greek tragedy about hubris. They were getting crushed by a market gone mad. It wasn't right. It wasn't fair.

Asness sat down at his desk and stared at his computer screen. *More red numbers.* He hauled back and lunged with a roar, punching the screen with his fist. The screen cracked and flipped back off his desk, falling to the floor, destroyed.

Asness shook his head, gazing out the window at the browning foliage of Greenwich beyond. He knew he wasn't the only hedge fund taking a beating as 2007 drew to a close. The global financial crisis was metastasizing like a cancer. A reckoning for the high-flying industry was under way, pummeling even the savviest operators. AQR had long been considered one of the smartest, most advanced funds in the business. But starting in August 2007, it all seemed to be coming undone. All the math, all the theory—none of it worked. Whatever AQR did to try to right its ship proved the wrong move as wave after wave of deleveraging ripped across the system.

Part of the problem lay at the core of AQR's modus operandi. Value-oriented investors such as AQR snap up stocks when they are unloved, expecting them to advance once their true worth—once the Truth—is recognized by Mr. Market, that all-knowing wise man whose moniker was coined by value king (and Warren Buffett tutor) Benjamin Graham. But in the great unwind that began in 2007, value investors were burned repeatedly as they swept up beaten-down stocks, only to see them beaten down even more. Mr. Market, it seemed, was on an extended vacation.

Many of those battered stocks were banks such as Bear Stearns and Lehman Brothers, whose value spiraled lower and lower as they kept taking billions in write-downs on toxic assets. The models that had worked so well in the past became virtually worthless in an environment that was unprecedented.

Throttled quants everywhere were suddenly engaged in a prolonged bout of soul-searching, questioning whether all their brilliant strategies were an illusion, pure luck that happened to work during a period of dramatic growth, economic prosperity, and excessive leverage that lifted everyone's boat.

The worst fear of quants such as Asness was that their Chicago School guru, Eugene Fama, had been right all along: the market is efficient, brutally so. Long used to gobbling up the short-term inefficiencies like ravenous piranhas, they'd had a big chunk taken out of their own flesh by forces they could neither understand nor control.

It was a horrible feeling. But Asness was still confident, still upbeat. *It would all come back*. All those years of data, the models, the rationale behind them—momentum, value versus growth, the crucial factors—it would come back.

He knew it.

It was an unusually warm morning in Chicago in November 2007 as Ken Griffin walked briskly toward his private jet, which was prepped for the two-hour flight to New York City. As he was boarding the plane, he got an urgent call from Joe Russell, head of Citadel's credit investments operation.

A big Citadel holding, online broker E*Trade Financial, was getting crushed in the market, Russell told him. Its shares, having tumbled nearly 80 percent that year already, had been cut in half yet again just that morning, a Monday.

"We need to focus on this fast," Russell said. A savings and loan owned by E*Trade had been dabbling in subprime mortgages, and now it was paying the price. There was talk of bankruptcy for the former dot-com darling. Russell said Citadel should start buying shares of E*Trade to stabilize the market.

"Let's go," Griffin said, giving the plan the thumbs-up.

Within days, Griffin, along with a crack team of sixty Citadel analysts and advisors, swept into E*Trade's New York headquarters, just a few blocks from Citadel's New York branch, and pored over its books. Griffin racked up the miles on his Global Explorer, flying to New York in the morning and jetting back to Chicago at night three times during the talks.

On November 29, just weeks after that first call from Russell, a deal was struck. Citadel agreed to invest roughly $2.6 billion in the company. It purchased $1.75 billion worth of E*Trade shares and notes with a fat interest rate of 12.5 percent. It also snapped up a $3 billion portfolio of mortgages and other securities from the online broker for what seemed like a bargain-basement price of $800 million. The investment represented about 2.5 percent of Citadel's investment portfolio.

Griffin was certain the market had become overly pessimistic, and he sensed a fantastic buying opportunity. He'd seen markets like this before, when panicked sellers dump good assets while the savvy investors sit back and pick them off. Like AQR, Citadel was in many ways a value investor gobbling up battered assets, expecting them to surge ahead once the smoke cleared, once the Truth was recognized by the masses.

"The market is pricing assets like things are going to get really bad," Griffin told the *Wall Street Journal* soon after the deal. "But the more likely outcome is for the economy to slow for two or three quarters, and then strengthen."

The E*Trade deal was the biggest in Griffin's career, another headline-grabbing coup on top of the Amaranth trade of 2006 and the

Sowood rescue in July. Adding to the pressure, his wife, Anne Dias Griffin, was due to give birth to the first scion of the Griffin dynasty in December.

Griffin showed little sign of stress, however. The blue-eyed billionaire seemed to be hitting on all cylinders. The speed with which he completed the E*Trade deal was the envy of competitors who lacked the mental muscle and sheer guts—not to mention the cash—to pull it off. Griffin had moved into the rarefied big leagues of money managers able to shift billions at the drop of a hat to take advantage of distressed companies willing to do anything, to sell at any price, in order to survive.

Meanwhile, Citadel's high-frequency powerhouse, Tactical Trading, run by the Russian math whiz Misha Malyshev, continued to rack up gains despite the August quant quake. It was on track to pull in $892 million in 2007, and even more the following year. The firm's options trading business run by Matthew Andresen, Citadel Derivatives Group, was also raking in cash, having grown to become the largest options market maker in the world. Griffin, who personally owned a large chunk of each business, decided to split Tactical and the derivatives group out of his hedge-fund operations. The move helped diversify Citadel's business lines ahead of the planned IPO.

It also helped Griffin get a bigger chunk of Tactical, which was becoming one of the most consistently profitable business lines at the fund, if not in the world. Investors in the hedge fund were given the chance to put cash into Tactical, but it had to be in addition to their current investments. About 60 percent of investors took Griffin up on the offer. The rest of the fund's capacity was taken by Citadel head honchos—mostly Griffin.

In the fund's annual town hall meeting for Citadel's staff at the Chicago Symphony Orchestra that November, Griffin was riding high. Citadel was in charge of roughly $20 billion in assets. It had dominated competitors in 2007, gaining 32 percent despite the quant meltdown in August. The firm had pulled off its E*Trade coup the week before, and the Sowood deal was shaping up nicely. Citadel's stock-options electronic market-making business had become the biggest in the world.

Speaking before the troops, roughly four hundred in all, Griffin was like a charged-up football coach preparing his team for the biggest game of their lives. After ticking off Citadel's accomplishments, Griffin shifted into corporate manager cliché mode. "Success has never been measured in home runs," he said, "it's the singles and doubles that got us here and will take us beyond. The best times are yet to come. Yes, there will be obstacles, but obstacles are opportunities for people who know how to get the job done. If you're up for that, you're in the right place."

The well-heeled crowd clapped and cheered. Griffin may be a hard driver, but he was a winner and had made everyone in the room incredibly wealthy. Citadel seemed on the cusp of greatness. The downturn the economy was suffering from the collapse in the housing market would be short-lived, Griffin thought, a brief hiccup in the global economy's unstoppable growth cycle. Indeed, he believed he could already see the light at the end of the tunnel. Good times were coming soon.

There's an old Wall Street proverb about such opportunism: the light at the end of the tunnel is an oncoming train. Ken Griffin was stepping right in front of it.

"Aaargh!"

Cliff Asness leapt from the card table, grabbed the first lamp in reach, and smashed it against the wall. He stood seething before the wide hotel window. It was late 2007, and a light dusting of snow fell over New York. Christmas lights adorned a number of the apartment windows of the luxury high-rise across from the hotel.

"What the hell is wrong with you?" Peter Muller said, looking up, startled, from his seat at the table.

There he goes again. Asness had lost another hand. Bad luck. But why did he care so much? What was with the temper tantrums? Asness's hedge fund made its money based on math, on cold-blooded rationality that ruthlessly cuts away the irrational, human element of trading. But when the chips were down at the poker table, Asness lost it.

Neil Chriss shook his head. "Cliff, you make and lose that much in a matter of minutes every day," he said. "I think some perspective is in order."

Why did Asness always take losing so personally? Why did he get so angry? He'd always had a temper, and hated to lose, especially to other quants.

"Screw it," Asness said, breathing heavily as he moved back to the card table.

In the previous year, Asness had been increasingly prone to outbursts. The pots seemed to keep rising, easily hitting five digits, sometimes more. Not that Asness couldn't afford it. He was the richest guy in the room. But his fortunes seemed to be dwindling every day as AQR hemorrhaged cash. And Asness's skills at the poker table seemed to track AQR's P&L—they waned at the same time his fund started to skid. Just my luck, he thought. Or lack of luck. It was nuts.

The quant poker games were brutal marathon sessions lasting until three, four in the morning. Not that Asness would stick around for the whole affair. He had two pairs of twins, born back-to-back in 2003 and 2004, waiting for him back at his mansion in Greenwich. He liked to call the sequential birth of the twins "a gross failure of risk control."

Risk control seemed to get thrown out the window for the poker game, too, or so it might seem to an outsider. The buy-in was $10,000. For certain games attended by the more serious players of the group, such as Muller and Chriss, the buy-in could vault as high as fifty grand.

The players didn't toss it all on the table on the first hand, of course. They could stuff the chips in their pockets and keep them there all night, at least until their luck ran out, if that's how they wanted to play it. But who cared? Fifty grand was Monopoly money to them. It was all about who won and who lost. And although winners sometimes could take home winnings measured in six figures, it wasn't going to change any of their lives.

But Asness wasn't winning. He was losing. Just like AQR.

"Ante up," said Muller, dealing another hand.

Asness pulled a stack of chips from his pocket and tossed them into the pot. He watched the cards as they fell around the table. He looked up at Muller, who was staring blankly at his hand. He didn't know how Muller could stay so calm. He'd lost more than half a billion in August over the course of a few days, yet acted like it was another day on the beach in Hawaii. But AQR had lost even more, much more. Sure, things had bounced back—a lot—but the speed of the meltdown had been unnerving. And now, as the credit crisis ground on in late 2007, AQR was facing even more losses.

Picking up his cards, Asness winced. Nothing.

He wasn't ready to give up yet, not even close. AQR held its traditional Christmas party at Nobu 57, a swank Japanese restaurant in midtown Manhattan. But there were signs that the bloom was off the rose. Spouses and guests weren't allowed, unlike previous years. The stressed Greenwich quants let loose, swilling sake and Japanese beer by the gallon. "It turned into a drunkfest," said one attendee.

The quants were also haunted by another fear: systemic risk. The August 2007 meltdown showed that the quants' presence in the market wasn't nearly as benign as they had believed. As with a delicate spiderweb, a tear in one part of the financial system, in this case subprime mortgages, could trigger a tear in another part—and even bring down the web itself. The market was apparently far more intertwined than they had ever realized.

MIT finance professor Andrew Lo, and his student Amir Khandani, published a definitive study of the meltdown in October 2007 called "What Happened to the Quants?" Ominously, they evoked an apocryphal Doomsday Clock for the global financial system. In August 2007, the clock ticked nearer to midnight, perhaps the closest it had come to financial Armageddon since Long-Term Capital's implosion in 1998.

"If we were to develop a Doomsday Clock for the hedge-fund industry's impact on the global financial system," they wrote, "calibrated to five minutes to midnight in August 1998, and fifteen minutes to midnight in January 1999, then our current outlook for the state of systemic risk in the hedge-fund industry is about 11:51 P.M. For the moment, markets seem to have stabilized, but the clock is ticking."

One of the central concerns, Lo and Khandani explained, was the weblike interconnectedness of the system. "The fact that the ultimate origins of this dislocation were apparently outside the long-short equity sector—most likely in a completely unrelated set of markets and instruments—suggests that systemic risk in the hedge-fund industry has increased significantly in recent years," they wrote.

There was also the worry about what happened if high-frequency quant funds, which had become a central cog of the market, helping transfer risk at lightning speeds, were forced to shut down by extreme market volatility. "Hedge funds can decide to withdraw liquidity at a moment's notice," they wrote, "and while this may be benign if it occurs rarely and randomly, a coordinated withdrawal of liquidity among an entire sector of hedge funds could have disastrous consequences for the viability of the financial system if it occurs at the wrong time and in the wrong sector."

It wasn't supposed to be this way. The quants had always thought of themselves as financial helpers, greasing the churning wheels of the Money Grid. Now it seemed that they posed significant systemic risk—pushing the world closer to doomsday. Sitting at the poker table, holding another dud hand, Asness would have been justified in shutting his eyes and thinking back to his days as the most brilliant student at the University of Chicago.

Where had it all gone wrong?

One quant gadfly had been predicting a crackup in the financial system for years: Nassim Nicholas Taleb, the former hedge fund trader and author who'd squared off against Peter Muller at Neil Chriss's wedding several years back. In January 2008, Taleb arrived at AQR's office in Greenwich to give a lecture. Aaron Brown had asked him to explain his theories about why quantitative models work fine in the physical world but are dangerous wizardry in the world of finance (a view Brown didn't necessarily share).

Taleb's audience was sparse. Asness, drained, passed. Aaron Brown had been a friend of Taleb's for years—Taleb had provided a blurb for Brown's book, *The Poker Face of Wall Street*—and was interested in what he had to say, even if he didn't agree with it.

"Hey, Nassim, how goes it?"

"Not bad, my friend," Taleb said, stroking his beard. "I hear you have been having a bad time of it."

"You wouldn't believe it," Brown replied. "Or maybe you would, I don't know. I'd say we've definitely seen one of the blackest swans of all time. But things seem to be cooling off."

Taleb quickly set up his PowerPoint demonstration and began to talk. One of the first slides in the talk showed a clip from a *Wall Street Journal* article from August 11 about Matthew Rothman's description of the quant meltdown.

"Matthew Rothman is used to working with people who pride themselves on their rationality," the article said. "He's a 'quant,' after all, one of a legion of Ph.D.'s on Wall Street who use emotionless rules of mathematics to pick trading positions. But this week, he caught a whiff of panic."

Taleb's slide was titled "Fallacy of Probability." Rothman had described the quant meltdown as something models predicted would happen once in ten thousand years—but it had taken place every day for several days in a row. To Taleb, that meant something was wrong with the models.

"These so-called financial engineers experience events that can only happen once, in the history of mankind, according to the laws of probability, every few years," he told the room (full, of course, of financial engineers). "Something is wrong with this picture. Do you see my point?"

Another slide showed a giant man sitting on the right side of a scale, tipping it heavily, while a group of tiny people scatter and fall on the left side. The slide read "Two Domains: Type 1—Mild 'Mediocristan' (Gauss, etc.); Type 2—Wild 'Extremistan.' "

The slide was a key to Taleb's vision about extreme events in the market and why the mathematics used in the physical world—the science used to put a man on the moon, fly an airplane across the ocean, microwave a sandwich—doesn't apply in the world of finance. The physical world, he said, is "Mediocristan." Bell curves are perfect for measuring the heights or weights of people. If you measure the height of a thousand people, the next measurement isn't likely to change the average.

In finance, however, a sudden swing in prices can change everything. This is Taleb's world of "Extremistan." Income distributions, for instance, exhibit signs of Extremistan, a discovery Benoit Mandelbrot had made more than half a century before. Measure the wealth of a thousand people plucked off the street. On a typical day, the distribution will be normal. But what if you select Bill Gates, the richest man in the world? The distribution is suddenly, massively skewed. Market prices can also change rapidly, unexpectedly, and massively.

Taleb continued to address the sparse audience for another thirty minutes. He talked about fat tails. Uncertainty. Randomness. But he could tell his audience was fried. They didn't need to be told about black swans. They'd just seen one, and it had terrified them.

Still, few could believe that the downturn would get much worse. A year of unfathomable volatility was just beginning. Later that January, it emerged that a thirty-one-year-old rogue trader at Société Générale, a large French bank, lost $7.2 billion on complex derivatives trades. The trader, Jérôme Kerviel, used futures contracts tied to European stock indexes to build up a staggering $73 billion worth of positions that were basically one-way bets that the market would rise. After the bank discovered the trades, which Kerviel covered up by hacking its risk-control software, it decided to unwind them, triggering a staggering global market sell-off. In response to the volatility, the Federal Reserve, which didn't know about the SocGen trades, slashed short-term rates by three-quarters of a point, a bold move that frightened investors because it smacked of panic.

Still, even as the system teetered on the edge, many of the smartest investors in the world couldn't see the destructive tsunami heading directly for them. The implosion of Bear Stearns in March was a wake-up call.

The Doomsday Clock was ticking.

Around 1:00 p.m. on March 13, 2008, Jimmy Cayne sat down at a card table in Detroit and began to craft his strategy. The seventy-four-year-old chairman of Bear Stearns, seeded fourth in a group of 130 in the IMP Pairs category of the North American Bridge Championship, was squarely focused on the cards in his hand.

Bridge was an obsession for Cayne, a product of Chicago's hardscrabble South Side, and he wasn't going to let his company's troubles get in the way of one of the most important competitions of the year.

At the same time, back at Bear's New York headquarters on Madison Avenue, about forty of the firm's top executives had gathered in a twelfth-floor dining area to strategize. Everyone knew trouble was brewing. Bear's anemic stock price told the story all too clearly. But no one was sure exactly how bad it was. Around 12:45 P.M., Bear chief executive Alan Schwartz appeared to assure the troops that all was well.

No one was buying it. Bear Stearns, founded in 1923, was teetering on the edge of collapse as its trading clients pulled billions from the bank in a white-hot panic. Insiders at the firm knew it was serious when one of its most cherished clients pulled out more than $5 billion in the first half of March. The client: Renaissance Technologies. Then another top client bolted for the exits with $5 billion more in hand: D. E. Shaw.

The quants were killing Bear Stearns.

To this day, former Bear Stearns employees believe the firm was taken out in a ruthless mugging. During its final week as a public entity, it had $18 billion in cash reserves on hand. But once Bear's blood was in the water, jittery clients who traded with Bear weren't willing to wait around to see what happened. The worry was that the bank would implode before they could pull out their money. It wasn't worth the risk. There were other investment banks more than willing to take their funds, such as Lehman Brothers.

By March 15, 2008, a Saturday, Bear Stearns was nearly finished. Federal Reserve and Treasury Department officials and bankers from J. P. Morgan roamed the halls of its midtown Manhattan skyscraper like scavengers picking over a cadaver. Bear executives were frantic, worried about a shotgun wedding and jamming the phones for any kind of last-minute salvation. Nothing worked. On Sunday, Cayne and the rest of Bear's board agreed to sell the eighty-five-year-old institution to J. P. Morgan for $2 a share. A week later, the deal was boosted to $10 a share.

For a time, optimistic investors believed the death of Bear marked the high-water mark of the credit crisis. The stock market shot up. The system had seen its moment of crisis and come through largely unscathed. Or so it seemed.

Dick Fuld was putting on a classic performance. The Lehman Brothers CEO, known as the "Gorilla" for his heavy-browed Cro-Magnon glare, monosyllabic grunts, and fiery rampages, had been ranting for more than a half hour to a roomful of managing directors.

Fuld screamed. Jumped up and down. Shook his fists in defiance.

It was June 2008. Lehman's stock had been getting hammered all year as investors fretted about the firm's shaky balance sheet. Now it was getting worse. The firm had just posted a quarterly loss of $2.8 billion, including $3.7 billion in write-downs for toxic assets such as mortgages and commercial real estate investments. It was the bank's first quarterly loss since 1994, when it was spun off from American Express. Despite the losses, Fuld and his lieutenants had kept a straight face publicly, insisting everything was fine. It wasn't.

Fuld had called a meeting of the firm's managing directors to clear the air and explain the situation. He began with an announcement: "I spoke to the board this weekend," he said. Some in the room wondered whether he'd offered to resign. Just a week earlier, the sixty-two-year-old CEO had scrambled the firm's executive office, replacing president Joe Gregory with his longtime partner Herbert "Bart" McDade. Was it Fuld's turn to fall on his sword? Some in the room hoped so.

"I told them," Fuld said, "I'm not taking a bonus this year."

The room seemed to release an audible sigh of despair. Fuld quickly started going through the math, laying out how strong Lehman was, how solid its balance sheet remained. He talked about how the firm would crush the short sellers who'd been pile-driving Lehman's stock into dust.

Someone raised a hand. "We hear everything you're saying, Dick. But talk is cheap. Acting is louder than words. When are you going to buy a million shares?"

Fuld didn't miss a beat. "When Kathy sells some art."

Fuld was referring to his wife, Kathy Fuld, known for her expensive art collection. Was he joking? Some wondered. Fuld wasn't laughing. There was the classic furrowed brow. It was a moment when some of Lehman's top lieutenants started to wonder in earnest whether Lehman was in fact doomed. Their CEO seemed detached from reality.

When Kathy sells some art?

There was a yell, a smash, the sound of glass breaking and crashing to the floor. AQR's researchers and traders jolted in their seats, looking up shocked from their computer screens toward John Liew's office, where the sudden crash had come from, breaking the standard office calm typified by the constant low hum and snick of quants typing furiously at keyboards.

Through the windows, they could see their boss, Cliff Asness, peering back at them, smiling sheepishly. He opened the door.

"Everyone is okay," he said. "Calm down."

It was another outburst. Asness had hurled a hard object at the wall, scoring a direct hit on a framed picture in Liew's office, shattering the glass. Asness had already destroyed several computer screens as well as an office chair as AQR's fortunes continued to sour. It was late summer 2008. The mood in the office had grown tense. The carefree days of just over a year ago were long gone, replaced by paranoia, fear, and worry. Some believed the firm was losing direction, but no one dared challenge the mercurial boss. Asness had surrounded himself with yes-men, some complained, and brooked no deviation from the carefully wrought models that had made him wildly rich. "It will all come back," he said repeatedly, like a mantra. "When the insanity goes away."

Others weren't so sure, and some employees were getting increasingly alarmed by the fund manager's outbursts. "He was losing it a little more and more every day," said a former employee. "Things were spinning out of control."

A key player had abandoned ship. Earlier in the year, Mani Mahjouri, one of AQR's whiz kids who'd been with the firm since 2000, had quit. He'd grown tired of Asness's tongue-lashings, the battle-axe emails. Manjouri had been an idol of the younger quants at AQR. A student of Ken French's at MIT in the 1990s with degrees in math, physics, and finance, he was on the verge of becoming a partner, living proof that a young gun could rise to the top in a culture dominated by Goldman veterans. He was also the class clown of the fund, turning his office into a haunted house during Halloween, decorating the cubicles of a researcher on his or her birthday with balloons and party hats (unbeknownst to the researcher), and hacking into the target's email and writing: "Today is my birthday, please come to my cubicle and celebrate with me," sending the message to the entire firm— hugely embarrassing to certain antisocial quants.

The fun and games were over. Mahjouri was gone. The IPO was history, a bad reminder of better days. As the summer of 2008 neared an end, few of the quants at AQR could fathom—probably Asness most of all—that the pain was about to get much worse.

By September 9, Dick Fuld's confidence in Lehman Brothers was visibly shaken. In his thirty-first-floor office at the bank's midtown Manhattan headquarters, equipped with a shower, library, and expansive views of the Hudson, the Wall Street mogul raged against his tormentors like Ahab on the deck of the *Pequod*. That morning, news broke that Lehman's white knight, the Korea Development Bank, had decided not to purchase a stake in the bank. Making matters worse, if not catastrophic, J. P. Morgan's cochief of investment banking, Steven Black, called Fuld and told him that Morgan needed $5 billion in extra collateral and cash. Lehman had been margin-called. It was a dagger. Lehman's shares were in free fall, down more than 40 percent.

"We've got to act fast so this financial tsunami doesn't wash us away," Fuld said to his underlings, a manic tone in his voice.

But it was too late. The firm that Fuld had joined in 1969 was in a death spiral. Over the weekend of September 13, 2008, Lehman's fate was decided among a select group of individuals at the Federal Reserve's concrete fortress on Liberty Street in downtown Manhattan. Fuld wasn't even present. Instead, Hubert McDade and Alex Kirk, a fixed-income expert, sat at the table with Treasury secretary Paulson and New York Fed president Tim Geithner, President Obama's future Treasury secretary.

Fuld machine-gunned phone calls to the meeting, frantically making offers, spinning new deals. "How about this? How about this?"

Nothing worked. London banking giant Barclays, run by Bob Diamond, briefly considered ponying up some cash for Lehman, so long as the Fed backed the deal as it had with Bear. Paulson said no.

Derivatives traders, frantic about the demise of one of the world's largest banks, convened at the New York Fed's office Saturday night. The goal was to create a game plan for settling trades in case Lehman imploded. Among those traders was Boaz Weinstein. Deutsche Bank had done a significant amount of trading through Lehman, and Weinstein was concerned about the impact of a Lehman collapse on his positions. He seemed calm and relaxed, as poker-faced as ever. Beneath his calm exterior, Weinstein was nervous, realizing that he could be facing the biggest test of his trading career.

Sunday morning a consortium of bankers briefly cobbled together a deal to back a Barclays-led buyout, but the plan fell apart. Regulators in the United Kingdom had gotten cold feet and wouldn't sign off. It spelled doom for Lehman. Sunday night McDade returned to Lehman's midtown headquarters and told Fuld the bad news. Lehman would have to file for bankruptcy.

"I want to throw up," Fuld moaned.

That Sunday, Lehman quant Matthew Rothman was furious. His bank was teetering. And still his bosses wanted him to fly to Europe for a series of quant conferences in London, Paris, Milan, Frankfurt, and Zurich? *Idiots.*

He checked his schedule. He was on tap to give the keynote speech for Lehman's quantitative conference in London the following day. The previous week he'd sent an email to the team in Europe organizing the conference: "We may be filing for bankruptcy; there's a good chance we may not even be here." The response: *You're crazy.*

Rothman's boss, Ravi Mattu, was bombarded with complaints about Rothman. *He's not a team player. He's psycho. Of course Lehman Brothers isn't going to declare bankruptcy!*

Rothman was incredulous. He wanted to be available for his team in case anything happened. Like a platoon sergeant in a foxhole, he didn't want to leave his troops when the shit hit the fan. And he could see it coming. So he reached a compromise: he'd take the red-eye to London for Monday's conference, then head straight back to Heathrow for the red-eye back to New York. It would suck, but at least he'd be around in case anything happened.

Sunday afternoon, he took a car from his home in Montclair, New Jersey, to JFK Airport. All along the way he was checking his BlackBerry, looking for news or emails from his colleagues at Lehman. At the airport, as he was checking into the terminal, he sent one last email to Ravi: "Do you want me to go to this conference?"

Just as Rothman was about to go through security, he got a response. "Cancel the trip."

Rothman's first emotion was relief. Then it hit him: Lehman was dying. Numb with the realization of what had happened, he took a cab back home to Montclair and immediately hopped in his wife's station wagon, leaving his '96 Honda Civic behind. He needed the extra room, he thought. For boxes.

Nearly every Lehman employee who could make it streamed toward the bank's New York office that night. Ranks of cameras and news teams lined Seventh Avenue. Rumors were flying around that the bank would shut its doors at midnight. There was no time to lose.

Inside the bank, there was relative calm. Employees were busy packing up their belongings. It was a surreal scene, like a wake. Another rumor came down: the computer systems were going to shut down. Everyone started sending emails, saying their goodbyes, attaching email addresses where they could be reached in the future, "It's been great to work with all of you," et cetera. Rothman sent his own email, picked up his belongings, and carried them out to his wife's station wagon.

Monday morning, chaos gripped Wall Street. Lehman had declared bankruptcy. Merrill Lynch had disappeared into Bank of America. American International Group, the world's largest insurer, teetered on the edge of collapse.

Outside Lehman's office, hordes of cameramen perched like vultures, pouncing on any bedraggled, box-laden Lehman employee scurrying from the building. Satellite dishes stacked atop vans lined the western verge of Seventh Avenue at the feet of Lehman's spotlit sky-scraper. Mutating pixels of images and colors slithered robotically across the bank's twenty-first-century façade, a triple-deck stack of massive digital screens. A bulky man in a blue suit and candy-striped tie, bald with a bushy white mustache—a beat cop dressed for a funeral—protected the doors to the besieged building.

A man in a scruffy white jacket and green cap shuffled back and forth in front of the building's entrance, eyes shooting toward the turnstiles. "The capitalist order has collapsed," he shouted, waving a fist as cameramen snapped the idle shot. "The whole scam is falling apart." Security men quickly shooed him away.

In the executive suite on the thirty-first floor, Dick Fuld looked down upon the spectacle below. His global banking empire lay in ruins beneath his feet. To protect himself from fuming employees, Fuld, who'd taken home a $71 million paycheck in 2007, had staffed up on extra bodyguards. A garish painting of Fuld, perched on the side-walk outside the building, was covered in angry messages scrawled in marker, pen, pencil. "Greed took them down," read one. Another: "Dick, my kids thank you."

Credit markets were frozen as trading began. Investors were struggling to make sense of Lehman's collapse and the black cloud hanging over AIG. Later that Monday, rating agencies slashed AIG's credit. Since AIG had relied on its triple-A rating to insure a number of financial assets, including billions in subprime bonds, the change pushed it toward the edge of insolvency. Rather than let AIG fail, the U.S. government stepped in with a massive bailout.

A unit of AIG, called AIG Financial Products, was behind the blowup. Known as AIG-FP, the unit had gobbled up $400 billion of credit default swaps, many of which were tied to subprime loans. AIG-FP's headquarters were in London, where it could sidestep tricky U.S. banking laws. It had a AAA rating, which made its business at-tractive to nearly every investor imaginable, from hedge funds to highly regulated pension funds. The sterling rating also allowed it to sell products cheaper than many competitors.

AIG-FP had sold insurance on billions of dollars of debt securities tied to asset-backed CDOs packed with everything from corporate loans to subprime mortgages to auto loans to credit-card receivables. Since AIG-FP had such a high credit rating, it didn't have to post a dime of collateral on the deals. It could just sit back and collect fees. It was a form of infinite leverage based on AIG's good name. The collateral was the soul and body of AIG itself.

The models that gauged the risk of those positions were constructed by Gary Gorton, a quant who also taught at Yale University. The models were replete with estimates about the likelihood that the bonds AIG was insuring would default. But defaults didn't torch AIG-FP's balance sheet: AIG-FP was killed by margin calls. If the value of the underlying asset insured by the swaps declined for whatever reason, the protection provider—AIG-FP—would have to put up more collateral, since the risk of default was higher. Those collateral calls started to soar in the summer of 2007. Goldman Sachs, for instance, had demanded an extra $8 billion to $9 billion in collateral from AIG-FP.

It was a case of model failure on a massive scale. AIG had rolled the dice on a model and had crapped out.

Meanwhile, the hasty exodus of Lehman employees that Sunday night had proven premature. The following week, Barclays purchased Lehman's investment banking and capital markets units, which included Rothman's group. But the damage had been done, and regulators were scrambling to contain it.

On Thursday, September 18, Fed chairman Ben Bernanke, Treasury secretary Hank Paulson, and a select group of about sixteen top legislators, including New York senator Chuck Schumer, Nevada senator Harry Reid, and Connecticut senator Chris Dodd, gathered around a polished conference table in the offices of House Speaker Nancy Pelosi. Bernanke began to talk. The credit markets had frozen, he explained, likening the financial system to the arteries of a patient whose blood had stopped flowing.

"That patient has had a heart attack and may die," Bernanke said in a somber tone to the dead-quiet room. "We could have a depression if we don't act quickly and decisively."

Bernanke spoke for about fifteen minutes, outlining a looming financial Armageddon that could destroy the global economy. The

Money Grid was collapsing. The elected officials who had been faced with terrorist attacks and war were stunned. The loquacious Chuck Schumer was speechless. Chris Dodd, whose state pulled in billions from hedge fund taxes, turned talcum white.

The infusion of cash came quickly. The government stepped in with an $85 billion bailout of AIG, which soared to about $175 billion within six months. In the following weeks, the Treasury Department, led by Hank Paulson, former CEO of Goldman Sachs, unveiled a plan to pump $700 billion into the financial system to jolt the dying patient back to life. But no one knew if it would be enough.

Andy Lo's Doomsday Clock was nearing midnight.

A FLAW

Alan Greenspan sat in the hot glare of ranks of TV cameras on Capitol Hill, sweating. On October 23, 2008, the former chairman of the Federal Reserve faced rows of angry congressmen demanding answers about the cause of a credit crisis ravaging the U.S. economy. For more than a year, Greenspan had argued time and again that he wasn't to blame for the meltdown. Several weeks earlier, President George W. Bush had signed a $700 billion government bailout plan for a financial industry devastated by the housing market's collapse.

In July, Bush had delivered a blunt diagnosis for the troubles in the financial system. "Wall Street got drunk," Bush said at a Republican fund-raiser in Houston. "It got drunk, and now it's got a hangover. The question is, how long will it sober up and not try to do all these fancy financial instruments?"

The credit meltdown of late 2008 had shocked the world with its intensity. The fear spread far beyond Wall Street, triggering sharp downturns in global trade and battering the world's economic engine. On Capitol Hill, the government's finger-pointing machinery cranked up to full throttle. Among the first called to account: Greenspan.

Greenspan, many in Congress believed, had been the prime enabler for Wall Street's wild ride, too slow to remove the punch bowl of low interest rates earlier in the decade. "We are in the midst of a once-in-a-century credit tsunami," Greenspan said to Congress in his characteristic sandpaper-dry voice. To his left sat the stone-faced Christopher Cox, head of the Securities and Exchange Commission, in for his own grilling later in the day.

Representative Henry Waxman, a Democrat from California overseeing the hearings, shifted in his seat and adjusted his glasses. A patina of sweat glistened on his egglike dome. Greenspan droned on about the causes of the crisis, the securitization of home mortgages by heedless banks on Wall Street, the poor risk management. It was nothing new. Waxman had heard it all before from countless economists and bankers who had testified before his committee that year. Then Greenspan said something truly strange to viewers unfamiliar with the quants and their minions.

"In recent decades, a vast risk management and pricing system has evolved combining the best insights of mathematicians and finance experts supported by major advances in computer and communications technology," he said. "A Nobel Prize was awarded for the discovery of the pricing model that underpins much of the advance in derivatives markets," he added, referring to the Black-Scholes option model. Greenspan kept his eyes glued to the speech laid out on the long wooden table before him.

"The modern risk management paradigm held sway for decades," he said. "The whole intellectual edifice, however, collapsed in the summer of last year."

Waxman wanted to know more about this intellectual edifice. "Do you feel that your ideology pushed you to make decisions that you wish you had not made?" he asked, indignant.

"To exist you need an ideology," Greenspan replied in his signature monotone. "The question is whether it is accurate or not. And what I'm saying to you is, yes, I have found a flaw. I don't know how significant or permanent it is. But I have been very distressed by that fact."

"You found a flaw in the reality?" Waxman asked, seeming genuinely bewildered.

"A flaw in the model that I perceived is the critical functioning structure that defines how the world works, so to speak."

The model Greenspan referred to was the belief that financial markets and economies are self-correcting—a notion as old as Adam Smith's mysterious "invisible hand" in which prices guide resources toward the most efficient outcome through the laws of supply and demand. Economic agents (traders, lenders, homeowners, consumers, etc.) acting in their own self-interest create the best of all possible worlds, as it were—guiding them inexorably to the Truth, the efficient market machine the quants put their faith in. Government intervention, as a rule, only hinders this process. Thus Greenspan had for years advocated an aggressive policy of deregulation before these very same congressmen in speech after speech. Investment banks, hedge funds, the derivatives industry—the core elements of the sprawling shadow banking system—left to their own devices, he believed, would create a more efficient and cost-effective financial system.

But as the banking collapse of 2008 showed, unregulated banks and hedge funds with young quick-draw traders with billions at their disposal and huge incentives to swing for the fences don't always operate in the most efficient manner possible. They might even make so many bad trades that they threaten to destabilize the system itself. Greenspan wasn't sure how to fix the system, aside from forcing banks to hold a percentage of loans they make on their own balance sheets, giving them the incentive to actually care about whether the loans might default or not. (Of course, the banks could always hedge those loans with credit default swaps.)

Greenspan's confession was stunning. It marked a dramatic shift for the eighty-two-year-old banker who for so long had been hailed variously as the most powerful man on the planet and the wise central banker with a Midas touch. In a May 2005 speech he'd hailed the system he now doubted. "The growing array of derivatives and the related application of more sophisticated methods for measuring and

managing risks had been key factors underlying the remarkable re-
silience of the banking system, which had recently shrugged off severe
shocks to the economy and the financial system."

Now Greenspan was turning his back on the very system he had
championed for decades. In congressional testimony in 2000, Vermont
representative Bernie Sanders had asked Greenspan, "Aren't you concerned with such a growing concentration of wealth that if one of
these huge institutions fails it will have a horrendous impact on the
national and global economy?"

Greenspan didn't bat an eye. "No, I'm not," he'd replied. "I believe that the general growth in large institutions has occurred in the
context of an underlying structure of markets in which many of the
larger risks are dramatically—I should say fully—hedged."

Times had changed. Greenspan seemed befuddled by the meltdown, out of touch with the elephantine growth of a vast risk-taking
apparatus on Wall Street that had taken place under his nose—and by
many accounts had been encouraged by his policies.

After his testimony ended, Greenspan stood and walked, hunched
over, out of the hot glare of the television lights. He seemed shaken,
and it was painfully clear that Greenspan, once hailed as the savior of
the financial system after orchestrating the bailout of Long-Term Capital Management in 1998, was a fragile and elderly man whose better
days were long behind him.

Watching the telecast of the congressional hearings from his hedge
fund in Greenwich, Cliff Asness couldn't believe what he was hearing.
If anyone personified the system Greenspan called into question, it
was Asness. A product of the University of Chicago's school of finance,
which preached the dogma of free market libertarianism like a new
religion, Asness believed with every fiber in his body and brain in the
economic model Greenspan now seemed to reject. *There is no flaw.*

"Traitor," he muttered to his TV set. Greenspan was turning his
back on a theory about the efficiency of free markets simply to salvage
his reputation, Asness thought. "Too late, old man."

The way Asness saw it, Greenspan had been right about free
markets; his mistake was leaving interest rates too low for too long,

helping inflate the housing bubble that fed the whole mess in the first place. That's what Greenspan should have apologized for, not his support of free markets.

Everything Asness believed in seemed under siege. Greenspan was turning his back on a movement that, Asness thought, had generated unprecedented wealth and prosperity for America and much of the rest of the world. Capitalism worked. Free markets worked. Sure, there were excesses, but the economy was in the process of purging those excesses out of the system. *That's how it worked.* To see Greenspan lose faith and betray the creed at its moment of weakness seemed the most extreme form of cretinism.

Far worse for Asness, AQR itself was under siege. It had lost billions in the market meltdown. Rumors had started to crop up that AQR was close to shutting down.

AQR wasn't the only fund suffering such rumors in October 2008. Another major hedge fund was perched on the very edge of a death spiral: Citadel.

Ken Griffin marched into a brightly lit conference room on the thirty-seventh floor of the Citadel Center on South Dearborn Street, sat down before a polished wooden table, and donned a headset. Beside him sat Gerald Beeson, Citadel's green-eyed, orange-haired chief operating officer, the son of a cop who'd grown up on Chicago's rough-and-tumble South Side. Beeson was one of Griffin's most trusted lieutenants, a veteran of the firm since 1993. It was Friday afternoon, October 24, one day after Greenspan's testimony on Capitol Hill. More than a thousand listeners were on the line waiting for Griffin and Beeson to explain what had become of Citadel.

Rumors of Citadel's collapse were spreading rapidly, even hitting TV screens on the financial news network CNBC. Citadel, traders said, was circling the drain. The market turmoil after the collapse of Lehman Brothers had led to massive losses in its giant convertible bond portfolio. If Citadel went under, many feared, the ripple effects would be catastrophic, causing other funds with similar positions to tumble like so many dominoes.

According to former senior executives at Citadel, Griffin decided to push some employees out as Citadel's fortunes grew more precarious. Joe Russell, head of Citadel's credit trading group and the key man in the E*Trade deal, had been agitating for more power. Griffin wouldn't give it to him, and his ruthless side emerged. The word around Citadel was that Griffin and Russell engaged in a furious shouting match that left little doubt they'd never work together again.

But Griffin was still confident that Citadel could withstand the pressure. One major unknown kept him up at night: Goldman Sachs. Goldman's stock had been plunging, and some feared it, too, would follow in the wake of Bear Stearns and Lehman Brothers. Goldman was a key counterparty to Citadel in numerous trades and also extended credit to the fund. Throughout the crisis, Griffin and Goldman CEO Lloyd Blankfein held numerous discussions about the state of the markets. As the system spiraled out of control, the impossible suddenly seemed all too possible. If Goldman went down, Griffin believed, Citadel would certainly follow.

The thought of Goldman Sachs collapsing seemed incredible. Impossible. But Bear had gone down. So had Lehman. Morgan Stanley was on the ropes. AIG, Fannie Mae, Washington Mutual. Even Ken Griffin's fortress of money was crumbling. He'd do everything in his power to keep that from happening. Even the unthinkable: hold a conference call open to the press.

Earlier that day, James Forese, Citigroup's head of capital markets, had called Griffin with a warning. "Ken, you guys are getting killed in the rumor mill," Forese said. "Most of these things are just blatantly false. If you get out there and say you're fine, it will mean a lot to the market right now."

And so, setting aside his penchant for secrecy, Griffin cleared his throat and prepared to explain what had happened to Citadel.

Trouble was, everything wasn't fine.

■   ■   ■

In nearly two decades, Griffin had lost money in only a single year, 1994. Now his fund was on the verge of collapse. The suddenness of its downturn was head-spinning and spoke to the severity of the market's post–Lehman Brothers turbulence.

Citadel had been flushed into the public eye by the dramatic upheaval. The implosion of Lehman and the panic sparked by the near-collapse of AIG were like massive earthquakes rattling through the global financial system. At first the shock waves seemed manageable. Markets were dislocated in the few days following Lehman's bankruptcy filing on September 15, but not so dramatically that Citadel would feel threatened. Griffin later described it as a huge wave that passes unfelt beneath a ship as it heads treacherously toward shore.

Among the first to feel the crushing impact of the wave once it hit shore were credit-trading powerhouses Citadel and Boaz Weinstein's Saba, which dabbled heavily in corporate bonds and credit default swaps. Citadel's flagship fund, Kensington, lost a staggering 20 percent in September. By late October, it was down 35 percent for the year. Saba was also gravely wounded, losing hundreds of millions in positions in companies such as General Motors and Washington Mutual, the Seattle thrift and subprime-mortgage giant seized by federal regulators and sold to J. P. Morgan shotgun-wedding-style for $1.9 billion in late September. Weinstein had been making bets that financial firms deemed systemically important would survive the crisis, but the relentless violence of the credit meltdown crushed his optimistic forecasts.

Now Citadel and Saba were in the crosshairs. The rumors of Citadel's collapse were adding to the market's already volcanic volatility, triggering big downturns and wild swings. One of the most damaging rumors, popping up on message boards and financial blogs, was that Federal Reserve officials had swooped into Citadel's Chicago headquarters and were combing through its positions to determine whether it needed a bailout—bad memories of LTCM's 1998 bailout a decade ago still lingered among many Wall Street veterans.

Citadel denied it was in trouble, but the Fed rumors were partially true. Officials from the central bank were privately worried about the prospects of a collapse by Citadel. The fund sat on nearly $15 billion worth of corporate bonds in its convertible-bond arbitrage book, which was the most highly leveraged portion of the fund, according to people familiar with the fund. While the amount of leverage was a closely guarded secret, one bank's assessment put it north of 30 to 1 in 2007, though the leverage had been reduced to 18 to 1 by the summer of 2008.

The convertible-bond arbitrage book, whose roots went all the way back to Ed Thorp's breakthrough insights in the 1960s, was Citadel's hot zone. If the fund failed and started dumping bonds on the market, the system would sustain yet another brutal shock. It was already on the very cusp of doom. To gauge the risk, regulators from the Fed's New York branch started questioning the fund's major counterparties such as Deutsche Bank and Goldman Sachs about their exposure to Citadel, worried that Citadel's collapse could threaten yet another bank.

Inside Citadel's Chicago office, the mood was grim but professional. Traders went to work as they did every day, showing up early, staying late—often much later than usual. Inside, many were quietly terrified by the huge losses they saw on their screens.

Griffin knew he had to stop the bleeding. Egged on by Wall Street bankers such as Forese, he made a snap decision that late October Friday to hold a conference call with Citadel bondholders to quell the rumors. It was set to begin at about 3:30 P.M. Eastern time. In keeping with the nerve-wracking tenor of the moment, nothing was working the way it was supposed to. The lines were such hot commodities that many listeners couldn't get through. A technical glitch created by the demand led to a twenty-five-minute delay, an embarrassing gaffe for a fund that prided itself on its military-style precision.

By the time the call started, Beeson seemed flustered by the huge turnout, stumbling on his opening lines. "Today we'd like to thank you for taking . . ." He started again, his voice flat: "Today we'd like to thank you for taking the time to join us on this conference call on short notice."

Griffin chimed in, curtly thanking his team for its hard work, then turned the call back over to Beeson, who sounded almost in awe of the destructive powers of the market meltdown.

"To call this a dislocation doesn't go anywhere near the enormity of what we've seen," he said. "What have we seen here? We have seen the near-collapse of the world's banking system."

Beeson described the impact the powerful deleveraging was having on Citadel's positions. Just as investors plowed into cash or Treasury bonds during Black Monday in 1987 and the collapse of Long-Term Capital in 1998, a torrent of money had flowed into highly liquid assets following Lehman's collapse. At the same time, investors dumped less-safe assets such as corporate bonds like a panicked mob fleeing a burning building.

Normally Citadel wouldn't have even been singed too severely by such a move. Like any good quant fund, it had hedged its bets with credit default swaps. The swaps were supposed to gain in value if the price of the bonds declined. If a GM bond fell 10 percent, the credit default swap insuring the bond would gain 10 percent. Simple. As Boaz Weinstein liked to say, it wasn't rocket surgery.

But in the financial tsunami of late 2008, the swaps were dysfunctional. The deleveraging had grown so powerful that most banks and hedge funds weren't willing to buy insurance from anyone; that meant the swaps that were supposed to protect investors weren't working as promised. Many were afraid the seller of the insurance might not be around much longer to pay up if the underlying bond defaulted. Banks essentially stopped lending, or clamped down on lending terms tighter than a cinch knot, making it extremely hard for many investors, including hedge funds such as Citadel, to fund their trades—which were almost entirely conducted with leverage. No leverage, no trading, no profits.

It was the same problem that always occurred during financial crises: when the shit hit the fan, the fine-tuned quant models didn't work as panicked investors rushed for the exits. Liquidity evaporated, and billions were lost. Like frightened children in a haunted house, investors had grown so skittish that they were running from their own shadows. The entire global credit market suffered a massive panic attack, threatening to bring down trading powerhouses such as Saba and Citadel in its wake.

Another blow came from the federal government's ban on short selling in the weeks following the Lehman-AIG debacle. Shares of financial firms across the board—even stalwarts such as Goldman Sachs and Morgan Stanley—were collapsing. To keep the situation from spiraling out of control, the Securities and Exchange Commission in September instituted a temporary ban on shorting about eight hundred financial stocks. Citadel, it turned out, had short positions in some of those companies as part of its convertible bond arbitrage strategy. Just as Ed Thorp had done in the 1960s, Citadel would buy corporate bonds and hedge the position by shorting the stock. With the short-selling ban, those shares surged dramatically in a vicious short squeeze that inflicted huge losses on hedge funds. Shares of Morgan Stanley, a bank squarely in the short sellers' crosshairs, surged more than 100 percent in a matter of days from about $9 to $21 in early October when the ban was in place.

Before the ban took effect, Griffin got SEC chairman Christopher Cox on the phone.

"This could mean a catastrophe for us, and a lot of other funds like us," Griffin told Cox. "The ban could also inject greater uncertainty and risk into the market," he said.

The chairman was unmoved. "The financial system is in crisis, Ken," he said. "The people need to be protected from a collapse."

It was a quant nightmare. Markets were at the mercy of unruly forces such as panicked investors and government regulators. As the conference call proceeded, Beeson kept repeating a single word: *unprecedented*. Citadel's losses, he said, were due to "the unprecedented deleveraging that took place around the world over the past several weeks."

To quants, *unprecedented* is perhaps the dirtiest word in the English language. Their models are by necessity backward-looking, based on decades of data about how markets operate in all kinds of conditions. When something is unprecedented, it falls outside the parameters of the models. In other words, the models don't work anymore. It was as if a person flipping a coin a hundred times, expecting roughly half to turn up heads and the rest tails, experienced a dozen straight flips where the coin landed on its edge.

Finally Griffin took charge of the call. "Again, good afternoon," he said, quickly reminding listeners that while he might be a forty-year-old whippersnapper, he'd been in the game for a long time, having seen the crash in 1987, the debt panic of 1998, the dot-com bust. But this market was different—unprecedented.

"I have never seen a market as full of panic as I've seen in the past seven or eight weeks," he said. "The world is going to change on a going-forward basis."

Then the stress broke through. Griffin's voice cracked. He seemed on the verge of tears. "I could not ask for a better team to weather the storm that we are going through," he said in a sentimental flourish. "They are winning on a going-forward basis," he said, sounding almost wistful even as he lapsed into the most generic corporatese.

After just twelve minutes, the call ended. The rumors about Citadel's collapse had been quieted, but not for long.

Griffin was growing more worried, convinced that rival hedge funds and take-no-prisoners investment bank traders were taking bites out of his fund, sharks smelling blood in the water and trying to swallow Citadel whole. Inside his fund, he fumed at white-knuckled bond traders who refused to keep adding positions in the market's madness. He clashed with his right-hand man, James Yeh, a reclusive quant who'd been at Citadel since the early 1990s. Yeh thought his boss was making the wrong move. After the Bear Stearns debacle, as the crisis was heating up, Citadel had taken on huge blocks of convertible bonds. Griffin had even been eyeing pieces of Lehman Brothers before the firm collapsed. Yeh and others at Citadel, however, were far more bearish than Griffin and thought the best move was to batten down the hatches and wait for the storm to pass.

That wasn't how Ken Griffin played the game. In past crises, when everyone else was ducking for cover, Griffin had always been able to make money by wading into the market and scooping up bargains—the LTCM debacle of 1998, the dot-com meltdown, the Enron implosion, Amaranth, Sowood, E*Trade. Citadel always had the firepower to make hay while others cowered in fear. As the system cratered in late 2008, Griffin's instincts were to double down.

Griffin's signature trade, however, worked against him this time. The market wasn't stabilizing. Values kept sinking, bringing Citadel down with them.

As the meltdown continued, Griffin began personally buying and selling securities. Griffin, who hadn't personally traded in size for years, seemed to be trying to save his firm from catastrophe using his own market savvy. There was one problem, traders said: The positions were often losers as the market kept spiraling lower.

But Griffin, like Asness, was certain the situation would stabilize. When it did, Citadel, as always, would be on top.

Citadel's lenders, big Wall Street banks, weren't so confident. Citadel depended on the banks to bankroll its trades. In the spring of 2008, its hedge funds held about $140 billion in gross assets on $15 billion in capital, or the stuff it actually owned. That translated to a 9-to-1 leverage ratio. Most of the extra positions came in the form of lines of credit or other arrangements with banks.

Concerned about the impact a Citadel collapse would have on their balance sheets, several banks organized ad-hoc committees to strategize for the possibility. J. P. Morgan was playing hardball with Citadel's traders regarding the financing of certain positions, according to traders at the fund. Regulators, meanwhile, pressed the banks not to make drastic changes in their dealings with Citadel, worried that if one lender blinked, the others would also flee, triggering another financial shock as the entire system teetered on the edge.

Investors were clearly worried. "There's a rumor a day about how Citadel is going to go out of business," Mark Yusko, manager of Citadel investor Morgan Creek Capital Management in North Carolina, told his clients on a conference call.

Inside the firm, as the carnage dragged on, employees were running ragged. Visitors noted dark rings around traders' bloodshot eyes. The three-day beards, the loose, coffee-stained ties. As rumors about Citadel's situation spread, traders were barraged by calls from outside the firm asking whether Federal Reserve examiners were scouring the premises. At one point an exasperated trader stood and shouted into his phone, "Sorry, I don't see any Fed here." Another quipped: "I just looked under my desk and didn't see any Fed."

Beeson, meanwhile, was the front man for Citadel as the firm suffered more losses. He leapt into damage-control mode, shuttling nonstop between Chicago and New York to meet with edgy counterparties, trying to reassure them that Citadel had enough capital to make it through the storm. Traders were frantically unloading assets to raise cash and trim the firm's leverage. At one point, as flagship fund Kensington's net worth continued to plunge, Citadel arranged an $800 million loan from one of its own funds, the high-frequency machine Tactical Trading run by Misha Malyshev that had been spun out of the flagship fund in late 2007, according to people familiar with the fund. Investors who learned of the odd but completely legal financing manoeuvre took it as a sign of desperation and realized it meant the firm was truly on the precipice—if it was lending itself its own money, that could mean it was having a hard time getting a decent loan elsewhere.

Several days after the bond-holder's call, Griffin distributed an email to Citadel's employees around the world. Citadel would survive and thrive, he said, ever the optimist. The fund's situation reminded him of Christopher Columbus's journey across the Atlantic in 1492, he explained. When land was nowhere in sight and the situation seemed desperate, Griffin said, Columbus wrote two words in his journal: Sail on.

It was a rallying cry for Citadel's beleaguered employees. Just the year before, Citadel had been one of the mightiest financial forces in the world, a $20 billion powerhouse on the verge of greater things. Now it was faced with disaster. While the situation might seem bleak, Griffin said, and calamity imminent, land would eventually be found.

Some reading the email thought back to their history lessons and recalled that Columbus had been lost.

Soon after, Griffin held his fortieth-birthday party at Joe's Seafood Prime Steak and Stone Crab in downtown Chicago, a dozen blocks from Citadel's headquarters. Employees presented Griffin with a lifeboat-sized replica of one of Columbus's ships. Griffin laughed and accepted the gift gracefully, but there was a sense of overhanging doom, a chill in the air, that killed any sense of festivity. Everyone could feel it: Citadel was sinking.

At Morgan Stanley, Peter Muller and PDT were in crisis mode. The investment bank's shares were collapsing. Many feared it was the next Lehman, destined for Wall Street's mounting scrap heap. The market was making insane moves. The volatility was out of control, like nothing ever seen before. Muller decided to reduce a large portion of PDT's positions, putting a hoard of its assets into cash before everyone else did.

"The types of volatility we were seeing had no historical basis," said one of PDT's traders. "If your model is based on historical patterns and you're seeing something you've never seen before, you can't expect your model to perform."

It was a tumultuous time for Muller on other fronts. Ever the restless globetrotter, he'd decided to pull up stakes again. His girlfriend was pregnant, and he wanted to put down roots in a place he truly loved. He purchased a luxurious house with a three-car garage and a pool in Santa Barbara, California. Still manning the helm of PDT from afar, he was making trips to New York one or two weeks a month, where he would meet up with his poker pals.

Morgan Stanley, meanwhile, was under heavy fire. Hedge funds that traded through Morgan tried to pull out more than $100 billion in assets. Its clearing bank, the Bank of New York Mellon, asked for an extra $4 billion in capital. It was a move from the same playbook that had taken down Bear Stearns and Lehman Brothers.

In late September, Morgan and Goldman Sachs scrapped their investment banking business model and converted into traditional bank holding companies. Effectively, Wall Street as it had long been known ceased to exist. The move meant the banks would be far more beholden to bank regulators and would be subject to more restrictive capital requirements. The glory days of massive leverage, profits, and risk taking were a thing of the past—or so it seemed.

Days later, Morgan CEO John Mack orchestrated a $9 billion cash infusion from Japan's Mitsubishi UFJ Financial Group. Goldman negotiated a $5 billion investment from Warren Buffett's Berkshire Hathaway.

Catastrophe seemed to have been averted. But the financial mayhem continued to churn through the system. PDT was riding it out on a much-diminished cushion of cash while Muller set up house in sunny Santa Barbara and played the odd gig in Greenwich Village. Seemingly little had changed for Muller, although behind the scenes he was drafting major changes for PDT that would come to light several months later. The same couldn't be said for Boaz Weinstein.

By outward appearances, Boaz Weinstein was sailing through the credit meltdown unfazed. Internally, he was deeply worried. Saba was taking massive hits from the credit market. The Deutsche Bank trader watched in disbelief as his carefully designed trades came unglued.

Weinstein had rolled into 2008 at the top of his game. He and a colleague in London, Colin Fan, were overseeing all global credit trading for Deutsche. Saba was in control of nearly $30 billion in assets, a monster-sized sum for the thirty-five-year-old trader. Weinstein's boss, Anshu Jain, had offered him the powerful position of head of all global credit trading. But Weinstein turned him down flat. He'd already drawn up plans to break away from Deutsche in 2009 and launch his own hedge fund (to be called Saba, naturally).

After the collapse of Bear Stearns in March 2008, Weinstein believed the worst of the credit crisis was in the rearview mirror. He wasn't alone. Griffin thought the economy was stabilizing. Morgan's John Mack told shareholders that the subprime crisis was in the eighth or ninth inning. Goldman Sachs CEO Lloyd Blankfein was somewhat less optimistic, saying, "We're probably in the third or fourth inning."

To capitalize on depressed prices, Weinstein scooped up the distressed bonds of companies such as Ford, General Motors, General Electric, and Tribune Co., publisher of the *Chicago Tribune*. And, of course, he hedged those bets with credit default swaps. At first the bets paid off as corporate bonds rallied, giving Saba a tidy profit.

Weinstein continued to plow cash into bonds through the summer, and Saba cruised into September 2008 in the black for the year.

Then everything fell apart. The government took over the mortgage giants Fannie Mae and Freddie Mac. Lehman declared bankruptcy. AIG teetered on a cliff, threatening to pull the entire global financial system over with it.

Just like Citadel, Saba was getting mauled. As the losses mounted, the flow of information among Saba's traders ground to a halt. Normally junior traders on the group's desks would compile profit-and-loss reports summarizing the day's trading activities. With no warning or explanation, the reports stopped circulating. Rumors of huge losses were bandied about around the water cooler. Some feared the group was about to be shut down. The weekly $100 poker games held off Saba's trading floor came to a halt.

Weinstein's hands were tied. He watched in horror as investors avoided risky corporate bonds like three-day-old fish, causing prices to crater. Like Citadel, its positions were hedged with credit default swaps. But investors, worried about whether the counterparties to the traders would be around to fulfill their obligations, wanted nothing to do with the swaps. Typically, the price of the swaps, which are traded every day on over-the-counter markets between banks, hedge funds, and the like, fluctuate according to market conditions. If the value of the swaps Saba held increased in value, it could mark those positions higher on its books, even if it didn't actually trade the swaps itself.

But as the financial markets imploded and leverage evaporated, the swaps market became dysfunctional. The trades that would indicate the new value for the swaps simply weren't happening. Increasingly, Weinstein's favorite investing vehicle, which he'd helped spread across Wall Street since the late 1990s, was seen as the fuse to the powder keg that blew up the financial system.

Weinstein remained outwardly calm, quietly brooding in his office overlooking Wall Street. But the losses were piling up rapidly and soon topped $1 billion. He pleaded with Deutsche's risk managers to let him purchase more swaps so he could better hedge his positions, but the word had come down from on high: buying wasn't allowed, only selling. Perversely, the bank's risk models, such as the notorious

VAR used by all Wall Street banks, instructed traders to exit short positions, including credit default swaps.

Weinstein knew that was crazy, but the quants in charge of risk couldn't be argued with. "Step away from the model," he begged. "The only way for me to get out of this is to be short. If the market is falling and you're losing money, that means you are long the market—and you need to short it, as fast as possible."

He explained that the bank's ability to see around the subprime model in 2007 had earned it a fortune. Now the right move was the same—think outside the quant box.

It didn't work. Risk management was on autopilot. The losses piled up, soon reaching nearly two billion. Saba's stock trading desk was instructed to sell nearly every holding, effectively closing the unit down.

Weinstein was rarely seen on Saba's trading floors as his losses ballooned. The trader was holed up in his office for long periods of time, often late into the night, conferring with top lieutenants about how to stop the bleeding. No one had answers. There was little they could do.

Paranoia took hold. It seemed as if the group could be shut down at any moment. Several of the group's top traders, including the equity trader Alan Benson, were laid off. In late November, a trader was conducting a tour of Saba's second-floor operation. "If you come back two weeks from now, this space will be empty," he said.

He was a little early, but not by much.

A month after Greenspan's testimony, in mid-November, Waxman's committee grilled another group of suspects in the credit crisis: hedge fund managers.

And not just any hedge fund managers. Waxman had summoned the top five earners of 2007 for a televised grilling about the risks the shadowy industry posed to the economy. The lineup, men whose take-home pay averaged $1 billion in 2007, included famed tycoon George Soros. Also on the hot seat was Philip Falcone, whose hedge fund, Harbinger Capital, boasted a 125 percent return in 2007 from a big bet against subprime. His gains paled beside those of fellow witness John Paulson, whose Paulson & Co. posted returns as high as nearly 600 percent from a massive wager against subprime, earning him a one-year bonanza of more than $3 billion, possibly the biggest annual return for an investor ever.

The other two managers arrayed before Waxman's House Committee on Oversight and Government Reform were Jim Simons and Ken Griffin. The quants had come to Capitol Hill.

Griffin, for one, had prepared for his appearance with Citadel's typical discipline. Having flown to Washington from Chicago on his private jet just that morning, he was coached by a battery of lawyers, as well as Washington power broker Robert Barnett. In 1992, Barnett had helped Bill Clinton prepare for the presidential debates, acting as the stand-in for George H. W. Bush. He'd acted as a literary agent for Barack Obama, former British prime minister Tony Blair, *Washington Post* reporter Bob Woodward, and George W. Bush's defense secretary Donald Rumsfeld.

The move was classic Ken Griffin. Money was no object. When he inevitably veered off script during his testimony, lecturing the congressmen on the value of unregulated free markets, that was also classic Ken Griffin.

But for the most part, the hedge fund kingpins made nice, agreeing that the financial system needed an overhaul but shying away from calling for direct oversight of their industry. Soros expressed outright scorn for the hedge fund industry, made up of copycats and trend followers destined for extinction. "The bubble has now burst and hedge funds will be decimated," Soros said in his gruff Hungarian accent, a gleeful prophet of doom. "I would guess that the amount of money they manage will shrink by between 50 and 75 percent."

Coming into 2008, hedge funds were in control of $2 trillion. Soros was estimating that the industry would lose between $1 trillion and $1.5 trillion—through either outright losses or capital flight to safer harbors.

Simons, looking every bit the frumpy professor with his balding pate, chalk-white beard, and rumpled gray jacket, said Renaissance didn't dabble in the "alphabet soup" of CDOs or CDSs that triggered the calamity. His testimony provided little insight into the problems behind the meltdown, though it did offer a rare glimpse into Renaissance's trading methods.

"Renaissance is a somewhat atypical investment management firm," he said. "Our approach is driven by my background as a mathematician. We manage funds whose trading is determined by mathematical formulas. . . . We operate only in highly liquid publicly traded securities, meaning we don't trade in credit default swaps or collateralized debt obligations. Our trading models tend to be contrarian, buying stocks recently out of favor and selling those recently in favor."

For his part, Griffin sounded a note of defiance, fixing his unblinking blue eyes on the befuddled array of legislators. Hedge funds weren't behind the meltdown, he said. Heavily regulated banks were.

"We haven't seen hedge funds as the focal point of the carnage in this financial tsunami," said Griffin, clad in a dark blue jacket, black tie, and light blue shirt.

Whether he believed it or not, the statement smacked of denial, overlooking the fact that Citadel's dramatically weakened condition in late 2008 had added to the market's turmoil. Regulators had been deeply concerned about Citadel and whether its demise would trigger even more blowups.

Griffin also opposed greater transparency. "To ask us to disclose our positions to the open market would parallel asking Coca-Cola to disclose their secret formula to the world."

Despite Griffin's warnings, Congress seemed to be heading toward greater oversight of hedge funds, which it saw as part of a shadow banking system that had caused the financial collapse. "When hedge funds become too big to fail, that poses a problem for the financial system," MIT's Andrew Lo, he of the Doomsday Clock, told the *Wall Street Journal*.

Citadel didn't fail, though it came dangerously close. Griffin, who'd once nurtured grand ambitions of a financial empire that could match the mightiest powerhouses of Wall Street, had been brought low.

But Griffin knew that the high-flying hedge fund fantasy of the past two decades would never again be the same. The mountain-moving leverage and ballsy billion-dollar bets on risky hands were all consigned to another age.

Griffin put a brave face on. As he said on the conference call that Friday afternoon in October: "We need to face the fact that we need to evolve. We will embrace the changes that are part of that evolution, and we will prosper in the new era of finance."

His investors weren't so sure. Many were asking for their money back. In December, after redemption requests totaling about $1.2 billion, Citadel barred investors from pulling money from its flagship funds. Assets at Citadel had already shrunk to $10.5 billion from $20 billion. To comply with further requests, Griffin would have to unload more positions to raise the funds, a bitter pill to swallow in a depressed market.

Investors had little choice but to comply. But the move had infuriated many, who saw it as a strong-arm tactic by a firm that had already lost them countless millions that year.

Griffin was also suffering a big hit to his mammoth pocketbook. Few outsiders knew exactly how much of Citadel Griffin owned, but some estimated that he held roughly 50 percent of the firm's assets heading into the crisis, putting his personal net worth at about $10 billion, far higher than most believed. The 55 percent tumble by his hedge funds, therefore, hurt no one more than Griffin. Adding to the pain, he'd used $500 million of his own cash to prop up the funds and pay management fees typically borne by investors. Of course, he was also the biggest investor in the firm's high-frequency quant powerhouse, Tactical Trading, which had pulled in $1 billion.

Citadel, meanwhile, was severely hobbled. The gross assets of its hedge funds had tumbled sharply in the meltdown, falling from $140 billion in the spring of 2008 to just $52 billion by the end of the year. The firm had unloaded nearly $90 billion of assets in its frantic effort to deleverage its balance sheet, a wave of selling that had added further pressure to a panicked post-Lehman market.

Griffin had plenty of company, of course, in the great hedge-fund shakeout of 2008—including Cliff Asness.

Cliff Asness was furious. The rumors, lies, and the cheap shots had to stop.

It was early December 2008. The small town of Greenwich, Connecticut, was in turmoil. The luxury yachts and streamlined power-boats lay moored in the frigid docks of the Delamar on Greenwich Harbor, a luxury hotel designed in the style of a Mediterranean villa. Caravans of limousines, Bentleys, Porsches, and Beamers sat locked in their spacious custom garages. Gated mansions hunched in the Connecticut cold behind their rows of exotic shrubbery, bereft of their traditional lacings of Christmas glitz. Few of the high-powered occupants of those mansions felt much like celebrating. It was a glum holiday season in Greenwich, hedge fund capital of the world.

Making matters worse, a multibillion-dollar money management firm run by a reclusive financier named Bernard Madoff had proved to be a massive Ponzi scheme, one that Ed Thorp had already unearthed in the early 1990s. The losses rippled throughout the industry like shock waves. A cloud of suspicion fell upon an industry already infamous for its paranoia and obsessive secrecy.

Ground zero of Greenwich's hedge fund scene was Two Greenwich Plaza, a nondescript four-story building beside the town's train station that once had housed a hodgepodge of shippers, manufacturers, and stuffy family law firms. That was before the hedge fund crowd moved in.

One of the biggest hedge funds of them all, of course, was AQR. Its captain, Cliff Asness, was on a rampage. He wasn't quite rolling steel balls around in his hand like Captain Queeg on the *Caine*, but he wasn't far off. The battered computer monitors Asness destroyed in anger were piling up. Some thought Asness was growing too agitated. He seemed to be slipping into a kind of frenzy, the polar opposite of the rational principles he'd based his fund upon. Driving his fury was the persistent chatter that AQR was blowing up, rumors such as AQR had lost 40 percent in a single day . . . AQR was on the verge of shutting its doors forever . . .

AQR was melting down and tunneling to the center of the earth in a crazed China syndrome hedge fund catastrophe . . .

Many of the rumors cropped up on a popular Wall Street blog called Dealbreaker. The site was peppered with disparaging comments about AQR. Dealbreaker's gossipy scribe, Bess Levin, had recently written a post about a round of layoffs at AQR that had included Asness's longtime secretary, Adrienne Rieger.

"Uncle Cliff is rumored to have recently sacked his secretary of ten years, and as everyone knows, it's the secretaries who hold the key to your web of lies and bullshit and deceit, and you don't get rid of them unless you're about to go down for the dirt nap," she wrote.

Dozens of readers posted comments on Levin's report. Asness, reading them from his office, could tell that many came from axed employees or, worse, disgruntled current employees sitting in their cubicles just outside his office. Some of the posts were just plain mean. "I guess the black box didn't work," read one. Another: "AQR is an absolute disaster."

On the afternoon of December 4, Asness decided to respond. Unlike Griffin, who held a conference call, Asness was going to confront the rumormongers in their den: on the Internet. From his third-floor corner office, he sat before his computer, went to Dealbreaker's site, and started to type.

"This is Cliff Asness," he began. He sat back, wiped his mouth, then leaned forward into the keyboard:

All these inside references, yet so much ignorance and/or lies. Obviously some of these posts are bitter rants by people not here anymore, and obviously some are just ignorance and cruelty. Either way they are still lies. . . . For good people we had to let go I feel very bad. For investors who are in our products that are having a tough time I feel very bad and intend to fix it. Frankly, for anyone who is in a tough spot I feel bad. But for liars, and bitter former employees who were let go because we decided we needed you less than the people you now lie about . . . and little men who get off on anonymous mendacity on the internet, ---- YOU and the keyboard you wrote it on. Sorry I can't be more eloquent, you deserve no more and will hear no more from me after this post. I'm Cliff Asness and I approved this message.

Asness posted the rant on the site and quickly realized he'd made a terrible mistake—later he'd call it "stupid." It was a rare public display of anger for a widely respected money manager. It became an immediate sensation within AQR and throughout the hedge fund community. Morale at the fund had been on the wane as its fortunes suffered. Now the founder of a firm known for rationality and mathematical rigor seemed to have let his emotions get the best of him.

Investors didn't seem to mind the dustup. What they did mind were the billions of dollars AQR had lost. But Asness was convinced the following year would be better. The models would work again. Decades of research couldn't be wrong. The Truth had taken a shot in the mouth, but it would eventually come back. When it did, AQR would be there to clean up.

The travails of AQR, once one of the hottest hedge funds on Wall Street, and the intense pressures placed on Asness captured the plight of an industry struggling to cope with the most tumultuous market in decades.

The market's chaos had made a hash of the models deployed by the quants. AQR's losses were especially severe in late 2008 after Lehman Brothers collapsed, sending markets around the globe into turmoil. Its Absolute Return Fund fell about 46 percent in 2008, compared with a 48 percent drop by the Standard & Poor's 500-stock index. In other words, investors in plain-vanilla index funds had done just about as well (or poorly) as investors who'd placed their money in the hands of one of the most sophisticated asset managers in the business.

It was the toughest year on record for hedge funds, which lost 19 percent in 2008, according to Hedge Fund Research, a Chicago research group, only the second year since 1990 that the industry lost money as a whole. (In 2002, hedge funds slid 1.5 percent.)

The Absolute Return Fund had lost more than half of its assets from its peak, dropping to about $1.5 billion from about $4 billion in mid-2007. AQR in total had about $7 billion in so-called alternative funds and about $13 billion in long-only funds, down sharply from the $40 billion it sat on heading into August 2007, when it was planning an IPO. In a little more than a year, AQR had lost nearly half its war chest.

AQR's poor performance shocked its investors. So-called absolute return funds were supposed to provide positive risk-adjusted returns in any kind of market—they were expected to zig when the market zagged. But Absolute Return seemed to follow the S&P 500 like a magnet.

One reason behind the parallel tracks: in early 2008, AQR had made a big wager that U.S. stocks would rise. According to its value-centric models, large U.S. stocks were a bargain relative to a number of other assets, such as Treasury bonds and markets in other countries. So Asness rolled the dice, plowing hundreds of millions into assets that mirrored the S&P 500.

The decision set the stage for one of the most frustrating years in Asness's investing career. AQR also made misplaced bets on the direction of interest rates, currencies, commercial real estate, and convertible bonds—pretty much everything under the sun.

As the losses piled up, investors were getting antsy. AQR was supposed to hold up in market downturns, just as it had in 2001 and 2002 during the dot-com blowup. Instead, AQR was racing to the bottom along with the rest of the market.

In October and November Asness went on a long road trip, visiting nearly every investor in his fund, traveling in a private jet to locations as far afield as Tulsa, Oklahoma, and Sydney, Australia. For the rare down moments, he pulled out his Kindle, Amazon.com's wireless reading device, which was loaded with books ranging from *How Math Explains the World* to *Anna Karenina* to *When Markets Collide* by Mohamad El-Erian, a financial guru at bond giant Pimco.

But Asness had little time for reading. He was trying to keep his fund alive. His goal was to convince investors that AQR's strategies would eventually reap big returns. Many decided to stick with the fund despite its dismal performance, testimony to their belief that Asness would, in fact, get his mojo back.

By December, as the market continued to spiral lower, the pressure ratcheted up on Asness. He'd become obsessed with a tick-by-tick display that tracked Absolute Return's dismal performance. The stress in AQR's office became intense. Asness's decision to lay off several researchers as well as Rieger, his secretary, raised questions about the firm's longevity.

Chatter about AQR's precarious state became rampant in hedge fund circles. Asness and Griffin frequently exchanged rumors they'd heard about the other's fund, tipping each other off about the latest slander.

Both onetime masters of the universe knew the glory days were over. In a telling sign of his diminished, though defiant, expectations, Asness coauthored a November article for *Institutional Investor*, with AQR researcher Adam Berger, called "We're Not Dead Yet." The article was a response to a question from *Institutional Investor* about whether quantitative investing had a future.

"The fact that we have been asked this question suggests that many people think the future of quantitative investing is bleak," Asness and Berger wrote. "After all, upon seeing a good friend in full health—or even on death's doorstep—would you really approach the person and say, 'Great to see you—are you still alive?' If you have to ask, you probably think quant investing is already dead."

Asness knew the quants weren't dead. But he knew they'd taken a serious blow and that it could take months, if not years, before they'd be back on their feet and ready to fight.

Ken Griffin was also fighting the tide. But the bleeding was relentless. By the end of 2008, Citadel's primary funds had lost a jaw-dropping 55 percent of their assets in one of the biggest hedge fund debacles of all time. At the start of January, the firm had $11 billion left, a vertiginous drop from the $20 billion it had had at the start of 2008.

What is perhaps more remarkable is that Citadel lived to trade another day. Griffin had seen his Waterloo and survived. His personal wealth fell by an estimated $2 billion in 2008. It was the biggest decline of any hedge fund manager for the year, marking a stunning fall from the heights for one of the hedge fund world's elite traders.

Not every hedge fund lost money that year. Renaissance's Medallion fund gained an astonishing 80 percent in 2008, capitalizing on the market's extreme volatility with its lightning-fast computers. Jim Simons was the hedge fund world's top earner for the year, pocketing a cool $2.5 billion.

Medallion's phenomenal surge in 2008 stunned the investing world. All the old questions came back: How do they do it? How, in a year when nearly every other investor got slaughtered, could Medallion rake in billions?

The answer, at the end of the day, may be as prosaic as this: The people in charge are smarter than everyone else. Numerous ex–Renaissance employees say that there is no secret formula for the fund's success, no magic code discovered decades ago by geniuses such as Elwyn Berlekamp or James Ax. Rather, Medallion's team of ninety or so Ph.D.'s are constantly working to improve the fund's systems, pushed, like a winning sports team's sense of destiny, to continue to beat the market, week after week, year after year.

And that means hard work. Renaissance has a concept known as the "second forty hours." Employees are each allotted forty hours to work on their assigned duties—programming, researching markets, building out the computer system. Then, during the second forty hours, they're allowed to venture into nearly any area of the fund and experiment. The freedom to do so—insiders say there are no walled-off segments of the fund to employees—allows for the chance for breakthroughs that keep Medallion's creative juices flowing.

Insiders also credit their leader, Jim Simons. Charismatic, extremely intelligent, easy to get along with, Simons had created a culture of extreme loyalty that encouraged an intense desire among its employees to succeed. The fact that very few Renaissance employees over the years had left the firm, compared to the river of talent flowing out of Citadel, was a testament to Simons's leadership abilities.

Renaissance was also free of the theoretical baggage of modern portfolio theory or the efficient-market hypothesis or CAPM. Rather, the fund was run like a machine, a scientific experiment, and the only thing that mattered was whether a strategy worked or not—whether it made money. In the end, the Truth according to Renaissance wasn't about whether the market was efficient or in equilibrium. The Truth was very simple, and remorseless as the driving force of any cut-throat Wall Street banker: Did you make money, or not? Nothing else mattered.

Meanwhile, a fund with ties to Nassim Taleb, Universa Investments, was also hitting on all cylinders. Funds run by Universa, managed and owned by Taleb's longtime collaborator Mark Spitznagel, gained as much as 150 percent in 2008 on its bet that the market is far more volatile than most quant models predict. The fund's Black Swan Protocol Protection plan purchased far-out-of-the-money put options on stocks and stock indexes, which paid off in spades after Lehman collapsed as the market tanked. By mid-2009, Universa had $6 billion under management, up sharply from the $300 million it started out with in January 2007, and was placing a new bet that hyperinflation would take off as a result of all the cash unleashed by the government and Fed flooding into the economy.

PDT also had a strong run riding the volatility tiger, posting a gain of about 25 percent for the year, despite its massive liquidation in October. Muller's private investment fund, Chalkstream Capital Group, however, had a very bad year due to its heavy investments in real estate and private equity funds, losing about 40 percent, though the fund rebounded solidly in 2009. Since Muller had a great deal of his personal wealth in the fund, it was a doubly hard blow.

Weinstein, meanwhile, decided it was time to break out into the wide world on his own. But he was leaving a tangled mess behind him. By the end of the year, Saba had lost $1.8 billion. In January 2009, the group was officially shut down by Deutsche, which, like nearly every other bank, was nursing a massive hangover from its venture into prop trading and was radically scaling back on it.

Weinstein left Deutsche Bank on February 5, slightly more than a decade after he'd first come to the firm as a starry-eyed twenty-four-year-old with dreams of making a fortune on Wall Street. He'd made his fortune, but he'd been bruised and bloodied in one of the greatest market routs of all time.

THE DEVIL'S
WORK

Paul Wilmott stood before a crowded room in the Renaissance Hotel in midtown Manhattan, holding up a sheet of paper peppered with obscure mathematical notations. The founder of Oxford University's first program in quantitative finance, as well as creator of the Certificate in Quantitative Finance program, the first international course on financial engineering, wrinkled his nose.

"There are a lot of people making things far more complicated than they should be," he said, shaking the paper with something close to anger. "And that's a guaranteed way to lose $2 trillion." He paused for a second and sniggered, running a hand through his rumpled mop of light brown hair. "Can I say that?"

It was early December 2008, and the credit crisis was rampaging, taking a horrendous toll on the global economy. Americans' fears about the state of the economy had helped propel Barack Obama into the White House. The Dow Jones Industrial Average had crashed nearly 50 percent from its 2007 record, having dived 680 points on December 2, its fourth-biggest drop since the average was launched in 1896. The United States had shed half a million jobs in November, the biggest monthly drop since 1974, and more losses were coming. Economists had stopped speculating about whether the economy was sliding into a recession. The big question was whether another depression was on the way. Bailout fatigue was in the air as more revelations about losses at financial institutions from Goldman Sachs to AIG filled the airwaves.

Taxpayers wanted someone to blame. But the crisis was so confusing, so full of jargon about derivatives and complex instruments, that few of the uninitiated knew who was at fault.

Increasingly, fingers were pointing at the quants. The tightly coupled system of complex derivatives and superfast computer-charged overleveraged hedge funds that were able to shift billions across the globe in the blink of an eye: It had all been created by Wall Street's math wizards, and it had all come crumbling down. The system the quants had designed, the endlessly ramifying tentacles of the Money Grid, was supposed to have made the market more efficient. Instead, it had become more unstable than ever. Popular delusions such as the efficient market hypothesis had blinded the financial world to the massive credit bubble that had been forming for years.

Jeremy Grantham, the bearish manager of GMO, an institutional money manager with about $100 billion in assets, wrote in his firm's early 2009 quarterly letter to clients—titled "The Story So Far: Greed + Incompetence + A Belief in Market Efficiency = Disaster"—that EMH and the quants were at the heart of the meltdown.

"In their desire for mathematical order and elegant models," Grantham wrote, "the economic establishment played down the inconveniently large role of bad behavior . . . and flat-out bursts of irrationality." He went on: "The incredibly inaccurate efficient market theory was believed in totality by many of our financial leaders, and believed in part by almost all. It left our economic and government establishment sitting by confidently, even as a lethally dangerous combination of asset bubbles, lax controls, pernicious incentives, and wickedly complicated instruments led to our current plight. 'Surely, none of this could be happening in a rational, efficient world,' they seemed to be thinking. And the absolutely worst part of this belief set was that it led to a chronic underestimation of the dangers of asset bubbles breaking."

In a September 2009 article titled "How Did Economists Get It So Wrong" in the *New York Times Magazine*, Nobel Prize–winning economist Paul Krugman lambasted EMH and economists' chronic inability to grasp the possibility of massive swings in prices and circumstances that Mandelbrot had warned of decades earlier. Krugman blamed "the profession's blindness to the very possibility of catastrophic failures in a market economy. . . . As I see it, the economics profession went astray because economists, as a group, mistook beauty, clad in impressive-looking mathematics, for truth."

While the collapse had started in the murky world of subprime lending, it had spread to nearly every corner of the financial universe, leading to big losses in everything from commercial real estate to money market funds and threatening major industries such as insurance that had loaded up on risky debt.

But not every quant had been caught up in the madness. Few were sharper in their criticism of the profession than Paul Wilmott, one of the most accomplished quants of them all.

Despite the freezing temperature outside, the bespectacled British mathematician was clad in a flowery Hawaiian shirt, faded jeans, and leather boots. Before Wilmott, spread out in rows of brightly colored plastic molded chairs, sat a diverse group of scientists in fields ranging from physics to chemistry to electrical engineering. Members of the motley crew had one thing in common: they were prospective quants attending an introductory session for Wilmott's Certificate in Quantitative Finance program.

Wilmott wanted this bright-eyed group to know he wasn't any ordinary quant—if they hadn't already picked up on that from his getup, which seemed more beach bum than Wall Street. Most quants, he said, were navel-gazing screwups, socially dysfunctional eggheads entranced by the crystalline world of math, completely unfit for the messy, meaty world of finance.

"The hard part is the human side," he said. "We're modeling humans, not machines."

It was a message Wilmott had been trying to pound into the fevered brains of his number-crunching colleagues for years, mostly in vain. In a March 2008 post on his website, Wilmott.com, he lambasted Wall Street's myopic quant culture. "Banks and hedge funds employ mathematicians with no financial-market experience to build models that no one is testing scientifically for use in situations where they were not intended by traders who don't understand them," he wrote. "And people are surprised by the losses!"

Wilmott had long been a gadfly of the quants. And he had the mathematical firepower to back up his attacks. He'd written numerous books on quantitative finance and published a widely read magazine for quants under his own name. In 1992, he started teaching the first financial engineering courses at Oxford University. Single-handedly he founded Oxford's mathematical finance program in 1999.

He'd also warned that quants might someday blow the financial system to smithereens. In "The Use, Misuse and Abuse of Mathematics in Finance," published in 2000 in *Philosophical Transactions of the Royal Society*, the official journal of the United Kingdom's national academy of science, he wrote: "It is clear that a major rethink is desperately required if the world is to avoid a mathematician-led market meltdown." Financial markets were once run by "the old-boy network," he added. "But lately, only those with Ph.D.'s in mathematics or physics are considered suitable to master the complexities of the financial market."

That was a problem. The Ph.D.'s might know their sines from their cosines, but they often had little idea how to distinguish the fundamental realities behind why the market behaved as it did. They got bogged down in the fine-grained details of their whiz-bang models. Worse, they believed their models were perfect reflections of how the market works. To them, their models *were* the Truth. Such blind faith, he warned, was extremely dangerous.

In 2003, after leaving Oxford, he launched the CQF program, which trained financial engineers in cities from London to New York to Beijing. He'd grown almost panicky about the dangers he saw percolating inside the banking system as head-in-the-clouds financial engineers unleashed trillions of complex derivatives into the system like a time-release poison. With the new CQF program, he hoped to challenge the old guard and train a new cadre of quants who actually understood the way financial markets worked—or, at the very least, understood what was and wasn't possible when trying to predict the real market using mathematical formulas.

It was a race against time, and he'd lost. The mad scientists who'd been running wild in the heart of the financial system for decades had finally done it: they'd blown it up.

On a frigid day in early January 2009, several weeks after addressing the crowd of hopeful quants at the Renaissance Hotel, Wilmott boarded a plane at Heathrow Airport in London and returned to New York City.

In New York, he met with über-quant Emanuel Derman. A lanky, white-haired South African, Derman headed up Columbia University's financial engineering program. He was one of the original quants on Wall Street and had spent decades designing derivatives for Goldman Sachs, working alongside legends such as Fischer Black.

Wilmott and Derman had become alarmed by the chaotic state of their profession and by the mind-boggling destruction it had helped bring about. Derman believed too many quants confused their elegant models with reality. Yet, a quant to the core, he still held firmly that there was a central place for the profession on Wall Street.

Wilmott was convinced his profession had run off track, and he was growing bitter about its future. Like Derman, he believed that there was still a place for well-trained, and wise, financial engineers.

Together that January, they wrote "The Financial Modelers' Manifesto." It was a cross between a call to arms and a self-help guide, but it also amounted to something of a confession: *We have met the enemy, and he is us.* Bad quants were the source of the meltdown.

"A spectre is haunting markets—the spectre of illiquidity, frozen credit, and the failure of financial models," they began, ironically echoing Marx and Engels's *Communist Manifesto* of 1848.

What followed was a flat denunciation of the idea that quant models can approximate the Truth:

> Physics, because of its astonishing success at predicting the future behavior of material objects from their present state, has inspired most financial modeling. Physicists study the world by repeating the same experiments over and over again to discover forces and their almost magical mathematical laws. . . . It's a different story with finance and economics, which are concerned with the mental world of monetary value. Financial theory has tried hard to emulate the style and elegance of physics in order to discover its own laws. . . . The truth is that there are no fundamental laws in finance.

In other words, there is no single truth in the chaotic world of finance, where panics, manias, and chaotic crowd behavior can overwhelm all expectations of rationality. Models designed on the premise that the market is predictable and rational are doomed to fail. When hundreds of billions of highly leveraged dollars are riding on those models, catastrophe is looming.

To ensure that the quant-driven meltdown that began in August 2007 would never happen again, the two über-quants developed a "modelers' Hippocratic Oath":

- I will remember that I didn't make the world, and it doesn't satisfy my equations.
- Though I will use models boldly to estimate value, I will not be overly impressed by mathematics.
- I will never sacrifice reality for elegance without explaining why I have done so.
- Nor will I give the people who use my model false comfort about its accuracy. Instead, I will make explicit its assumptions and oversights.
- I understand that my work may have enormous effects on

society and the economy, many of them beyond my comprehension.

While the manifesto was well-intentioned, there was little reason to believe it would keep the quants, in years to come, from convincing themselves that they'd perfected their models and once again bringing destruction to the financial system. As Warren Buffett wrote in Berkshire Hathaway's annual report in late February 2009, Wall Street needs to tread lightly around quants and their models. "Beware of geeks bearing formulas," Buffett warned.

"People assume that if they use higher mathematics and computer models they're doing the Lord's work," observed Buffett's longtime partner, the cerebral Charlie Munger. "They're usually doing the devil's work."

For years, critics on the fringes of the quant world had warned that trouble was brewing. Benoit Mandelbrot, for instance, the mathematician who decades earlier had warned the quants of the wild side of their mathematical models—the seismic fat tails on the edges of the bell curve—watched the financial panic of 2008 with a grim sense of recognition.

Even before the fury of the meltdown hit with its full force, Mandelbrot could tell that the quantitative underpinnings of the financial system were unraveling. In the summer of 2008, Mandelbrot—a distinctly European man with a thick accent, patchy tufts of white hair on his enormous high-browed head, and pink blossoms on his full cheeks—was hard at work on his memoirs in his Cambridge, Massachusetts, apartment, perched on the banks of the Charles River. As he watched the meltdown spread through the financial system, he still chafed at the quants' failure to listen to his alarums nearly half a century before.

His apartment contained bookshelves packed with his own writings as well as the weighty tomes of others. One day that summer he pulled an old, frayed book from the shelf and, cradling it in his hands, opened the cover and proceeded to leaf through it. The book, edited by MIT finance professor Paul Cootner, was called *The Random Character of Stock Market Prices*, a classic collection of essays about market theory published in 1964. It was the same book that helped Ed Thorp derive a formula for pricing stock warrants in the 1960s, and the first collection to include Bachelier's 1900 thesis on Brownian motion. The book also contained the essay by Mandelbrot detailing his discovery of wild, erratic moves by cotton prices.

The pages of the copy he held in his hand were crisp and ochered with age. He quickly found the page he was looking for and started to read.

"Mandelbrot, like Prime Minister Churchill before him, promises us not utopia but blood, sweat, toil, and tears," he read. "If he is right, almost all of our statistical tools are obsolete. . . . Surely, before consigning centuries of work to the ash pile, we should like to have some assurance that all our work is truly useless."

The passage, by Cootner himself, was a stern rebuke to Mandelbrot's essay detailing strange characteristics he'd observed in the behavior of cotton prices. Market prices, Mandelbrot had found, were subject to sudden violent, wild leaps. It didn't matter what caused the jumps, whether it was self-reinforcing feedback loops, wild speculation, panicked deleveraging. The fact was that they existed and cropped up time and again in all sorts of markets.

The upshot of Mandelbrot's research was that markets are far less well behaved than standard financial theory held. Out at the no-man's-land on the wings of the bell curve lurked a dark side of markets that haunted the quants like a bad dream, one many had seemingly banished into subconsciousness. Mandelbrot's message had been picked up years later by Nassim Taleb, who repeatedly warned quants that their models were doomed to fail because unforeseen black swans (which reputedly didn't exist) would swoop in from nowhere and scramble the system. Such notions threatened to devastate the elegant mathematical world of quants such as Cootner and Fama. Mandelbrot had been swiftly attacked, and—though he remained a mathematical legend and created an entire new field known as fractal geometry and pioneering discoveries in the science of chaos—was soon forgotten in the world of quants as little more than a footnote in their long march to victory.

But as the decades passed, Mandelbrot never changed his mind.

He remained convinced the quants who ignored his warnings were doomed to fail—it wasn't a question of if, only when. As he watched the markets fall apart in 2008, he saw his unheeded warnings manifest themselves in daily headlines of financial meltdowns that presumably no one—or almost no one—could have foreseen.

If vindication gave him any pleasure, Mandelbrot didn't show it. He wasn't so cavalier about the pain caused by the meltdown as to enjoy any sort of last laugh.

"The only serious criticism of my work, expressed by Cootner, was that if I am right, all of our previous work is wrong," Mandelbrot said, staring out his window at the Charles. "Well, all of their previous work *is* wrong. They've made assumptions which were not valid."

He paused a moment and shrugged. "The models are bad."

In February 2008, Ed Thorp gazed out of the windows of his twelfth-floor corner office in the exclusive city of Newport Beach, California. The glistening expanse of the whitecapped Pacific Ocean stretched far into a blue horizon past Newport Harbor toward the green jewel of Catalina Island. "Not a bad view," he said to a reporter with a smile.

Thorp was angry even though the full fury of the crisis was yet to strike. The banks and hedge funds blowing up didn't know how to manage risk. They used leverage to juice returns in a high-stakes game they didn't understand. It was a lesson he'd learned long before he founded his hedge fund, when he was sitting at the blackjack tables of Las Vegas and proving he could beat the dealer. At bottom, he learned, risk management is about avoiding the mistake of betting so much you can lose it all—the mistake made by nearly every bank and hedge fund that ran into trouble in 2007 and 2008. It can be tricky in financial markets, which can exhibit wild, Mandelbrotian swings at a moment's notice. Banks juggling billions need to realize the market can be far more chaotic over short periods of time than standard financial models reflect.

Thorp stood ramrod straight from his habit of continual exercise. Until 1998, when he injured his back, he ran a few marathons a year. He was trim, six feet tall, with the etched features of an aging athlete. His gaze was clear and steady behind a pair of square gold-framed glasses. Thorp had been taking a large number of pills every day, as part of his hope that he will live forever. After he dies, his body will be cryogenically frozen. If technology someday advances far enough, he'll be revived. Thorp estimates that his odds of recovering from death are 2 percent (he's quantitative literally to the end and beyond). It is his ultimate shot at beating the dealer.

Even if corporeal immortality was unlikely, Thorp's mark on Wall Street was vast and indelible. One measure of that influence lay in a squat chalk-white building, its flat-topped roof flared like an upside-down wedding cake, a short walk from his office in Newport Beach.

The building houses Pimco, one of the largest money managers in the world, with nearly $1 trillion at its disposal. Pimco is run by Bill Gross, the "Bond King," possibly the most well-known and powerful investor in the world besides Warren Buffett. A decision by Gross to buy or sell can send shock waves through global fixed-income markets. His investing prowess is legendary, as is his physical stamina. When he was fifty-three, he decided to run a series of marathons—five of them, in five days. On the fifth day, his kidney ruptured. He saw blood streaming down his leg. But Gross didn't stop. He finished the race, collapsing into a waiting ambulance past the finish line.

Gross would never have become the Bond King without Ed Thorp. In 1966, while a student at Duke University, Gross was in a car accident that almost killed him—he was nearly scalped, as a layer of skin was ripped from the top of his head. He spent six months recovering in the hospital. With lots of time to kill, he cracked open *Beat the Dealer*, testing the strategy in his hospital room over and over again.

"The only way I could know if Ed was telling the truth was to play," said Gross later that day in a conference room just off Pimco's expansive trading floor. His red tie hung jauntily untied around his neck like a scarf. A tall, lanky man with combed-back orange-tinted hair who meditates daily, Gross appeared so relaxed it was as if he were getting an invisible massage as he sat in his chair. "And lo and behold, it worked!" Thorp, sitting to Gross's right, gave a knowing chuckle.

After he recovered from his accident, Gross decided to see if he could make the system pay off in the real world, just as Thorp had done in the early 1960s. With $200, he headed out to Las Vegas. In rapid fashion, he parlayed that into $10,000. The wad of cash helped pay for graduate school at the University of California, Los Angeles, where Gross studied finance. That's where he came across *Beat the Market*. Gross's master's thesis was based on the convertible-bond investment strategies laid out in the book—the same strategies Ken Griffin used to build Citadel.

Soon after reading Thorp's book, Gross had an interview at a firm then called Pacific Mutual Life. He had no experience trading and had little chance of landing a job. But his interviewer noticed that his thesis was on convertible bonds. "The people who hired me said, 'We have a lot of smart candidates, but this guy is interested in the bond market.' So I got my job because of Ed," said Gross.

As Gross and Thorp sat together in Pimco's conference room, they got to musing about the Kelly criterion, the risk management strategy Thorp used starting with his blackjack days in the 1960s. Pimco, Gross noted, uses a version of Kelly. "Our sector concentration is predicated on that—blackjack and investments," he said, gesturing toward the trading floor. "I hate to stretch it, but professional blackjack is being played in this trading room from the standpoint of risk management, and that ultimately is a big part of our success."

Thorp nodded in agreement. The key behind Kelly is that it keeps investors from getting in over their heads, Thorp explained. "The thing you have to make sure of is that you don't overbet," he said.

The conversation turned to hedge funds and leverage. A river of money had flowed into hedge funds in recent years, turning it from an industry with less than $100 billion under management in the early 1990s to a $2 trillion force of nature. But the amount of actual investing opportunities hadn't changed very much, Thorp said. The edge had diminished, but hedge fund managers' and bankers' appetite for gigantic profits had only grown more voracious. That led to massive use of leverage—in other words, overbetting. The inevitable end result: gambler's ruin on a global scale.

"A classic example is Long-Term Capital Management," Thorp said. "We'll be seeing more of that now."

"The available edge has been diminished," Gross agreed, noting that Pimco, like Warren Buffett's Berkshire Hathaway, used very little leverage. "And that led to increased leverage to maintain the same returns. It's leverage, the overbetting, that leads to the big unwind. Stability leads to instability, and here we are. The supposed stability deceived people."

"Any good investment, sufficiently leveraged, can lead to ruin," Thorp said.

After about an hour, Gross stood, shook hands with the man responsible for getting him started, and walked onto Pimco's trading floor to keep an eye on the nearly $1 trillion in assets he ran.

Thorp walked back to his own office. It turned out that he was doing a little trading himself.

Sick and tired of watching screwups by managers he'd hired to care for his money, Thorp had decided to take the reins himself once again. He'd developed a strategy that looked promising. (What was it? Thorp wasn't talking.) In early 2008, he started running about $36 million with the strategy.

By the end of 2008, the strategy—which he called System X to outsiders—had gained 18 percent, *with no leverage.* After the first week, System X was in positive territory the entire year, one of the most catastrophic stretches in the history of Wall Street, a year that saw the downfall of Bear Stearns, AIG, Lehman Brothers, and a host of other institutions, a year in which Citadel Investment Group coughed up half of its money, a year in which AQR fell more than 40 percent and Saba lost nearly $2 billion.

Ed Thorp was back in the game.

DARK POOLS

On a sultry Tuesday evening in late April 2009, the quants convened for the seventh annual Wall Street Poker Night in the Versailles Room of the St. Regis Hotel in midtown Manhattan.

It was a far more subdued affair than the heady night three years earlier when the elite group of mathematical traders stood atop the investing universe. Many of the former stars of the show—Ken Griffin, Cliff Asness, and Boaz Weinstein—were missing. They didn't have time for games anymore. In the new landscape, the money wasn't pouring in as it used to. Now they had to go out and hustle for their dollars.

Griffin was in Beverly Hills hobnobbing with former junk bond king Michael Milken at the Milken Institute Global Conference, where rich people gathered, some for the primary purpose of reminding one another how smart they are. His IPO dreams had evaporated like a desert mirage, and he was furiously trying to chart a new path to glory. But the wind was blowing against him in early 2009. Several of his top traders had left the firm. And why not? Citadel's main fund, Kensington, had lost more than half its assets in 2008. In order to collect those lucrative incentive fees—the pie slice managers keep after posting a profit—the fund would need to gain more than 100 percent just to break even. That could take *years*. To instant-gratification hedge fund managers, you might as well say forever. Or how about never?

Griffin wasn't shutting down the fund, though. Instead, he was launching new funds, with new strategies—and new incentive fees. He also was venturing into the investment banking world, trying to expand into new businesses as others faded. The irony was rich. As investment banks turned into commercial banks after their failed attempt to become hedge funds, a hedge fund was turning into an investment bank.

Some saw it as a desperate move by Griffin. Others thought it could be another stroke of genius. The toppled hedge fund king from Chicago was moving to take over business from Wall Street as his competitors were shackled by Washington's bailouts. His funds had made something of a comeback, advancing in the first half of the year as the chaos of the previous year abated. Whatever the case, Griffin hoped investors would see the debacle of 2008 as a one-time catastrophe, never to be repeated. But it was a tough sell.

Weinstein, meanwhile, was in Chicago hustling for his hedge fund launch. He was busy trying to convince investors that the $1.8 billion hole he'd left behind at Deutsche Bank was a fluke, a nutty mishap that could only happen in the most insane kind of market. By July, he'd raised more than $200 million for his new fund, Saba Capital Management, a big fall from the $30 billion in positions he'd juggled for Deutsche Bank. Setting up shop in the Chrysler Building in midtown Manhattan, Saba was set to start trading in August.

Asness stayed home with his two pairs of twins and watched his beloved New York Rangers lose to the Washington Capitals in the decisive game seven of the National Hockey League's Eastern Conference playoff series. He was also busy launching new funds of his own.

AQR had even ventured into the plain-vanilla—and low-fee—world of mutual funds. In a display of confidence in his strategies, Asness put a large chunk of his own money into AQR funds, including $5 million in the Absolute Return Fund. He also put $5 million into a new product AQR launched in 2008 called Delta, a low-fee hedge fund that quantitatively replicated all kinds of hedge fund strategies, from long-short to "global macro." Several of AQR's funds had gotten off to a good start for the year, particularly his convertible bond funds—the decades-old strategy laid out by Ed Thorp in *Beat the Dealer* that had launched Citadel and hundreds of other hedge funds in the 1990s. Asness even dared to think the worst, finally, was behind him. He managed to find a bit of time to unwind. After working for months straight with barely a weekend off, Asness took a vacation in March to hike the craggy hills of Scotland. He even left his BlackBerry behind. But there were still reminders of his rough year. A newspaper article about AQR mentioned Asness's penchant for smashing computers. To his credit, he was now able to laugh at the antics he'd indulged in at the height of the turmoil, writing a tongue-in-cheek note to the editor protesting that it had "happened only three times, and on each occasion the computer screen deserved it."

But there was Peter Muller, walking briskly among the poker crowd in a brown jacket, well tanned, slapping old friends on the back, beaming that California smile.

Muller seemed calm on the outside, and with good reason: having earned north of $20 million in 2008, he was one of Morgan's highest earners for the year. Inside, he was seething. The *Wall Street Journal* had broken a story the week before that PDT might split off from Morgan Stanley, in part because its top traders were worried that the government, which had given the bank federal bailout funds, would curb their massive bonuses. Muller had been working on a new business model for PDT for more than a year but was biding his time before he went public with his plans. The *Journal* article beat him to the punch, causing him no end of bureaucratic headaches. PDT had, in a flash, become a pawn in a game of giants—Wall Street versus the U.S. government. The move looked to some as if Morgan had crafted a plan to have its cake and eat it, too—spin off PDT, make a big investment, and get the same rewards while none of the traders lost a dime of their fat bonuses.

To Muller, it was a nightmare. Ironically, Morgan insiders even accused Muller of leaking the story to the press. Of course, he hadn't: Muller didn't talk to the press unless he absolutely needed to.

But he had one thing to look forward to: poker. And when it came to poker, Muller was all business.

Jim Simons, now seventy-one years old, was in attendance, hunched over a crowded dining table in a blue blazer and gray slacks, philosophically stroking his scraggly gray beard. But all was not well in Renaissance land. While the $9 billion Medallion fund continued to print money, gaining 12 percent in the first four months of the year, the firm's RIEF fund—the fabled fund that Simons once boasted could handle a whopping $100 billion (a fantasy it never even approached)—had lost 17 percent so far in 2009, even as the stock market was rising, tarnishing Simons's reputation as a can't-lose rainmaker. RIEF investors were getting upset about the disparity between the two funds, even though Simons had never promised that it could even approach the performance of Medallion. Assets in Renaissance had fallen sharply, sliding $12 billion in 2008 to $18 billion, down from a peak of about $35 billion in mid-2007, just before the August 2007 meltdown.

There were other big changes in Simons's life, hints that he was preparing to step down from the firm he'd first launched in 1982. In 2008, he'd traveled to China to propose a sale of part of Renaissance to the China Investment Corp., the $200 billion fund owned and run by the Chinese government. No deal was struck, but it was a clear sign that the aging math whiz was ready to step aside. Indeed, later in the year Simons retired as CEO of Renaissance, replaced by the former IBM voice recognition gurus Peter Brown and Robert Mercer.

Perhaps most shocking of all, the three-pack-a-day Simons had quit smoking.

Meanwhile, other top quants mixed and mingled. Neil Chriss, whose wedding had seen the clash of Taleb and Muller over whether it was possible to beat the market, held session at a table with several friends. Chriss was a fast-rising and brilliant quant, a true mathematician who'd taught for a time at Harvard. He'd recently launched his own hedge fund, Hutchin Hill Capital, which received financial backing from Renaissance and had knocked the cover off the ball in 2008.

In a back room, before play began, a small private poker game was in session. Two hired-gun poker pros, Clonie Gowen and T. J. Cloutier, looked on, wincing from time to time at the clumsy play.

The crowd, still well heeled despite the market trauma, was dining on rack of lamb, puff pastry, and lobster salad. Wine and champagne were served at the bar, but most were taking it slow. There was still a lot of poker to play. And the party atmosphere of years gone by was diminished.

A chime rang out, summoning the players to the main room. Rows of tables with cards fanned out across them and dealers prim in their vested suits awaited them. Simons addressed the gathering crowd, talking about how the tournament had been getting better and better every year, helping advance the cause of teaching students mathematics. The quants in attendance somehow didn't think it ironic that their own profession amounted to a massive brain drain of mathematically gifted people who could otherwise find careers in developing more efficient cars, faster computers, or better mousetraps rather than devising clever methods to make money for the already rich.

Soon enough play began. The winner that night was Chriss, whose hot hand at trading spilled over to the poker table. Muller didn't make the final rounds.

It had been a wildly tumultuous three years on Wall Street, drastically changing the lives of all the traders and hedge fund managers who'd attended the poker tournament in 2006. A golden era had come and passed. There was still money to make, but the big money, the *insane* money, billions upon billions . . . that train had left the station for everyone but a select few.

Muller, ensconced in his Santa Barbara San Simeon, was hatching his plans for PDT. Its new direction wasn't just a change for Muller and company; it marked a seminal shift for Morgan Stanley, once one of the most aggressive kill-or-be-killed investment banks on Wall

Street. By 2009, PDT, even in its shrunken state, was the largest proprietary trading operation still standing at Morgan. Its departure, if it happened, would cement the historic bank's transformation from a cowboy, risk-hungry, money-printing hot rod into a staid white-shoe banking company of old that made money by making loans and doing deals—not by flinging credit default swaps like so many Frisbees through the Money Grid and trading billions in other tangled derivatives through souped-up computers and clumsy quant models.

Most assuredly, it would be a big change for PDT, once Morgan's secret quant money machine, and its mercurial captain.

Griffin, Muller, Asness, and Weinstein were all intent on making it work again, looking boldly into the future, chastened somewhat by the monstrous losses but confident they'd learned their lessons.

But more risk lurked. Hedge fund managers who've seen big losses can be especially dangerous. Investors, burned by the losses, may become demanding and impatient. If big gains don't materialize quickly, they may bolt for the exits. If that happens, the game is over.

That means there can be a significant incentive to push the limits of the fund's capacity to generate large gains and erase the memory of the blowup. If a big loss is no worse than a small loss or meager gains—since either can mean curtains—the temptation to jack up the leverage and roll the dice can be powerful.

Such perverse and potentially self-destructive behavior isn't countenanced by the standard dogmas of modern finance, such as the efficient-market hypothesis or the belief that the market always trends toward a stable equilibrium point. Those theories were increasingly coming under a cloud, questioned even by staunch believers such as Alan Greenspan, who claimed to have detected a flaw in the rational order of economics he'd long championed.

In recent years, new theories that captured the more chaotic behavior of financial markets had arisen. Andrew Lo, once Cliff Asness's teacher at Wharton and the author of the report on the quant meltdown of August 2007 that warned of a ticking Doomsday Clock, had developed a new theory he called the "adaptive market hypothesis." Instead of a rational dance in which market prices waltz efficiently to a finely tuned Bach cantata, Lo's view of the market was more like a drum-pounding heavy-metal concert of dueling forces that compete for power in a Darwinian death dance. Market participants were constantly at war trying to squeeze out the last dime from inefficiencies, causing the inefficiencies to disappear (during which the market returns briefly to some semblance of equilibrium), after which they start hunting for fresh meat—or die—creating a constant, often chaotic cycle of destruction and innovation.

While such a vision seems unnerving, it appeared to many to be far more realistic, and certainly captured the nature of the wild ride that started in August 2007.

Then there were the behavioral finance theories of Daniel Kahneman, who picked up a Nobel Prize for economics in 2002 (his colleague, Amos Tversk, had passed away years earlier). The findings of behavioral finance—often studies conducted on hapless undergraduate students in stark university labs—had shown time and again that people don't always make optimal choices when it comes to money.

A similar strand of thought, called neuroeconomics, was delving into the hardwiring of the brain to investigate why people often make decisions that aren't rational. Some investors pick stocks that sound similar to their own name, for instance, and others pick stocks with recognizable ticker symbols, such as HOG (Harley-Davidson). Evidence was emerging that certain parts of the brain are subject to a "money illusion" that blinds people to the impact of future events, such as the effect of inflation on the present value of cash—or the possibility of a speculative bubble bursting.

A small group of researchers at a cutting-edge think tank called the Sante Fe Institute, led by Doyne Farmer (the hedge fund manager and chaotician who briefly met Peter Muller in the early 1990s), was developing a new way to look at financial markets as an ecology of interacting forces. The hope was that by viewing markets in terms of competing forces vying for limited resources, much like Lo's evolutionary vision, economists, analysts, and even traders will gain a more comprehensive understanding of how markets work—and how to interact with those markets—without destroying them.

And while quants were being widely blamed for their role in the financial crisis, few—aside from zealots such as Taleb—were calling for them to be cast out of Wall Street. That would be tantamount to banishing civil engineers from the bridge-making profession after a bridge collapse. Instead, many believed the goal should be to design better bridges—or, in the case of the quants, better, more robust models that could withstand financial tsunamis, not create them.

There were some promising signs. Increasingly, firms were adapting models that incorporated the wild, fat-tailed swings described by Mandelbrot decades earlier. J. P. Morgan, the creator of the bell curve–based VAR risk model, was pushing a new asset-allocation model incorporating fat-tailed distributions. Morningstar, a Chicago investment-research group, was offering retirement-plan participants portfolio forecasts based on fat-tailed assumptions. A team of quants at MSCI BARRA, Peter Muller's old company, had developed a cutting-edge risk-management strategy that accounted for potential black swans.

Meanwhile, the markets continued to behave strangely. In 2009 the gut-churning thousand-point swings of late 2008 were a thing of the past, but stocks were still mired in a ditch despite an early-year rally; the housing market looked as if it would keep cratering until the next decade. Banks had dramatically reduced their leverage and promised their new investor—the U.S. government—that they would behave. But there were signs of more trouble brewing.

As early as the spring of 2009, several banks reported stronger earnings numbers than most expected—in part due to clever accounting tricks. Talk emerged about the return of big bonuses on Wall Street. "They're starting to sin again," Brad Hintz, a respected bank analyst, told the *New York Times*.

Quant funds were also suffering another wave of volatility. In April, indexes that track quant strategies suffered "some of the best and worst days ever ... when measured over approximately 15,000 days," according to a report by Barclays quant researcher Matthew Rothman (formerly of Lehman Brothers).

Many of the toxic culprits of the meltdown were dying away. The CDOs were gone. Trading in credit default swaps was drying up. But there were other potentially dangerous quant gadgets being forged in the dark smithies of Wall Street.

Concerns about investment vehicles called exchange-traded funds were cropping up. Investors seemed to be piling into a number of highly leveraged ETFs, which track various slices of the market, from oil to gold mining companies to bank stocks. In March 2009 alone, $3.4 billion of new money found its way into leveraged ETFs. Quant trading desks at banks and hedge funds started tracking their behavior using customized spreadsheets, attempting to predict when the funds would start buying or selling. If they could predict the future—if they knew the Truth—they could anticipate the move by trading first.

The worry was that with all the funds pouring money into the market at once—or pulling it out, since there were many ETFs that shorted stocks—a massive, destabilizing cascade could unfold. In a report on the products, Minder Cheng and Ananth Madhavan, two top researchers at Barclays Global Investors, said the vehicles could create unintended consequences and potentially pose systemic risk to the market. "There is a close analogy to the role played by portfolio insurance in the crash of 1987," they warned.

Another concern was an explosion in trading volume from computer-driven, high-frequency funds similar to Renaissance and PDT. Faster chips, faster connections, faster algorithms—the race for speed was one of the hottest going. Funds were trading at speeds measured in microseconds—or one-millionth of a second. In Mahwah, New Jersey, about thirty-five miles from downtown Manhattan, the New York Stock Exchange was building a giant data center three football fields long, bigger than a World War II aircraft carrier, that would do nothing but process computerized trades. "When people talk about the New York Stock Exchange, this is it," NYSE co-chief information officer Stanley Young told the *Wall Street Journal*. "This is our future."

But regulators were concerned. The Securities and Exchange Commission was worried about a rising trend of high-frequency trading firms that were getting so-called naked access to exchanges from brokerages that lent out their computer identification codes. While high-frequency firms were in many ways beneficial for the market, making it easier for investors to buy and sell stocks since there always seemed to be a high-frequency player willing to take the other side of a trade, the concern was that a rogue fund with poor risk-management practices could trigger a destabilizing sell-off.

"We consider this dangerous," said one executive for a company that provided services to high-frequency trading firms. "My concern is that the next LTCM problem will happen in less than five minutes."

The world of high-frequency trading leapt into the media spotlight in July 2009 when Sergey Aleynikov, a quant who'd just quit a job writing code for Goldman Sachs, stepped off a plane at Newark Liberty Airport after a trip to Chicago. Waiting for him at the airport were FBI agents. Aleynikov was arrested and charged with stealing code from Goldman's secretive high-frequency trading group, a charge he fought in court.

Adding to the mystery was a connection to a powerful quant Chicago hedge fund: Citadel. Aleynikov had just taken a position at Teza Technologies, which had recently been founded by Misha Malyshev, who'd been in charge of Citadel's highly lucrative Tactical Trading outfit. Six days after Aleynikov's arrest, Citadel sued Malyshev and several of his colleagues—also former Citadel employees—alleging that they'd violated noncompete agreements and could also be stealing code, allegations the defendants denied.

The court's decision was something of a draw, giving Citadel a sense of victory but allowing Teza to get back to work and open up for business. Along the way the suit spelled out previously unknown details about Citadel's superfast trading operation. The court learnt that the Tactical Trading offices, which required special codes to enter, came equipped with ranks of cameras and guards to ensure no proprietary information was stolen.

The suit also revealed that Tactical was a money-making machine, having raked in more than $1 billion in 2008, capitalizing on the market's volatility, even as Citadel's hedge funds lost about $8 billion.

All of the controversy alarmed regulators and everyday investors, who'd been largely unaware of the lightning-fast trading that had become a central component of the Money Grid, strategies first devised in the 1980s by innovators such as Gerry Bamberger and Jim Simons and furthered in the following decade by the likes of David Shaw and Peter Muller. But there were legitimate concerns that as computer-driven trading reached unfathomable speeds, danger lurked.

Many of these computer-driven funds were gravitating to a new breed of stock exchange called "dark pools"—secretive, computerized trading networks that match buy and sell orders for blocks of stocks in the frictionless ether of cyberspace. Normally, stocks are traded on public exchanges such as the Nasdaq and the NYSE in open view of anyone who chooses to look. Trades conducted through dark pools, as the name implies, are anonymous and hidden from view. The pools go by names such as SIGMA X, Liquidnet, POSIT, CrossFinder, and NYFIX Millennium HPX. In these invisible electronic pools, vast sums change hands beyond the eyes of regulators. While efforts were afoot to push the murky world of derivatives trading into the light of day, stock trading was sliding rapidly into the shadows.

Increasingly, hedge funds had been crafting new systems to game the pools, hunting for price discrepancies between them in the eternal search for arbitrage or even *causing* price changes with dubious tactics and predatory algorithms. Hedge funds were "pinging" the dark pools with electronic signals like submarines hunting prey, searching for liquidity. The behavior was largely invisible, and light-years ahead of regulators.

Dark pools were also opening up to superfast high-frequency trading machines. The NYFIX Millennium pool had narrowed its response time to client orders to three milliseconds. A flier Millennium sent to potential clients claimed that traders with "ninja skills succeed" in dark pools at "dangerously high speeds for the unprepared."

Mom and Pop's retirement dreams, meet Ninja Hedge Fund.

Whether such developments posed a broader risk to the financial system was unknown. Users of the technology said faster trades boosted "liquidity," making trading easier and cheaper. But as the financial panic of 2007 and 2008 had shown, liquidity is always there when you don't need it—and never there when you do.

Meanwhile, congressmen, President Obama, and regulators were making noise about reining in the system with new rules and regulations. Progress had been made in setting up a clearinghouse for credit default swaps to keep better track of the slippery contracts. But behind the scenes, the financial engineers were hard at work devising new methods to operate in the shadows.

Just look: exotic leveraged vehicles marketed to the masses worldwide, hedge funds gaming their returns, lightning-fast computerized trading robots, predatory ninja algorithms hunting liquidity in dark pools . . .

Here come the quants.

Notes

1 ▪ ALL IN

PAGE 2: **Simons had pocketed $1.5 billion:** *Alpha*, May 2006.

PAGE 3: **That night at the St. Regis:** Several details of the poker event were gleaned from *MFA News* 2, 1 (Spring 2006).

PAGE 11: **In 1990, hedge funds held $39 billion:** Based on data from Hedge Fund Research, a Chicago research group.

2 ▪ THE GODFATHER: ED THORP

PAGE 13: **Just past 5:00 A.M.:** I conducted numerous interviews with Ed Thorp and exchanged many emails. Many details about Ed Thorp's blackjack career, including a description of his foray into blackjack in 1961, were found in his colorful book *Beat the Dealer: A Winning Strategy for the Game of Twenty-One* (Vintage, 1962).

Other details were found in the excellent *Fortune's Formula: The Untold Story of the Scientific Betting System That Beat the Casinos and Wall Street*, by William Poundstone (Hill and Wang, 2005). I confirmed details I used from this book with Thorp.

PAGE 18: **The strategy was from a ten-page article:** "Getting a Hand: They Wrote the First Blackjack Book but Never Cashed In," by Joseph P. Kahn, *Boston Globe*, February 20, 2008.

PAGE 20: **He'd kept his roulette strategy largely secret:** "The Invention of the First Wearable Computer," by Edward O. Thorp (http://graphics.cs.columbia .edu/courses/mobwear/resources/thorp-iswc98.pdf.)

PAGE 21: **Science-fiction writer Arthur C. Clarke:** *Voice Across the Sea*, by Arthur C. Clarke (HarperCollins, 1975).

3 ▪ BEAT THE MARKET

PAGE 27: **On a typical day of desert sun:** Much like the blackjack chapter, many details of this chapter derive from interviews with Thorp, *Fortune's Formula*, and Thorp's second book, *Beat the Market: A Scientific Stock Market System*. That book is out of print, but Thorp kindly provided a Web-accessible version.

PAGE 39: **Huge, sudden leaps:** For more than a decade, Nassim Taleb has been criticizing quant models for leaving out huge market events, or black swans, and he deserves much credit for warning about such shortcomings of the models. I had numerous conversations with Taleb while writing this book.

PAGE 41: **Gerry Bamberger discovered stat arb:** The section on the discovery of statistical arbitrage is based almost entirely on interviews with Gerry Bamberger, Nunzio Tartaglia, and several other members of the original Morgan Stanley group that discovered and spread stat arb across Wall Street. Previous mention of this group can be found in *Demon of Our Own Design*, by Richard Bookstaber (John Wiley & Sons, 2007).

PAGE 43: **Morgan had hired Shaw:** The account of Shaw's departure from Morgan are based on interviews with Nunzio Tartaglia and others who were at APT.

4 ■ THE VOLATILITY SMILE

PAGE 47: **Sometime around midnight:** Many details of Black Monday were found in numerous *Wall Street Journal* articles written during the time, including "The Crash of '87—Before the Fall: Speculative Fever Ran High in the 10 Months Prior to Black Monday," by James B. Stewart and Daniel Hertzberg, December 11, 1987.

Other details, including the description at the opening of the chapter, were found in *An Engine, Not a Camera: How Financial Models Shape Markets*, by Donald MacKenzie (MIT Press, 2006), and *The Age of Turbulence: Adventures in a New World*, by Alan Greenspan (Penguin 2007), 105.

PAGE 49: **On the evening of September 11, 1976:** The best description of the invention of portfolio insurance that I know of can be found in *Capital Ideas: The Improbable Origins of Modern Wall Street*, by Peter L. Bernstein (John Wiley & Sons, 2005). Another source is "The Evolution of Portfolio Insurance," by Hayne E. Leland and Mark Rubinstein, published in *Portfolio Insurance: A Guide to Dynamic Hedging*, edited by Donald Luskin (John Wiley & Sons, 1988).

PAGE 53: **"Even if one were to have lived":** The age of the universe is 13.5 billion years, not 20 billion.

PAGE 54: **When German tanks rumbled into France:** Some details of Mandelbrot's life come from a series of interviews with Mandelbrot in the summer of 2008. Many also come from the book *The (Mis)Behavior of Markets: A Fractal View of Financial Turbulence*, by Benoit Mandelbrot and Richard L. Hudson (Basic Books, 2006).

PAGE 61: **"I realized that the existence of the smile":** *My Life as a Quant*, by Emanuel Derman (John Wiley & Sons, 2004), 226.

PAGE 61: **A squad of fifty armed federal marshals:** Certain details come from *Den of Thieves*, by James Stewart (Simon & Schuster, 1991).

PAGE 62: **He also worked as a consultant:** I learned the fascinating story of Thorp's discovery of the Madoff fraud in several interviews with Thorp in December 2008 as the fraud was discovered. I confirmed his story with the firm involved and through several pertinent documents.

5 ▪ FOUR OF A KIND

PAGE 64: **In 1990, Ed Thorp took a call:** The details of Thorp's connection to Citadel was told to me by Thorp, Frank Meyer, Justin Adams, and Ken Griffin.

PAGE 70: **Griffin set up shop:** I learned a number of details about Griffin's and Citadel's history during a single interview with Griffin and numerous interviews with people who worked for him. Other details were found in the following articles: "Citadel's Griffin: Hedge Fund Superstar," by Marcia Vickers, *Fortune*, April 3, 2007; "Citadel Returns 26 Percent, Breaks Hedge Fund Mold, Sees IPO," by Katherine Burton, Bloomberg News Service, April 29, 2005; "Will a Hedge Fund Become the Next Goldman Sachs?" by Jenny Anderson, *New York Times*, April 4, 2007.

PAGE 71: **When he was ten years old:** I learned a number of details about Peter Muller's life in a series of interviews with people who knew him. Other details, such as the trip to Europe, were taken from an essay he wrote in the book *How I Became a Quant*, edited by Richard R. Lindsey and Barry Schachter (John Wiley & Sons, 2007).

PAGE 77: **The muscular professor strode:** I've never attended a Fama course, but I did speak with a number of people who took his courses, including Cliff Asness, and I conducted several interviews with Fama. This is a depiction of what his course may have been like and what he may have said based on those interviews.

PAGE 80: **As a child, Clifford Scott Asness:** I learned a number of details about Asness's life in a series of interviews with Asness and people who knew him. Other details about Asness's early life were taken from an essay he wrote in the book *How I Became a Quant*.

I conducted numerous interviews with current and former employees of AQR. Other sources include "Beta Blocker: Profile of AQR Capital Management," by Hal Lux, *Institutional Investor*, May 1, 2001, and, "The Quantitative, Data-Based, Risk-Massaging Road to Riches," by Joseph Nocera, *New York Times Magazine*, June 5, 2005.

PAGE 81: **Born near the end of the Great Depression:** Fama interview.

PAGE 83: **Kendall found no such patterns:** Quoted from *An Engine, Not a Camera: How Financial Models Shape Markets*, 63.

PAGE 86: **Fama and French cranked up:** The paper was called "The Cross Section of Expected Stock Returns," published in the June 1992 edition of *Journal of Finance*.

PAGE 90: **One day in the early 1980s:** Nearly all of the details of Boaz Weinstein's life and career come from interviews with Weinstein and people who knew and worked with him.

PAGE 95: **In 1994, John Meriwether:** A number of details of LTCM's demise were taken from *When Genius Failed: The Rise and Fall of Long-Term Capital Management*, by Roger Lowenstein (Random House, 2000), and *Inventing Money: The Story of Long-Term Capital Management and the Legends Behind It*, by Nicholas Dunbar (John Wiley & Sons, 2000).

6 ▪ THE WOLF

PAGE 102: **On a spring afternoon in 1985:** The Liar's Poker account is taken from *The Poker Face of Wall Street*, by Aaron Brown (John Wiley & Sons, 2006), as well as interviews and email exchanges with Brown.

PAGE 107: **The Culver Spy Ring sprang up:** "Setauket: Spy Ring Foils the British," by Tom Morris, *Newsday*, February 22, 1998.

PAGE 108: **As a toddler growing up:** Despite numerous requests, James Simons declined to grant me an interview. Details of Renaissance Technologies were learned through interviews with former employees Elwyn Berlekamp, Robert Frey, Nick Patterson, Sandor Straus, and others who asked not to be identified. Other details were found in "Simons Doesn't Say," by John Geer, *Financial World*, October 21, 1996, and "Simons at Renaissance Cracks Code, Doubling Assets," by Richard Teitelbaum, Bloomberg News, November 27, 2007.

PAGE 116: **In December 2003, Renaissance sued:** "Ex-Simons Employees Say Firm Pursued Illegal Trades," Katherine Burton and Richard Teitelbaum, Bloomberg News, June 30, 2007.

7 ▪ THE MONEY GRID

PAGE 119: **Griffin's fortress for money:** A number of details about Citadel's performance and assets were taken from Citadel offering documents and other Citadel documents.

PAGE 119: **One of Citadel's early trades:** Griffin interview.

PAGE 123: **Muller and Elsesser:** Interviews with Kim Elsesser.

PAGE 124: **A founder of Prediction Company:** Interviews with Doyne Farmer.

PAGE 128: **In 1995, a young quant named Jaipal Tuttle:** Interviews with Jaipal Tuttle.

PAGE 133: **When Cliff Asness took a full-time job:** Accounts of Asness's time at Goldman and the rise of AQR were taken from news articles previously listed, as well as interviews with John Liew, David Kabiller, Cliff Asness, and others who asked not to be identified.

PAGE 135: **Black believed in rationality:** Many details of Black's life derive from interviews with people who knew him, including Asness, Emanuel Derman, and others, as well as his biography, *Fischer Black and the Revolutionary Idea of Finance*, by Perry Mehrling (John Wiley & Sons, 2005).

PAGE 146: **One day Weinstein was strolling:** "Young Traders Thrive in Stock, Bond Nexus," by Henny Sender, *Wall Street Journal*, November 28, 2005.

8 ▪ LIVING THE DREAM

PAGE 152: **Griffin was quietly building:** Some information about Tactical Trading's performance derives from testimony in Citadel's 2009 lawsuit against Malyshev and two other ex-Citadel employees filed in the Chancery Division of Cook County, Ill., Circuit Court.

PAGE 155: **A $10 billion hedge fund called Amaranth Advisors:** "How Giant Bets on Natural Gas Sank Brash Hedge-Fund Trader," by Ann Davis, *Wall Street Journal*, September 19, 2006.

PAGE 157: **They also like to party:** "The Birthday Party," by James B. Stewart, *New Yorker*, February 11, 2008.

PAGE 164: **But one evening a colleague:** "Going Under, Happily," by Pete Muller as told to Loch Adamson, *New York Times*, June 8, 2003.

PAGE 165: **In May 2002, he attended the wedding:** The wedding account is based on interviews with Nassim Taleb, John Liew, and Neil Chriss.

PAGE 165: **His peripatetic life had shown him:** The brief account of Taleb's life is based on numerous interviews with Taleb and his longtime trading partner Mark Spitznagel, as well as the articles "Blowing Up: How Nassim Taleb Turned the Inevitability of Disaster into an Investment Strategy," by Malcolm Gladwell, *New Yorker*, April 22 and 29, 2002, and "Flight of the Black Swan," by Stephanie Baker-Said, *Bloomberg Markets*, May 2008.

PAGE 167: **Once or twice a month:** The subjects of this book did not discuss this poker game *often*. A number of details were learned from people familiar with the game.

PAGE 169: **The frenzy that greeted the IPO:** "Newest Hot Internet Issue Raises Question: How to Price It Fairly?" by Dunstan Prial, *Wall Street Journal*, November 30, 1998.

PAGE 173: **AQR's flagship Absolute Return Fund would gain:** "The Geeks' Revenge," by Josh Friedlander, *Absolute Return*, July/August 2006.

PAGE 175: **One day in 2005, Boaz Weinstein:** The chess match is based on several interviews with Deutsche Bank employees who witnessed the match. Weinstein corroborated the account.

PAGE 178: **Boaz Weinstein dealt crisply:** The account of the game is based on interviews with people who attended. Some incidental details, such as Muller's victory and the amount bet, were created to add verisimilitude to the account. Muller is known to be the ace of the group, Asness the rookie. Other fund managers not named also frequently played in the game.

9 ▪ "I KEEP MY FINGERS CROSSED FOR THE FUTURE"

PAGE 184: **Growing up in Seattle, Brown had:** Interviews with Aaron Brown.

PAGE 190: **Enter the credit default swap:** "The $12 Trillion Idea: How Blythe Masters and the 'Morgan Mafia' Changed the World of Finance," by Gillian Tett, *FTMagazine*, March 25–26, 2006.

PAGE 191: **The first Bistro deal:** "Credit Derivatives: An Overview," by David Mengle, International Swaps and Derivatives Association, published for the 2007 Financial Markets Conference held by the Federal Reserve Bank of Atlanta, May 15, 2007.

PAGE 193: **That solution came from a Chinese-born quant:** "Slices of Risk: How a Formula Ignited Markets That Burned Some Big Investors," by Mark Whitehouse, *Wall Street Journal*, September 12, 2005.

PAGE 196: **Magnetar's presence in the CDO world:** "A Fund Behind Astronomical Losses," by Serena Ng and Carrick Mollenkamp, *Wall Street Journal*, January 14, 2008.

PAGE 198: **The carry trade was fueling:** "Global Credit Ocean Dries Up," by Ambrose Evans-Pritchard, *The Telegraph*, February 28, 2006.

PAGE 201: **Regulators lent a helping hand:** "Agency's '04 Rule Let Banks Pile Up New Debt," by Stephen Labaton, *New York Times*, October 2, 2008.

PAGES 205–206: **news emerged that a pair of Bear Stearns hedge funds:** The Bear Stearns meltdown has been extensively covered and I used multiple sources. The best were a series of articles written by *Wall Street Journal* reporter Kate Kelly, who also wrote an excellent book documenting Bear's meltdown, *Street Fighters: The Last 72 Hours of Bear Stearns, the Toughest Firm on Wall Street* (Portfolio, 2009).

10 ▪ THE AUGUST FACTOR

PAGE 210: **Cliff Asness walked to the glass partition:** Virtually all of the information in this chapter derives from dozens of interviews with the participants, including many who requested anonymity. A number of details of PDT's turmoil were first reported in "August Ambush: How Market Turmoil Waylaid the 'Quants,'" by Scott Patterson and Anita Raghavan, *Wall Street Journal*, September 7, 2007.

PAGE 217: **At the headquarters of Goldman Sachs:** Most of the information about GSAM is based on an interview with Katinka Domotorffy, who took over Global Alpha and several other quant funds at GSAM after Mark Carhart and Raymond Iwanowski left Goldman in 2009.

PAGE 222: **Matthew Rothman was still groggy:** Interviews with Matthew Rothman.

PAGE 229: **"A massive unwind is occurring":** "Behind the Stock Market's

Zigzag—Stressed 'Quant' Funds Buy Shorted Stocks and Sell Their Winners," by Justin Lahart, *Wall Street Journal*, August 11, 2007.

PAGE 239: **"These shocks reflected one of the most"**: "Loosening Up: How a Panicky Day Led the Fed to Act—Freezing of Credit Drives Sudden Shift," by Randall Smith, Carrick Mollenkamp, Joellen Perry, and Greg Ip, *Wall Street Journal*, August 20, 2007.

11 ▪ THE DOOMSDAY CLOCK

PAGE 245: **"We need to focus on this fast"**: Part of the Citadel-E*Trade deal details derive from "Why Citadel Pounced on Wounded E*Trade," by Susanne Craig, Gregory Zuckerman, and Matthew Karnitschnig, *Wall Street Journal*, November 30, 2007.

PAGE 247: **Cliff Asness leapt from the card table**: Asness's poker-playing rampage is based on accounts from people familiar with the games. As with the other poker game, some incidental details were created to add verisimilitude to the account.

PAGE 250: **One quant gadfly**: The account is based on interviews with Nassim Taleb and Aaron Brown.

PAGE 254: **Dick Fuld was putting on a classic performance**: The account is based on an interview with a person who attended the meeting.

PAGE 255: **There was a yell, a smash**: The account is based on interviews with people who were present.

PAGE 257: **"I want to throw up"**: Several details of Lehman's last days, including this quote, derive from "Burning Down His House: Is Lehman CEO Dick Fuld the True Villain on the Collapse of Wall Street?" by Steve Fishman, *New York*, December 8, 2008.

PAGE 260: **The models that gauged the risk**: "Behind AIG's Fall, Risk Models Failed to Pass Real-World Test," by Carrick Mollenkamp, Serena Ng, Liam Pleven, and Randall Smith, *Wall Street Journal*, October 31, 2008.

PAGE 260: **"That patient has had a heart attack"**: The account is based on an interview with New York senator Chuck Schumer.

12 ▪ A FLAW

PAGE 264: **In a May 2005 speech**: "Risk Transfer and Financial Stability," by Alan Greenspan, remarks made to the Federal Reserve Bank of Chicago's Forty-first Annual Conference on Bank Structure, Chicago, Illinois, May 5, 2005.

PAGE 267: **"Ken, you guys are getting killed"**: Several details of Citadel's late-2008 turmoil, and the conference, are based on an interview with Ken Griffin and interviews with numerous people familiar with the fund who requested anonymity.

Others, including the James Forese quote, are based on "Citadel Under Siege: Ken Griffin's $15 billion Firm Was Flirting with Disaster This Fall," by Marcia Vickers and Roddy Boyd, *Fortune*, December 9, 2009; and "Hedge Fund Selling Puts New Stress on Market," by Jenny Strasburg and Gregory Zuckerman, *Wall Street Journal*, November 7, 2008; and "A Hedge Fund King Comes Under Siege," by Jenny Strasburg and Scott Patterson, *Wall Street Journal*, November 20, 2009.

PAGE 274: **It was a rallying cry:** Columbus did not write "Sail on" in his 1492 journal.

PAGE 276: **By outward appearances, Boaz Weinstein:** A number of details of Saba's final days were first reported in "Deutsche Bank Fallen Trader Left Behind $1.8 Billion Hole," by Scott Patterson and Serena Ng, *Wall Street Journal*, February 6, 2008.

PAGE 282: **Cliff Asness was furious:** Several details of AQR's struggles in 2008 were first reported in "A Hedge-Fund King Is Forced to Regroup," by Scott Patterson, *Wall Street Journal*, May 23, 2009.

PAGE 288: **a fund with ties to Nassim Taleb:** Universa's gains were first reported in "October Pain Was 'Black Swan' Gain," by Scott Patterson, *Wall Street Journal*, November 3, 2008.

13 ▪ THE DEVIL'S WORK

PAGE 289: **Paul Wilmott stood before a crowded room:** The account is based on firsthand reporting and interviews with Paul Wilmott.

PAGE 293: **Together that January, they wrote:** The full "manifesto" can be found on Wilmott's website, http://www.wilmott.com/blogs/eman/index.cfm/2009/1/8/The-Financial-Modelers-Manifesto.

PAGE 295: **"They're usually doing the devil's work":** Interview with Charlie Munger.

PAGE 295: **Even before the fury of the meltdown hit:** The account is based on a series of interviews with Mandelbrot in his Cambridge apartment.

PAGE 297: **In February 2008, Ed Thorp gazed:** The account is based on a meeting with Ed Thorp in his office, and a subsequent meeting with Thorp and Bill Gross in Pimco's office. The Q&A appeared in "Old Pros Size Up the Game—Thorp and Pimco's Gross Open Up on Dangers of Over-Betting, How to Play the Bond Market," by Scott Patterson, *Wall Street Journal*, March 22, 2008.

14 ▪ DARK POOLS

PAGE 301: **On a sultry Tuesday evening:** The account of the poker night is first-hand.

PAGE 303: **Muller had been working on a new business model:** "Morgan Stanley Eyes Big Trading Change," by Aaron Lucchetti and Scott Patterson, *Wall Street Journal*, April 24, 2009.

PAGE 304: **There were other big changes in Simons's life:** "Renaissance's Simons Delays Retirement Plans," by Jenny Strasburg and Scott Patterson, *Wall Street Journal*, June 11, 2009.

PAGE 308: **"They're starting to sin again":** "After Off Year, Wall Street Pay Is Bouncing Back," by Louise Story, *New York Times*, April 26, 2009.

PAGE 311: **a new breed of stock exchange:** In part derived from "Boom in 'Dark Pool' Trading Networks Is Causing Headaches on Wall Street," by Scott Patterson and Aaron Lucchetti, *Wall Street Journal*, May 8, 2008.

Glossary

Arbitrage: The act of buying and selling two related securities that are priced differently with the expectation that the prices will converge. If gold costs $1,000 an ounce in New York and $1,050 in London, an arbitrageur will buy the New York gold and sell it in London. Quants use formulas to detect historical relationships between assets such as stocks, currencies, and commodities, and place bets that any disruption in the relationships will revert back to normal in time (*see* **statistical arbitrage**). Such bets are placed under the assumption that past performance in the market is predictive of future performance—an assumption that isn't always true.

Black-Scholes option-pricing formula: A mathematical formula that describes the price of a stock option, which is a contract that gives its owner the right to buy a stock (a call option) or sell a stock (a put option) at a certain price within a certain time. The formula has many components, one of which is the assumption that the future movement of a stock—its volatility—is random and leaves out the likelihood of large swings (*see* **fat tails**).

Brownian motion: First described by Scottish botanist Robert Brown in 1827 when observing pollen particles suspended in water, Brownian motion is the seemingly random vibration of molecules. Mathematically, the motion is a random walk in which the future direction of the movement—left, right, up, down—is unpredictable. The average of the motion, however, can be predicted using the law of large numbers, and is visually captured by the bell curve or normal distribution. Quants use Brownian motion mathematics to predict the volatility of everything from the stock market to the risk of a multinational bank's balance sheet.

Credit default swap: Created in the early 1990s, these contracts essentially provide insurance on a bond or a bundle of bonds. The price of the insurance fluctuates depending on the riskiness of the bonds. In the late 1990s and 2000s, more and more traders used the contracts to make bets on whether a bond would default or not. At Deutsche Bank, Boaz Weinstein was a pioneer in the use of CDS as a betting instrument.

Collateralized debt obligation: Bundles of securities, such as credit-card debt or mortgages, that are sliced up into various levels of risk, from AAA, which is deemed relatively safe, to BBB (and lower), which is highly risky. In the late 1990s, a team of quants at J. P. Morgan created "synthetic" CDOs by bundling credit default swaps linked to bonds and slicing them up into various portions of risk. In the credit meltdown of 2007 and 2008, billions in high-rated CDO and synthetic CDO slices plunged in value as borrowers defaulted on their mortgages in record numbers.

Convertible bonds: Securities issued by companies that typically contain a fixed-income component that yields interest (the fixed part), as well as a "warrant," an option to convert the security into shares at some point in the future. In the 1960s, Ed Thorp devised a mathematical method to price warrants that anticipated that Black-Scholes option-pricing formula.

Efficient-market hypothesis: Based on the notion that the future movement of the market is random, the EMH claims that all information is immediately priced into the market, making it "efficient." As a result, the hypothesis states, it's not possible for investors to beat the market on a consistent basis. The chief proponent of the theory is University of Chicago finance professor Eugene Fama, who taught Cliff Asness and an army of quants who, ironically, went to Wall Street to try to beat the market in the 1990s and 2000s. Many quants used similar Fama-derived strategies that blew up in August 2007.

Fat tail: The volatility of the market is typically measured using a bell curve, which represents the normal distribution of market movements captured by Brownian motion. The tails of the distribution—the left and right sides of the curve—slope downward. A fat tail represents a highly unlikely "black swan" event not captured by the bell curve, and visually is captured by a bulge on either side of the curve. Benoit Mandelbrot first devised methods to describe such extreme market events in the 1960s, but he was largely ignored.

Gaussian copula: A model developed by financial engineer David X. Li that predicted the price correlations between various slices of collateralized debt obligations. Copulas are mathematical functions that calculate the connections between two variables—in other words, how they "copulate." When X happens (such as a homeowner defaulting), there's a Y chance that Z happens (a neighboring homeowner defaults). The specific copulas Li used were named after Carl Friedrich Gauss, the nineteenth-century German mathematician known for devising a method to measure the motion of stars through the bell curve. The connections among the default risks of the slices in a CDO were, therefore, based on the bell curve (a copula is essentially a multidimensional bell curve). In the credit crisis that began in August 2007, the model failed as the correlations between CDO slices became far tighter than expected.

Hedge fund: Investment vehicle that is open only to wealthy individuals or institutions such as pension funds and endowments. Hedge funds tend to use copious amounts of leverage, or borrowed money, and charge high fees, typically 2 percent of assets under management and 20 percent or more of profits. One of the first hedge funds was launched in 1949 by Alfred Winslow Jones, a reporter, who "hedged" positions by taking offsetting long and short positions in various stocks. Ed Thorp started a hedge fund in 1969 named Convertible Hedge Associates, later changed to Princeton/Newport Partners.

Law of large numbers: The law states that the more observations one makes, the greater the certainty of prediction. Ten coin flips could produce 70 percent heads and 30 percent tails. Ten thousand coin flips are far more likely to approach 50 percent heads and 50 percent tails. Thorp used the LLN to win at blackjack and went on to use it on Wall Street. Many quant formulas are based on it.

Statistical arbitrage: A trading strategy in which computers track the relationships between hundreds or thousands of stocks and implement trades based on those relationships. The computers look for periods when the long-term relationship breaks down and makes bets that the relationship will revert back. The strategy was first deployed by a computer programmer, Gerry Bamberger, at Morgan Stanley in the 1980s. It quickly became one of the most powerful and popular trading methods ever devised, helping launch the giant New York hedge fund D. E. Shaw and others. Peter Muller at Morgan Stanley's Process Driven Trading was one of the most adept stat arb traders. The strategy imploded in the quant crisis of August 2007.

Acknowledgments

A cast of thousands, it seems, helped me with this book, including a multitude of unnamed sources behind the scenes who explained the inner workings of these highly secretive investors. My agent, Shawn Coyne, helped bring the idea to life and deserves enormous credit for helping develop it. My editor, Rick Horgan, and his gifted associate editor, Julian Pavia, had a wealth of ideas that gave a healthy kickstart to the book when it needed it. Mitch Zuckoff was an ideal sounding board and provided fantastic insights into how to put the book together and make the ideas understandable. Thanks to my editors at *The Wall Street Journal*, particularly Jon Hilsenrath and Nik Deogun, who encouraged my interest in writing about this strange group of traders; and Anita Raghavan, who helped me crack open the quant group at Morgan Stanley. A virtual army of traders and professors helped me better understand the world of the quants, including Mark Spitznagel, Nassim Taleb, Paul Wilmott, Emanuel Derman, Aaron Brown, Benoit Mandelbrot, and so many others. Ed Thorp devoted far too much time to help me understand the true nature of trading and risk management, as well as his own amazing career. As promised, I'd like to thank ANONYMOUS. Mostly, I thank my wife, Eleanor, whose understanding, patience, and constant encouragement over the past few years made this book possible.

Index

A. W. Jones & Company, 34
Absolute Return Fund, 173, 235, 284–285, 303
Adams, Justin, 69–70, 161
Adaptive market hypothesis, 306
Adjustable interest rates, 197
ADT Security Services, 119
Ahmed, Shakil, 125, 126, 133, 165, 168
AIG (American International Group), 100, 258–261, 267, 268, 277, 300
AIG Financial Products (AIG-FP), 100, 259–260
Alcoa, 229
Aldinger, William, 205
Aleynikov, Sergey, 310
Alpha, 8–9
Alpha magazine, 8
Alphabuilder system, 9, 76
Amaranth Advisors, 155, 160, 177, 234, 245, 272
American Bankers Association, 47
American Express, 254
American Home Mortgage Investment, 207
American Management Systems, 185
American Mathematical Society, 23
Andresen, Matthew, 153, 246
AOL Time Warner, 146
Applied Quantitative Research Capital Management (AQR), 4, 5, 7, 11, 118, 141–143, 144, 159, 169–171, 173–175, 178, 183–184, 197, 205, 208, 210–213, 216, 217, 221, 224–227, 230, 234–238, 242–244, 247–250, 255, 256, 266, 282–286, 303
AQR (*see* Applied Quantitative Research Capital Management (AQR))
Arbitrage, 35–37, 71, 91
ART, 224
Art prices, 156
Arthur D. Little, 136
Asness, Clifford Scott, ix, 4–7, 9–12, 15, 63, 79–81, 85, 88–90, 91, 106, 117, 118, 133–135, 138–143, 147, 148, 154, 167–168, 170–176, 178, 179, 181, 182, 183, 200, 205, 208, 210–213, 220, 224–226, 229, 230, 234–238, 242–244, 247–250, 255, 256, 265–266, 282–286, 301, 302–303, 306
Astashkevich, Alexander, 116
Automated Proprietary Trading (APT), 42–45, 112, 128
Avenue Capital Group, 4
Ax, James, 110–111, 113, 287
Axcom Ltd., 110

Bachelier, Louis, 29, 30, 39, 57, 58, 82–84, 296
Bacon, Louis Moore, 65
Bahl, Lalit, 114
Baldwin, Roger, 18
Bamberger, Gerry, 41–42, 44–45, 123, 126, 191, 311
Bank of America, 170, 211, 258
Bank of Japan, 198
Bank of New York Mellon, 275
Bankers Trust, 93
Barbarians at the Gate (Burrough and Helyar), 53
Barclays Bank, 256–257, 260
Barclays Global Investors, 216, 222, 309

Barnett, Robert, 279
Barr Rosenberg Associates, 73
BARRA Inc., 9, 72–77, 106, 123, 161, 178
Basel Accord, 199
Basis Capital Fund Management, 207
Baum, Lenny, 109–110
Baum-Welch algorithm, 109–110
Bear Stearns, 12, 97, 100, 203, 205–207, 221, 223, 243, 244, 252–253, 257, 267, 272, 275, 300
Beat the Dealer: A Winning Strategy for the Game of Twenty-One (Thorp), 24, 25, 45, 90, 92, 143, 147, 184, 298, 303
Beat the Market: A Scientific Stock Market System (Thorp and Kassouf), 32, 35, 38, 45, 68, 90, 185, 299
Beazer Homes USA, 229
Beeson, Gerald, 266, 269–271, 274
Behavioral finance theories, 307
Bell curve, 30, 56, 57, 84, 96, 194, 295, 307–308
Bell Labs, 103
Belopolsky, Alexander, 116
Benson, Alan, 213–214, 226, 238, 278
Berger, Adam, 286
Berkshire Hathaway, 33, 78, 107–108, 148, 211, 276, 295, 300
Berlekamp, Elwyn, 110–113, 287
Bernanke, Ben, 11, 260
Bernard L. Madoff Investment Securities, 63, 282
Beta, 8, 81, 86, 88
Binary number system, 19
Bistro (Broad Index Secured Trust Offering), 191, 192
Black, Fischer, 38, 51, 61, 75, 85, 88, 119, 133, 135–138, 194, 293
Black, Steven, 256
Black Monday, October 19, 1987, 46–48, 51–54, 59–61, 68, 69, 110, 166, 233, 238, 270
Black-Scholes option-pricing formula, 38–40, 46, 49, 50, 60, 61, 83, 85, 136, 194, 263
Black Swan Protocol Protection plan, 288
Black swans, 59, 296

Blackjack, 13–15, 18–20, 22–25, 31, 37, 111, 143, 146–147, 194, 298, 299
BlackRock, 145
Blackstone Group, 157, 158, 175
Blankfein, Lloyd, 267, 276
Bloom, David, 198
Bloomberg, Michael, 119, 158
BNP Paribas, 233
Bonfire of the Vanities (Wolfe), 53
BOSS Partners, 44–46
Brewster, Caleb, 107
Brown, Aaron, x, 102–106, 183–190, 192, 197–199, 201–205, 221, 226, 241, 250–251
Brown, Peter, 113–115, 304
Brown, Robert, 28–29, 38, 39, 95
Brownian motion, 29, 31, 39, 54, 56, 58, 61, 82, 84, 96, 166, 296
Bruck, Connie, 53
"Bubble Logic: Or, How to Learn to Stop Worrying and Love the Bull" (Asness), 171–173
Buffett, Warren, 33, 78–79, 87, 99, 107, 148, 156, 211, 244, 276, 295, 298, 300
Bunning, David, 121
Burnett, Erin, 210
Burrough, Bryan, 53
Bush, George W., 184, 262
Busson, Arpad "Arki," 142

California utilities strike, 145
Call options, 27
Campos, Roel, 201
Canadian Imperial Bank of Commerce (CIBC), 193
Cantey, Wilbert, 18
Capital asset pricing model (CAPM), 86, 88, 287
Capital reserve requirements, 201
Capital structure arbitrage, 148
Carhart, Mark, 140, 212, 213, 217, 230
Carnegie Mellon, 140
Carry trade, 174, 197–198, 217, 233, 237, 240
Caxton Associates, 65, 224
Cayne, Jimmy, 252, 253
CDOs (*see* Collateralized debt obligations [CDOs])

CDS (*see* Credit default swaps [CDS])
Center for Public Integrity, 197
Center for Research in Security Process (CRSP), 81, 87
Chalkstream Capital Group, 288
Chaos theory, 124
Chapel Funding, 179
Cheng, Minder, 309
Chern, Shiing-Shen, 109
Chern-Simons theory, 109
Chicago School, 137, 171
China Investment Corporation, 304
Chriss, Neil, 6, 140, 147–148, 165, 167, 247–248, 250, 304, 305
Cioffi, Ralph, 206, 207, 223
Cisco Systems, 172
Citadel Derivatives Group Investors, 153, 246
Citadel Investment Group, 4, 9, 11, 36, 45, 65, 67, 70, 100, 119–122, 148, 152–161, 175, 178, 197, 208, 216, 217, 234, 244–247, 266–275, 277, 280–282, 287, 300, 302, 303, 310
Citigroup, 12, 100, 129, 145, 168, 192, 198, 199, 243
Clarke, Arthur C., 21
Cloutier, T. J., 2, 9, 305
Cohen, Steve A., 6
Collateralized debt obligations (CDOs), 180–181, 183, 190–198, 202–208, 223, 242, 259, 280, 308
Collateralized mortgage obligations (CMOs), 187
Collins, Jim, 153
Commodity Corporation, 65
Continental Illinois, 48
Convertible bond arbitrage, 36–37, 67, 68
Convertible Hedge Associates, 35, 68
Cooper, Tom, 76
Cootner, Paul, 58, 295–297
Correlation, 180–181, 192–194, 203
Countrywide Financial, 203, 207, 210, 211, 239
Courant Institute, 140
Cox, Christopher, 263, 271
Cramer, Jim, 210
Crawford, Steve, 199

Credit default swaps (CDS), 8, 93–95, 100–101, 145–146, 148–149, 181, 189–194, 196, 208, 259, 264, 268, 270, 276–278, 280, 308
Credit derivatives, 92–94, 146
Crouhy, Michael, 194
Cruz, Zoe, 203, 227, 228
Cryptography, 113–115

D. E. Shaw, 44, 45, 126, 173, 216, 230, 253
Daily Telegraph, 198
Dall, Bob, 186
Dark pools, 311–312
Dealbreaker, 283–284
Dean Witter Discover & Company, 199
Della Pietra, Stephen, 114
Della Pietra, Vincent, 114
Delta hedging, 37, 38, 42, 68
DeLucia, David, 91, 92
Derman, Emanuel, 61, 293–295
Deutsche Bank, 6, 11, 12, 93–95, 100, 101, 118, 143–149, 151, 155, 175–179, 181, 194, 200, 208, 257, 269, 276, 277, 288, 302
Diamond, Bob, 256–257
Discount window, 240
Diskovery Educational Systems, 67
Dodd, Christopher, 260–261
Donaldson Lufkin Jenrette, 92
Dot-com stocks, 112, 169–173, 226, 272, 285
Doubling down, 23
Dow Jones Industrial Average, 47, 50, 51, 198, 210, 233, 239, 290
Dresdner Kleinwort, 154
Drexel Burnham Lambert, 62, 103

EarthWeb Inc., 169–170
Economist, The, 174
Efficient-market hypothesis (EMH), 32, 53, 75, 78, 79, 82–85, 89, 113, 172, 222, 244, 287, 290, 291
Einhorn, David, 3–4, 9, 153
Einstein, Albert, 29, 31, 38
Elsesser, Kim, 123–125, 127, 130–132, 162
Empirica Fund, 166
Enron Corporation, 122, 146, 155, 272

Entropy, law of, 20–21
Equity Office Properties, 157
E*Trade Financial, 244–246, 267, 272
Eurodollar futures contracts, 129, 166
Exchange-traded funds (ETFs), 309

Falcone, Philip, 278
Fama, Eugene, 32, 53, 75, 77–89, 106, 113, 136, 138, 139, 172, 212, 222, 224, 225, 244, 296
Fan, Colin, 276
Fannie Mae, 267, 277
Farmer, Doyne, 124, 126, 128, 307
Fat tails, 57–58, 166, 167, 215, 252, 295, 307
Federal funds rate, 240
Federal Reserve, 11, 47, 53, 99, 120, 127, 170, 210, 216, 239, 252, 253, 256–257, 268, 269
Fidelity Investments, 79, 84
"Financial Modelers' Manifesto, The" (Wilmott and Derman), 293–294
Fooled by Randomness (Taleb), 59, 165
Ford Motor Company, 170, 276
Forese, James, 267, 269
Fortress Investment Group, 157, 175
Fortune magazine, 122, 158
Fraser, Laurel, 170–171
Freddie Mac, 243, 277
Free market libertarianism, 265–266
French, Kenneth, 81, 86–89, 106, 225, 256
Frey, Robert, 45, 112, 116, 125
Friedman, Jacques, 212
Friedman, Milton, 39
Fuld, Dick, 254–257, 259
Fuld, Kathy, 254

Gates, Bill, 184
Gauss, Carl Friedrich, 194
Gaussian copula, 193–195, 197, 203, 208
Geffen, David, 156
Geithner, Timothy, 256
General Electric, 276
General Motors, 73, 94, 149, 150, 170, 213, 268, 276

Generalized autoregressive conditional heteroscedasticity model (GARCH), 166
Gerard, Ralph, 33
Giuliani, Rudolph, 62, 65
Glass-Steagall Act of 1933, 145
Glenwood Capital Management, 65
Global Alpha Fund, 9, 135, 138–141, 151, 174, 197, 200, 212, 213, 217, 224, 225, 230, 236
Global Equity Opportunities Fund, 212, 217, 235, 237
Goldman Sachs, 4, 5, 12, 45, 51, 61, 85, 88, 91–92, 97, 100, 106, 133–142, 151, 156, 158, 170, 171, 174, 176, 178, 194, 199–201, 203, 206, 212, 213, 221, 224, 238, 260, 267, 268, 271, 275, 293
Goldman Sachs Asset Management (GSAM), 89–90, 217–218, 225–226, 230–231, 235–237, 240
Golkin, Saul, 68
Gorton, Gary, 260
Gowen, Clonie, 2, 6, 9, 10, 305
Graham, Benjamin, 33–34, 244
Grantham, Jeremy, 290–291
Great Depression, 12, 34
Great Hedge Fund Bubble, 12
Greenberg, Ace, 144
Greenlight Capital, 3, 153
Greenspan, Alan, 11, 47–48, 60, 120, 170, 262–266, 306
Gregory, Joe, 254
Griffin, Anne Dias, 122, 246
Griffin, Ken, ix, 4, 7, 9–12, 15, 36, 45, 63–70, 91, 118–123, 148, 151–161, 169, 175, 207, 208, 216, 234, 236, 244–247, 266–276, 279–281, 286, 287, 301–302, 306, 310
Gross, Bill, 90, 298–300
Growth versus value stocks, 87, 224, 225
Gutfreund, John, 104

Hand, Eddie, 24
Harbinger Capital, 278
Hedge Fund Research, 284
Helyar, John, 53
Herron, Natasha, 165

Hibbs, Albert, 17
Hidden Markov process, 109–110
High-frequency trading, 173, 309–311
Hintz, Brad, 308
Housing prices, 11, 84, 179, 197, 204 (*see also* Subprime mortgage market)
Houthakker, Hendrik, 55–56
"How Did Economists Get It So Wrong" (Krugman), 291
HSBC Finance Corporation, 205, 243
HSBC Holdings, 205
Hubler, Howard, 203, 204, 206–207, 243
Hull, Blair, 45
Hume, David, 92
Hunter, Brian, 155, 177
Hurst, Brian, 134
Hutchin Hill Capital, 305

IBM Corporation, 55–57, 86, 113, 114
Icahn, Carl, 4
Illinois Income Investors (III/Triple I), 66, 69, 70
IndyMac Bancorp, 205
Information theory, 19–21, 115
Inside Mortgage Finance, 204
Institute for Defense Analysis (IDA), 108–109
Institutional Investor, 286
Intelligent Investor, The (Graham), 33
Interest rates, 120, 170, 173, 174, 197, 216, 233, 239–240, 252, 263, 266
Investment Company Act of 1940, 33
Invisible hand theory, 264
Island ECN, 153
Israel, Ronen, 212
It's a Wonderful Life (movie), 186
Iwanowski, Ray, 140, 212, 213, 217, 230

J. P. Morgan, 93, 96, 100, 144, 155, 188, 190–193, 216, 253, 256, 268, 273
Jackwerth, Jens Carsten, 53
Jain, Anshu, 148, 276
Jones, Alfred Winslow, 33–34, 35
Jones, Paul Tudor, 65
Jones, Robert, 51, 225
Journal of Fixed Income, 193

Journal of the American Statistical Association, 18

Kabiller, David, 141, 142, 226, 235
Kahneman, Daniel, 307
Kassouf, Sheen, 28, 32, 36–38
Kelly, John, Jr., 22–23, 37, 39, 110
Kendall, Maurice, 83
Kensington Fund, 120, 154, 268, 274, 302
Kepler Financial Management, 112
Kerkorian, Kirk, 149, 150
Kerviel, Jérôme, 252
Keynes, John Maynard, xi
Khandani, Amir, 249–250
Kidder, Peabody & Company, 102, 103, 105–106
Kimmel, Emmanuel "Manny," 24–25, 41
Kirk, Alex, 256
Korea Development Bank, 256
Kovner, Bruce, 65–66
Krail, Robert, 134, 142
Krispy Kreme Doughnuts, 86, 229
Krizelman, Todd, 169
Krochuk, Tim, 229
Krugman, Paul, 291

Large versus small stocks, 87–88
Larson, Jeffrey, 159, 160
Lasry, Marc, 4–5
Laufer, Henry, 112, 117
Law of large numbers, 14, 31, 87, 194
Law of one price (LOP), 36
Lehman Brothers, 12, 97, 100, 200, 203, 204, 221, 231, 232, 238, 243, 244, 253–260, 266–268, 270, 272, 275, 277, 284, 288, 300
Leland, Hayne, 49–50
Leland, John, 49
Leland O'Brien Rubinstein Associates Inc. (LOR), 50
Leperq, de Neuflize & Company, 185–188
Levin, Asriel "Uzi," 222–223, 232
Levin, Bess, 283
Lévy, Paul, 57
Lévy distribution, 57

Lewis, Michael, 53, 103, 104
Li, David X., 193–194, 203
Liar's Poker, 102–105, 183, 186
Liar's Poker (Lewis), 53, 103, 104
Liew, John, 134, 142, 165, 226, 227, 235, 255
Lipper TASS Database, 224
Lippmann, Greg, 208
Litowitz, Alec, 121–122, 196
Lo, Andrew, 80, 249–250, 261, 280, 306, 307
Loeb, Daniel, 153, 154
Long-Term Capital Management (LTCM), 60, 95–101, 104, 120, 142, 143, 145, 154, 155, 167, 170, 191, 225, 231, 233, 235, 239, 249, 265, 268, 270, 272, 299, 309
Lowenstein, Roger, 98
LTCM (*see* Long-Term Capital Management [LTCM])
Lynch, Peter, 79

Mack, John, 124–126, 199–203, 227, 228, 276
Madhavan, Ananth, 309
Madoff, Bernard, 63, 282
Magellan Fund, 79
Magnetar Capital, 122, 196
Mahjouri, Mani, 255–256
Maisel, Herbert, 18
Malkiel, Burton, 83
Malyshev, Misha, 152, 234, 246, 274, 310
Mandelbrot, Benoit, x, 54–60, 167, 215, 252, 291, 295–297, 308
Maptest, 176–177
Margin calls, 223, 240, 260
Markov, Andrey, 109
Markov process, 109
Markowitz, Harry, 81, 82, 95
Martingale betting, 23
Mattu, Ravi, 257, 258
McDade, Herbert "Bart," 254, 256, 257
McDermott, James, 18
Medallion Fund, 66, 75, 107–108, 110–113, 115–117, 127, 152, 227, 230, 234, 286–287, 304

Melamed, Leo, 47–48
Mendelson, Michael, 205, 212–213, 235
Menta Capital, 222
Mercer, Robert, 113–115, 304
Meriwether, John, 95–98, 104
Merrill Lynch, 91, 92, 100, 206, 243, 258
Merton, Robert, 40, 60, 75, 83, 95, 97, 119, 136, 137
Meyer, Frank, 64–67, 70, 120
Midas, 126, 133, 215
Milken, Michael, 3, 62, 103, 301
Millennium Partners, 116
Miller, Merton, 82
Mitsubishi UFJ Financial Group, 276
Monemetrics, 109, 110
Monte Carlo simulations, 84
Moore Capital Management, 65
Morgan Creek Capital Management, 273
Morgan Stanley, 2, 3, 6, 7, 9, 12, 41–45, 76–77, 100, 106, 112, 118, 123, 124–133, 151, 162, 165, 168–169, 183, 184, 191, 194, 198–207, 214, 219–220, 227–228, 242–243, 267, 271, 275–276, 303, 305–306
Morningstar, 308
Mozilo, Angelo, 210
MSCI BARRA, 308
Muller, Peter, ix, 1–7, 9–12, 15, 45, 63, 71–77, 91, 106, 117, 118, 123–128, 130–133, 140, 147, 148, 154, 161–165, 167–169, 178–179, 181, 182, 200, 202, 208, 214, 216, 218–220, 224, 227–229, 233, 236–237, 243, 247–250, 275–276, 288, 303, 305–306, 308, 311
Munger, Charlie, 295
My Life as a Quant (Derman), 61

Nash, John, 18
National Academy of Sciences, 19, 20, 23
Natural gas prices, 155
Neilson, Lars, 212
NetJets, 148, 168, 175
Neuroeconomics, 307
New Century Financial, 159, 203, 205
New York Cotton Exchange, 56

New York Times Magazine, 5, 108, 175, 291

Newhouse, S. I., 156

Newsweek magazine, 53

Newton, Isaac, 7, 12

Nickerson, Ken, 125, 126, 133

Normal Two-Dimensional Singularities (Laufer), 112

Nova Funds, 112, 125

"OAS Models, Expected Returns, and a Steep Yield Curve" (Asness), 90

Obama, Barack, 209, 279, 289, 312

O'Brien, John, 50

O'Connor, Terrence, 69

Off-balance-sheet accounting, 188, 192, 202, 207, 243

"On Default Correlation: A Copula Function Approach" (Li), 193

Overstock.com, 229

Pacific Mutual Life, 299

Pandit, Vikram, 129, 133, 168

Parallel processing, 43

Paraschivescu, Andrei, 9–10

Paternot, Stephan, 169

Patterson, Nick, 115, 116

Paulson, Henry, 138–140, 200, 256–257, 260, 261

Paulson, John, 279

Paulson & Company, 279

PDT (*see* Process Driven Trading [PDT])

Pelosi, Nancy, 260

Pension funds, 11, 173, 186

Pimco, 90, 177, 298–300

Poker Face of Wall Street, The (Brown), 205, 250

Portfolio insurance, 49–53, 61, 100, 309

Portfolio System for Institutional Trading (POSIT), 116

Predators' Ball, The (Bruck), 53

Prediction Company, 124, 126

Price-to-book value, 86–87, 170, 229

Prince, Chuck, 168

Princeton/Newport Partners, 35, 40–41, 44–46, 52, 61–63, 65–67, 70, 119, 121

Probability theory, 14, 53

Process Driven Trading (PDT), 2–3, 123, 125–133, 151, 152, 162, 163, 165, 167–169, 173, 176, 202, 203, 208, 214–216, 219, 220, 227–230, 233, 236, 241, 275–276, 288, 303, 305–306, 309

Purcell, Phil, 199–200

Quantitative Research Group (QRG), 133–134, 137, 140

Rabobank, 189

Random Character of Stock Market Prices, The (ed. Cootner), 28, 29, 58, 295–296

Random Walk Down Wall Street, A (Malkiel), 83

Random walk theory, 30–32, 38, 39, 59, 61, 65, 78, 83, 109

Ranieri, Lewis, 186, 187

Reagan, Ronald, 49

Reagan Revolution, 50

Rechtschaffen, Andrew, 53

Reed, Mike, 125, 126, 129, 214–216, 229, 230, 233

Regan, Jay, 34–35, 38, 40, 41, 44, 46, 62

Reid, Harry, 260

Renaissance Institutional Equities Fund (RIEF), 224, 227, 233, 234, 304

Renaissance Technologies, 2, 11, 45, 66, 75, 106–108, 110–117, 121, 125, 126, 127, 152, 159, 173, 208, 216, 224, 226–227, 230, 241, 253, 279–280, 286–287, 304, 309

Resolution Trust Corporation, 188–189

Ridgeline Partners, 97, 121, 151

Rieger, Adrienne, 283, 286

Risk magazine, 144

RiskMetrics, 188

Robertson, Julian, 66, 142

Rosenberg, Barr, 72–74, 119

Rosenberg Institutional Equity Management, 73

Rothman, Matthew, 222–225, 230–231, 238, 251, 257–258, 308
Roulette, 16–18, 20–22, 124
Royal Bank of Scotland, 100
Rubin, Robert, 136
Rubinstein, Mark, 50, 53
Rudd, Andrew, 76
Rukeyser, Louis, 91, 144
Rule of threes, 186
Russell, Joe, 244–245, 267
Russian default, 98, 101, 145, 191

S&P 500, 32, 37, 40, 41, 48, 50–52, 78, 129, 172, 197, 284, 285
Saba, 6, 178, 197, 208, 213, 226, 268, 271, 276–278, 288
Saba Capital Management, 302
Salomon Brothers, 93, 95–98, 106, 119, 130, 186–188, 202
Samuelson, Paul, 82–83, 113
Sanders, Bernie, 265
Savage, Leonard "Jimmie," 82
Savings and loans, 186–189
Saxon Capital, 202
Scholes, Myron, 38, 40, 60, 95, 97, 99, 136, 163, 194
Schumer, Chuck, 260–261
Schwartz, Alan, 253
Schwarzman, Stephen, 157–158
Searching for Bobby Fischer (movie), 90
Securities and Exchange Commission (SEC), 34, 175, 201, 203, 211, 271, 309
Securitization market, 179–180, 183, 186–190, 192, 195, 197, 198, 202, 203, 207, 233, 243
Shannon, Claude Elwood, 19–22, 110
Sharpe, William, 81, 82, 86, 88
Shaw, David, 43–44, 66, 311
Shearson Lehman Brothers, 50
Short sale, defined, 214
Sierra Partners, 65
Simons, James Harris, ix–x, 2–4, 11, 12, 45, 66, 75, 108–113, 115–117, 118, 127, 227, 233–234, 236, 279–280, 287, 304, 305, 311
Sinha, Gyan, 206
Small versus large stocks, 87–88

Smelcer, Wilma, 48
Smith, Adam, 264
Smith, Derek, 178
Smith, Harold, 24–25
Snyder, Dan, 122
Société Générale, 252
Soros, George, 3, 34, 65, 93, 99, 278, 279
Sosnick, Aaron, 224
South Sea Bubble, 12
Sowood Capital Management, 159–160, 207, 216, 234, 246, 272
Speech recognition, 113–115
Spitznagel, Mark, 288
Statistical arbitrage, 41–45, 112, 121, 126, 128, 152, 191, 200, 225
Stevens, Chad, 143
Stevens, Ross, 134
Stock warrants, pricing, 27–28, 31–33, 35, 37, 185, 296
String theory, 109
Subprime mortgage market, 158, 159, 179–181, 183, 188, 192, 195–198, 202–208, 211, 220, 221, 223, 224, 239, 240, 242, 243, 245, 249, 259, 268, 278, 279
Survival analysis, 193
Susquehanna International Group, 67
Synthetic CDOs, 190–194, 202
System X, 300
Systemic risk, 249–250

T. Rowe Price, 84
Tactical Trading Fund, 152–153, 234, 246, 274, 281, 310
Taleb, Nassim Nicholas, 59, 165–167, 250–252, 288, 296, 307
Tallmadge, Benjamin, 107
Tanemura, Ronald, 93–95, 144
Tannin, Matthew, 206, 207
Tartaglia, Nunzio, 42–45, 112, 123, 125, 128, 200
Taser International, 229
Taylor, Fred, 44
Taylor, Maxwell, 108
Texas Instruments, 40
Theglobe.com, 169
Theobald, Tom, 48

"Theory of Speculation, The" (Bachelier), 29

Thorp, Edward Oakley, x, 13–28, 31–42, 44–46, 52–53, 58, 61–64, 66–68, 70, 73, 85, 92, 93, 97, 100, 106, 110, 119, 121, 122, 124, 135, 136, 147, 149, 151–152, 154, 184, 194, 269, 271, 282, 296, 297–300, 303

Thorp, Vivian, 17–18

Tiger Management, 66, 142–143

Time Warner, 146

Total Securitization newsletter, 196

Townsend, Robert, 107

Tracinda Corporation, 149

Travelers Group, 98

Treasury, U.S. Department of, 253, 261

Treasury bonds, 95, 98

Tribune Company, 276

Trout, Monroe, Jr., 134

"Turbulent Times in Quant Land" (Rothman), 232

Tuttle, Jaipal, 128, 129, 132, 133

Tversk, Amos, 307

27-standard-deviation event, 53, 54

Tykhe Capital, 226

UBS, 100, 221

Universa Investments, 288

Value-at-risk (VAR), 96–97, 99, 278, 308

Value versus growth stocks, 87, 224, 225

"Variation of Certain Speculative Prices, The" (Mandelbrot), 57

Viniar, David, 238

Volatility, 31, 32, 38, 39, 59–60, 81, 88, 96, 97, 166–167, 217, 230–231, 275, 308

Volatility smile, 60–61

Volfbeyn, Pavel, 116

Vonage Holdings, 229

Waitzkin, Joshua, 90–91

Walford, Roy, 17

Wall Street (movie), 53

Wall Street Journal, 40, 196, 229, 239, 245, 280, 303

Wall Street with Louis Rukeyser (television show), 91

Walt Disney, 229

Wang, Bing, 146, 150

Washington, George, 107

Washington Mutual, 205, 267, 268

Waxman, Henry, 263–264, 278

Weapons Systems Evaluation Group, 108

Weinstein, Boaz, ix, 6–9, 11, 12, 15, 63, 90–95, 100–101, 118, 143–150, 151, 167, 175–178, 181, 183, 189, 191, 200, 208, 213–214, 226, 236, 238, 257, 268, 270, 276–278, 288, 301, 302, 306

Welch, Lloyd, 109

"We're Not Dead Yet" (Asness and Berger), 286

Whalen, Christopher, 160

"What Happened to the Quants?" (Lo and Khandani), 249–250

When Genius Failed (Lowenstein), 98

White, Harrison, 184

Whitehouse, Kaja, 232

Wilmott, Paul, x, 289, 291–295

Wilson, Charlie, 185

Winkler, Charlie, 155

Wolfe, Tom, 53

Wong, Amy, 125, 214–216, 228

Woodward, Bob, 279

WorldCom, 146

Yeh, James, 272

Young, Stanley, 309

Yusko, Mark, 273